THE PHYSICIAN LEADER'S GUIDE

SECOND EDITION

Edited by Richard Burton, MD, PhD, MBA

From the Publisher of
THE QUALITY LETTER
for Healthcare Leaders
in cooperation with
The American College of Physician Executives

CPI
Capitol Publications Inc.

1101 King Street, Suite 444 • Alexandria, Virginia 22314

Marjorie Weiner, Publisher
Amy Beth Miller, Executive Editor of the Health Division

Printed in the United States of America

ISBN: 1-56925-107-x $99

Table of Contents

Table of Contents (Cont.)

Table of Contents (Cont.)

Table of Contents to Figures

Table of Contents to Figures (Cont.)

Forward

Times have changed. With the emergence of the Internet; the new innovations in medical technology; the standardization of quality issues; and the changing role of physicians as communicators, negotiators, strategists and leaders, all involved in the medical field are in need of a resource to keep them abreast of current issues affecting them. ***The Physician Leader's Guide, Second Edition*** will help you do just that.

Written by chief medical officers, professors and top-notch consultants in the healthcare industry, each chapter draws on their personal experiences, helping you to:

- Take advantage of proven financial principles, management techniques and problem-solving methods already used by other successful senior healthcare executives;
- Make breakthroughs in the areas important to you and your staff such as credentialing, CQI and team development; and
- Successfully handle managed care issues, staff organization, delineating privileges and responsibilities and much more.

New to this edition are more than 15 additional chapters, including a whole new section on managed care. Topics range from "The Role of the Physician Executive in 2005" to "Physician Compensation in Managed Care Environments." Figures throughout the book help you easily decipher the information, reiterating important points in the chapter. The appendix contains more than 50 medical terms for your use.

Keeping up with today's trends in the healthcare industry can be challenging and complex. Information on each specific topic is readily available, but can be overwhelming. The compilation of chapters in ***The Physician Leader's Guide*** puts you in touch with that information in one easy-to-read resource.

I hope ***The Physician Leader's Guide, Second Edition*** is a useful addition to your healthcare library.

Sincerely,

Amy Beth Miller
Executive Editor of the Health Division

Acknowledgments

Many thanks are due to people who have contributed to the second edition of this publication. Thanks are due to:

All of the authors who volunteered their time and effort to make this publication happen.

- Meg de Guzman for serving as the project manager; contacting authors, compiling the information and editing.
- Robin Jones-Williams for coordinating the publication of the book.
- Richard Burton, MD, MBA, PhD for serving as our technical editor.
- Amy Beth Miller, Executive Editor of the healthcare group, for proofing the publication.
- Rosette Graham, Director of Production, for the page design and layout.
- Judy Denton, Art Director, for the cover design.

Thanks to you all.

Roles and Responsibilities

The Role of the Physician Executive in 2005

By Michael B. Guthrie, MD, MBA, FACPE

From 1965 to 1998, the institutions involved in providing healthcare services in American communities have changed substantially in scope and variety. Parallel to these changes, there has been a significant diversification of roles for physicians interested in management and leadership.

Where physicians once practiced medicine and identified themselves primarily or exclusively as physicians, today there are a number of men and women with experience as a physician and a role as an executive. With each passing year, they are developing and executing a wider variety of roles that span several components of the healthcare industry and beyond.

Despite the education and experience required to be successful in these new roles, many physicians are responding to the opportunities and becoming leaders and executives, in positions both formal and informal, throughout the industry. More organizations are recognizing the importance of the unique perspective and values of the qualified, experienced physician who also can produce effective organizational results in a management role.

◆ ◆ ◆

Dr. Marcus Welby hopped out of the cab at 52nd and Madison streets and entered the high-rise where he worked as medical director for a large group practice. He rode the elevator to the 32nd floor, where he exited, greeted the receptionist, and walked directly to his office; his first task was to review his voice mail. Today, Dr. Welby had 12 new messages—several from physicians interested in having their practices acquired, two from medical directors in different regions of his territory with questions about contract issues, and one from a physician on the group's board of directors. What's more notable is what was not on his voice mail: no requests for consults or referrals and no calls from patients.

As depicted above, the role of the physician executive has evolved dramatically in the past decade or so, and the pace of change is not expected to slow anytime soon. Physicians have served in executive roles for a long time, of course. What's remarkable is the increased number of such roles and the expanding variety of opportunities for men and women interested and qualified to assume non-clinical positions.

According to various benchmarks and sources, the number of physicians engaged at least part-time in medical administrative or executive duties has soared. For example, membership in the American College of Physician Executives has increased from approximately 60 people in the early 1970s to more than 13,000 today. The American Medical Association's master file provides similar trend information, showing a 29% increase between 1970 and 1994 in the number of physicians who list "administration" as part or full use of their time, according to the *Physician Characteristics and Distribution in the United States 1995/1996.*

Responsibilities

As providers have been pressed by the changing economics of health delivery to form various enterprises, physicians have been asked to manage at the interface between other physicians and managers, between clinical practice and economic incentives, and between physicians and regulatory or market demands. The physician executive's role frequently is defined by key needs within the organization, such as a need for communication among and education of clinical personnel. Physician executives also are perceived as being well positioned by training and experience to lead quality management and improvement efforts and to balance conflicts between economic incentives and appropriate clinical interventions. Managed care organizations are pressing many medical groups and hospital medical staffs to respond to higher expectations about clinical results and service excellence. Physicians with management training and experience are perceived to be able to interpret these new demands for heightened clinical accountability for their physician colleagues while understanding the limits and requirements of quality medical practice. Furthermore, physicians can presumably better lead or educate their colleagues than nonphysician managers.

As a result, many physician executives in provider organizations begin their managerial careers in roles that require communicating the organization's mission and vision to practicing physicians and educating them about continuous quality improvement. The next logical step is to manage nonphysician clinicians. From there, physician managers graduate to leading whole sectors or divisions of provider institutions. As they move from medical affairs to vice president and then perhaps to chief executive officer, some physician executives are becoming focused on the business side of healthcare, far beyond managing clinical effectiveness alone.

Health maintenance organizations (HMOs), in particular, have created new roles for physicians to have a voice in running health plans. In an HMO, a physician executive will likely be called upon for his or her clinical expertise, as well as specialized abilities such as actuarial skills or population management. Similar to such positions with payers, a number of new roles have emerged for physician leaders within independent practice associations (IPAs), medical groups and physician practice management companies. All of them need medical directors, presidents with clinical expertise and physician members on their boards.

There are also many physicians involved in healthcare regulation—both in and beyond government. They combine their technical aptitude with abilities in politics, quality improvement, law and/or public health to craft or influence policy affecting patient care on a broad scale. Physicians in executive roles are also increasingly found in pharmaceutical and manufacturing companies. Here their responsibilities may begin with science and research functions, but evolve into managing teams of other professionals and finally broad-based executive responsibilities for the business aspects of the organization. These roles emphasize combinations of clinical and scientific knowledge with finance and marketing understanding, as well as general organizational skill.

In the past ten years, several other venues for physician executive leadership have developed in emerging entrepreneurial environments. Senior physician managers occupy positions in information systems companies, venture capital firms, biotech startups, and medical device manufacturers. Roles for them also have been created in specialty advertising and marketing companies as well as in accounting firms responsible for benefits design and consulting to industries outside of healthcare.

Many of these roles leave the practice of medicine far behind as the physician executive takes increasing responsibility for overall business structure, staffing, budgeting, planning, accounting and marketing. Though fewer in number than their compatriots in the delivery side of the business, these individuals represent a changing model for cross-functional personnel with perspectives from unique combinations of clinical experience and industry knowledge with personal aptitude. *(See Figure 1 below)*.

FIGURE 1: REPRESENTING TITLES FOR PHYSICIAN EXECUTIVES

- Medical Director (medical groups, PPMCs*, hospitals, HMOs, other)
- Vice President for Medical Affairs (medical groups, PPMCs*, hospitals, HMOs, other)
- Chief Medical Officer (medical groups, PPMCs*, hospitals, HMOs, other)
- Chief Operating Officer (medical groups, PPMCs*, hospitals, HMOs, other)
- Vice President for Business Development
- Vice President for Clinical Affairs
- Dean
- Vice Provost for Health Affairs
- Chief Executive Officer (medical groups, PPMCs*, hospitals, HMOs, other)
- Chief Financial Officer (medical groups, hospitals, consultancy)
- Vice President for Health Services
- Vice President for Development (hospitals, PPMCs*, other)
- President (medical groups, PPMCs*, hospitals, HMOs, other)
- Chief Transformation Officer (hospitasl)
- Vice President for Information Systems
- Chief Medical Informatics Officer

*Physician practice management companies

Skills

A number of challenges face any physician who wants to cross the line from clinical practice to management. While some are dealt with through education and training, others can be overcome only through acquiring experience and perspective. Either way, acquiring specific skills is as essential for voluntary, part-time medical leaders as it is for those interested in a full-time career in management. The necessary skills encompass the following areas:

- Relationship management (i.e., good, old-fashioned people skills);
- Change management;
- Process improvement; and
- Persuasion (i.e., selling ideas and alternatives and being able to explain what's realistic).

Of course, doctors who wish to move into full-time management are increasingly being expected to pursue formal training in business so they have a grasp of various accounting methods, finance, law and marketing. Until just a few years ago, a master's in business or health administration was more an exception than the rule among physician candidates for upper-level positions in management. But that's just the beginning. Management-bound physicians also must acquire on-the-job experience in progressively complex positions of authority and responsibility. Much has been written about how to acquire these skills, and there are many routes to doing so. In essence, a physician who wants to become a leader must demonstrate in every position an ability to lead people to constructive ends. The most tangible evidence of such leadership will be the production of results valued by the organization. *(See "Other Sources of Information for the Up and Coming Physician Leader" at the end of this chapter, page 18.)*

Personal Transition

Even when a physician is first elected to a voluntary medical staff position, he or she experiences changed relationships with peers. Any leadership position poses personal, as well as professional, demands on doctors. Authority exists, even in these modest roles, and should be exercised properly if the organization or group is to achieve its objectives. This changes the relationship of the leader to the other members of the team, for better and for worse. While preparation and guidance from more senior friends and teachers eases the transition, conscious and thoughtful experience is the best teacher over time. Therefore, any physician with an eye toward management would be well served to fill even the least powerful leadership roles as they arise.

As the physician leader's role becomes more significant and complex, the transitional challenges also become more significant. Most advisors suggest mentors, positive working relationships, formal training and on-the-job experience.

Impact

A frequent question is why physicians move from the practice of medicine to management or leadership. The answers are as multiple and complex as the individuals involved, but there is some consistency.

Physicians as a population are smart and energetic and strongly inclined to seek significance in both their work and personal life. As a consequence, many who are aware of the changes occurring in the profession and in healthcare overall feel compelled to take action in an attempt to make a positive difference. Physicians who transition into management frequently report that they did so in part because they hoped to make healthcare better for a population of patients, as opposed to caring for one patient at a time. The significance of management in a health delivery organization, however, can cut either way: It may be broad and deep, or the results can be dilute and long delayed.

Physicians bring their special perspective to management, even when they have been away from bedside or office clinical practice for some time. They are physicians first in most instances and managers (or even leaders) second.

Physicians also are focused most of the time on the care of all patients, perhaps all in a given disease category or population, but all nonetheless. This perspective is close to setting policy or crafting optimal care and procedures in the point of view it establishes. As a consequence, many physicians are naturally drawn to the process of setting guidelines for care and monitoring progress toward an ideal in patient management.

What impact do physician executives actually have on organizations? This is a tough question to answer with detailed data or factual information. A review of the medical literature for the past five years revealed just one study published in the fall 1994 issue of *Health Care Management Review*. According to an unpublished study conducted in 1996 by Richard Burton, MD, MBA, ACPE, the impact may be as much as a savings of $2 to $5 per member per month in mature health plans. At any rate, the conventional wisdom is physicians in leadership positions make significant, positive differences in the function of their organizations—a difference that can only sometimes be mirrored by nonphysician executives. More information over time will tell.

How Far Do You Want to Go?

Finally, a few words about your career and potential future. Many physician executives begin their transition without visualizing how high in an organization they might rise, or how large a role they might actually enjoy and do well. Usually, after a few years of working in organizations it becomes conceivable to some of us that we might like to be the top executive, or near the top, and not "just" the medical director. This is another significant transition and implies a new set of values and objectives that are dramatically different from our core medical training and socialization.

Do you want to become the chief executive officer? If the answer is yes, you must train for it and work your way up through a wide variety of executive responsibilities. Smart organizations don't hire people as CEO just because they have "medical doctor" behind their name. You must demonstrate through your experience, not just training, that you can do the work and achieve the expected results. Being certified, licensed, trained and having a degree in management is insufficient, although helpful, for getting advanced to senior management positions.

Also, if you do want to make the leap to senior executive management, seek experience outside of areas focused exclusively on medicine or healthcare delivery in your organization. Don't be marginalized as "just a physician" if you want to be CEO. Ask to be responsible for operating results, and then prove you can make a positive differ-

ence.
That being said, it isn't necessary to be CEO or advance to the upper hierarchy in management in order to have a successful and rewarding career. Many positions that do not require changing your "spots" from physician to manager are exciting and challenging, as well as important to an organization's success.

◆ ◆ ◆

Other Sources of Information for the Up and Coming Physician Leader

Curry, Wes, Ed. *The Physician Executive*, 2nd ed. Tampa, FL: American College of Physician Executives, 1994.
McCall, M., and Claire, J. "In Transit from Physician to Manager: Part I." *Physician Executive* 18(2):3-9 (March/April, 1992).
Sheldon, A. *Managing Doctors*. Irwin, IL: Dow Jones, 1986.

About the Author

Michael B. Guthrie, MD, MBA, FACPE, is executive vice president for Premier Practice Management, where he's responsible for development and medical management. He is also executive vice president for Premier Inc., the nation's largest alliance. Dr. Guthrie is a past president of the American College of Physician Executives.

Delineating Responsibility in Practice

By Robin L. Smith, MD, Hara J. Schwartz, MD and David B. Nash, MD, MBA

Today, as a result of all the requirements from managed care organizations, and a need to document outcomes, a solo practitioner may find it exceedingly difficult to fulfill the Hippocratic oath. Therefore, the organizational structure of medicine is changing. As responsibilities are being delegated and medicine is fragmenting, who will be responsible to do what?

We will begin by exploring the role of the generalist versus the specialist, and review the data available in the medical literature to support the need for segmentation in treatment of specific diseases. We will then focus on the expanding role and the need for physician extenders in today's practice of medicine. We will continue by examining a new breed of physicians called "hospitalists." The hospitalist specializes in acute medicine, and is equipped to improve physician access, efficiency and quality of care in the hospital setting, while allowing the outpatient practitioners to focus their time and attention in the office setting. Lastly, we will discuss the economic and time impact of medical education and the need to reevaluate the role of the educator and setting of medical education in a healthcare system heavily weighted toward managed care.

◆ ◆ ◆

Specialist vs. Generalist

There is no question that the scope of medical knowledge has exceeded the capabilities of any single physician, and that specialty care is needed and adds value. However, specialization—which aims to unleash an armamentarium of care against a disorder of a specific organ system—may conflict with other indicators of high-quality care, such as patient accessibility, continuity of care and open physician-patient communication.[1] The result of this complex interface of primary and specialty care, and overlapping responsibilities, may ultimately pit one group's interests against the other's. Moreover, little is known about: the best way to coordinate care between two or more clinicians; patient perceptions of this potential dichotomy; how reimbursement changes the impacts; and how this impact drives care delivery.

Specialty care is perhaps more important today than at any other time in medical history. The delineation of specialties is unsettled, however, leaving room for anxiety and mistrust. In order to maintain profitability in a managed care environment, specialists are continuously being pressured to increase the number of patients they see. This is becoming more difficult in a gatekeeper system, where the primary care physicians are being encouraged to treat illnesses and perform procedures without the assistance of specialists. One mechanism specialists are using to increase patient volumes is to broaden their repertoire of diseases they treat. This may infringe upon procedures that were previously performed by other specialists.

In an effort to define provider roles and responsibilities, the federal Agency for Health Care Policy and Research (AHCPR) convened a panel of experts. These experts were charged to identify the information needed to help define the roles and competencies of generalists and specialists and determine who does what best.[2]

Data are rapidly becoming available. One interesting finding seen when surveying generalists and specialists is the perceptual differences in the definition of quality. The American College of Physicians solicited opinions to determine the volume of electrocardiograms (EKGs) a physician was required to read to become competent in this area. Whereas the mean recommend number to achieve competency was 750, program directors, internists and cardiologists felt only 100 were necessary.[3] What is the right number of EKGs that a physician must read in order to become competent? The answer may depend on the definition of competence. The number recommended EKGs by general internists may reflect their assessment of the number necessary to achieve "basic" competence, defined as "the ability to read the majority of EKGs, but still require consultation and referral on a minority of EKGs." The number recommended by cardiologists may reflect the number necessary to achieve "master" competence in EKGs, defined by the ability to read all EKGs and answer referrals about difficult to interpret EKGs. The American College of Cardiology has attempted to develop standards for EKG interpretation by developing a standardized four-hour test and self-assessment program. The first certifying tests were given in June 1996. Presumably, certification through this exam would imply "master" competence in EKG interpretation. However, the degree of competence that a primary care physician should have is not addressed by this process. Should only physicians who have been certified through this test be deemed competent read EKGs? Or can primary care physicians read EKGs that they feel comfortable with, and refer the rest? This is an area where empirical data is sorely needed to bolster expert opinion alone.

Recent data have shown that specialty care for some diseases leads to better outcomes. The following examples support this conclusion.

- The care endocrinologists provide for patients with diabetic foot ulcers than the care provided by family practitioners or general internists.[4]

- Cardiologists were found more likely to provide proper care defined by clinical practice guidelines of acute myocardial infarction than internists or family practitioners.[5,6]

- Horner et al. showed an unadjusted, increased survival rate of individuals suffering an acute ischemic stroke who were treated by neurologists compared to generalists. When risk adjustments were considered, estimated survival was not significantly affected and the data continued to support better outcomes for acute ischemic stroke patients when treated by a neurologist .[7,8,9]

- A strong correlation of experience, expertise and quality has been shown in the intensive care setting where an intensivist is present.[10,11]

- AIDS also has been shown to be diagnosed and treated more expediently by AIDS specialists as opposed to internists and family practitioners.[12,13,14,15]

Physician Extender vs Physician

Nurses, physician assistants and physician extenders are no longer utilized only in rural or underserved populations, but have become a critical part of many urban and suburban practices. They provide patient education, preventative and routine care in the healthcare setting. Additionally, as technology increases, it is impossible for physicians to learn and maintain currency on each procedure "tool." This has led to the increasing need for physician support when administering treatment and performing procedures. Today it is common that certified physician extenders be present when particular procedures or therapeutics are administered. This requirement is often written into guidelines. As stated in the guidelines for Administration of Cancer Chemotherapeutic and Biological Response Modifiers "adequate nursing and pharmacy support is essential for optimal administration of these drugs..." For percutaneous transluminal coronary angioplasty (PTCA), the critical role of "environment," as well as reliance upon the cardiac care team are acknowledged as crucial ingredients in the guideline. High technology demands technical expertise that may necessitate knowledge and skills that a physician does not, and is not, required to possess. Many high technology guidelines recommend using ancillary staff for many of the procedures, such as: Bone Marrow Aspiration and Biopsy; Exercising Testing; and Aphoresis. All contain the general requirement that such personnel be under the supervision of a specialist or another physician certified as competent to perform the procedure. The guideline for Aphoresis, perhaps the most lax in this regard, states that while it is the supervising physician's responsibility to maintain donor/patient selection and safety, "it should not be necessary...to be able to set up and personally run each of the multiple available devices."[16] In contrast is the guideline for Hemodynamic Monitoring, in which "relegating total responsibility for equipment setup, trouble-shooting, calibration, or other technical details to nursing or tech. personnel is unacceptable because integrity of the data is always the physician's responsibility."[17] Coordination of responsibilities between the supervising physician and technical staff is imperative.

In addition to serving as administrators of complex therapeutics and diagnostic modalities, physician extenders are also educators and providers. In an outpatient setting, physician extenders act as educators, and may provide routine primary care services as well as screen "sick" visits. In the hospital, they may make preliminary rounds, coordinate and arrange testing, communicate with families and providers, arrange for home care and discharge and may be the common link with the doctors of a large group practice. With extenders comes the concept of team approach.

Primary Care Physician vs Hospitalist

A new concept in the United States is that of the hospitalist.[18, 19] This practitioner specializes in inpatient medicine and takes care of the sick and critically ill hospitalized patients.[20] This enables primary care physician to specialize in outpatient medicine.

Today there are approximately 2000 recognized hospitalists.[21] The majority received training in internal medicine, pulmonary medicine or critical care. Many are double or triple boarded. Hours are flexible, salaries are competitive ($130,000-$200,000) and jobs are plentiful.[22] Some hospitalists work year round in the hospital setting, while other hospitalists rotate with other members of their practice doing one week, a month or two month stints.

The Scripps Clinic and Foundation in La Jolla, Calif., uses a form of hospitalist. In this scenario, a community primary care physician turns over coordination of care to another primary care physician specifically assigned to inpatients at that particular hospital, to streamline the hospitalization process. At the Scripps Clinic, the decision to adopt this policy was an attempt to combat inefficiencies arising from the need to follow a defined office schedule and no time for rounds, seeing only one or two patients. The absence of these attendings from the hospital led to delays in responding to test results, changing diets, consulting with specialists and, most importantly, initiating discharge planning. At Scripps, team members are internists who take weekly rotations directing a group of professionals (nurses, social workers, etc.) in managing hospitalized patients.[23]

Hospitalists may work directly for the hospital, for a managed care organization or contract directly with primary care providers or provider groups. Thus, who pays the hospitalist has been inconsistent to date. The market for the hospitalist is immature, with tremendous potential to develop and shape the role of this specialty. In order to impact the delivery of inpatient healthcare, the hospitalist may chose to become involved in quality assurance, continuous quality improvement and development of critical pathways. Hospitalists may become the primary educators for the inpatient portion of medical education.

Hospitals and managed care organizations are using the hospitalist to improve efficiency and decrease length of stay. Hospitalists can "restore the sanctity of office hours" and protect the primary care providers from disruption at unpredictable and inconvenient times. Some argue that this jeopardizes continuity of care, however this shortcoming may be more than compensated by quick physician access, efficiency and technical expertise.

Provider vs Educator

Medical education is at a crossroads in terms of reorganization to accommodate the changing role of the physician in today's society.[24] There has been an articulate call for the reform of medical education to help practitioners not only deal with professional knowledge, but also provide the skills to make them effective caregivers in the evolving new environment of healthcare.[25]

The dilemma of teaching remains. Who will be responsible to teach physicians, and who will pay for it? Differences in missions between academic medical centers and managed care organizations have made teaching collaborations difficult. Academic medical centers are committed to providing high quality education to doctors and ancillary practitioners, conducting research and providing care regardless of the individuals ability to pay for it. Managed care organizations are committed to providing high-quality, low-cost care to their members. Teaching initiatives for the managed care organization are targeted at inefficient providers who demonstrate overutilization of resources. Additionally, continuing medical education for providers is a requisite for many hospital privileging boards and accreditation by the National Committee for Quality Assurance.

There are, however, synergistic opportunities for collaboration. As teaching continues to move toward outpatient medicine, training needs include more outpatient exposure. Managed care organizations offer more teaching sites in their primary care doctors' offices, and in turn help influence trainees to chose primary care as their specialty.[26]

Managed care organizations benefit from teaching cost-effective medical practice to doctors in training. There is an additional public relations benefit for managed care because teaching carries prestige and demonstrates a commitment to quality.

In 1993 more than 75% of physicians were involved in one or more managed care contracts.[27] Today this number is closer to 90%. Managed care organizations look for efficiency and productivity in their physicians, and thus the need and necessary cost of becoming involved in medical education must be recognized. How can physicians be efficient, see high volumes of patients and take the time to teach in a managed care environment? This represents a challenge because student teaching in an ambulatory setting increases costs and lowers productivity. Managed care organizations have to acknowledge the financial and time burdens of teaching. In addition, they must provide some form of compensation for this activity in order for physicians to succeed while teaching in an environment heavily weighted toward managed care. Managed care organizations must accept part of the financial burden to train physicians in the 21st century.

Traditional inpatient medical education will continue to exist, since significant pathophysiology and exposure to acute life threatening illness is not available in the ambulatory setting. The cost of care at teaching hospitals is approximately 20% higher than at non-teaching hospitals.[28, 29, 30] This is not compatible with today's cost-effective emphasis. Hospitals are struggling to survive as length of stay decreases, leaving a surplus of hospital beds. Perhaps inpatient teaching also will become one of the roles of the hospitalist.

Conclusion

In summary, we have described a new world where physicians' roles, responsibilities and expectations have dramatically changed coincident with the growth of managed care. We have attempted to show how physicians have adapted to this changing environment and the role definitions that we have described are a tribute to the flexibility and creativity of current day practitioners.

After evaluating all of the economic, job function and relationship changes among physicians, there are two remaining challenges for the coming years. The first relates to the function of credentialing and how hospitals, third parties and possibly even the government will adapt to the rapidly changing delineation of responsibilities. Multiple credentialling sources lead to conflicting performance criteria which will undoubtedly be amplified by continued fragmentation in the field. Additionally, without a single nationally recognized credentialling entity, resources are wasted and quality is compromised. The American Medical Association in collaboration with specialty, state and local medical societies has responded to this dilemma by forming the American Medical Accreditation Program (AMAP). The AMAP is a physician driven, nonprofit, nongovernment comprehensive accreditation program that uses national standards, in the form of credentials, personal qualifications, clinical performance, patient care results and environment of care to accredidate physicians and ensure quality. Perhaps this will become the credentialling body of the 21st century.

The second, and most important, relates to the maintenance and sanctity of the patient-physician relationship. After all is said and done, the latter has to be protected and, it is hoped, enhanced as economic and time pressures eat away at this fundamental component of the art of medicine.

◆ ◆ ◆

References

[1]Barr, D.A. "The Effects of Organizational Structure on Primary Care Outcomes Under Managed Care." *Annals of Internal Medicine*, 122(5):353-59, 1995.

[2]Gaus, C.R., and Clancy, C.M. "Research at the Interface of Primary Care." *Journal of the American Medical Association (JAMA)*, 274(18)1419, 1995.

[3]Seltzer, J. and Nash, D.B. "The Evolution of Physician Quality Assessment." *Models for Measuring Quality in Managed Care: Analysis and Impact*, 1-34. New York, NY: Faulkner and Grey Inc., 1997.

[4]Greenfield, S., Roger, W., Mangotich, M., et al. "Outcomes of Patients with Hypertension and Non-Insulin-Dependent Diabetes Mellitus Treated by Different Systems and Specialists." *JAMA*, 274(18):1436-1444, 1995.

[5]Ayanian J.Z., Hauptman, P.J., Gaudagnoli, E., et al. "Knowledge and Practices of Generalist and Specialist Physicians Regarding Drug Therapy for Acute Myocardial Infarction." *New England Journal of Medicine (NEJM)*, 331(17):1136-1142, 1995.

[6]Nash, I.S., Nash, D.B., and Fuster, V. "Do Cardiologists Do It Better?" *Journal of the American College of Cardiologists*, 29:475-8, 1997.

[7]Barry, H.C. "Knowledge of Drugs for Myocardial Infarction: Generalists versus Specialists," *NEJM*, 332(7):472, 1995.

[8]Justice, A.C. "Knowledge of Drugs for Myocardial Infarction: Generalists versus Specialists," *NEJM*, 332(7):472-473, 1995.

[9]Horner, R.D., Matchar, D.B., Divine, G.W., et al. "Relationship Between Physician Specialty and the Selection and Outcomes of Ischemic Stroke Patients." *Health Services Research*, 30(2):275-287, 1995.

[10]Pollack, M.M., Katz, R.W., Ruttimann, U.E, et al. "Improving the Outcome and Efficiency of Intensive Care: The Impact of an Internist." *Critical Care Medicine*, 16:11-17, 1988.

[11]Li, T.C., Phillips, M.C., Shaw, L., et al. "Onset Physician Staffing in a Community Hospital Intensive Care Unit: Impact on Test and Procedure Use and Patient Outcome." *JAMA*; 252:2023-2027, 1984.

[12]Paauw, D.S., Wenrich, M.D., Curtis J.R., et al. "Ability of Primary Care Physicians to Recognize Physical Findings Associated with HIV Infection." *JAMA*, 274(17):1380-1382, 1995.

[13]Kitahata, M.M., Koepsell, T.D., Deyo, R.A., et al. "Physician's Experience with the Acquired Immunodeficiency Syndrome as a Factor in Patients' Survival." *NEJM*, 334:701-706, 1996.

[14]Stone, V.E., Seage, G.R. III, Hertz, T., et al. "The Relation Between Hospital Experience and Mortality for Patients with AIDS." *JAMA*, 268:2655-2661, 1992.

[15]Turner, B.J., McKee, L., Fanning, T., et al. "AIDS Specialist versus Generalist Ambulatory Care for Advanced HIV Infection and Impact on Hospital Use." *Medical Care*, 32:902-916, 1994.

[16]Phillips, G., Armitage, J., Bearman, S., et al. "American Society for Blood and Marrow Transplantation Guidelines for Clinical Centers." *Biological Blood Marrow Transplant*, 1(1):54-5,1995.

[17]Ginosar, Y., Thijs, L.G., and Sprung, C.L. "Raising the Standard of Hemodynamic Monitoring: Targeting the Practice or the Practitioner?" *Critical Care Medicine*, 25(2):209-11, 1997.

[18]Frieden, J. "Internist Limits Practice to Hospital." *Internal Medicine News*, Vol. 29, 1,9, 1996.

[19]Moore, J.J. "The Inpatient's Best Friend. 'Hospitalists' Specialize in Managing Care of the Very Ill." *Modern Healthcare*, 27:54-56, 58-62, 1997.

[20]Wachter, R.M. and Goldman, L. "The Emerging Role of 'Hospitalists' in the American Health Care System." *NEJM*, 335(7):514-516, 1996.

[21]Wiebe, Christine. "Physicians Turn to Hospital Practice in New 'Specialty.'" *AMA News*, 40(33):1,23, 1997.

[22]Ibid.

[23]Bradner, J. "Will Hospital Rounds Go the Way of the House Call?" *Managed Care Review*,19-28, July 1995.

[24]Wilkes, M. "The Changing Role of Medical Education in the Face of Pressure to Reform Health Care." *Drug Information Journal*, 29:461-468, 1995.

[25]Greenlick, M.R. "Educating Physicians for the Twenty-first Century." *Academic Medicine*, 70:179-185, 1995.

[26]Larsen, R.R., Robinson, J.W., Smith, R. et al., "Residency Training in an HMO." *Managed Care Medicine*, 1(10);34-39, 1994.

[27]Emmons, D.W., and Simon, C.J. *Physicians' Marketplace Report: Recent Trends in Managed Care*. Chicago, IL: American Medical Association, 1993.

[28]Dobson, A., Coleman, K. and Mechanic, R. *Analysis of Teaching Hospital Costs*. Fairfax, VA: Lewtn-VHI Inc., August, 1994.

[29]Andrson, C.F. and Lave, J.R. "Financing Graduate Medical Education and Biomedical Research: Whose Responsibility?" *Health Policy*, 7:8-12, 1987.
[30]Thorpe, K.E. "Why are Urban Hospital Costs so High? The Relative Importance of Patient Source of Admission, Teaching, Competition, and Case Mix." *Health Services Research*, 22:821-835, 1988.

About the Authors

Hara Schwartz, MD, is currently a fellow in the U.S. Quality Algorithms Managed Care Fellowship between U.S. Healthcare and Thomas Jefferson Medical College. As a board certified Internist, she serves as a clinical attending physician in primary care at the Wilmington Veteran's Affairs Hospital in Delaware.

Dr. David B. Nash, MD, MBA, FACP is the founding Director of the Office of Health Policy and Clinical Outcomes at Thomas Jefferson University Hospital and Associate Professor of Medicine at Jefferson Medical College in Philadelphia. In December 1996, Dr. Nash assumed additional responsibilities as the first Associate Dean for Health Policy at Jefferson Medical College.

Robin Smith, MD, is a Specialist Project Consultant to the Department of Health Policy and Clinical Outcomes at Thomas Jefferson Medical College. She is a Primary Care Attending at the Wilmington Veteran's Affairs Hospital in Delaware and an Associate Medical Director at Aetna-U.S. Healthcare.

The Role of Physicians in Prioritizing the Work of Teams and the Organization

By J. Edward McEachern, MD, and
Jonathan T. Lord, MD

In this article, the authors discuss key survival issues for physician leaders and healthcare organizations, including the importance of:

- *Developing a value-based, patient-centered relationship between medical staffs and healthcare organizations;*
- *Redesigning medical staffs to include physician executives as well as volunteer physician leaders;*
- *Developing effective physician leaders; and*
- *Evaluating the performance of those leaders.*

◆ ◆ ◆

The 1990s are bringing significant, fundamental changes in the financing and organization of healthcare services. These changes are placing increased responsibilities on physician leaders, particularly those serving in a voluntary capacity. The shifting roles of medical staffs and their leaders can be best understood in the context of the dramatic changes under way in healthcare.

New Delivery Systems Spell New Skills

Increasingly, patients, practitioners, healthcare institutions and payers must cope with a very different world. Access to care has been broadened for many of those without financial means, while patients with health insurance may have fewer options open to them. Financial incentives reward efficiency and cost-effectiveness, and both the public and major purchasers expect providers to demonstrate the value of their services. Competition is heightened, especially for fast-growing ambulatory services and urban centers. Separate reimbursements for individual services have yielded to a payment system in which hospitals, physicians and other providers share in per case or per capita payments.

As markets move toward more controlled forms of paying providers, providers develop key core competencies in order to be successful in the marketplace. (*See Figure 1 on page 28.*)

Figure 1: Market Progression to Capitation

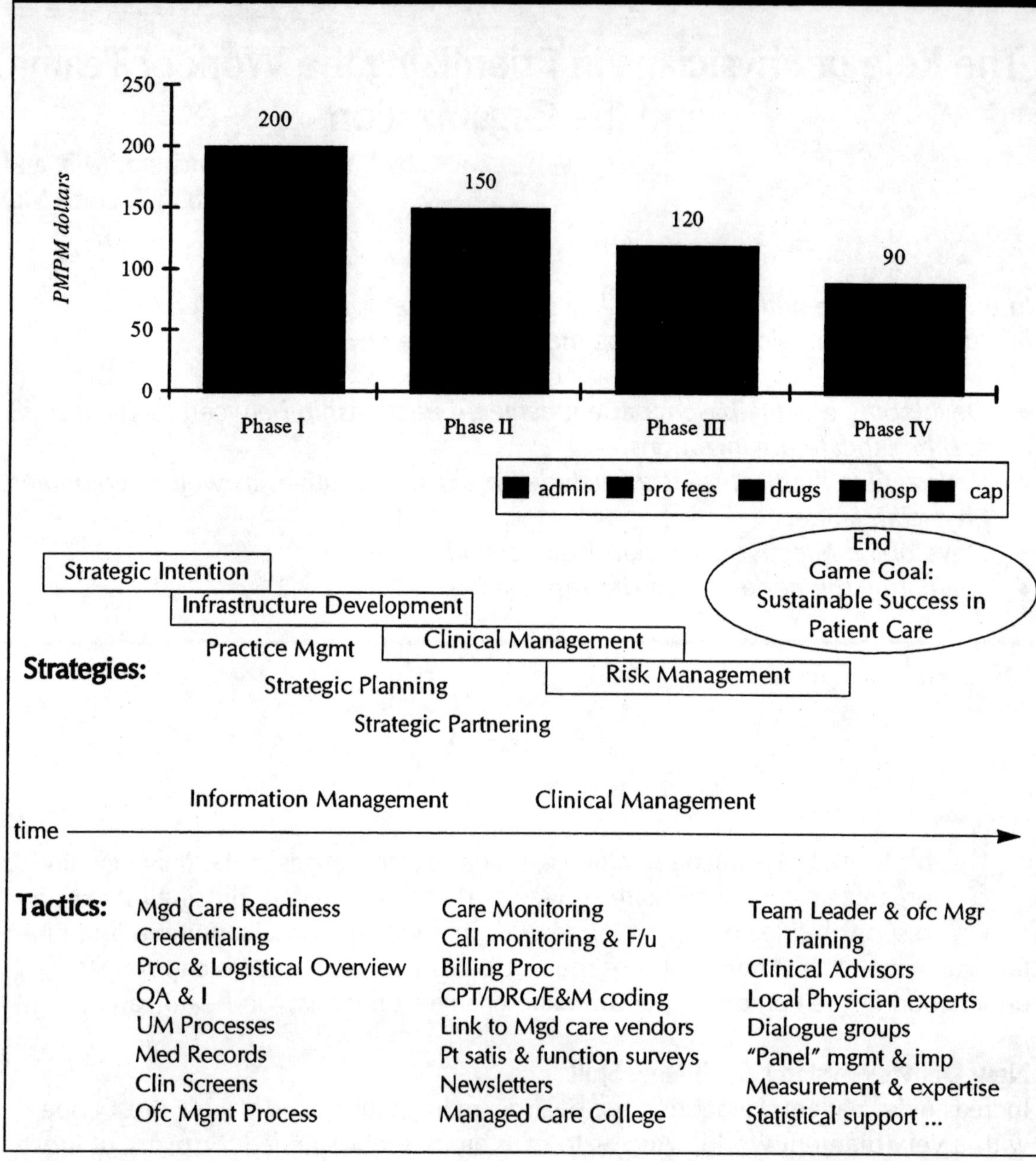

Markets progress more or less toward capitation such that lower total payments are received by providers. At each phase of market progression, providers develop key core competencies, strategies and tactics to ensure market success. Core competencies include having a strategic intention and a working, explicit business model; developing infrastructure that facilitates the acceptance of risk; and developing clinical management systems that provide excellent care at lower total cost. Core competencies dictate strategies for providers, who in turn must become proficient at practice management, strategic planning, strategic partnering, information management and epidemiologically relevant "panel" management. Fortunately, there are a number of tactics that providers and hospitals can undertake together as the market develops. Market progression dictates new strategies and tactics for success. *(See Figure 2 on page 29.)*

FIGURE 2: MARKET PROGRESSION TO NEW STRATEGIES AND TACTICS

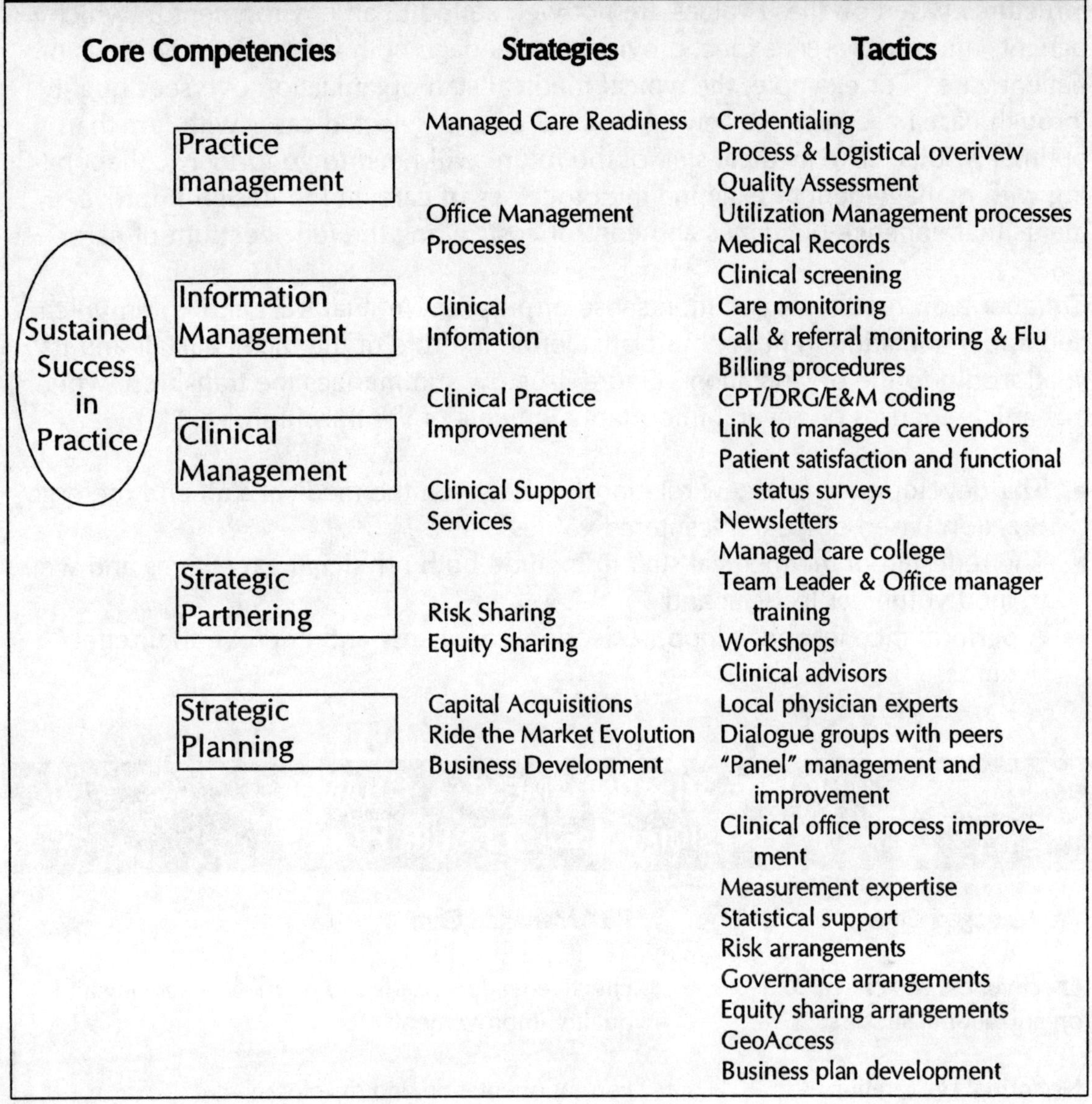

These and other changes call for physicians and healthcare delivery organizations to collaborate as never before, and physicians will be asked to play increasingly important roles in the management of healthcare organizations.

Unfortunately, the medical staff structure of many healthcare organizations is not well positioned for this new environment. It reflects, instead, the values of past times, particularly:

- Separation from administration, in order to preserve physicians' traditional autonomy;
- Representation of doctors' interests to management and the board;
- Focus on ensuring the quality of medical care, but not on nonmedical aspects of care and not on the costs of care;

- Assistance in meeting regulatory and accreditation requirements; and
- Voluntarism, with physicians taking brief turns in leadership positions.

Structures based on these values are not well suited to an environment in which patients and purchasers expect providers to manage both the quality and costs of patient care. For example, the typical medical staff organization oversees quality through case-based peer review of medical care in selected cases with less-than-optimal results. The medical staff of the future will need to go further, collaborating with management to examine the processes of care and to design improvements that enhance outcomes and control costs along the full spectrum of care.

Collaboration requires a common sense of purpose, mutual trust and communication and a transition in how physicians define the role of the medical staff and its relationship to the organization. Figure 3 below summarizes the transition, while this article focuses on several important elements of the transition:

- The development of a new relationship between the medical staff and the organization based on patient-centered values;
- The redesign of the medical staff to include both physician executives and well-trained volunteer leaders; and
- A performance feedback loop, so leaders can assess and improve their effectiveness.

FIGURE 3: FUNDAMENTAL CHANGES IN PHYSICIAN LEADERSHIP ROLES

Pre-Managed Care	Post-Managed Care
Effectiveness not critical to organizational success	Effective leaders needed to promote efficiency and quality improvement
No formal preparation	Formal orientation and development
Leaders selected by rotation	Leaders selected based on qualifications
All volunteer	Some compensated, including physician executives
Advocate medical staff interests to administration	Advocate broader patient care interests

Organizations Grow Through Cycles of Success, Harvest and Decay

The administrative model of hospital and physician relationships has been especially stagnant since the times of Graham Gray Ward, MD, E. A. Codman, MD, and Malcomb MacEachern, MD. As organizations experience success, commonly based on a set of (usually) unarticulated beliefs, assumptions and explicit behaviors, they develop methods and structures to respond to the market and current environment. If the beliefs, assumptions and behaviors are correct for the time, they are rewarded with market success, leading the system's "founding fathers" to develop a paradigm fix point, which further solidifies the methods that grew out of the initial assumptions, beliefs and behaviors regarding the environment at the time. As time goes on, the founding fathers move on, but those working in the system are left with methods and systems that preserve the fix point. These behaviors in turn develop another set of assumptions, beliefs and behaviors in current workers, again preserving the paradigm fix point.

For a while, this model will allow the organization to harvest the market's rewards, but after a fashion, its success blinds the workers' ability to see the future from any perspective other than the one that made their system successful. The organization then either spins into decay or promotes leaders who can articulate a new paradigm that may lead to more market success and harvest.

FIGURE 4: CYCLE OF GROWTH, HARVEST, NEW PARADIGM/DECAY

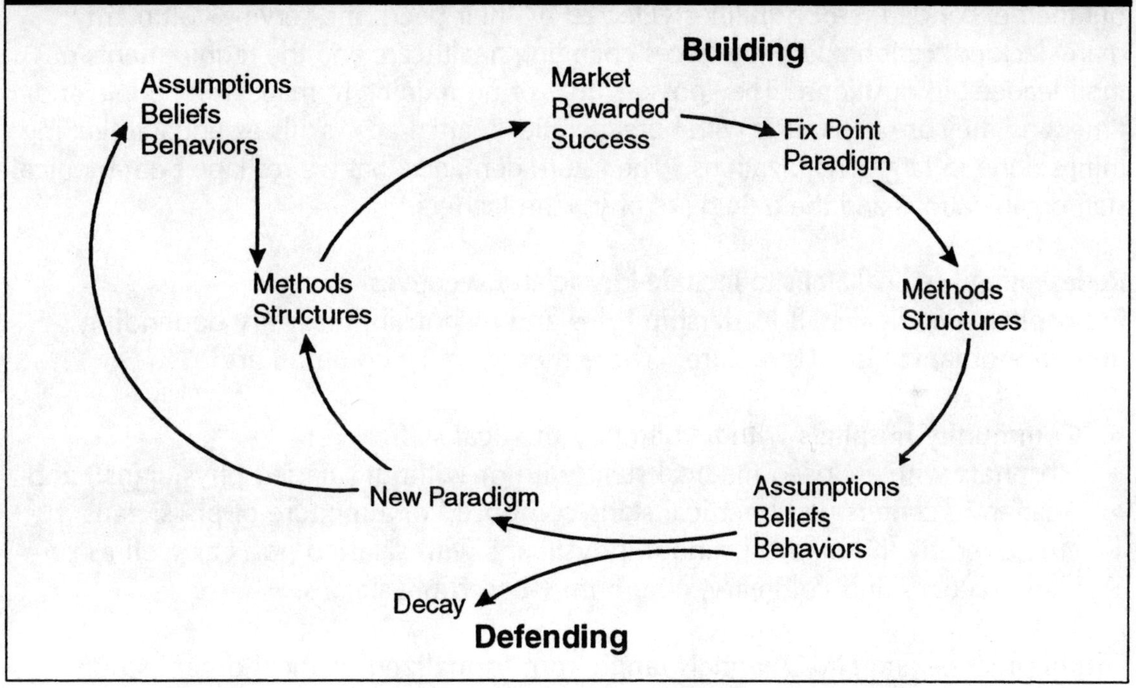

The current structure that serves as the mental model for most medical staffs dates back to E.A. Codman's 1928 treatise on hospital efficiency. It's reiterated in Malcomb MacEachern's landmark book, *Hospitals*, which dates from the early 1940s. If we're living with such antiquated structures, perhaps we're in need of a new paradigm and paradigm fix point.

A Value-Based, Patient-Centered Relationship

Any change in the *status quo* is unsettling, especially changes as far-reaching as those facing today's healthcare providers. Change also can provide opportunities for improvement, however. Medical staffs and healthcare organizations that seize the opportunity to re-examine basic structures and formulate a new relationship based on a set of common values will be able not only to cope with change but also to improve because of it. Fundamental to these values is a focus on the needs of patients—individually and collectively—as the community they serve. By virtue of their training and experience, physicians and other healthcare workers are driven by values that focus on the needs of patients, including respect for the individual, access to healthcare for all, and innovation in treatment and delivery systems to improve care.

Hospitals and other healthcare organizations are also driven by these values. Within the hospital, patients, their families and staff are bound together by intense human emotions—joy, fear, relief and grief. Patients are the common bond; meeting their needs can be a common goal.

Healthcare organizations and physicians that have forged an alliance based on common values and goals will find themselves better positioned to meet the financial, personal and societal challenges facing them. In turn, such alliances require capable and competent medical leadership. But physician leaders are often not prepared to carry out their expanded responsibilities. Elected by their peers and serving voluntarily, many lack education about the forces changing healthcare and the requirements of their leadership positions. They possess little or no training in managing people and time, and they are unfamiliar with bureaucratic "martial arts" skills essential to getting things done in large organizations. The future demands that we reshape both medical staff organizations and the training of physician leaders.

Redesigning Medical Staffs to Include Physician Executives

In hospitals, medical staff leadership roles and responsibilities vary depending upon the organizational structure. Three models most common are:

- Community hospitals with a voluntary medical staff;
- Hospitals with a closed medical staff (with or without salaried physicians); and
- Academic centers with medical staffs composed of a mixture of physicians employed by the medical school, physicians with salaried posts as well as private practices and voluntary, community-based physicians.

Group practice and HMO models range from formalized medical organizations like Kaiser's Permanente Group to less formal assignments of medico-administrative duties to selected physicians.

The predominant organizational model, however, is the community hospital with a voluntary medical staff. Its physician leaders generally include medical staff officers, department and committee chairs and leaders of other organized activities who serve on a voluntary basis. Physicians usually hold leadership positions for a limited period of time, so turnover is common.

The paid executive. In acknowledgment of the demands of a changing environment, many organizations and medical staffs have recognized the need for paid

FIGURE 5: MEDICAL STAFF ORGANIZATION

	TRADITIONAL	CONTINUOUS IMPROVEMENT IN QUALITY
Transition of Roles & Responsibilities	• Assuring the quality of medical care • Self-governance of medical staff bylaws Credentials review and privileging Corrective actions Structure • Positively influencing the management of the institution	• Continuous improvement • Quality of care Accessibility of care Scope of care Performance • Expanded input from/to: Board Administration Nursing • Integral component of leadership team
Transition of Structure	• Executive committee Department chairpersons, CEO, officers of medical staff • Departments MDs only QA staff • Committees Reactions to external mandated function • Officers One- to two-year terms Focus on medical staff activities Limited role at Board and administrative functions	• Executive committee Expanded participants: Board, nursing • Departments, service line groups, multi-disciplinary teams Staffed Planned • Committees and quality improvement teams Collaborative • Officers and leaders Leadership development and continuity Integral participants Board Strategic planning Finance Operations Focus on institutional activities "Professional" support
Transition of Bylaws	• Focus on: Regulatory issues Legal considerations Define credentials mechanisms • Developed by: Attorney with input/approval by the medical staff • Implementations Acknowledged (but not read) by new staff members Used occasionally (problem cases or procedural issues)	• Focus on: Role of medical staff in the context of mission of the organization Established ethics and values of medical staff Defines leadership responsibilities and development • Developed by: Medical staff leadership with input from attorney • Implementation Integral to orientation for new staff members Used frequently to guide decision process
Transition of Relationships	• Activities primarily internal to medical staff organization Quality assurance Credentials Medical capital equipment Limited interaction with Board, management team (except CEO), nursing • Behaviors are directive Apathy Complaints Negative incentives • Relationships are: Perfunctory Competitive	• Activities encompass internal medical staff, institutionwide and external functions Strategic planning Operational Community services Regionwide, statewide, and national levels of participation • Behaviors are collaborative Participatory Innovation Positive incentives • Relationships are: Supportive Collaborative
Transition of Functions	• Driven by: Regulation Events/problems • Key functions Monitoring & evaluation Credentials review and privileging Policies/bylaws CME • Peer review Case based Negative Reactive Minimal, sporadic	• Driven by: Ethics/values Future needs/mission Innovation/improvement • Key functions Planning Educational Institutional performance Community leadership • Peer review Aggregate level Positive Proactive Ongoing

Source: Reprinted with permission from IQA^2: Continuous Performance Improvement Through Integrated Quality Assessment. *Published by American Hospital Publishing, Inc., © 1992.*

medical administrative positions in addition to volunteer physician leadership. A growing number of community hospitals, as well as academic medical centers, have created at least one salaried physician executive position during the past decade. This individual manages the activities of the medical staff and channels the perspectives of the medical staff into the operations of the organization.

Salaried physician executive positions are as varied as the hospitals in which they are found. The nature of the position reflects the local culture, politics and geographical location. Some physician executive positions are full-time posts, others are part-time. Most physician executives' salaries are paid by the hospital. Only on rare occasions are salaries paid by the medical staff or financed jointly by the hospital and medical staff. (In the past few years, a variant of this position has emerged—the "circuit riding" medical director who serves multiple hospitals). In some hospitals, physician executives report to the CEO; in others, they report jointly to the CEO and the president of the medical staff.

Candidates for this position must demonstrate strong interpersonal and communication skills, knowledge of healthcare regulation and the forces of change and basic management skills. To be successful, the individual must hold the mutual respect and support of the administration and medical staff, and actively participate at the leadership levels of the organization, particularly at the board and senior management levels.

Physician Leadership Development

Even with a highly qualified physician executive, medical staffs still need voluntary leaders who can effectively manage medical staff issues and positively influence the leadership and management of the healthcare organization. There is simply so much to do that the organization needs a cadre of strong physician leaders. Physician leaders do more than serve as advocates for the medical staff. Based on their strong linkages with patients and the community, and their ongoing contacts with nursing, ancillary, administrative and support staff, physician leaders have valuable "customer" perspectives to share with other institutional leaders.

Traditionally, physician leaders have learned their responsibilities by observing colleagues and from personal trials by fire. This informal apprenticeship approach means that physician leaders come to their jobs with inconsistent and insufficient preparation. But the growing complexities of healthcare will not permit survival of organizations that depend on haphazard management skills. Healthcare organizations need to establish a formal and continuous educational process for medical staff leaders. Organizations that recognize the importance of leadership and commit to programs that actively foster and develop leaders will more likely attain marketplace success. Leadership values should be clearly articulated in the medical staff and hospital bylaws.

Training. Orientation sessions for new leaders should emphasize the values of the organization and the medical staff, as well as their commitment to collaborative efforts. The agenda for an orientation program developed by the law firm Horty, Springer and Mattern for physician leaders at Ellis Hospital, Schenectady, N.Y., appears in Figure 6. *(See page 33.)* Physician leaders should receive a manual that includes the corporate and medical staff bylaws; job descriptions and terms of office for leaders; discussions of key medical staff functions, such as credentialing and quality assessment; policies and procedures for dealing with disruptive or impaired physicians; management techniques, such as staff development and effective meeting skills; and important references, such as sample committee minutes,

Figure 6: Sample Department Chief and Medical Staff Leader Orientation

the Health Care Quality Improvement Act of 1986, and key Joint Commission standards.

The Physician Leader's Guide is designed to supplement the orientation materials provided to leaders by their organizations. In the chapters to follow, experienced physician leaders and other knowledgeable individuals share thoughts and techniques on medical staff roles, quality improvement, credentialing and management methods.

In addition, physician leaders should have continuing education opportunities.

Outside seminars, speakers brought to the hospital, and professional readings on medical management contribute to ongoing leadership development.

Training resources include courses developed by the American College of Physician Executives (ACPE), the Joint Commission, the American Hospital Association and various state hospital associations. Medical staff officers (secretary/treasurer, vice president and president) should be urged to attend ACPE's physician-in-management series (I, II and III) or a similar program as they progressively advance to each position. Similarly, department chairs and assistant chairs should avail themselves of courses in quality improvement sponsored by the Joint Commission and ACPE.

Compensation. Leadership takes time, patience, vision and planning. One issue that needs to be dealt with early on is compensation for the time physician leaders voluntarily take away from their practice and family to participate in medical staff related activities. A growing number of hospitals directly compensate some physicians who do extensive leadership work through monthly stipends. Sometimes, the costs are borne either by the hospital or the medical staff; in other cases, the costs are shared by both. Some organizations offer indirect compensation, such as CME credits, recognition or reimbursement of expenses for spouses to accompany physicians to outside meetings.

In any event, the chore of medical staff leadership is so large and complex that it involves a significant time commitment for training and staff duties. That commitment needs to be recognized with some compensation for the time an individual devotes to making the medical staff work effectively.

Performance Evaluation

All physician leaders should receive feedback about their performance so they can identify opportunities for improvement. Officers and committee chairs may be evaluated by all members of the medical staff, while department and section heads should be assessed by the physicians in their respective departments. A sample, generic performance appraisal for clinical department chairs is shown in Figure 7 *(See page 37)* and can be adapted to meet the needs of each clinical specialty.

The performance appraisal focuses on various aspects of leadership, including how well the individual:

- Serves as an advocate for his or her clinical service;
- Manages administrative functions such as budgeting and long-range planning;
- Fairly enforces medical staff bylaws; and
- Effectively manages credentialing and privileging activities.

For each performance element, physician leaders are rated on a scale, such as from one ("Excellent/Consistently Exceeds Expectations") to five ("Poor/Inconsistently Meets Expectations").

Figure 7: Sample Appraisal Form for Clinical Chairs

Department:________________

Please use the following scale to evaluate specific performance elements.

Excellent/Consistently Exceeds Expectations		Fair/Consistently Meets Expectations		Poor/Inconsistently Meets Expectations
1	2	3	4	5

Performance Elements						
A. Serves as an advocate for the needs of the department.	1	2	3	4	5	N/A*
B. Supports the goals of the medical staff and hospital.	1	2	3	4	5	N/A
C. Actively directs quality assurance and improvement activities of the department.	1	2	3	4	5	N/A
D. Manages department administrative functions (*eg*, budget, planning, and equipment requirements) effectively.	1	2	3	4	5	N/A
E. Consistently conducts well-organized meetings.	1	2	3	4	5	N/A
F. Consistently provides feedback from the Medical Staff Executive Committee and other administrative activities.	1	2	3	4	5	N/A
G. Supports continuing medical education activities.	1	2	3	4	5	N/A
H. Fairly enforces medical staff bylaws and department rules.	1	2	3	4	5	N/A
I. Encourages development of new procedures and technologies.	1	2	3	4	5	N/A
J. Effectively manages the department credentials review and privileging activities.	1	2	3	4	5	N/A

Comments:________________________________

________________ **Signature** ________________ **Date**

* Circle No Answer (N/A) if you do not know enough about this element to form an opinion.

NOTE: UNSIGNED EVALUATIONS WILL NOT BE CONSIDERED

Performance reviews should be conducted annually. After the evaluations have been tallied, the physician executive or chief of staff should meet with each physician leader to review the overall scores for each element and to discuss specific comments and/or issues brought up on the appraisal forms. This individual could work with another physician leader(s) who received an overall score of four or five for any element to develop an individualized program for improving skills and performance.

An Understanding of Successful Physician Enterprise

Essential to physicians' success in the new enterprise is working well together in groups. Typically, by the nature of their work, medical staff leaders take part in shaping physician group culture, even though these groups may not be a formal part of the medical staff. Successful physician groups create a new organizational culture, engage in clinical reengineering to manage risk in panels, become financially integrated and create workable management and governance structures.

As David Ottensmeyer, MD, president and CEO of Lovelace Medical Foundation, once said, culture is "the underlying beliefs that affect the way things are done around here." It is built upon the trust and belief that comes from making medical decisions. In medicine, the current cultural shift reflects an entirely different paradigm of efficiency and effectiveness, which can be uncomfortable.

But medicine is not unique in its externally driven need for cultural change; industries such as banking, telecommunications, automobile manufacturing, steel, computers and others are undergoing similar overhauls. It is always confusing. Change rarely happens slowly and most often occurs at the peripheries of an industry. The most successful in the new world order tend to be those who were among the most disadvantaged in the old one. Finally, the kind of seismic shift that has seized healthcare puts everyone on a level playing field, so the old rules for success may not apply. Prosperous clinical groups will pay attention to and actively manage their cultural environments.

Perhaps to buy time or perhaps because they really don't know what's going on, some organizations mask their failure to achieve real progress with activities that appear to be future oriented. These activities can distract physicians from preparing for the new imperative of risk management and include a carte blanche out

FIGURE 8: KEYS TO SUCCESS

- Understand Market and Political Forces
- Understand Evolution of FFS to Capitation
    - Structure and Function
    - Premium Dollar Flow
    - Patient Care Management Team Models
    - Quality, Outcomes and Information Systems
- Understanding Capital Acquisitions Strategies
- Understanding Business Development
    - Managed Care Vision
    - Governance/Organizational Development
    - PCP Group Formation
    - Market Forecasts
    - Pro Forma Financials
- Understanding Quantitative Partnering Options

sourcing of management services, contracting for discounted fee-for-service reimbursement and externally driven and directed utilization management (UM). Activities that foster change include putting physicians in control of UM, integrating financially and getting physicians involved in management and on the board.

Risk assumption's benefits usually outweigh the costs of learning how to accept fiscal risk for patient care. Management of full risk requires an understanding of epidemiology, actuarial evaluation, pricing, long-term implications of contracts, and the systems to manage health and financial risk across the spectrum of care. Similarly, financial integration holds advantages for physicians but requires skills that are atypical for most medical staffs and will not be accomplished with the totality of the medical staff.

Through a common management structure only occasionally linked to the formal medical staff structure, financially integrated physician groups are able to vote with one voice, vest single-signature authority, align incentives and achieve economies of scale. Some physicians will elect to participate in such risk-sharing arrangements; others will not. Medical staff leaders often are responsible for helping those who want to participate in hospital-sponsored programs, as well as helping those who eschew them.

Medical staff leadership will need the ability to navigate through a maze of options to manage the changes necessary for building a successful enterprise. Keep in mind, though, that the essential skills will be different from those that are key to success in the traditional medical staff structure. Leading the medical staff for this decade and into the next will be challenging, frustrating and, it is hoped, ultimately rewarding. Some may prefer to stand on the sidelines and criticize, but if physicians do this, they and the quality of healthcare will be poorer for it. Healthcare today is a collaborative enterprise of patients, physicians, other health professionals and healthcare delivery organizations working under tremendous constraints. We may not like all the changes and choices placed upon us, but healthcare organizations need our knowledge and professionalism to make the best possible decisions. Leadership roles offer physicians an opportunity to affect the transformations going on around us in both the practice of medicine and the management of healthcare organizations.

◆ ◆ ◆

References

Codman, E.A. *A Study in Hospital Efficiency*. Boston: Thomas Todd Co., 1915.

MacEachern, Malcolmb. *Hospital Organization and Management*, 1st ed. Chicago: The Physicians' Record Co., 1935.

ABOUT THE AUTHORS

J. Edward McEachern, MD, is the vice president for medical affairs at St. Alphonsus Regional Medical Center in Boise, Idaho. Previously, Dr. McEachern was vice president for medical affairs at Hospital Corp. of America (HCA)'s West Paces Ferry Hospital in Atlanta, and quality improvement consultant for direct patient care to HCA's corporate office in Nashville, Tenn. He is the author of four books and numerous articles on quality improvement, and is on the editorial review board of three newsletters.

Jonathan T. Lord, MD is the AHA's chief operating officer. Previously Dr. Lord was the director for quality assurance for the Department of the Navy and served as an advisor to the secretary of the navy during a major reorganization of Navy medicine. He is a member of the American College of Physician Executives and the American Medical Association.

Tomorrow's Vice President for Medical Affairs

By Stephen J. Williams, ScD, and
Charles M. Ewell, PhD

The vice president for medical affairs (VPMA) is an increasingly important management position. This executive is critical to operations, strategic decision-making and day-to-day management, and also has a high degree of vested responsibility within the nation's healthcare system.[1] The appropriate role and duties for this position need to be addressed to understand and ensure medical leadership for the future. The complex issues that impinge on the success of the VPMA in the evolution and operation of the nation's healthcare system are explored utilizing data from a national panel survey conducted by The Governance Institute.

◆ ◆ ◆

Previous Research

Limited data is available to empirically analyze the nature of the vice president for medical affairs position. Various surveys have been conducted of physician leaders.[2,3,4,5,6] Previous research on physician executives has characterized the VPMA as a white male in his mid-50s with responsibility for quality assurance, credentialing, risk management and performance review.[5] Communication skills, clinical credibility, concern for quality of care and leadership qualities have been identified as important characteristics of these administrators.[7] A literature review indicates a more delineated and aggressive stance for medical leadership in the future.[8]

Key Concepts: Vice President Affairs/Medical Leadership Performance Success

The role of medical leadership in hospitals and health systems is under constant scrutiny and change. The nature of the vice president for medical affairs (VPMA) position and its relationship to leadership in the healthcare system is explored through a national panel survey conducted recently. The effective VPMA will: be an aggressive manager able to implement change, and address strategic planning and quality of care issues; have a high level of integrity; and be a good communicator and problem solver. The results of the research are presented in three sections. The first section describes the background characteristics and compensation of the VPMAs who participated in the survey. The second section focuses on the current role of the VPMA, including duties and responsibilities, job performance barriers and required skills. The final section addresses respondents' perceptions regarding areas for improvement in the role of the VPMA, as well as projections for future changes in this position.

The national panel survey results provide a detailed analysis of the duties, characteristics, responsibilities and ideal specifications for the VPMA position. Other aspects of this medical leadership role are explored, such as compensation arrangements. The data provide a framework for clarifying the role of VPMA leadership in operational responsibility for the nation's healthcare system.

Panel Selection, Composition and Survey

Issues addressed in this study were formulated based on a national panel survey of hospital chiefs of staff, interviews with physician leaders and a review of the professional literature. Topics were oriented toward identifying characteristics of the effective physician executive and delineating current and appropriate future roles for the VPMA. Attention was also directed toward the evolution of medical leadership from a traditional focus to a broader health system and payer perspective.

The data were derived from a national panel survey of 69 leading U.S., mostly not-for-profit, hospitals. The participating institutions are members of The Governance Institute, a service provider for hospitals and health systems, whose mission is to improve organizational effectiveness by strengthening members' medical leadership, boards of directors and management.

Questionnaires were addressed to the VPMA or the equivalent position. The questionnaire consisted of a multi-part form and was divided into three sections:

(1) respondent's socio-demographic and background characteristics;
(2) current practices and characteristics for the VPMA position within the institutional setting; and
(3) perspectives on priorities for future roles and responsibilities for this position, and its changing nature in the evolving healthcare system.

VPMA Profile

Of those VPMAs participating in this survey, the median age was 57 years. Although the ages ranged from 37 to 72 years of age, the majority of VPMAs were mature, seasoned professionals. All participants were males, although nationally, female physicians are increasingly assuming administrative responsibilities in this and related positions. Of the 69 participants, 62 were white, although the diversity of ethnic background in medical executive and leadership positions continues to broaden.

The respondents were experienced clinicians—they reported a mean of 25 years of clinical experience in their medical or surgical specialty, as well as a mean of nearly 10 years in medical administration. In a parallel finding, participants reported a mean length of time in their current positions slightly over five years. The average work week was 46 hours, with a range three to 70 hours. They reported devoting little time to clinical medicine, with a mean practice time of six and a half hours per week.

Average cash compensation for VPMAs participating in the survey was $168,111 *(See Figure 1, page 43)*. Larger facilities are generally associated with higher compensation levels. However, with the changing nature of health services and increasing VPMA responsibility for other than inpatient services, bed size may be a less valuable measure of size than in past years.

Few respondents reported holding a formal degree in management. Although all but one respondent was a physician, only three held an advanced degree in public health, business or law. Rather, on-the-job training was much more common, with two-thirds of respondents having held other medical management positions prior to assuming their current position.[9, 10] Virtually all respondents who were physicians, also were board certified in a medical or surgical specialty."

Figure 1: Mean Cash Compensation of VPMAs by Hospital Size

Hospital Bed Size (Beds)	Mean Cash Compensation (Dollars)
0 - 249	119,385
250 - 399	172,602
400+	185,933
All	168,111

Figure 2: VPMA Management Styles, Now and in the Future

Management Style	Current	Future
Highly aggressive	6	18
Moderately aggressive	67	82
Non-aggressive	27	0

—Williams & Ewell

Perspectives on Medical Leadership

The respondents' perspectives on their duties and responsibilities provide insight into the nature of this position. These results also set the stage for the presentation of future perspectives in the following section.

- **Management Styles.** Asked to characterize their management styles, respondents predominantly indicated that they were either moderately aggressive or non-aggressive managers. However, when asked about the appropriate leadership style for the year 2000, there was significant shift in responses toward more highly aggressive styles. (See *Figure 2.)*

- **Barriers to Job Performance.** Respondents were asked to rank order barriers that inhibited their ability to perform their job function to the highest degree of their own satisfaction. The most significant barriers identified by the respondents were resistance to change in their hospital, difficulties in

Figure 3: VPMA Job Performance Barriers

Barrier	Percent Indicating Most Significant Barrier
Resistance to change in hospital	19
Difficulties moving to managed care	16
Lack of medical staff compliance	15
Inadequate role clarification	10
Overwhelming responsibilities	9
Medical staff hostility	9
Not enough time as VPMA	7
Communication problems with medical staff	3
Communication problems with administration	1
Inadequate support from governing entity	1
Inadequate CEO support	1
Barriers to PHO (or similar entity) implementation	1
Other/none	8

moving to managed care and lack of medical staff compliance. These barriers represent significant concerns in light of the direction in which healthcare is moving and the need to adapt to change at the institutional and system levels. (*See Figure 3 on page 43.*) Other barriers were inadequate role clarification, the overwhelming nature of responsibilities, medical staff hostility and inadequate time available to devote to the role of VPMA. These results suggest the complexity of the VPMA position and the difficulties in achieving performance.

VPMA Administrative Responsibilities

Respondents were asked to identify which of their administrative responsibilities were most important in achieving success in their position. The results indicate that the duties that were rated very or highly important to VPMA success included involvement in institutional strategic planning, cost containment, administrative committee liaison, risk management and utilization review, information systems and medical staff credentialing. (See *Figure 4.*) The least important administrative responsibilities for facilitating VPMA success included marketing and physician contract negotiations. The importance of administrative control and organizational responsibilities is particularly notable in assessing which VPMA administrative responsibilities facilitate or are associated with successful job performance.

Figure 4: Important Administrative Responsibilities in Facilitating VPMA Success

Responsibility Area	Percent Indicating Very or Highly Important
Institutional strategic planning	85
Cost containment	78
Committee liaison	71
Risk management/UR	66
Information systems	62
MD staff credentialing	62
Physician recruitment	55
MD staff discipline	53
Coordination with others	47
Community relations	44
MD practice development	43
CME involvement	43
MD contract negotiations	36
Marketing	18

—Williams & Ewell

Time Commitments

What are the most common responsibilities on which respondents spend much of their time? Most notably, improving the quality of care and organizational issues, such as defining organizational goals, dealing with staff and board issues, communicating goals to staff and improving medical staff organization. (*See Figure 5 on page 45.*) Relatively less time is spent on determining governing board agenda items, teaching and research, dealing with community leaders, improving medical staff organization and policies, interacting with the media, determining services termination or reductions, disciplining physicians, communicating organizational goals to the public and generating philanthropic support.

When asked where VPMAs should devote substantially more effort (*See Figure 6 on page 45*), respondents indicated that more time should be spent on improving the quality of care, having greater involvement in information systems, and doing more to evaluate physicians' performance regarding the cost of services provided. Overall, however, respondents indicated that the time allotted to the various responsibilities is appropriate to the demands of their positions.

Figure 5: Five Most Common Responsibilities on which VPMAs Spend Much Time

Responsibility Area	Percent of Respondents Spending "Much" Time On Area
Improving quality of care	71
Defining organizational goals	46
Dealing with staff and board issues	42
Communicating goals to staff	39
Improving medical staff organization	39

—Williams & Ewell

What Does the Future Hold?

With the rapid and dramatic changes in the nation's healthcare system, the respondents' perspectives regarding directions for medical leadership is germane. More than half of the respondents project a moderate or greater increase in the number of medical administration positions in healthcare organizations in the future. Three-fourths indicated that the VPMA position will become more important. Most respondents think that the focus of medical leadership and administration will continue to lie in the hospital, while a smaller percentage suggested that the focus will shift to other organizations, such as medical groups and insurance entities.

Figure 6: Five Most Common Responsibilities on which VPMAs Believe They Should Be Spending More Time

Responsibility Area	Percent of Respondents*
Improving quality of care	49
Dealing with information systems	43
Evaluating physician performance	41
Communicating organizational goals	32
Developing new programs	32

**Percent of respondents indicating they should be spending more time on responsibility area.*

—Williams & Ewell

Figure 7: Five Greatest Strengths in Carrying out VPMA Role

Greatest Strength	Percent of Respondents Indicating Strength
Personal integrity	31
Listening skills	19
Communications	12
Planning	7
Problem Solving	6

—Williams & Ewell

What are the greatest perceived strengths of VPMAs in carrying out their duties? The most prominent responses included personal integrity, listening ability, communications ability, planning and problem solving. (*See Figure 7.*) The greatest indicated weakness was managing time effectively. What are the top five areas of knowledge and skills that are most important to the VPMA role? Respondents overwhelmingly concluded interpersonal and communications skills, followed by knowledge of organizational dynamics and negotiating skills. Asked which of these skills they believe will be most important in the year 2000, the respondents again indicated interpersonal and communications skills, followed by knowledge of quality assurance and organizational dynamics.

The Role of Medical Leadership

The role of medical leadership, and of physicians in particular, is one of increasing importance in the evolution of the nation's healthcare system. The ability to lead, organize and manage physicians and other clinicians will be essential ensuring that the radical changes in organizing and financing health services under way is facilitating the provision of care. [12, 13]

Those in medical leadership positions disproportionately bear this burden, at least based on historical precedent.[14] The executive position of VPMA, or its equivalent, is gaining much more importance as organizational controls over physicians and healthcare providers have increased.

The results of this survey suggest that the VPMA is an experienced clinician with considerable prior experience in medical leadership and administration. Few respondents in this survey had a formal degree in management, suggesting that considerable on-the-job experience is a principal prerequisite.[15,16] A modestly aggressive management style is typical of those responding to the survey, but not reflective of their perceptions of future requirements, which tend toward a more aggressive stance. This perhaps reflects perceptions of the increasing need to provide stronger and more directed leadership in light of ongoing changes in the control and financing of healthcare.[17]

Barriers to successful job performance include difficulties interacting with the medical staff, resistance to change and problems in moving to managed care, all of which may mirror the transition from an indemnity to a managed system. Interaction with administration and governance bodies did not appear to a problem.

Administrative responsibilities that facilitate successful job performance include involvement in cost containment. The allocation of time to quality of care issues, and the suggestion that even more time is needed in this area is consistent with other reports, as is the value of being involved with organizational goal definition and communication.[18,19] The suggestion that more time should be allocated to involvement in information systems and evaluating physician performance is interesting in light of the changing emphasis on control mechanisms and information flows.

Perhaps it is a self-serving observation, but respondents overwhelmingly indicated that the VPMA will increase in importance. In light of the need to better integrate clinicians into the organizational goals of the delivery system, especially with regard to productivity and quality performance, this result is of considerable importance.

The high ranking assigned to personal integrity as an important strength in successful job performance is striking. Communication and problem-solving skills are also of considerable importance in physician executive job success. Time management is an area that needs greater attention. For the future, communication skills, knowledgeable organizational dynamics and negotiating skills are of considerable importance.

In summary, little empirical evidence is available regarding the duties, responsibilities and ideal characteristics of the vice president for medical affairs. Yet, this position has increasing responsibility for shaping the nation's healthcare system.[20] The research reported here is a further step in identifying the duties and characteristics of effective physician executives in decision-making positions of authority and leadership.

◆ ◆ ◆

References

[1]Brown, M. ed., *Physicians and Management in Health Care.* Gaithersburg, MD: Aspen Publishers, 1992.

[2]"Survey of Hospital Medical Staff Organization—1991." Chicago, IL: American Hospital Association, 1992.

[3]Noie, N., Shortell, S.M., and Morrissey, M.A. "A Survey of Hospital Medical Staff—Part 1: New Data Reveal Surprises in Size, Composition, Committee Structure, and Participation in Governance." *Hospitals*, 57:80-84, 1983.

[4]Morrissey, M.A., Shortell, S.M., and Noie, N.E. "A Survey of Hospital Medical Staff—Part 2: Reporting on Changes in Credentialing, Compensation, and Multiple Hospital Appointments." *Hospitals*, 57:91-94, 1983.

[5]Lloyd, J.S., and Guilfoyle, F.M. "Physician Executives in the '90s: Report of a National Survey." *Physician Executive*, 23-29, 1991.

[6]The Governance Institute. "Medical Leadership Trend at 69 Leading Hospitals: 1995 Panel Survey of Vice Presidents for Medical Affairs of Hospital and Health Systems." La Jolla, CA: The Medical Leadership Forum of The Governance Institute,1996.

[7]Tabenkin, H., Zyzanski, S.J. and Alernagno, S.A. "Physician Managers: Personal Characteristics Versus Institutional Demands." *Health Care Management Review, 14*(2): 185-189, 1989.

[8]Kindig, D., and Lastiri-Quiros, S. "The Changing Managerial Role of Physician Executives." *The Journal of Health Administration Education, 3*(2): 169-74, 1985.

[11]Hagland, M. "Physician Execs Bring Clinical Insight to Nonclinical Challenges." *Hospitals, 20*(65): 42-48, 1991.

[12]Royer, T. "Physician Executives of the Future Moving from Management to Leadership." *MGM Journal,* 10,12 (Jan./Feb. 1995).

[13]Johnson, J. "How to Give MDs a Greater Role Management." *Hospitals, 20*(66): 64, 1992.

[14]Riley, P. "Health Care Administration in the Year 2000: Practitioners' Views of Future Issues and Job Requirements." *Hospitals and Health Services Administration*, 38: 181-195, 1993.

[15]Ottensmeyer, D.J., and Key, M.K. "Lessons Learned Hiring HMO Medical Directors." *Health Care Management Review,* 16(2): 199-204, 1991.

[16]McCall, M.W., and Clair, J.A. "In Transit from Physician to Manager—Part 1." *Physician Executive*, 18(2): 3, 1992.

[17]Johnson, J. "Proactive Executives: Prospering Tough Times." *Hospitals*, 22-27, March 1991.

[18]Kirschman, D., and Grebenschikoff, J. "Quality Management Remains Top Medical Manager Responsibility." *Physician Executive*, 42-44, (Sept./Oct. 1992).

[19]Ashmos, D.P., and McDaniel, R.R., Jr. "Physician Participation in Hospital Strategic Decision Making: The Effect of Hospital Strategy and Decision Content." *Health Research*, 26(3): 375-401, Aug. 1991.

[20]Coddington, D.C., Moore, K.D., and Fischer, E.A. *Integrated Health Care: Reorganizing the Physician. Hospital and Health Plan Relationship.* Englewood, CO: Center for Research in Ambulatory Health Care Administration, 1994.

About the Authors

Stephen J. Williams, ScD, is professor of public health and head of the Division of Health Services Administration for the Graduate School Public Health at San Diego State University, in California.

Charles M. Ewell, Ph.D., is president of The Governance Institute in La Jolla, Calif.

Conflict and Cooperation: The Chief Medical Officer and the Chief of Staff As a Team

by Kenneth C. Cummings, MD, FACPE

The roles of the chief medical officer (CMO) and the chief of staff (COS) are not always fully understood. This can cause conflict and misunderstanding between the two positions. In this article, the author outlines an approach chief medical officers and chiefs of staff can use to foster teamwork and collaboration.

◆ ◆ ◆

The position of chief medical officer is not a new phenomenon in the hospital setting. It has evolved over time in response to organizational need and development. Historically, the position was filled by part-time volunteers, chiefs of staff elected or appointed by the medical staff itself.

As hospitals have grown in size and complexity and as time and energies have increased, a number of healthcare organizations have added a physician executive position of salaried medical director (part- or full-time) and, more recently, vice president for medical affairs, while also retaining the elected chief of staff position. The senior physician executive usually is accountable to the CEO, although medical staffs are almost always consulted on hiring and firing for physician executive positions.

No single model defines the organizational relationship between physician executive and chief of staff. Rather, myriad arrangements can be found. Many, however, fall into one of the following categories:

- A full-time, salaried vice president for medical affairs, with or without a subordinate salaried medical director, both of whom work with a volunteer chief of staff elected by the medical staff;
- A full-time, salaried medical director who works with a volunteer chief of staff elected by the medical staff;
- A full-time, salaried medical director working with an elected or appointed chief of staff who is paid a modest stipend. In this arrangement, the chief of staff's responsibilities are likely to exceed those of a volunteer chief;
- A part-time, salaried medical director serving with a volunteer or modestly compensated chief of staff. Smaller organizations frequently adopt this model;

- A full-time, salaried medical director working with a figurehead chief of staff who wields less power than clinical department heads. The dynamics of this model, found in some academic medical centers, can pose interesting challenges; or
- A full- or part-time, salaried medical director who also serves as an officer of the medical staff. The duality of this model is clear; the individual serving in this capacity must continually balance organizational objectives with medical staff perspectives.

Regardless of the staffing model adopted by the organization, the potential exists either for collaboration or conflict between these positions. Typically, a chief of staff's loyalties are heavily weighted in favor of his or her profession and fellow physicians. Physician executives, though seasoned clinicians, must take a more balanced position, of course protecting the patients and the clinicians' prerogatives, but also protecting the rights and interests of the hospital or institution. Given their divided loyalties, and in many cases, their overlapping responsibilities, the prognosis for genuine cooperation between physician executives and chiefs of staff could be dim.

From the organization's point of view, cooperation between these individuals is critical to its ability to ensure quality and to its overall success in the marketplace. Ongoing conflict between a physician executive and chief of staff can ensure failure amidst the burgeoning competition among healthcare providers. How, then, can the organization, as well as its two (or more) key physician leaders, minimize conflict and maximize cooperation?

Clearly define the roles. As a first measure, the physician executive and chief of staff need to have clearly defined roles and responsibilities. Sample position descriptions developed by the American Medical Association appear in Figures 1 and 2, pages 51 and 52. If any aspect of the relationship is left ambiguous, the potential for conflict increases. Ambiguity also arms others. Either physicians or nonphysician administrators can use the tension between the two leaders to advance their own agendas. Clearly defined and mutually agreed upon roles and responsibilities do not ensure that the physician executive and chief of staff will be able to work effectively together. Their relationship will be determined, to a large extent, by the culture of the organization. If an underlying lack of trust exists between the organization and the medical staff, then the physician executive and chief of staff's most well-intentioned efforts to work together in a cooperative and constructive manner will not likely succeed. Conversely, if these two individuals are locked in personal conflict, they will poison collaborative efforts initiated by the board, administration or medical staff.

The Chief Medical Officer (CMO) (also commonly entitled the vice president for medical affairs, or VPMA)

The CMO/VPMA must possess the set of skills defined for the medical director in Figure 1 on page 51, but must also possess other skills and perspectives. He/she must be a more strategic thinker, both internally and externally; must have knowledge and/or skill for marketing, business venture development, finance, planning,

Figure 1: Responsibilities of the Medical Director

The medical director is usually responsible for most of the administrative responsibilities of the hospital medical staff and is accountable to the hospital governing board who hired him or her for the management of medical staff functions.

Traditional hospital/medical staff relationships may be altered with the establishment of this position. The medical director assumes many of the administrative functions and responsibilities of the president or chief of staff of the medical staff:

- Acting as liaison between the institution's governing and administrative bodies and the medical staff and between the institution and regulatory and accrediting agencies.
- Attending all medical staff meetings and committee meetings.
- Enforcing and implementing medical staff bylaws, rules and regulations.
- Implementing and assuring compliance with institutional bylaws and required policies from regulatory and accrediting agencies.
- Representing the medical staff to the governing an administrative bodies of the hospital, keeping each informed on issues of mutual concern.
- Monitoring all medical staff activities and periodically reporting the findings to the hospital governing board and administration.
- Serving as chief quality assurance officer, establishing and maintaining review analysis and evaluation of medical staff performance in all department/services.
- Establishing and maintaining channels of communication.
- Monitoring and maintaining professional standards and criteria regarding application for appointment and reappointment to medical staff membership.
- Establishing and maintaining continuing medical education programs.
- Providing direction and guidance to department chairmen and committees in establishing and fulfilling proper functions of the medical staff.
- Directing efficient operation and organization of the medical staff.
- Administering any other duties as assigned.

Source: Organization: A Guide for Hospital Medical Staffs. © American Medical Association, 1985

higher level negotiation, corporate management and business environment; and political savvy.

Further, the CMO position requires principle-based leadership, change process leadership and unusual ability for clear, straightforward and honest communications.

The Medical Director

The inherent tension in the medical director's position has been termed the dual-role dilemma of doctor and administrator. The medical director needs to apply a range of skills to bridge the two perspectives.

Figure 2: Responsibilities of the Chief of Staff

- Presiding at general medical staff meetings.
- Serving as chairman of the executive committee, preparing agendas and presiding at meetings.
- Serving as liaison between the institution's governing and administrative bodies and the medical staff.
- Making necessary preparations, attending and presiding at committee meetings other than the executive committee as defined in the medical staff bylaws.
- Serving, consulting and advising other committees, either in an official capacity or as an ex officio member as defined in the medical staff bylaws.
- Enforcing and implementing medical staff bylaws, rules, regulations and sanctions, in compliance with standards of ethical conduct and professional demeanor.
- Appointing committee members and chairmen as required in the medical staff bylaws.
- Representing the medical staff to the governing body and administration of the institution, and keeping each informed on issues of mutual concern.
- Transmitting to the appropriate authority medical staff views, concerns and recommendations on matters affecting policy, planning, operations, governance and relationships with external agencies.
- Serving as chief quality assurance officer.
- Directing the efficient operation of the medical staff.

Source: Organization: A Guide for Hospital Medical Staffs. © American Medical Association, 1985

A good listener. Some years ago, when I was a newly appointed medical director, a medical staff member said to me, "Doctor, you are hearing my words, but are you hearing my heart?" Members of the medical staff know the medical director is accountable to administration, but they expect this individual to be sensitive to their views and needs as well. He or she is, after all, a physician. To serve dual masters effectively, the medical director must not only be a good listener, but also be perceived as one by the medical staff. He or she must also be empathetic and diplomatic, both allowing and encouraging others to fully state their views and feelings.

Inevitably, the medical director will have to make decisions that fail to meet all the medical staff's expectations. If this individual is not viewed as being sensitive to medical staff needs and a fair and honest decision maker, the medical staff will withdraw its support, and institutional conflict is likely to result. Aroused to battle, the medical staff can be a formidable foe.

A consensus seeker. My clinical practice in pathology almost always involved communicating across specialties and stimulating specialists to communicate. A surgical colleague suggested that one reason I was successful as a medical director is my clinical specialty. What this colleague was identifying is the importance of seeking consensus. The organization wants a medical director who is firmly in touch with the medical staff, but it also needs an individual who will subscribe to and promote the goals and objectives of the hospital. Management needs a medical director to be a consensus builder between the hospital and medical staff, one who can find the common ground and mutual benefits in difficult situations. If the medical director is found wanting in this regard, the organization will seek another individual to fill the role.

Role clarification. The transitional nature of our healthcare delivery system has placed greatly increased stress on managers and practitioners alike. Much of the stress can be reduced or accommodated more effectively by rigorous role clarification. The medical director must have a clear understanding not only of his or her own role in the organization, but also that of the chief of staff. Further, the medical director must play a key role in helping the chief of staff understand the new realities in medical leadership in the hospital and a larger health system or community. Much conflict can be avoided or more easily resolved if the chief of staff is the medical director's emissary to the medical staff. While this may shift some of the conflict to the chief of staff, this individual is almost always better positioned to successfully handle it. This will help the medical director if he or she supports the chief of staff whenever possible. However, if too much conflict is shifted, or if it is shifted on a regular and ongoing basis, the chief of staff will tire of the turmoil. Again, the likely result is the replacement of the medical director.

Negotiating skills. The duality of the medical director's role demands well-honed negotiating skills. The medical director must help management and the medical staff resolve their differences through enlightened give and take. If the medical director maintains an open and probing mind, a win-win resolution is more likely to occur. If one side or the other must be supported, it is often helpful for the medical director to consider the issue from the patient's point of view. In my opinion, it is much easier for both sides to agree on what constitutes the best answer for the patient; negotiations can proceed from there.

Long-term gain. Effective leaders take the long-term view, understanding that myriad small steps—some forward, some backward—lead to success. Ultimate satisfaction comes from attaining the long-term goal, not from the steps themselves. Long-term success requires patience and a high degree of selflessness. The medical director must develop these characteristics and cultivate them in those with whom he or she works. Conflicts become unresolvable only when the parties involved lock themselves into positions from which they cannot or will not retreat.

Some years ago, as a newly recruited medical director, I was confronted with a 10-year-old complex clinical/administrative situation with multiple players, each out of patience and ruling out potential solutions because their short-term objectives might not be met. In subsequent meetings that spanned many hours, we reassessed what the issues really were and developed an expanded list of solutions, one of which was ultimately adopted and remains functional to this day.

Open communication. I have found that information received from, for example, a floor nurse, secretary or QA/UR staff member can be extremely valuable for understanding problems or behaviors and for reaching a solution. To ensure that the dialogue remains open and concentrated on mutually acceptable compromise, the medical director will need to have informal communication with affected parties and with others who can contribute. The director of nursing or director of pharmacy, for instance, could hold the key to resolving a conflict between the medical staff and the hospital's financial staff. If the medical director has good contacts with these third parties, he or she can bring their contribution to the main discussions.

The medical director acts as an intermediary and a sounding board, gathering input from a wide range of individuals and ensuring that information is communicated accurately and in a timely fashion to all involved.

The Chief of Staff

Like the medical director, the chief of staff needs to apply a range of skills in the pursuit of collaboration. Also, like the medical director, he or she must clearly understand his or her role.

Elected representative. The chief of staff needs to be seen by the medical staff as representing its interests in dealing with the hospital. No matter how accomplished the medical director is in fulfilling his or her duties, it is the chief of staff who is viewed as the medical staff's "friend." Even in cases when the chief of staff is compensated by the hospital for his or her administrative tasks, the person is viewed as an extension of the medical staff and not as a member of the management team.

Communication skills. The relationship between the medical director and the chief of staff is two-way. The interpersonal skills critical for the medical director also apply to the chief of staff. The chief of staff must have firm knowledge of the wishes of the medical staff and must be able to effectively communicate those wishes to the medical director.

Whenever possible, the chief of staff must be able and willing to support the medical director and to take his or her views back to the medical staff. In this regard, communication skills are just as necessary as they are for the medical director. The chief of staff cannot discharge his or her liaison function between the medical staff and the administration if there is poor acceptance or understanding of the administration's goals or an inability to communicate those goals dispassionately to the medical staff.

The modern day chief of staff is expected to quickly learn, or already have, an understanding of many of the functions of the CMO, but practiced in the context of the chief's role of physician advocate and spokesperson. The CMO must have a willingness to learn, since many of the skills required of chiefs of staff aren't part of medical training or experience. If the COS is dealing with the VPMA, issues are usually more significant, politically and economically more complex and the requirement for a decision on both sides to be collaborative as opposed to adversarial is even more essential.

Overlapping Responsibilities

Regardless of the personal characteristics that these physician leaders bring to their respective roles, the potential for conflict is always present. Were it not, there would be less need for these positions.

Part of their job is to see that conflicts are averted or, when they occur, that they are resolved with minimum disruption to the organization, the medical staff and patient care. Key to any collaboration between the physician executive and chief of staff is their ability to reach an agreement on how difficult overlapping responsibilities will be handled. Several questions are illustrative.

Who has the responsibility for credentialing and privileging decisions, and who has the right to take disciplinary action? The medical director and chief of staff must develop a mutually agreeable division of responsibility for these processes. Medical staff credentialing, privileging and disciplinary processes, which traditionally have been the purview of the medical staff, are ultimately accountable to the governing board. Procedures must be clearly outlined in the medical staff bylaws and strictly adhered to. Regardless of who has primary control over these functions, the other individual has to be well connected at critical steps. Both the administration and the medical staff must be assured that their representatives are fully knowledgeable of all administrative functions.

Generally, the medical director performs the administrative functions associated with credentialing, privileging and disciplinary activity, such as management of information gathering, assembling performance profiles and ensuring that the bylaws are being followed. It is the chief of staff's duty to hold medical staff officers and department heads accountable for performing peer review and making recommendations to the board. Figure 3 on page 55 illustrates how a medical director and chief of staff might delineate overlapping credentialing responsibilities.

Who speaks to the board on behalf of the medical staff? The short answer is, both do, but each from a slightly different perch. The medical staff has long been accustomed to a special relationship with the board of trustees. In fact, much of the tension between the administration and the medical staff can stem from this relationship. With the hiring of a physician executive, the relationship is altered, and the medical director or VPMA, acting as the chief medical officer and usually reporting to the CEO, is seen by the board as a primary source of medical information.

At the same time, if the chief of staff has been elected by the medical staff, it is his or her duty to represent the interests of the medical staff to the administration and the board. In these situations, the chief of staff generally sits ex-officio on the hospital board. Both the chief of staff and the medical director must assure the medical staff, on an ongoing basis, that their positions are being represented in a fair and impartial manner, and that they are receiving an open hearing from the board. Conflicts will arise when the medical director is viewed as an inadequate or biased representative by the medical staff or the administration. One way to circumvent this is to have a "joint conference committee" made up of board members, medical

Figure 3: Example of Mutual Agreement on Handling Overlapping Responsibilities

Typical Credentialing Responsibilities	Medical Director	Chief of Staff
Assembling credentials files	Manages the process.	Advises on what files should contain.
Developing performance profiles for reappointments	Develops a system for assembling and displaying valid data.	Advises on data and format. Holds clinical chairs accountable for reviewing the profiles.
Reviewing malpractice cases	Manages the process for gathering information for review by clinical chairs; prepares draft case summaries.	Holds clinical chairs accountable for review of malpractice information.
Recommending approval or disciplinary acton	Coordinates the process, ensuring that recommendations are timely and well documented.	Ensures that the clinical chairs, credentials committee, and MEC have done a thorough review.

staff officers, physician executives and administrators to process all medical staff related issues prior to board review.

Who has responsibility for medical quality management? In most cases, the medical director retains organizational responsibility for designing and implementing both the traditional medical staff QA, QI and UR systems. However, cooperation between the medical director and the chief of staff is imperative.

Too often in the past, physicians perceived QA, QI and UR as thinly disguised attempts to "beat up on" the medical staff. As a result, physicians have greeted each new initiative—from quality assurance and continuous quality improvement through outcomes management and clinical protocol development—with reluctance if not outright resistance.

If the medical director hopes to achieve the promise of these systems, he or she must persuade the chief of staff of their efficacy, so that the chief of staff can help overcome any resistance from the medical staff.

Who has responsibility for settling departmental turf wars? The larger and more complicated the medical staff structure, the more likely it is that major territorial battles will erupt. Neither the medical director nor the chief of staff may be directly involved, but both will have to play roles in easing or settling the turf battles.

Ideally, prime responsibility for settling interdepartmental disputes should fall on the chief of staff and the medical staff organization as a whole. The medical director should provide backing and information and be kept fully informed about how the issue is resolved. The medical director should take an active role only if the chief of staff and the medical staff cannot resolve the issue themselves.

In practice, the chief of staff frequently has several professional or personal reasons to avoid the conflict. Commonly, what actually evolves is that the medical director is expected, by the chief of staff, to bring about resolution of the issue, with his or her input.

Turf battles can quickly deteriorate into no-win situations. It is best for future relationships between the medical director and the chief of staff if the medical director is isolated from the main segments of the battlefield, being brought on only as a last resort.

Beyond the above, there are a number of hospital issues that provide the opportunity for considerable conflict or harmony and synergy. A list of these, to name but a few, would include: (1) the hiring of full-time, salaried intensivists; (2) economic pressure to develop an exclusive physician-panel organization as part of a physician-hospital organization; and (3) via exclusive contract or board of trustees fiat, closure of a specialty service or function to other members of the medical staff or community.

To sum up, the physician executive and chief of staff can succeed if they view their relationship as a team effort. The former focuses on the managerial role, the latter on the representational role, and together, they agree how to share overlapping realities.

About the Author

Kenneth C. Cummings, MD, FACPE, is executive vice president of physician integration and services, Carondelet Health, Kansas City, MO.

What the Governing Board Expects From Physician Leaders and What Physician Leaders Should Expect in Return

By Barry S. Bader

In an open letter to physician leaders, the author:

- *Explains why, from the perspective of a hospital trustee, effective physician leaders are critical to organizational excellence;*
- *Shares a trustee's expectations of physician leaders; and*
- *Articulates what hospital boards should pledge to physicians in return for their service in leadership positions.*

◆ ◆ ◆

Dear Doctor:

I am a trustee, a member of the governing board of a hospital like the one at which you and your colleagues practice. Like most trustees on the boards of hospitals, health systems and other types of healthcare delivery organizations, I am here for many reasons, but one is paramount: I hope to put to work my knowledge, experience, judgment and position in the community for the good of the organization and its patients.

Similarly, you have accepted a position as an elected officer, chair of a clinical department, or chair of a medical staff committee. As a physician leader, you are voluntarily fulfilling a professional responsibility to enhance the quality of patient care through participation in the organization's policy making, decision making and peer review activities.

While our backgrounds differ, I believe trustees and physician leaders share common goals that revolve around excellent patient care. If we each can better understand the other's needs and expectations, we can work in a collaborative way to meet and exceed our shared objectives. In this letter, I hope to clarify from at least one trustee's perspective the board's expectations of physician leaders. In turn, I want to delineate the things you and your fellow physicians have a right to expect from me and my colleagues on the board.

Why We Serve

Trustees come from varied backgrounds. Many are successful business people, financiers, civic leaders or attorneys, and they serve in order to give something back to the communities that have treated them so well. Others are professionals drawn from the organization itself—physicians, nurses, the chief executive officer—who have been elevated to a special position of trust and responsibility. Their expertise and insights are invaluable. Some trustees are men and women from religious communities, serving the institution as an embodiment of their sacred life commitment. However diverse their backgrounds, though, trustees come united to the board to serve its mission and its future, to help it achieve excellence in challenging times.

What the Board Needs

As board members, trustees bring knowledge from outside the organization, but we depend heavily on the organization's internal leaders to inform and help us carry out our difficult roles and responsibilities. We look to the chief executive officer for strategic direction and managerial expertise. Similarly, we look to physicians in leadership positions for guidance in our work that affects clinical care and services.

We are responsible for deciding who is allowed to practice in this institution. As board members, we have to decide how to allocate limited resources, such as whether we can afford both a new CT scanner and a new endoscopy suite, or whether one purchase will have to wait until next year. We have to decide whether the medical staff development plan that guides efforts to recruit and retain physicians meets the mission, community need and strategic goals; complies with legal requirements; and is fair to the physicians on staff. We need to determine whether physicians returning from treatment for substance abuse should be allowed to regain their clinical privileges and, if so, under what conditions. To make these and countless other medically related decisions wisely, we need your counsel and support.

Specifically, trustees seek the following from their interactions with physician leaders:

- Acceptance of your role as a physician leader;
- Medical expertise;
- Translation of medical jargon;
- Objectivity based on information;
- Thoroughness;
- Organizational perspective;
- Voice of the customer;
- Consistency;
- Management of dualities of interest; and
- Attendance.

I will discuss and give examples of each of these before going on to what physician leaders have a right to expect in return from trustees.

Leadership. First and foremost, the board looks to you to be a *leader*. The focus of the leader is meeting not only the demands of today but also the challenges of tomorrow. Leaders are visionaries, seeing the needs of the future and the changes required to get there. Leaders take time out for education to understand the forces of change, and they emphasize communication and collaboration in the pursuit of strategic responses.

Many changes are neither understood nor welcomed initially by those affected. Hospital outpatient care centers, physician recruitment, cooperation with managed care organizations and a greater board role in credentialing are examples of changes required of hospitals and greeted less than warmly by many physicians. The board looks to physician leaders to use their positions to understand the need for change, communicate it to their peers and help shape responsible change strategies.

Medical expertise. Substantively, trustees look to physician leaders for the clinical expertise that goes into sound policymaking and decision making at the board level. For example, we look to physician leaders to help us answer such questions as:

- Do physicians applying to the staff and seeking reappointment have the requisite training, experience and current clinical and behavioral competence to be granted privileges to practice in this institution?

- Does a proposed new medical technology meet clinical standards of efficacy, and how will it benefit our patients if the organization acquires it?

- What should be the organization's policies on difficult matters of medical ethics, such as do-not-resuscitate orders, advance patient directives or testing of healthcare workers for the AIDS virus?

As trustees, we cannot make intelligent decisions on matters such as these without clinical input.

Translation and interpretation of medical jargon. Relatively few trustees have clinical experience. We need physician leaders to put clinical terms and procedures into language and analogies we can understand.

As a physician leader, you can nurture a positive climate for learning in the board room by presenting medical topics without jargon, encouraging questions and, when they arise, answering them directly and clearly. Be wary of inadvertent patronization, such as prefacing explanations with a statement like, "You nonphysicians probably wouldn't understand...." When you use a clinical term or abbreviation, think about using a phrase trustees are familiar with, such as replacing CABG with cardiac bypass surgery or transurethral prostatectomy (TURP) with prostate surgery.

Objectivity based on information. Trustees also need medical information to be presented as objectively as possible. While trustees respect physicians' judgment, it's important that we understand the basis of recommendations for credentialing decisions, medical policies and other proposed actions.

This is the same way that I and my fellow trustees operate our businesses. For instance, if my vice president for information services says, "Buy this computer for $100,000," I trust that judgment, but I want to know how he or she came to that conclusion. Has the VP considered other alternatives, researched the proposed vendor and consulted our employees who will use the computer? In other words, what are the objective facts that support the recommendation?

Trustees know from experience that an analytical process leads to more informed, better decisions, and we want to apply that model to medically related decisions we must make as board members. For example:

> The Medical Executive Committee has voted unanimously to recommend termination of Dr. Z.'s privileges. Dr. Z.'s care was judged substandard by peer review of patient charts in two of Dr. Z.'s cases, one of which resulted in the patient's death.
>
> That's not enough information to support a decision by the board of trustees. To demonstrate that the peer review mechanism has been thorough and objective, the recommendation could be supported by additional facts such as:
>
> - The total number of cases that Dr. Z. treated, and results of quality reviews on those cases;
> - An understandable description of the objective performance indicators on which Dr. Z.'s care was assessed;
> - A comparison of Dr. Z.'s outcomes with those of his peers on the staff here and, if available, with national or other norms;
> - The opinions of external, independent peer reviewers, particularly if the physicians judging Dr. Z. are close economic competitors; and
> - Summaries of the findings of a hearing panel or whatever mechanism is provided by the bylaws to offer due process to Dr. Z.

By asking for such information to accompany an adverse credentialing recommendation, trustees are not questioning the judgment of physician leaders. They are verifying that an objective foundation for the action exists. With objective information, the board will be able to make a fact-based decision that protects the interests of patients and the institution. By insisting on facts, we respect the rights of the physician facing disciplinary action and safeguard the medical staff from antitrust allegations.

Thoroughness. Leadership makes tremendous demands on physicians' time, particularly for meetings and chart review activities. Trustees know physician leaders are busy people, with a practice to run and patients to see. Nevertheless, the board needs thoroughness in the clinical review and input that goes into the medical staff's recommendations. Hospital decisions to deny appointment or privileges have been overturned by courts because the staff's recommendations, although clinically justifiable, were not supported by thorough documentation and observance of due process requirements. We must all work together to use time efficiently, but time pressures can never be an acceptable excuse for cutting corners, whether by the medical staff, management or the board.

Organizational perspective. Perhaps the most difficult thing trustees need from physician leaders is for them to place their counsel to the board in an organizational perspective. The physician's primary duty is of course to the patient, and the physician leader also has a duty to the organization and the broader interests of all patients. The imperative of leadership is to place these interests uppermost. For example:

> Assume you are a surgeon and the chair of the Credentials Committee. You get many patient referrals from the internal medicine practice of Drs. A, B and C.
>
> Drs. AB&C recruit Dr. D., who is recommended for privileges by the chair of medicine, who this year is Dr. A. Dr. D. has a checkered history, with past problems involving both clinical care and professional behavior.
>
> The board looks to the chair of the Credentials Committee and, in turn, the Medical Executive Committee, to place personal interests aside and take an organizational perspective on Dr. D.'s application. The board can grant privileges based only on documentation of current clinical and behavioral competence. The law and accreditation standards are quite specific about this. We need to be sure the medical staff has made a thorough review of Dr. D. and not just rubber stamped his application to avoid antagonizing Drs. AB&C.

Trustees understand the difficulties posed by such situations, including the potential loss of patient referrals to leaders acting on their convictions. However, the physician leader's overriding obligation is to the hospital patients that Dr. D. will treat—the same patients that the trustees of the organization have a duty to protect.

Voice of the customer. In business parlance, physicians are customers of the hospital—the largest customer group really, since they admit the patients and order the majority of services, from tests to drugs to procedures. Physician leaders provide a vital channel of communication between members of the medical staff and the leaders of the board and management.

By your involvement in such processes as strategic planning, capital budgeting, continuous quality improvement and technology assessment, you can help ensure that the organization meets the needs of its physician customers and, by so doing, enhances the quality of care and services provided to patients and the community.

Consistency. As a board member, I expect other trustees, executives and physician leaders to explore issues thoroughly, gathering facts and airing various viewpoints. Diversity is productive in the fact-finding and deliberative phases of decision making. Once agreement is reached, however, we need to move forward as a team. Physician leaders, board members and executives need to be able to count on each other.

When this process breaks down, it's very destructive of trust. For example, one hospital was planning a major facility modernization. The chief of the medical staff accompanied the CEO to round after round of meetings with clinical departments and the Medical Executive Committee, seeking advice on the renovations. At each meeting, the chief spoke out in support of the modernization effort and emphasized the CEO's willingness to respond to physicians' suggestions. Many physicians' ideas were incorporated into the plans. But at the board meeting to approve the final plan, the chief of staff stood up and said he'd talked to some doctors who were opposed (although they'd never taken the opportunity to come to any meetings to air their views). Then came the *coup de grace*: The chief of staff said he was opposed, too! The CEO was aghast; he'd been working hand-in-hand with the chief of staff for more than a year.

The trustees at this hospital wanted physician leaders to speak their mind. But they also needed consistency. If the process of gathering and responding to physician input was flawed, the chief had an obligation to voice this earlier, not to reverse direction at the 11th hour.

Management of dualities of interest. A conflict or duality of interest occurs when an organizational leader has, or appears to have, a duty to both the organization's interests and a personal or professional interest. For instance, a trustee who is an investment banker has a conflict if his or her firm seeks to manage the organization's investments. So do trustees who provide legal or accounting services, medical supplies, or other products and services to the organization.

Such potential dualities of interest are inevitable; what counts is how they are handled. All leaders occupy a position of trust; we must not only *do* the right thing, we must also *appear* to be doing the right thing.

On the board, we have rules to govern such situations. For instance, the investment banker/trustee would declare the conflict and excuse himself or herself from a discussion and vote on the choice of a firm to manage the organization's investments. That can be tough, because the rest of the board will miss the trustee's expertise. However, our fiduciary responsibility requires us to be very careful in this regard. We have to be ready to demonstrate our impartiality.

Similarly, the board expects physician leaders to follow the two bywords for conflict of interest situations: disclosure and, depending on the circumstances, disassociation from the discussion and/or decision. For example:

When a physician joins a practice, his or her partners would have a duality of interest if one of them were a leader responsible for conducting the required medical staff interview or, as department chair, making a recommendation for appointment and privileges. In such a case, the partner needs to recognize the potential conflict and allow someone else to conduct the interview and make the credentialing recommendation.

Similarly, if the board is discussing acquisition of technology or initiation of a service that would significantly enhance or harm the business of a physician board member, that individual should disclose it and probably not vote.

Duality of interest is always a sensitive matter. Many people are uncomfortable disclosing parts of their professional and private lives. However, whenever dualities of interest occur, leaders have an obligation to be open and aboveboard in order to preserve their integrity and influence.

Attendance. Finally, trustees need physician leaders to participate. We recognize that an abundance of required meetings coupled with the unpredictable timing of patient care make it hard for physicians to maintain a perfect attendance record. Emergencies, unexpectedly long surgery, responsibilities in the office and at other facilities, and the need to cover for colleagues are common.

As a trustee, I want your patients to come first. However, physician leaders have been asked to serve in their positions for important reasons, and that responsibility deserves their time and attention. In order for the organization to benefit from their expertise, physician leaders need to make meeting attendance a high priority.

What Physician Leaders Should Expect

The board/physician leader relationship is not a one-way street; it's a partnership. In return for your service, you should expect a number of commitments from the board of trustees. To begin with, trustees need to parallel every expectation I've delineated for physician leaders:

- To be visionary leaders, emphasizing communication and collaboration;
- To provide expertise from our specialties in business, finance, law and other aspects of management;
- To bring the voice of the community to our deliberations;
- To interpret business and legal jargon in understandable terms;
- To be objective, thorough, and consistent;
- To act in the best interests of the organization and its mission;
- To manage conflicts of interest with scrupulous diligence; and
- To participate fully.

In addition, trustees need to support effective physician leadership in a number of special ways:

Appreciation and recognition. Physician leaders face tremendous practice pressures, from legal, payment and regulatory arenas. As a trustee, I need to make it known that the organization appreciates the work you do as a leader. Physician leaders take time from their practices and patients to help a less tangible group of patients, the organization and the community at large. Sometimes, it's hard to see how the work in board and medical staff forums benefits patients. The government accreditation bodies and other external bureaucracies seem to be the focus of our efforts. In fact, I believe our efforts do promote quality and organizational effectiveness. Effective credentialing contributes to medical quality, as does physician participation in continuous quality improvement activities. As trustees, we appreciate your contributions and promise to recognize them every chance we get.

Mission. The board will make decisions from the cornerstone of its commitment to the mission of the organization and not from any personal or professional interest. As trustees, we will put the interests of patients and the community first. We will seek your early involvement in the decision-making process for new programs and services.

Openness. We will constantly seek a range of views, including yours, that help us serve as trustees. We are always ready to hear from you and always ready for new and different thinking. Together we will learn, and our patient care organization will grow and prosper.

Due consideration and objective decision making. We promise to carefully consider your advice and recommendations. Oftentimes, the board must balance competing interests and cannot entirely follow physicians' advice, but we promise to weigh your counsel heavily. When we depart from your recommendations or must choose between equally meritorious alternatives, we will explain the rationale for the decision.

Support/resources. We pledge to give you, through the organization, the support and resources you need to be an effective physician leader. This includes training in leadership skills, orientation and reference manuals, and access to experts, including legal counsel on difficult credentialing matters. We also pledge to support the allocation of administrative resources, such as personnel and computerization for QI and credentialing.

Some physician leaders say the time they spend deserves compensation. I and many of my fellow trustees support this concept. Compensation is appropriate for some leadership positions when the administrative demands are significant, when accountability accompanies compensation, and when physicians themselves feel that compensation will not compromise their professional integrity. In the community hospital medical staff, compensation of physician leaders is a complex matter in which different organizations will come to different solutions. As a trustee, I am open to looking at the options and crafting a workable solution.

Confidentiality. Every member of the governing board must respect the confidentiality of discussions, especially those concerning patients and physicians with possible performance problems. On this there can be no compromise.

Trust and Respect. Underlying all of the expectations discussed here is the concept of mutual trust and respect. As a trustee, I pledge to respect each physician's clinical training, your oath to your patients, and the difficulty of your profession. I recognize the economic constraints you face. And I respect the time you devote to your leadership responsibilities. In return, I ask you to respect the voluntary commitment I and other trustees make, and trust that we are here for the same purpose as you: excellence in the provision of patient care.

No group of people can function without mutual trust and respect. We all bring something different to the table: clinical expertise, community knowledge, financial acumen, legal background and so forth. Time and again, I have seen boards make better decisions because of the range of knowledge and perspectives contributed by a diverse membership and supported by the recommendations of physician leaders.

Most leaders with whom I come in contact display this strong mutual trust and respect. If one of our colleagues does not exemplify these essential baseline values, it's our job to counsel our own, for without respect there can be no trust, without trust no communication and without communication, no collaboration.

So, doctor, these are the expectations of one trustee and, in return, my commitment to you and your fellow physician leaders. I think most of my fellow trustees would concur with these statements. I hope you will take them in the spirit of collaboration in which they are offered. Healthcare institutions face immense challenges today, challenges we cannot face down unless we combine our knowledge and skills as physicians, trustees and executives alike. I look forward to facing the challenges of the future with you.

About the Author

Barry S. Bader is a trustee of Suburban Hospital, Bethesda, MD, and chairman of its Medical Affairs Committee. He has worked with boards and medical staffs throughout the United States and Canada.

Physician Leadership in Group Practice

by Henry S. Berman, MD, FACPE and
Jack M. Dutzar, MD

With more and more physicians practicing in groups today, there is a need for real leadership within these groups, but where do you begin? In this chapter the authors examine this issue by focusing on:

- *The nature of the physician group and its method for selecting leaders;*
- *The challenges the group and its leaders face, including quality improvement, increasing cost effectiveness, competing effectively, and recruiting and retaining physicians;*
- *The leadership skills needed; and*
- *The job requirements and personal challenges of leadership.*

◆ ◆ ◆

A number of forces are contributing to the increase in the percentage of U.S. physicians practicing in groups. Many physicians are entering practice with significant amounts of debt, and an increasing number of physicians are putting predictable hours and other quality of life issues ahead of maximizing income. These factors have modest implications for physician leadership. Other forces, such as the increasing influence of managed care and the emerging emphasis in healthcare on total quality (including the developing field of outcomes management) cry out for effective physician leadership. This chapter will look at the critical challenges physician leaders in group practice face, discussing some of the variables that influence just how important these issues will be in a given practice and what determines the leaders' priorities.

What Type of Group Practice Is It?

Group practices can be organized in a number of ways. They can be partnerships, or the physicians can be employees; they can be primarily fee-for-service, or prepaid; they can be single specialty, multispecialty with an emphasis on primary care, or multispecialty with an emphasis on specialty care. Serving in a leadership capacity in any type of group practice, however, is substantially different from being a physician leader in a hospital or medical school.

Most hospitals and medical schools are organized into fiefdoms (called departments). Each is composed of a number of highly independent knights (the physicians). Commonly, the physician leader can, at best, be a King Arthur, gathering all the knights to the Round Table, hoping to convince them that they have mutual interests that could cause them to modify their behavior.

In most hospitals, the physicians are not employed by the institution. They may even work at a number of hospitals. The department chief or medical director has very little leverage in such cases. Physician leadership in medical schools is another world in itself. Although the physicians are employed by the institution, between tenure, faculty associations, and the three competing goals of teaching, research and practice, the priorities of physician leaders in these jobs are much different.

One study of administrative tasks performed by physician executives found that improving the organizational quality of care was the first priority in hospitals, third in group practices and HMOs, but only 10th in educational institutions. In the latter organizations, developing and improving teaching and research was the third priority of physician executives. This area did not make the top 15 for either hospitals or group practices.[1]

In group practices, the physicians have made the conscious decision to entrust their career to the group (or to the organization that forms the group, such as a staff-model HMO). Their professional and financial success will be tied to the success of the group. Therefore, there will be a potential leadership opportunity, if the leader is so inclined, and if the group will permit it.

Different Approaches to the Selection of Leaders

There is wide variation in the way physician leaders are chosen in group practice, and the way they do their job cannot be separated from the way they are chosen. At one extreme is the physician partnership that elects a president and/or medical director, who is then accountable to an elected board of directors. At the other extreme is the organization headed by a nonphysician senior executive (chairman, president, CEO) who hires/fires the senior physician executive (vice president of medical affairs, medical director) the same way he or she hires/fires other senior executives.

Between these extremes lie a number of alternatives. The physician partnership may elect its board of directors and give the board authority to name the physician executive, or it may elect a nominating committee and then vote on the alternatives proposed by that group. In some staff-model HMOs, the medical director reports directly to a board of directors that is elected by consumers or appointed by some group other than plan physicians. In other staff-model HMOs, the medical director reports to the chief executive officer, but the physician group has formal input into the selection process (whereas the members of the marketing or finance departments would not have such a role in the selection of the head of their departments). The priorities and stresses of the job are substantially different depending on the selection and reporting arrangement. This will be discussed later.

Challenges Facing Group Practice

With the increasing complexity of modern healthcare, and the increasing demands put on healthcare organizations by individual consumers, purchasers and regulators, the day of the solo practitioner, or even the two- or three-physician partnership, is clearly waning. One of the most qualified experts on this trend, Arnold Relman, MD, former editor of *The New England Journal of Medicine*, wrote recently, "Of no less importance in controlling costs is a change in the way medical practice is organized. ...a new emphasis on prepaid insurance plans would encourage many more practitioners to join groups and affiliate with HMOs. Group practices, controlled by physicians, provide an environment favorable to the practice of cost-effective medicine and the maintenance of professional standards."[2] For group practices to fulfill the role asked of them, their leaders must be able to deal effectively with a number of diverse challenges.

Improving quality. No word in healthcare today is more ubiquitous than "quality." Quality assessment (QA) has long been an expected activity in healthcare organizations, but traditionally it involved only tedious retrospective review of the process of delivering care, and did not really consider whether QA activities actually resulted in improved care. Industrial America, in an attempt to regain competitiveness with burgeoning foreign economies, has returned the principles of quality management exported in the '50s to Japan by Deming, Crosby and Juran to our shores. In the past few years, these principles have been seized upon by healthcare in the hope that they might be an answer for reducing the chaos and uncontrolled inflation that plague it. The Joint Commission and other regulatory agencies have made incorporation of total quality improvement (QI) initiatives essentially a requirement.

For the healthcare executive, and especially physician managers, this represents a difficult challenge. Learning new QI principles and techniques, as well as changing the entire focus of their management activities require flexibility. Healthcare institutions are reluctant to change, largely because of the basic conservatism of physicians, without whom change is impossible.

In addition, payers and regulators are increasingly demanding that medical delivery systems demonstrate their effectiveness in terms of outcomes. In the past, it was acceptable to merely demonstrate that physicians followed "standard" approaches when diagnosing and treating disease. The newer, much more difficult, requirement is that we demonstrate that what is done results in positive outcomes for patients.

Increasing cost effectiveness. Currently, it is nearly impossible to find anyone who believes that our healthcare delivery system will survive the next decade. Access to care and high quality are both at issue, but cost is the engine for change because of the very real risk that continued, uncontrolled growth will destroy the economy and our position in world markets. In healthcare organizations, physicians are the people who write the checks, and when cost concerns are raised, physician managers are expected to be able to respond with new systems that address the issues. In group practices, this results in conflict with colleagues who view cost issues as secondary to high quality. Also, for many physicians, their economic self-interest is threatened by these developments.

Competing effectively. Another sign of the changing times is the relatively recent development of competition among physicians and physician groups for more than just individual patients. Today, the trend toward physicians forming groups to compete effectively for the institutional healthcare dollar is nearly universal. Group practices, whether prepaid or fee-for-service, are uniquely positioned to bargain for contracts that ensure them a steady supply of insured patients.

HMOs and PPOs, in their myriad forms, are looking for ways to use their bargaining power to get the most quality for the least cost. The physician manager plays a pivotal role in these negotiations: traditional managers are unable to ensure the best outcomes, and the physicians in the group, whose services are the basic commodity at issue, demand that one of their own represent their concerns.

Recruitment and retention. Physicians are not a happy group. They suffer from general dissatisfaction arising from uncertainty and the sense they are doing more and more for less and less. Where once they were a stable group of professionals, it is becoming commonplace for physicians to change careers, location and practice style. In this environment, inspiring loyalty and commitment is perhaps the physician manager's greatest challenge. Turnover is destructive to any group's ability to respond to the environment. In addition, each group needs all of its members to be committed to a collective vision. This is difficult to achieve without some sense of continuity and shared destiny.

One of the outcomes of change in American medicine over the past 30 to 40 years is the shift from primary care to specialty-focused care. No other country has 70 percent of its physicians in the ranks of consultant specialists. It is clear that the linchpin of humane and cost-effective medical care is the primary care physician. The shortage is critical and will most probably worsen. This is a substantial challenge for all medical groups, even those bastions of specialized medicine, the multispecialty group practice. The most traditional of these groups realize that they cannot be competitive without a stable base of primary care physicians. It falls to the physician manager to recruit and retain primary care physicians.

Critical Skills Required of Physician Leaders

Before we discuss the specific skills needed by physician leaders in group practice, it is useful to note how those skills will differ depending upon a number of factors, including:

- The type of practice;
- The way leadership is selected; and
- The environment in which the practice functions.

A physician who is elected directly by his or her partners, and who wishes to have a long-term position as a leader, for example, is not likely to stray far from the explicit or implicit agendas of the voters. By contrast, the physician who is appointed directly by a nonphysician executive must be highly responsive to that person's priorities. The medical director of a fee-for-service group generally has the maximization of group income as a (perhaps the) priority; the medical director of a staff-model HMO has the success of the organization as a (perhaps the) priority. The medical director of a multispecialty group will inevitably have negotiating the relative compensation of the various specialties as a priority, which is not much of an issue in a group composed of primary care physicians.

There is a paradox that the physician leader must deal with if he or she is to be effective. Kindig describes the physician executive as having a "boundary-spanning role." He states, "The role of the physician executive consists of a set of responsibilities that span the boundary between general managerial tasks and the management of clinical activities and physicians."[3] To successfully span this boundary, physician leaders must promote the points of view for which they are not primarily accountable. For example, the physician elected by peers must strive to teach those peers that their long-term interest is served best by increasing the priority of quality, cost effectiveness and improving access—not just by maximizing this year's physician earnings. In contrast, the physician appointed by a "hard-headed" business person must convince that person that the organization will be successful only if the physicians have active involvement not only in those decisions that affect them directly but also in all important areas of the organization.

How the Environment Affects Skills Needed

The more challenging the environment—escalating demands by purchasers and regulators, significant competition faced by the group or the HMO—the greater the importance of having skills in what Kindig calls "general managerial tasks." These include defining organizational goals and course, communicating those goals to the staff, reviewing organizational financial performance and dealing with information systems. The tasks must be developed to complement the skills in "clinical internal management," which include developing new professional services and programs, improving quality of care, dealing with ethical and legal issues in patient care and dealing with liability risk—the more traditional priorities of physician leaders.

The more demanding the environment, the greater the need for the physician leader to position the group for long-term success. Figure 1 shows potential problems in doing this.

Figure 1: Leadership Matrix

		Environmental Challenge	
		Mild	Severe
Process for Choosing' Leadership	Elected	1	2
	Appointed	3	4

The physician leader operating out of box No. 1 has the least challenge—perhaps the group is the only real player in town—and direct election by the physicians is no obstacle to keeping the organization on course. The physician in box No. 4 has a great challenge, but has the authority to meet it. The appointing body or individual (board, CEO) will presumably have the organization's success as the goal and will be prepared to support the physician leader in his or her decisions.

The physician in box No. 3 may feel some discomfort. In a less challenging environment, it is not likely to be clear to the front-line physicians why they need to respond to the organizational priorities (reduce costs, expand services) that are the marching orders to the physician executive. But the toughest situation by far is box No. 2—the democratically elected physician leader who must help the organization move forward in a challenging environment. Physicians who find themselves in this situation may find it easier to change the way leaders are selected than to try endlessly to convince physicians of the need for change.

Job Requirements

The most dramatic change in the physician manager's role, as noted above, is the need to become involved in the day-to-day management of his or her organization. In the past, this has been confined to individuals trained in business who were either hired by the physician group or by the organization employing the physicians. With the increasing complexity of medical systems and the need to maximize the efficiency of physicians, management needs to have a solid understanding of what the delivery of care requires. The physician manager is uniquely positioned to offer this perspective, and is increasingly becoming less a consultant and more a participant. To be effective in this area, physician executives need to learn specialized skills in systems thinking and personnel management.

Managing healthcare professionals is no less important a role for the physician manager because of its traditional nature. The discipline involved in delivering care fosters an independence of thinking and action that complicates the management process. A "problem" physician will not respond to demands and threats as readily as to an objective discussion that is in his or her best interests to accommodate to the needs of the group. The physician manager is often called upon to intervene with physicians in conflict with the group when their behaviors are limiting their ability to contribute. This requires tact, sensitivity and a solid command of pertinent factual information.

Nothing rivals the process of contracting for its dramatic departure from traditional physician leadership responsibilities. Negotiating (sometimes with other physicians) for economic advantage is antithetical to the traditions of medicine. This is yet another circumstance where complexity and the deep involvement of clinical issues in negotiations require physician leaders to learn new skills and command a new body of information. Some physicians are "naturals" at this process; for those who are not, training and education are required to develop the skill.

Medical schools do not teach the arcane principles of double-entry accounting and how to look for the hidden "facts" in a balance sheet or cash summary. While physician managers virtually always have professional accountants addressing these issues in the groups they represent, physicians in leadership positions are increasingly expected to understand the language that accountants use. Because physician managers are also expected to be involved in the strategic decision-making process in their organizations, they must understand the financial implications of those decisions. This area may represent the most clear distinction between the physician leader and the physician who truly manages. The halcyon days of cost-plus reimbursement are gone forever and both business managers and physician leaders require a bridge of mutual understanding to produce the best decisions.

Requirements to Look for in a Physician Leader for a Group Practice

Physician leaders must:

- Be willing to get involved in the day-to-day management of the institution;
- Intervene with "problem physicians" with tact, sensitivity and pertinent factual information;
- Be willing and able to negotiate with different parties; and
- Have some knowledge of the language of accountants.

Personal Challenges

Physicians spend much of their early lives learning their chosen profession. The long training process and the subsequent experiences in their early career leave many physicians feeling as though nothing could be as demanding and complex as patient care. All too often, though, physicians who take on administrative duties are shocked to discover that managing people and making sound business decisions require a whole new body of knowledge and skills about which they know little. This can be discouraging and frequently results in self-doubt.

Another common "eye-opener" for new physician managers is the loss of identity with their peers. Physician leaders still consider themselves physicians, but their colleagues sense a change in character. The degree of management distrust in a physician group may vary but, even if the new physician manager is elected, he or she becomes set apart and different. This difference can be perceived as a decrease in status or an increase in some kind of ominous power that usually is not accepted in a positive light by peers. This commonly leads to a sense of isolation and, if a career decision is involved, it is not uncommon for there to be an actual period of mourning for their former clinical role.

Once physician managers adjust to the stresses and change involved in a career transition, they need to continue the process of learning the skills needed to perform well. In some groups this education is supported and new managers are groomed by being given increasing levels of responsibility.

As part of a plan for career change, some physicians pursue graduate education and some seek specialized education from professional organizations. In 1986, a survey found that fewer than 3 percent of physician executives had graduate management degrees other than an MPH. However, 86 percent of those surveyed said that formal graduate course work or degrees in management would be advisable or should be required in the future.[4]

There are almost as many reasons for organizations to choose to have physician managers as there are organizations in healthcare. Physicians can bring their unique perspective and understanding to issues pertaining to contracting, medical systems design, underwriting, benefits interpretation and a host of others. The activity that requires their presence in group practices is the management of physicians and, most especially, other physician leaders. Given their autonomy and self-reliance, working with physicians to adjust their priorities and behaviors in order to function well within a management group is a substantial challenge. For physician leaders, success comes from the progress they make forging a team with their colleagues that effectively and consistently addresses the needs of their patients.

◆ ◆ ◆

References

[1]Kindig, D.A., and Lastri-Quiros, S. "The Changing Managerial Role of Physician Executives." *The Journal of Health Administration,* 7(1):3346, Winter 1989.

[2]Relman, A. "Reforming the Health Care System." *The New England Journal of Medicine,* 323(14):99 1, Oct. 4, 1990.

[3]Kindig, D.A. and S. Lastri-Quiros. "The Changing Managerial Role of Physician Executives." *The Journal of Health Administration,* 7(1):42, Winter 1989.

[4]Kindig, D.A., and Lastri-Quiros, S. "Administrative Medicine: A New Medical Specialty?" *Health Affairs,* 5(4):146-56,1986.

About the Authors

Henry S. Berman, MD, FACPE, is president and CEO of Group Health Northwest in Spokane, WA. Jack M. Dutzar, MD, is vice president of medical affairs of Group Health Northwest. He is a member of the American College of Physician Executives.

Managed Care

Challenges of Managed Care: An Overview for Physician Groups and Enterprises

By Henry Golembesky MD

As managed care becomes an increasingly greater proportion of physician practices, the degree of change that the physician group must undergo should not be underestimated. In this chapter the author examines the major trends that are likely to occur.

◆ ◆ ◆

Changes in healthcare economics that will affect physician practices are likely to follow these trends:

- In the private sector, employers and purchasing coalitions are likely to remain key purchasers, along with a large and growing group of individual purchasers (e.g., seniors and individuals not under group coverage);
- Consumers will have much greater financial responsibility for healthcare services and will have access to and demand information for effective decision making (e.g., health system performance, disease/symptom-based protocols);
- Many public payment/delivery systems, as currently designed, will not be sustainable; solutions will have private-sector participation;
- Inadequate incentives to manage care will be present, despite the financing crisis;
- Solutions will include more effective health management, provider risk sharing and greater use of managed care options;
- Price will continue to be an important factor in purchasing decisions for most, but health systems will differentiate themselves based on health status and outcomes (which will be measurable and available to purchasers);
- Continued consolidation of health plans and providers coupled with the need to invest in technology, improve health status and reduce redundant cost will lead to strategic health plan/provider partnerships and varying levels of integration of financing and care delivery, with the majority of healthcare services purchased through these alliances;

- Health system economics will be heavily driven by the effectiveness of population health management (e.g., risk assessment, triage, disease-based protocols across the continuum of care); and

- Expected future growth in healthcare expenditures and major arbitrage opportunity though reduced utilization and true population health management will attract significant investment dollars.

Thus, in a managed care environment the creation of value, both economic and societal, will occur only through patient acquisition and retention and effective care management. Managing physician organizational dynamics and infrastructure will be a prerequisite to realizing value, but will create no market value in and of itself.

In light of that, the following hypotheses must be considered.

"Fully integrated" medical groups will have no *prima facie* advantage over looser affiliations of physicians who are bound together by effective contracting, care management systems and shared risk. Fully integrated medical groups have found that in advanced managed care marketplaces well organized independent practice associations can successfully compete with them to attract patients, and they also can compete with effective care management.

The time, money and political capital spent in trying to cobble together a large group of physicians who have no natural affiliation motives would be better applied to developing care management and shared risk infrastructure.

Successful disease management and population-based health management programs will create superior margins, market growth and network branding. This "success" will bond physicians to the network.

Industry consolidators, such as the national physician practice management companies, be they national or local, will need to demonstrate differentiation in attracting patients or managing care to overcome the inherent disadvantages of added administrative and capital costs.

The first step in value creation, then, is managing patient acquisition and retention.

Market segmentation/enrollee choice will become the norm; service offerings will need to be tailored by benefit design, and groups will use targeted marketing or specialized care management around the needs of a segment of the population. For example, groups may develop programs and services targeted at the Medicare population or specific conditions such as congestive heart failure or end-stage renal disease.

Most segments will be intolerant of poor service, requiring "re-education" of physicians and staff. As evidenced in many patient satisfaction surveys from health plans around the country, there is increasing dissatisfaction with appointment access, waiting times, interactions with the physicians and support staff, and patients, through their employers, are pressuring health plans and providers to improve these service issues or lose their contracts.

Effective contracting relationships will create value, not just prevent its loss. When physician providers aggregate into organized groups, they can develop contracting relationships with health plans that channel patients to the organization.

By aligning risk incentives physician groups will achieve different outcomes and, thereby, attract more patients in a managed care setting.

After the group has developed its strategy to acquire and retain patients, it must then manage enrollee health and patient care. In this context, managing enrollee health refers to programs designed to measure baseline health status and tailor programs to individual enrollees to maintain and/or improve their baseline health status (health maintenance). Patient care refers to those services related to the treatment of illness.

- Effective care management will require relationships/teamwork, protocols and data.
- Small groups of physicians (eight to12 members) can achieve superior outcomes but need to be linked for efficient operations and effective contracting.
- Specialists take over some PCP functions for selected patients, while PCPs will provide a broader range of services (including some historically provided by specialists). Disease state specific clinics will emerge as providers of care for certain conditions (e.g., asthma, diabetes).
- Nontraditional medicine, care sites and caregivers will grow exponentially. This will pose a challenge to physicians as to whether they should include these nontraditional approaches in their networks. A large, traditional health plan in California is already marketing an option that includes alternative medicine as covered benefits (chiropractic, acupuncture, herbal therapy, stress reduction, etc.).

In the near term, no universally accepted definition of quality will be forthcoming, so it will be important for physicians to assist in defining quality. After developing the group's strategy to create value through patient acquisition and retention, attention must then be paid to the successful (and efficient) operations of the physician group/network. The following areas will need particular care.

- Aligned incentives under risk contracts will outweigh traditional integration. Many integrated delivery systems have acquired physician practices and insulated the individual physician from the realities of the marketplace, and they find that even previously well functioning medical groups become dysfunctional with a deterioration not only in financial performance but also in patient service areas as well. By aligning individual physician financial incentive systems, they are discovering that the physician practice functions much more successfully in both of the above areas.

- Consensus decision making will yield to enfranchised leadership. However, it is critical to balance the time required to utilize a consensus-building process versus the need of the group to be able to make some decisions in a rapid time frame.

- Virtual integration (at least) will be required for the "teamwork" demands of care management. Information systems will provide access to real-time clinical information sharing by networks of physicians in multiple care settings so that optimal patient care can be achieved across the continuum of healthcare. That will also result in lower overall resource consumption.

- Performance management will be critical. The competitive marketplace of managed care will not tolerate inefficient operations for any length of time.

- Dissatisfied physicians (even "owned" ones) will look elsewhere unless a role in shared governance, an option for ownership, control over care management, and fairness in compensation are delivered

- No model will work forever in its current form—even the "benchmark" multispecialty groups are finding it necessary to adopt new approaches as their markets evolve.

The structure and operation of the physician organization can be thought of as a value exchange, where value is determined by thorough consideration of physician and system needs and capabilities. Increasingly, physicians are taking on administrative and board membership roles within integrated systems. *(See Figure 1, below.)*

As groups attempt to implement the above "value exchange" they will need to focus on clinical care management and physician compensation. Historically, physician compensation plans have been designed to:

FIGURE 1: VALUE EXCHANGE

Value physicians bring to the organization:	Value the organization brings to the physician:
• Architect of the patient's "care experience" (member acquisition and retention) • Chief determinant of clinical outcome (member acquisition and retention) • Clinical team leader • Manager of cost per covered life performance across system • Primary source of clinical innovation and technology	• Freedom to focus on clinical/academic activities • Affiliation status—access to managed care contracts • Infrastructure to support clinical excellence and clinical innovation • Network of high quality, like-minded colleagues • Income security (relative to market, by achieving market share, supporting price and reducing costs) • Economic upside through gain sharing • Meaningful voice in direction of the enterprise • Opportunity to pro-actively manage market force

- Attach physicians to the organization with minimum disruption from status quo, and maximum control for the organization;
- Attract competitive purchase prices (if acquiring pre-existing physician practices in a competitive market) and income guarantees;
- Preserve fee schedules that maintain the status quo for physicians, reinforcing the environment of "every man for himself" and not aligning the physician's incentives with the group; and
- Set the group up in a "monitoring" role, countering physician's needs and insulating them from the economic reality of the organization's performance.

In order to achieve the "value exchange" mentioned in Figure 1, groups must adopt:

- A medical loss model where physicians and other providers are not at risk for the total cost of medical care;

- Narrowly scoped, centrally enforced access controls at the expense of physician's autonomy needs. These approaches will reduce utilization initially but over time the physicians "learn" what documentation they must provide to obtain the required authorizations;

- Pre-certifications, pre-authorizations;

- Case managers assigned to high risk populations (not at physician direction);

- Centralized, enterprise-driven searches for clinical best practice, followed by poor-form dissemination to the physician community; and

- Data collections profiling is generally punitive where the physician is positioned as object to control and to keep fragmented.

Transitioning to a care management model that embodies the following approach will result in superior long-term performance:

- Case management model;
- Delegation of clinical management functions to autonomous, self-policing, risk-sharing groups of physicians at the local level;
- Physicians lead, the group supports;
- Economic risks are "felt" by accountable physician units;
- Ownership/governance matches risk;
- Explicit, direct gain-sharing motivates involvement and rewards/performance; and
- Significant infrastructure support provides an optimal centralization/decentralization mix:
  - ✓ Data management
  - ✓ Staff support.

The group will need to develop physician compensation programs that achieve the following results:

- Unique, meaningful economic opportunities for physicians to pursue common objectives with the group on an ongoing basis;
- Ownership/governance; and
- Income at risk:
  - ✓ Full capitation or global budgets to link to clinical performance;
  - ✓ Full gain-sharing with the enterprise on cost-effectiveness improvements; and
  - ✓ Link to market performance (member surveys, local market enrollment growth) with incentives created for physician-physician collaboration.

As the 1990s evolve, integrated delivery networks and physician groups will begin to segment member populations using risk assessment, triage, telemedicine and market research. A successful physician group over time will do the following:

- Profile risks using medical history and demographically targeted lifestyle information to segment members by health risk;
- Triage "lower risk" members to routine examinations with emphasis on prevention and self-help, and assign "higher risk" members to a case manager for selection of a wellness program including periodic diagnosis, treatment and education;
- Deliver quality acute care to members as needed, on a cost-effective basis;
- Increasingly rely upon "evidence-based medicine" as basis of patient care programs; and
- Reduce inappropriate admissions and clinic visits by providing members with increased telephone access to clinicians who speak the member's native language and who are supported with data on medical history, wellness programs and diagnostic algorithms.

Members also will be encouraged to self-administer simple diagnostics (e.g., blood pressure, blood sugars).

Tailor programs to meet member needs by using market research to identify major customer segments. Care-givers organize teams and information to evaluate existing programs, improve their quality and develop new programs for target populations.

Understanding the challenges physician groups will face as the healthcare market continues to evolve will enable them to implement the organizational changes that will be required for success. It is critically important not to underestimate how much of a challenge change management can be within a physician organization and beginning the change process early before the group begins experiencing performance declines will provide a greater chance for success in meeting these challenges.

About the Author

Henry Golembesky, MD, Principal, is a partner at APM Management Consultants in San Francisco. He co-directs the Physician Practice Services division. Formaly the medical director at Shar Rees-Stealy Medical Group, Dr. Golembesky has more than 15 years experience in healthcare management.

Linking Performance Evaluation to Care Delivery

Barry P. Chaiken, MD, MPH, Director,

The recent change in healthcare's economic forces—transferring the financial risk of care provision from insurance entities to providers of care—has sparked the development of a variety of reimbursement methodologies. They were constructed out of building blocks such as discounted fees, bonuses, withholds and capitation rates. Organizations use a melange of these financial incentives to obtain one particular economic and quality outcome. Irrespective of what method is used to compensate a provider, various performance metrics provide the basis for determining the level of compensation.

◆ ◆ ◆

Utilization of services drives the financial success of any healthcare organization. Therefore, initial compensation plans utilized numerical measures such as average lengths of stay, total cost per case and inpatient rates per thousand to determine compensation. As is often the case, the availability of data drove the use of specific measures. Although easy to collect and collate, these measures lack a defensible methodological basis. For example, these measures were often applied without risk adjustment, thereby making any comparisons suspect. In the absence of risk adjustment, many providers defended their rates by claiming their patient panels represented sicker patients.

Recent advances in information technology offer an opportunity to construct large, broad-based clinical data repositories. These repositories can provide sufficient data for establishing statistically meaningful provider norms and benchmarks across a large number of disease processes. Taking advantage of these improvements, many innovative organizations are moving beyond simple performance measures toward more clinically based, methodologically sound measures.

In developing any compensation matrix, an organization must link the performance measures to the overall strategic goals of the organization. For example, if an organization wants to decrease the costs associated with treatment of pediatric asthma, performance measures such as asthma emergency room visits and inpatient admissions need to be part of the compensation formula. In addition, providers need to receive regular reports on their performance so they can change behavior as required. Without such a feedback loop, providers have no means of gauging how they are performing in relation to compensation measures. For these reasons, managed care organizations continue to expand the implementation of provider profiling strategies.

Provider profiling tools allow plans to analyze the quality of care delivered, using transactional claims data and feedback metrics on quality, utilization, appropriateness, cost and preventive services. Compensation is then directly connected to the profiling results.

Data Sources

Available data sources for provider profiling are generally limited to common data sets readily available through transactional systems that process and collect data as part of the normal course of doing business. The most common types of transactional data sets are claims data.

Transactional systems provide tremendous advantages when performing provider profiling. Not to be overlooked — indeed the most valuable — is the relatively low cost of obtaining the data. For example, claims constitute a routine and necessary part of the healthcare process. Without claims, there is no reimbursement, so providers possess a strong motivation to complete and submit claims forms. Claims often include patient demographic information, as well as limited clinical information such as ICD-9 diagnosis and CPT-4 procedure codes. In addition, the data are widespread and readily available in a standardized format, perfect for analysis.

The lack of inexpensive, readily available alternative data sets promotes the use of claims data for profiling. The significant advantages of using claims sometimes mask the limitations inherent in the data. While the availability of advanced technology (i.e., computer systems, client-server arrangements, data cleansing) has increased the use of claims data for profiling, this increased ease of use must not influence or add undo validity to any generated performance measures.

Much of what is wrong with claims data is fairly obvious to anyone who has completed a claim form or worked with the data sets. The data collected on claims is there for only one purpose—to generate a reimbursement payment. The data are not submitted for quality improvement, risk management or provider profiling. Therefore, the information provided in a claim is often skewed, thereby making the clinical information suspect.

Because coding is an inexact science, questions concerning reliability and errors must be considered. There are difficulties in identifying accurate codes to reflect the documentation of the care processes as described in the medical record. Patients with multiple concurrent disease processes present a formidable challenge in recording accurate codes. Finally, claims data sets contain numerous duplications and omissions, which must be corrected before analysis.

Epidemiologists and other clinical researchers yearn to develop customized analytical databases. This offers control over the data set, including the data elements and the data collection process. Unfortunately, customized data sets require processes outside normal business operations. This presents significant obstacles to successful implementation, including increased costs coupled with a lack of additional revenue and a negative impact on productivity. Organizations focused on the bottom line have difficulty with data collection initiatives that do not provide immediate benefits or generate savings. As providers are asked to see more patients in less time, there will be little participation by those already overburdened.

By contrast, if the unique data set is integrated with the ongoing business of care delivery, it has a significantly greater chance of being both accepted and supplying quality data. It is important to evaluate and advertise the benefits of a new data collection process to obtain buy-in by those providing the data. If the participants understand the value to them and the organization, they are more likely to actively participate.

Unique data sets can be constructed from encounter forms. For managed care organizations that have eliminated claims (i.e., capitated providers), encounter forms help track services provided. Even under a capitated arrangement, collection of data on staff activities is necessary to allow for operational planning (e.g., staff schedules, capital improvements).

Although some of the transactional data sets have been around long enough to be tested for validity and reliability, a new unique data set, by definition, has not. Face validity—whether the data set, on the face of it, appears to capture the data it claims to capture—can be used to evaluate a unique data set, but care must be taken in reaching any far-ranging conclusions. Although face validity is not a rigorous concept, its importance cannot be ignored. Absence of face validity can be a serious barrier to overall confidence in the data, especially by physicians. Beyond face validity is testing the data sets for validity and reliability as a provider profiling data source, something most organizations do not have the staff available to perform.

Epidemiology–Risk Adjustment, Outcomes

Epidemiological principles and methods can be applied to a wide range of problems in many fields. These principles and methods relate to the description of human populations, to the investigation of the processes underlying their present state, to the interpretation and analysis of such information, and to the uses to which these data can be put. In the health field, epidemiology has three main uses: etiological, clinical and administrative. These aims relate to and, in fact, become intertwined in the pursuit of health policy's ultimate goal: the promotion and preservation of the population's health.

Choosing a data source for profiling requires a researcher to do the following:

- Set goals for collecting the data (e.g., increasing appropriate mammography screening);
- Develop a hypothesis (e.g., *acceptable* mammography screening for our network providers is 95%);
- Evaluate the data sources (e.g., claims data are readily available); and

- Understand the availability and impact of potential interventions (e.g., computer generated follow-up letters to members as reminders).

When planning to do provider profiling, you will never be able to devote enough time to planning the study. The data sources are so voluminous and the areas to examine so vast, a researcher can spend fantastic amounts of time analyzing the data and yet never reach a conclusion. Local experience combined with reports from distant colleagues and the literature provides clues as to what behaviors to profile. These sources can often lead to the identification of those areas that will bear the greatest results.

Expected results are a reflection of local knowledge and can impact greatly the data sources that are used. Investigations must match potential interventions, so that the results can be used to improve processes. Willingness to act is critical; there is no reason to study an issue if no intervention can reasonably occur to impact the finding. For example, a community hospital and a payer enter into a risk-sharing arrangement for all inpatient surgical care. Although all of the admitting surgeons are part of the risk-sharing arrangement, the cardiac surgeons refuse to participate, expecting to generate higher fees for themselves by accepting reimbursement on only an unlimited fee-for-service basis. Subsequent analysis of surgical profiling data revealed lengths of stay for the cardiac surgeons for coronary artery bypass graft surgery to be 35 percent greater than the norms for the region. The cardiac surgery program is a prestigious service that the hospital believes is critical to attracting and keeping lucrative employer contracts. The cardiac surgeons retain admitting privileges at both this community hospital and a second hospital across town. Although it is appropriate for the hospital to intervene to reduce the lengths of stay for coronary artery bypass grafts performed by these cardiac surgeons, the hospital is unwilling to act for fear that the surgeons will send their patients to the hospital across town. In this instance, the hospital benefits more from studying the lengths of stay for the surgeons that are sharing risk than this group of surgeons, over which it has little leverage.

In many instances the profiling effort must produce benefits, both monetary and otherwise, to substantiate the resources expended to perform the profiling. It makes great sense to choose goals that deliver a benefit—through implementation of an acceptable intervention—that is soon realized.

Statistics are a necessary skill to perform provider profiling. It is unreasonable to expect someone who does not work with the discipline on a regular basis to maintain an effective command of the concepts and techniques. On the other hand, there is no excuse for not obtaining the appropriate help from an epidemiologist or biostatistician to perform meaningful provider profiling.

As no two physicians see the same patients, adjustments need to be made to account for patient differences (e.g., diagnosis, age, comorbidity). Risk adjustment was conceived to enable practitioners and others to compare outcomes and costs associated with the care of patients, even though different, and to permit inferences about the relative effectiveness and efficiency of individual practitioners through practice patterns. Risk adjustment can be understood as a correction for the degree of difficulty in caring for a group of patients. These adjustments are made in the following manner:

Case Mix. Case mix adjustment utilizes age, sex and diagnosis to account for differences among patients. This methodology explains only a small amount of the variation seen among patients;

Episodes of Care. Episodes of care utilize age, sex, diagnosis, comorbidities and surgeries to construct categories that allow the grouping together of similar disease processes. These categories are then used to risk-adjust the data to allow comparisons among providers; and

Severity. Severity adjustment measures try to quantify the risks of the short-term outcomes for hospitalized patients. Severity includes measures that implicitly or explicitly define severity of resource use (e.g., cost, length of stay) and those that focus on more clinical definitions (e.g., risk of death, treatment difficulty, clinical instability).

Outcomes are defined as states or conditions of individuals and populations attributed or attributable to antecedent healthcare. They include changes in health status, changes in knowledge or behavior pertinent to future health status and satisfaction with healthcare (expressed as opinion or inferred from behavior).

Key issues in the use of outcomes in provider profiles include:

- Outcomes do not directly assess quality of performance. They only permit an inference about quality of the process and structure of care;
- The degree of confidence in that inference depends on the strength of the predetermined causal relationship between process and outcome (and structure and process). For example, clinicians know that the treatment of an otherwise healthy patient with community acquired bacterial pneumonia with a 10-day course of an antibiotic that the causative agent is sensitive to (i.e., process), generates an improved health status in the patient (i.e., outcome); and
- Because that causal relationship is modified by factors other than healthcare, corrections must be made for the effects of these factors, by risk adjustment, so that like can be compared with like.

Much of healthcare quality work in the past has focused on structure and process. *(See Figure 1 on page 90.)* Outcomes, although an important part of the quality triad, have lagged behind because of problems in methodology and data collection. Outcomes, when combined with process measures, offer an additional and important snapshot of provider performance.

Planning and Obtaining Value

In utilizing profiling tools for performance evaluation and provider compensation, both the profiling reports and compensation plan incentives must be linked. Key factors in any successful program include:

FIGURE 1: THE QUALITY TRIAD: INPUT, PROCESS OF CARE AND OUTCOMES

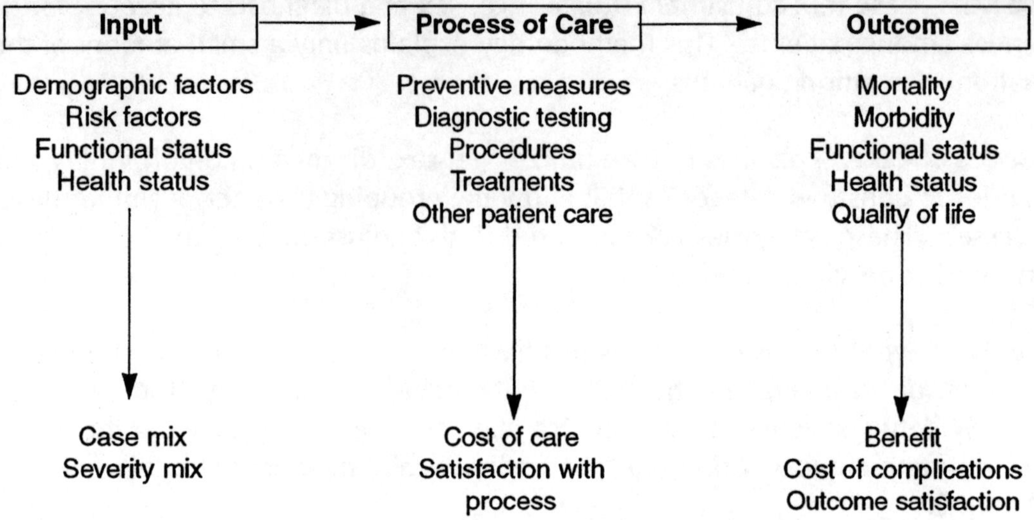

Source: Using Practice Guidelines to Evaluate Quality of Care, Volume 1, 1995, USDHHS, PHS, AHCPR, pub. No. 95-0045.

Addressing the Organizational Plan. Profiling reports and financial incentives need to parallel other organizational initiatives. In addition, these initiatives should contribute to the overall goals and objectives of the organization. For example, if a managed care company wants to demonstrate for marketing purposes that preventive services for women are at a high level, providers should receive profiling reports on their mammography screening activities;

Ease of Use. Profiling reports must be short, easily read, focused and make use of simplistic and easily understandable graphics. Summary data offers a quick view of current trends and should support whether any changes in behaviors are required; and

An Explanation of Methodology. All profiling tools contain limitations. To obtain credibility (not to mention being perceived as ethical), it is important to explain clearly the limitations of profiling reports and compensation formulas. Paradoxically, this approach only adds power to the results reported, because credibility is the key to successful profiling.

Changes in the economic factors driving healthcare move risk from payers to providers. Managers of this risk utilize profiling tools to measure physician performance and link results to levels of compensation. Choosing the right performance measures, measurement tools and compensation formula can lead to the delivery of high quality healthcare while managing the associated costs and financial risks.

◆ ◆ ◆

References

Graham, N.O. *Quality in Health Care: Theory, Application and Evolution.* Gaithersburg, MD: Aspen Publishers Inc., 1995.

Kongstevdt, P.R. *The Managed Health Care Handbook.* 3rd ed. Gaithersburg, MD: Aspen Publishers Inc., 1996.

Zablocki, E. *Changing Physician Practice Patterns.* Gaithersburg, MD: Aspen Publishers Inc., 1995.

Kongstvedt, P.R. *Essentials of Managed Health Care.* 2nd ed. Gaithersburg, MD: Aspen Publishers Inc., 1997.

Nash, D.B. *The Physician's Guide to Managed Care.* Gaithersburg, MD: Aspen Publishers Inc., 1994.

Iezzoni, L.I. *Risk Adjustment for Measuring Health Care Outcomes.* Ann Arbor, MI: Health Administration Press, 1994.

Goldfield, N. and Boland, P. *Physician Profiling and Risk Adjustment.* Gaithersburg, MD: Aspen Publishers, Inc., 1996.

Berwick, D. *Curing Health Care: Strategies for Quality Improvement.* Jossey-Bass, 1990.

Negroponte, N. *Being Digital.* New York: Alfred A. Knopf Inc., 1995.

Using Practice Guidelines to Evaluate Quality of Care, Volume 1. USDHHS, PHS, AHCPR, pub. No. 95-0045, 1995.

Knight, W. *Managed Care Contracting.* Gaithersburg, MD: Aspen Publishers Inc., 1997.

About the Author

Barry P. Chaiken, MD, MPH, Director, Medical Management Solutions Group, HPR Inc., provides medical leadership, strategic planning and product development support for this medical informatics solutions company. Dr. Chaiken is board certified in both general preventive medicine and public health, and quality assurance and utilization review. He is a diplomate, on the board of directors and second vice president of the American Board of Quality Assurance and Utilization Review Physicians (ABQAURP), and is currently chairman of the CME committee.

Physician Compensation in Managed Care Environments

Donald C. Wegmiller, FACHE and Robert J. Erra

Designers and administrators of physician compensation programs face three fundamental concerns:

- *Cost, because physicians are highly compensated as a rule.*
- *Cost effectiveness, because physicians are generally paid in proportion to the work they do.*
- *Cost pressures from third-party insurers.*

In this chapter the author takes a look at the economics of physician compensation and the different types of models.

◆ ◆ ◆

In most practice settings, physician compensation can be viewed as an equation addressing two important issues: a need to balance the program's patient charges with a need to pay physicians competitively and a need to balance individual fairness with the best interests of the physician group as a whole. The larger the number of involved physicians, the higher the economic stakes.

Most physician practices are break-even or money-losing operations. In partnership and proprietorship settings, money left over at the end of the year is distributed. In employment settings, pressures to increase compensation push costs up as far as they can go, within the constraints of affordability. For example, most emergency rooms lose money, partly because physician compensation costs more than reimbursement covers.

Virtually every physician compensation program needs to deal explicitly or implicitly with the relationship between reimbursement and the cost of physician compensation, and between pay and performance.

In most private practice settings, physician compensation is defined by billings (tying pay to performance and the market value of services provided) or collections (which connect to reimbursement levels).

In group practices, where reimbursement levels tend to be the ruling economic force, physician compensation is also tied to collections in one way or another.

In salaried settings, even when there are no apparent links between pay and performance or pay and reimbursement, relationships often are governed by extraneous factors such as mandatory performance standards or budgetary processes that match staffing levels with anticipated reimbursement levels.

All these principles apply to managed care environments as much as they do to fee-for-service settings, although managed care changes reimbursement formulas and may have an impact on the manner in which relationships are defined. Managed care also may limit reimbursement amounts, thereby forcing re-examination of the underlying economics of a relationship, i.e., the linkages between cost and affordability, and the value of services provided.

Some important rules-of-thumb for physician compensation planners to keep in mind:

- You can't afford to increase pay before you know where the money is coming from;

- If reimbursement is lower than you expected, there is less money available for physician compensation;

- If there is money left over at the end of the year, involved physicians will think it belongs to them;

- If Dr. Jones works "harder" or faster than Dr. Smith, Dr. Jones will expect to receive higher pay; and

- If a third-party payer allocates more for an OB/GYN's services than for those of a family practitioner, the OB/GYN will expect to be paid more.

The Economics of Physician Compensation

Before capitation, physicians viewed themselves as revenue producers in the fee-for-service environment. Their rewards were based on the work units they produced. Their income was based on what they charged for the services they rendered. Thus, the harder physicians worked, the more revenue they generated—and the more money they earned.

In those earlier days, physician fees were based on "usual and customary rates acceptable to the community," which varied from region to region throughout the country. Most indemnity plans of that day paid according to an 80/20 ratio. The insurance company paid 80 percent of the physician charge, and the patient paid the rest. The physician then received 100 percent of what everyone in the community might have expected to pay—the prevailing "usual and customary" charge. Should a physician charge a higher amount than the usual and customary, the charge would be reduced to the threshold payment levels (the usual and customary fees) of the community.

As healthcare costs escalated, insurance companies began to discount physicians' usual and customary charges by 20 percent to 30 percent. This meant a physician might get 70 percent of his bill from an insurer, and the patient had to pay the rest.

Although physicians continued to realize 100 percent of their charges in most instances, patients began to see that they were paying more out of pocket. Pressures on the reimbursement system to reduce patient charges began to mount.

Medicare was the first payer to act, implementing a policy requiring physicians to accept its payments in full and preventing them from balance-billing patients. A number of non-Medicare payers soon followed suit, giving rise to significant disparities between physician billings and collections.

At around the same time, payers began to adopt fee schedules—line-by-line payment itemizations covering virtually all medical procedures. Physicians then were asked to accept the schedules in their contracts. Again, patients were exempted from further cost sharing.

Fee schedules brought physicians to the realization that they had lost control of their revenues and income. No longer was it simply a matter of working harder to make more. It was now a matter of working harder to stay even—even to earn less.

The Transition to Capitation

Capitation—the managed care concept that allocates fixed amounts of money for the treatment of member patients—probably exerted the most profound impact on changing reimbursement patterns. It transformed physicians from revenue producers to cost centers—into resource consumers instead of resource creators.

Physicians who understood the dynamics of mature managed care marketplaces soon recognized that focusing on the cost of care presented the best opportunity to maximize practice revenues. Primary care physicians were among the first to redefine the medical services delivery apparatus in this way. They could garner a larger share of the capitation dollar, they realized, if they provided more of the necessary services instead of relinquishing them to specialists on referral. (Most specialists continued to practice on a fee-for-service basis in those early days of capitation.)

These strategies gave rise to a phenomenon known as the "primary care gatekeeper" model of medical care and service. Specialist reimbursement patterns evolved much as they had for primary care doctors as they embraced the managed care philosophy—with one important difference: Specialists, recognizing that they depended on primary physicians for referrals, conceded increases in their overheads, rationalizing that increased patient volumes would eventually offset such costs. Several prestigious groups—including the Scripps Clinics, the Virginia Mason Clinics and the Mayo Clinic—adopted the primary care gatekeeper model.

The transition to managed care ultimately led to an oversupply of specialists. Primary care physicians were taking on more and more of the sub-specialty services formerly provided by multi-specialty groups. Specialists in these groups soon faced a difficult decision: maintain their quality of life by reducing their ranks, or maintain their memberships by reducing their incomes proportionately.

The evolution to managed care led to more structured income distribution formulas containing certain incentives that would reward individuals, maximize revenues to their organizations and minimize costs.

All of this brings us to today's compensation climate in which physicians and physician groups face three basic concerns:

- A need to recruit and retain physicians within their organizations;
- A need to determine supportable numbers of physician specialists for their organizations; and
- Compensation models that create cultures based on unity rather than individuality.

Achieving unity of purpose within a physician organization depends on four compensation-based components:

1. **Base Salary**. Determination of the base or entry-level salary should reflect a group's wishes to guarantee income, regardless of individual production. Generally, base salary is determined as a percentage of a physician's total pay, ranging between 70 percent and 90 percent of what an individual might be expected to earn.

2. **Incentive Compensation.** Based on production or non-production incentives, this component of the compensation formula represents the difference between base salary and targeted income, according to internal and external peer group data.

3. **Cost Incentives.** These incentives attempt to reward physicians for their contributions to overall cost control.

4. **Benefits.** Retirement, life and disability insurance benefits should receive the same emphasis as cash compensation within an organization because of their value as retention devices.

Cash Compensation Components for Employed Physicians

There are several cash compensation components employed physicians should consider essential. When bundled together, they create a cash model that achieves several key objectives:

- Alignment of physician incentives with the organization's mission and goals;
- Enhanced ability to recruit and retain quality physicians;

- Generation of cash that is internally equitable and externally competitive;
- Physician rewards for high productivity;
- Physician rewards for non-production activities;
- Appropriate physician compensation under capitation; and
- Promotion of responsible resource stewardship.

Typical organizational cash models may include several components.

Base Salary
This element might range between 70 percent and 90 percent of the physicians' prior-year cash compensation, or be established as a flat minimum for all group members.

Productivity Incentive
Amounts available as productivity incentives depend on base salary levels. Thus, lower base salaries put more compensation at risk. If they are set too high, on the other hand, productivity motivation may decrease.

Additional compensation is paid after threshold measurements, tied to designated base salaries, have been exceeded. These measurements can be based on professional charges, either gross or net, or on relative value units (RVUs), Medicare's approach to equitable pay for physicians incorporating relative value units, instead of charges, to measure physician productivity. Patient visits are not considered effective physician productivity measures because they do not reflect patient acuity.

Expected Collection Rate
Expected collection rates, based upon historical experience, are applied to current professional production. They should be group rates that are also specialty specific. Individual collection rates tend to distract physicians from thinking and behaving as group members.

Non-production Incentive
The non-production incentive component rewards physicians for activities deemed important to the continued success of their organizations or group practices, but not directly linked to productivity. Criteria might include:

- Patient satisfaction;
- Quality of care indicators;
- Utilization review; and
- Teamwork.

Non-production incentive pools can represent five percent to 30 percent of a physician's cash compensation distributed according to a point system.

As capitation grows within a group practice, non-production incentive pools should also represent a greater portion of physician compensation.

Operating Unit Incentive

Recognizing that physicians have a significant influence on the cost structure of a practice, this incentive rewards them for their contributions to the reduction of practice overhead.

The Continuum of Physician Cash Compensation Models

Cash compensation models range from productivity-based models (compensation related to the physician's billings), to salary models (straight salary regardless of individual productivity), with variations in between.

Figure 1 below, shows how physician compensation trends evolved toward pure productivity-based and salary-based models between 1990 and 1993.

FIGURE 1: MEDICAL GROUP COMPENSATION METHODS 1990-1993

Type of Compensation Model	1990	1991	1992	1993
100% Productivity	21.1%	23.9%	28.8%	27.8%
51% to 99% Productivity	24.6%	26.3%	22.3%	18.8%
50% or Less Productivity	7.3%	9.7%	0.0%	0.0%
Salary Plus Bonus/Incentive	23.9%	22.3%	27.2%	26.6%
Straight Salary	5.0%	4.2%	9.5%	10.1%
100% Equal Share	11.6%	9.2%	9.3%	8.0%
Other	6.5%	4.3%	3.0%	8.8%

Source: Physician's Marketing and Management, December 1994, p. 148.

As managed care continues to influence physician practices, compensation shifts to straight-salary or salary-plus-incentives models, as shown in Figure 2.

FIGURE 2: COMPENSATION MODELS UNDER MANAGED CARE

Managed Care Percentage Penetration	Compensation Model
< 10-15%	Productivity Model
16-25%	Productivity Model With Incentives
26-45%	Salary Model With Productivity
> 45%	Salary Model With or Without Incentives

A number of cash compensation models are available to organizations employing physicians. A model's appropriateness will depend on many variables, including the culture of the organization, the mission and business strategy of the organization, the level of competition for physicians in the organization's market and the sophistication of available management systems.

Five Cash Model Designs Available to Employed Physicians

1. Productivity Model

The pure productivity model adapts the "keep what you earn" philosophy common in private solo practices. Individual physicians must produce to justify their compensation.

Advantages

Focuses on physician productivity.

Forms direct relationship between production and compensation.

Administers relatively easy.

Disadvantages

Physician recruitment may be impeded without salary guarantees.

No rewards for non-production activities such as patient satisfaction and teamwork.

In practices with capitation activity it's ineffective.

The productivity model is illustrated in Figure 3 below. This illustration is based on 100 percent productivity, with compensation tied to net professional production, and

FIGURE 3: PRODUCTIVITY MODEL

Base Year Activity	
Gross Professional Production	$275,000
Expected Collection Rate	90%
Net Professional Production	$247,500
Cash Compensation	$123,750

Projected Activity	**Year 1**	**Year 2**	**Year 3**
Gross Professional Production	$280,000	$290,000	$300,000
Expected Collection Rate	90%	88%	85%
Net Professional Production	$252,000	$255,200	$255,000
Compensation Payout Rate	50%	50%	50%
Cash Compensation	$126,000	$127,600	$127,500

with the organization establishing appropriate expected collection rates and compensation payout rates.

2. Salary Model

The physician's compensation is guaranteed under this model. It is established using either a step-salary method or salary ranges based on regional survey data. It also can be adjusted according to seniority, productivity and subjective performance criteria.

Advantages

Based on minimum standards.

Easy to administer.

Depending on parameters, equally paid group physicians at similar career points.

Appropriate in a practice with a large mix of capitated patients.

Disadvantages

Does not reward individual productivity.

Might lead to productivity problems due to lack of individual motivation.

When productivity influences salary, individuals must wait until the following year for the higher salary.

May generate internal equity issues among physicians.

The salary model is illustrated in Figure 4 on page 101. In this example, compensation is tied to a salary range. Survey data could be used to establish such a range. A physician's position within the range could be determined by production, seniority or other criteria deemed important by the organization.

3. Salary-Plus-Incentives Model

This model provides physicians with a reasonable base salary and an opportunity to increase their compensation through productivity and non-production activities.

Advantages

Provides physicians with minimum guaranteed salaries.

Rewards physicians for individual productivity.

FIGURE 4: SALARY MODEL

Base Year Activity

Gross Professional Production	$275,000
Cash Compensation	$123,750

Gross Professional Production Matrix	**Minimum Production**	**Targeted Production**	**High Production**
Gross Professional Production	$230,000	$290,000	$375,000
Salary Range Matrix[1]	$110,000	$130,000	$160,000

Projected Activity	**Year 1**	**Year 2**	**Year 3**
Gross Professional Production	$280,000	$290,000	$300,000
Compensation Payout Rate	N/A	N/A	N/A
Current Salary	$123,750	$125,000	$130,000
Next Year's Salary[2]	$125,000	$130,000	$131,000

[1]Starting salary for someone out of residency $105,000

[2]Current production determines the salary for next year

Rewards physicians for non-production activities.

Aligns physician incentives with organizational goals.

Puts a portion of pay at risk.

Disadvantages

Physicians may lose motivation if base salary is set too high.

Administration more complex. Requires generation of timely and accurate management reports for physicians.

Non-production incentive categories may be viewed as subjective.

The salary-plus-incentives model is illustrated in Figure 5 on page 102. This example is based on net professional production. The base salary, production threshold and the non-production incentive are based on the prior year's cash compensation.

4. Salary-Plus-Incentives-with-capitation Model

This model provides physicians with a reasonable base salary and an opportunity to increase their compensation through productivity and non-production activities. It also compensates physicians appropriately under capitation.

Figure 5: Salary-Plus-Incentives Model

Base Year Activity	
Gross Professional Production	$276,000
Expected Collection Rate	90%
Net Professional Production	$248,400
Cash Compensation	$124,200

Projected Activity	**Year 1**	**Year 2**	**Year 3**
Gross Professional Production	$280,000	$290,000	$300,000
Expected Collection Rate	90%	88%	85%
Net Professional Production	$252,000	$255,200	$255,000
Production Threshold	$223,560	$226,800	$229,680
Production Above Threshold	$ 28,440	$ 28,400	$ 25,320
Compensation Payout Rate	50%	50%	50%
Production Incentive	$ 14,220	$ 14,200	$ 12,660
Non-Production Incentive[1]	$ 6,210	$ 6,300	$ 6,380

Summary	**Year 1**	**Year 2**	**Year 3**
Prior-Year Cash Compensation	$124,200	$126,000	$127,600
Base Salary (85% of prior year cash)	$105,570	$107,100	$108,460
Production Incentive	$ 14,220	$ 14,200	$ 12,660
Non-Production Incentive	$ 6,210	$ 6,300	$ 6,380
Cash Compensation	$126,000	$127,600	$127,500

[1]Targeted at 5% of prior year cash compensation

Advantages

Similar to salary-plus-incentives model.

Compensates physicians appropriately under capitation.

Disadvantages

The introduction of capitation adds to administrative complexity. Simultaneous tracking of fee-for-service and capitation activities requires strong management system.

Managing a practice mixing fee-for-service with capitation may become a source of frustration for physicians and staff because of the difference in incentives.

Fairness in administering a primary care capitation pool shared by several physicians may become an issue.

The salary-plus-incentives-with-capitation model is illustrated in Figure 6, below. It incorporates primary care capitation activity and assumes that the capitation is distributed according to patient panel size.

Figure 6: Salary-Plus-Incentives-With-Capitation Model

Base Year Activity			
Gross Professional Production	$276,000		
Expected Collection Rate	90%		
Net Professional Production	$248,400		
Cash Compensation	$124,200		

Projected Activity	**Year 1**	**Year 2**	**Year 3**
Panel Size	200	300	500
Primary Care Capitation[1]	$ 26,400	$ 39,600	$ 66,000
Gross Professional Production	$280,000	$290,000	$300,000
Less: Capitated Professional Production	$ 29,000	$ 40,000	$ 68,000
FFS Professional Production	$251,000	$250,000	$232,000
Expected Collection Rate	0.90	0.88	0.85
Net Professional Production	$225,900	$220,000	$197,200
Plus: Primary Care Capitation	$ 26,400	$ 39,600	$ 66,000
Total Net Professional Production	$252,300	$259,600	$263,200
Production Threshold	$223,560	$203,310	$198,000
Production Above Threshold	$ 28,740	$ 56,290	$ 65,200
Compensation Payout Rate	0.5	0.5	0.5
Production Incentive	$ 14,370	$ 28,145	$ 32,600
Non-Production Incentive[2]	$ 6,210	$ 6,308	$ 7,084

Summary	**Year 1**	**Year 2**	**Year 3**
Prior Year Cash Compensation	$124,200	$126,150	$141,680
Base Salary (85% of prior year cash)	$105,570	$107,228	$120,428
Production Incentive	$ 14,370	$ 28,145	$ 32,600
Non-Production Incentive	$ 6,210	$ 6,308	$ 7,084
Cash Compensation	$126,150	$141,680	$160,112

[1]Assumes primary care capitation equal to $11pmpm (200 patients x 12 mo/yr x $11 pmpm)

[2]Targeted at 5% of prior-year cash compensation

5. The Relative Value Units (RVU) Model

This system, originally implemented Jan. 1, 1992, represents Medicare's approach to equitable pay for physicians. Incorporating relative value units, instead of charges, to measure physician productivity, it embraces three elements in arriving at total unit value per CPT code: physician work, practice costs and professional liability. Cash components described previously can also be utilized in the RVU model, which is illustrated in Figure 7 on page 104.

FIGURE 7: RELATIVE VALUE UNITS (RVU) MODEL

Assumptions (Base Year)	
RVU Professional Production	$ 5,300
RVU Conversion Rate	$ 26
Cash Compensation	$137,000

Projected Activity	**Year 1**	**Year 2**	**Year 3**
Current RVU Professional Production[1]	$ 5,300	$ 5,565	$ 5,843
RVU Professional Production Threshold[2]	$ 4,140	$ 4,140	$ 4,140
RVU Professional Production Above Threshold	$ 1,160	$ 1,425	$ 1,703
RVU Production Incentive (@ $26 per RVU)	$ 30,160	$ 37,050	$ 44,278
Non-Production Incentive[3]	$ 6,850	$ 6,851	$ 7,195

Summary	**Year 1**	**Year 2**	**Year 3**
Prior Year's Cash Compensation	$137,000	$137,010	$143,901
Base Salary[4]	$100,000	$100,000	$100,000
RVU Production Incentive	$ 30,160	$ 37,050	$ 44,278
Non-Production Incentive	$ 6,850	$ 6,851	$ 7,195
Cash Compensation	$137,010	$143,901	$151,473
Operating Unit Incentive[5]	0	0	0
Total Cash Compensation	$137,010	$143,901	$151,473

[1]Assumes constant production in Year 1, then 5% increase in Year 2 and Year 3
[2]RVU threshold corresponds to $100,000 base salary
[3]Targeted at 5% of prior year's cash compensation
[4]Base salary is guaranteed at $100,000
[5]For illustrative purposes only

Advantages

Provides an objective measure of physician productivity.

Pays higher for cognitive services versus surgical procedures.

Addresses historical distortions in physician services fee schedules.

Gains momentum as a system to compensate physicians.

Disadvantages

Physicians relate to charges better than units.

Information systems may not be compatible with RVU data requirements.

RVU system, as a method of compensation, may not correlate directly to how physicians are compensated.

Integration of RVUs in a capitation cash model difficult.

RVU data limited. Difficult to compare actual results to market survey data.

The relative value units model in Figure 7 is an example based on a primary care physician at a constant base salary for three years. The RVUs are based on "global" units (incorporating all three criteria).

When it comes to organizational structure, independent physician practices vary widely. Once affiliated, however, loosely connected groups of practices can be referred to generically as independent practice associations (IPAs).

Development and management of compensation arrangements for IPAs is characterized by two important components:

1. Determining how revenue will flow to and from the IPA; and
2. An income distribution formula.

The fund flow in and out of an IPA depends on the ownership of pertinent managed care contracts. In situations where healthcare organizations own all the contracts—and thus the total revenue stream—provider service agreements (PSAs) outline the amounts paid to IPAs for specific clinical services rendered to members of the various managed care organizations. When IPAs own the contracts, management services agreements (MSAs) are developed to allow them to designate the management services (e.g. contracting, practice management and risk management) they require from the provider organizations. Fees payable to the organization for the services are then negotiated, possibly on a per-month-per-member (PMPM) basis.

The most common income distribution formulas used by IPAs in managed care environments can be categorized under the primary care gatekeeper approach, which divides capitation funds available for ambulatory services into two separate pools, expressed as PMPM payments.

The first pool, representing PMPM payments ranging between $9 and $17, allocates primary care capitation payments to involved physicians. Under this model, each physician maintains an individual panel of patients (who may also be group specific). Minimum and maximum panel sizes are determined by the organization and adjusted according to the acuity of the patient mix. Each physician then receives monthly capitation payments equal to the total number of patients in his/her panel multiplied by the primary care cap rate. These payments, added to negotiated percentages of any discounted fee-for-service revenues generated, represent the physicians' base salaries.

The second pool is for specialty services. It generates payments to physicians equal to the total amount of ambulatory capitation available, less primary care capitation (generally between $9 PMPM and $17 PMPM). In smaller groups, specialists simply bill the organization for services they render according to an established fee schedule. These billings are then charged to the specialty pool.

Since primary care physicians control specialty services utilization under these arrangements, savings in the specialty services pool are distributed to them as incentive compensation for efficient utilization.

Distribution amounts depend on panel size. For example, if the specialty services budget was set at $32 PMPM and actual expenses amounted to only $30 PMPM, the primary care physicians would receive a bonus equal to the number of patients in their individual panels multiplied by the $2 PMPM savings in the specialty pool. Specialists in this model maintain more control of inpatient utilization; thus their incentives are based on institutional savings deriving from established hospital utilization targets.

In larger IPAs, it is often necessary to use zero-based budgeting when compensating specialists, an approach stemming from the RVU methodology. Target PMPMs for specialty services are multiplied by system membership totals to determine specialty compensation pool totals. The pools are then divided by RVU totals provided by participating specialists in order to determine unit values. The unit values are then applied to participant RVU totals to determine their compensation.

The effectiveness of this zero-based approach has led some organizations to experiment with a concept known as the specialty gatekeeper model. Under this approach, primary care physicians are capitated with a formula almost identical to the zero-based budget formula used for specialists in the primary care gatekeeper model. Budgeted PMPMs for primary care physicians are multiplied by membership totals to establish primary care compensation pools. These pools are then divided by primary care physician visit totals (RVUs also could be used) to arrive at unit values per visit. Individual primary care physicians are then paid according to the number of visits they provide multiplied by unit value per visit. At first glance, this approach seems to encourage "churning" of physician visits. With zero-based budgeting, however, the marginal value of each incremental visit decreases, and the economic value of churning is minimized.

Specialists are also paid from established compensation pools under the specialty gatekeeper model. Actuarial analyses determine what percentages of total specialty PMPMs can be designated for each specialty. These percentages are then applied to total available PMPMs to arrive at PMPM budgets by specialty.

Specialty-specific compensation pools are then established by multiplying organizational membership totals by each specialty-specific PMPM budget.

Pool distribution methods vary. The most common one is based on pro rata shares of "new referrals." New-referral definitions generally are based upon the length of time from the initial visit that must elapse before a patient can again be counted as a new referral. This system eliminates the risk of over-utilization of follow up visits and procedures by individual physicians.

About the Authors

Mr. Wegmiller is president of the Management Compensation Group/Healthcare Compensation with more than 30 years of experience in healthcare administration. Mr. Wegmiller formerly served as vice chairman and president of HealthSpan Health Systems Corp. (now Allina Health System).

Mr. Erra's distinguished career in healthcare management has emphasized organizational development, planning, team building and financial management. Before joining MCG/Healthcare, Mr. Erra was senior vice president and director of clinic operations at Scripps Clinic and Research Foundation in La Jolla, Calif. As an active member of the Medical Group Management Association, Mr. Erra also serves on the board of a publicly traded healthcare company and two private ventures.

Managed Care Contracts: A Strategy Approach to Evaluation and Negotiation

by Guy M. Masters, The Camden Group

This article provides guidelines for managed care contract evaluation and negotiation. It is not written from a legal perspective, but rather provides a strategic framework for assessing common contracting issues, using various benchmarks, guidelines and approaches that other providers have used in the past. The information herein does not constitute legal, clinical, accounting or other financial advice.

◆ ◆ ◆

It's late at night after a very busy day of seeing patients, and you're alone in the office with a few minutes to finally sort through the stack of in-box material that has grown to just within fire-hazard proportions. Using the glance-and-toss method of dispatch, you suddenly discover a thick, stapled document with a cover letter bearing the logo of that large, nationally based HMO that you've heard is coming to town—in a big way, with a ground-breaking Medicare risk product, besides the commercial benefit option that has just been picked up by the largest local employer. Scanning through the letter, you discover that if you're going to be part of the physician provider panel, a signed copy of the contract is due back to them by 5:00 p.m. tomorrow. What are you going to do?

Thumbing through the document, the contract appears to be about 50 pages in length, with several attachments that look like fee schedules for both the Medicare and commercial products, a lot of CPT codes, some other list labeled "Responsibility Matrix," and one titled "Risk Pool Formula and Distribution Schedule." Several thoughts cross your mind—*It's too late to call the attorneys or accountants, but maybe the contract should be faxed to them with a follow-up call in the morning? There's really no time for that, though. I hate to admit it, but I should have gone to the IPA meeting last week—wasn't there something on the agenda about this? Yes, they were going to review the key points and give a recommendation... but as a messenger model, the IPA is leaving it up to each physician to make the final decision to sign or not. Well, it's too late for any of those options, so I'll just wait until morning, and ask someone in the physician dining room at the hospital what they're going to do....*

If the foregoing sounds a little too familiar, the following points will be of interest to you. What follows is the outline of an approach to quickly assess key points of a managed care contract. The approach will be helpful regardless of whether you rely on a third party such as an IPA, PHO or other entity to ultimately influence or actually make the decision for you regarding signing managed care contracts. The evaluation approach and benchmarks outlined herein will provide several tools required for you to be familiar in a broad sense with the contract format and appropriateness.

1. **Get help from knowledgeable resources.** Contracts are complex, with obligations, terms and conditions that constantly change from draft to draft, and from payer to payer. Get some help. Health plans negotiate contracts with providers virtually every day of the year, and most physicians get involved once annually per agreement. So who is going to have the upper hand?

   Most individual physicians and their office administrators do not have the time or expertise to evaluate and make decisions about a contract's specific details, language and obligations. Many turn to outside advisors for help—an accountant,

FIGURE 1: TYPICAL COMPONENTS OF A PHYSICIAN PROVIDER SERVICES AGREEMENT (PSA)

1. Definitions
   a. Parties to the agreement
   b. Purpose and parameters of the agreement
   c. Service area
   d. Primary care/Specialist definition and delineation
   e. Enrollee/subscriber description
2. Obligations of Providers
   a. Type of services to be provided
   b. Hold harmless
   c. Credentialing, licensure, certification
   d. Credentialing
   e. Standard of care
   f. Compliance with policies and procedures
3. Compensation
   a. Payment methodology (e.g., capitation, fee schedule, case rates, other)
   b. Billing process
   c. Non-billing of prepaid patients
   d. Copayments/deductibles
   e. Coordination of benefits and third-party liability
   f. Indemnification
   g. Insurance
4. Term and Termination
   a. Term of contract
   b. With cause/without cause provisions
   c. Obligations upon termination
   d. Multiple products
5. Other Provisions
   a. Confidentiality
   b. Notices
   c. Assignment/delegation
   d. Utilization management/quality assurance/improvement
   e. Severability
   f. Grievances/appeals process/ arbitration
6. Exhibits
   a. Primary care physician responsibility service list
   b. Fee schedule
   c. Risk pool distribution formula
   d. Service responsibility matrix

actuary, consultant, attorney, peer, or some other healthcare professional or administrator. These individuals can often provide valuable information, benchmark data, and points of reference for making good contracting decisions.

The process for evaluating and negotiating physician managed care contracts in mature markets is often handled through third parties. Entities such as IPAs, PHOs, MSOs, group practice administrators and others often have the administrative personnel with expertise and delegated responsibility to gather information, review content and make recommendations to their members regarding specific contracts. In fact, many physicians join such organizations for this type of service and advice.

Don't sign a contract without doing some due diligence on the financial, clinical and strategic impacts of the contract's terms. Much of managed care is rooted in quantitative analysis and predictability of costs and utilization. You must be willing to learn the language of managed care, such as per unit costs, resource utilization expressed in per 1,000 lives, per member per month (PMPM), and other common measures.

2. **Create a financial flow-of-funds structure for the contract.** Read the contract through initially to get a feel for the broad picture—build a visual bridge between the contract terms and the actual service delivery process. Most contracts can overwhelm the average reader with legal definitions and descriptions. There are usually separate contracts for primary care and specialty physicians. While many sections of the contracts will be similar, the main difference will be in defining the different roles and responsibilities each type of physician will assume, the services to be provided, and the reimbursement methodology to be applied to each.

Figure 2: Example of Commercial Capitation Funds Flow Analysis

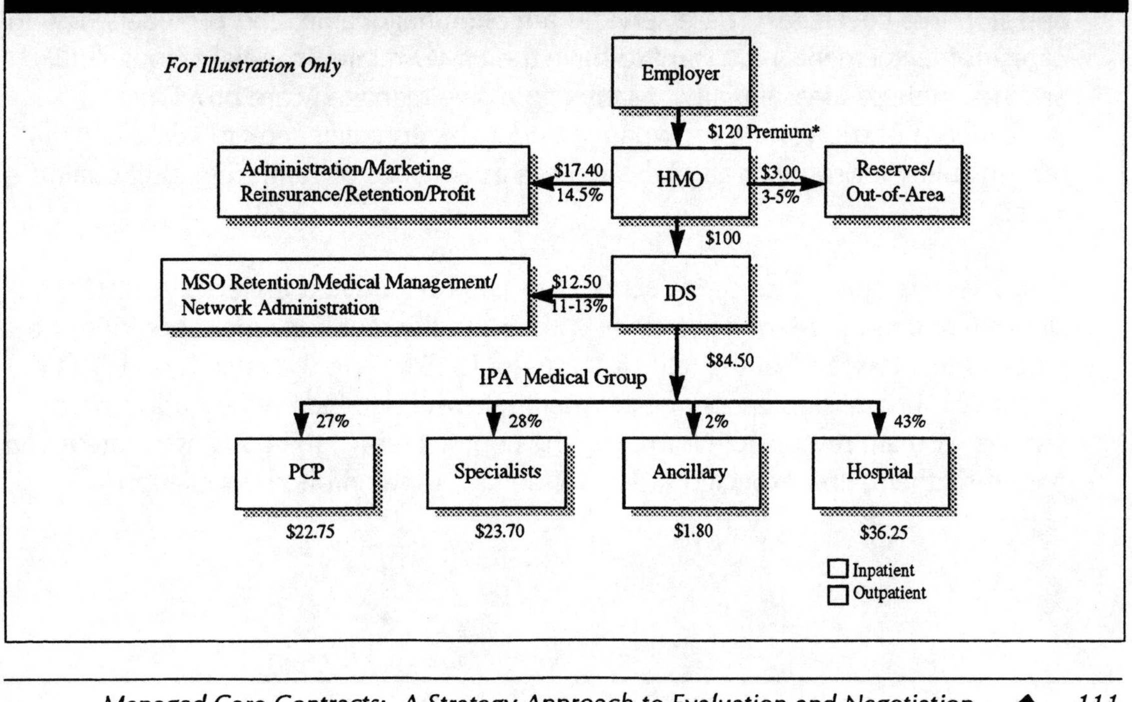

Review the contract to determine the scope of services to be provided. Does it pertain to a population of commercial (i.e., under age 65, employed), Medicare, Medicaid, or other enrollees? Is it a blanket contract covering multiple population types? Contract terms, payment rates and utilization performance standards will be different for various enrollee categories. *(See Figure 2 on page 111.)*

Your next step should be to review the contract with specific attention to how money flows to all the parties to the service delivery process. The following flow diagram is an example of financial allocations for an arrangement between an employer, the HMO, an integrated delivery system (e.g., PHO), an IPA, and a hospital provider.

Make the attempt to create a flow-of-funds diagram for your contract. While a physician agreement may not include the hospital payment allocation, it is possible to deduct what percentage of total premium is paid to them if you know the health plan's retained administrative percentage, and the amount or percentage paid to the IPA/physicians.

The percentage of the premium that the HMO will pay to all providers of services is referred to as the medical loss ratio (MLR). Most states require that HMOs report their average MLR on a regular basis, usually quarterly or annually. If you know the average MLR for the HMO you are dealing with, you have at least one benchmark to know if the contract you are evaluating is above or below its typical arrangement.

Many HMOs in mature managed care markets typically will have MLRs of between 80 percent and 85 percent for commercial benefit options. Medicare products may have lower MLRs, depending upon what services the HMO provides. The lower the MLR, the more services the HMO should be providing.

Pay close attention to whether or not the HMO is taking responsibility for covering benefits such as pharmacy, behavioral health, out-of-area care/emergencies, and stop-loss coverage. These services are often negotiable, and providers new to capitation agreements may want to have the HMO retain financial responsibility and risk in these areas initially. Many aggressive managed care providers with a track record of successful performance under risk contracts seek to take financial responsibility for some or all of these areas as a means of capturing additional revenue.

3. **Correlate the "flow of funds" to services to be provided and their designated reimbursement ranges.** Many physicians will turn to the reimbursement sections of a contract first to see what the rate structure looks like. Are the rates "good," "fair" or "bad?" The desirableness of a payment rate will depend entirely upon what services you are responsible for under the contract terms, the costs associated with providing them, and expected utilization rates for the enrolled population.

Figure 3: Example Contract Assessment Matrix— List of Services and Responsible Parties

Editor's note: Below is part of a sample template to be used for contract assessment.

Services	Primary Care	Specialists	PHO	Hospital	HMO
AIDS Professional Component					
Inpatient, Facility Component					
Allergy					
Testing					
Serum					
Ambulance					
Emergency					
In Area					
Out of Area					
Anesthetics, Administration of (Anesthesiology)					
Artificial Limbs (DME)					
Adult Day Care, Non-Medicare Covered					
Biofeedback					
Blood & Blood Products (Including Professional Component)					
From Blood Bank					
Autologous Blood Donation					
Cataract Surgery					
Professional component					
Facility component					
Implanted lenses					
Chemical Dependency Rehabilitation (Medicare)					
Inpatient Facility Component					
Inpatient Professional Component					
Outpatient Professional Component					
Outpatient Professional Component					
Chemotherapy					
Drugs					
Professional Component					
Facility component, if applicable					
Chiropractic					
Colostomy Supplies					
Outpatient					
Inpatient					
Cosmetic Surgery (Medically Necessary)					
Facility Component					
Professional Component					
Custodial Facilities, Non-Medicare Covered					

Typical reimbursement methods for physician services include capitation, fee schedules and case rates. The contract should have very precise language of how capitation rates are calculated and when payment will be made.

All payment rates should have some basis in an actuarial assessment of estimated costs and anticipated utilization per unit of service. Look in the contract exhibits or attachments for a "Service Responsibility Matrix" (see sample) or listing of services by procedure code to determine what you are responsible to provide. The matrix should list also what services responsibilities of the health plan and other providers. Some items may be shared, such as education, wellness and prevention services.

Whether a reimbursement rate is desirable or not will be a function of what services you are responsible to perform, the anticipated cost of those services and the expected potential utilization of those services by the population for which you are responsible. You should also perform a calculation to determine if the reimbursement is sufficient to cover your overhead for the expected patient visits during the contract period. *(See Figure 2 on page 113.)*

4. **Ask (and get an answer to) the "Golden Question" of managed care negotiations.** Good data has always been the breakfast of champions in the managed care process. Good data specifically is information that can help you make timely and effective decisions that will positively impact your financial and clinical outcomes. When negotiating and evaluating a managed care contract, you must know how your (and the IPA or provider group's) performance measures up relative to specific utilization and cost performance benchmarks. And you must know the financial breakeven point for each HMO contract, expressed in terms of key utilization measures (e.g., inpatient days per 1,000 covered lives). This is particularly important as you assess the likelihood of there being surplus funds available for distribution to physicians from any hospital risk pools.

   In fact, for PHO and hospital contracting, the Golden Question of managed care negotiations is expressed in this way: *"What is the breakeven point for the provider contract (specifically the hospital pool) expressed in terms of inpatient days per 1,000 lives?"* This question is essential to answer, whether by information from the HMO, or by your own research. You must be able to measure where your performance is now relative to a breakeven benchmark. This one measure will begin to help you understand how clinical practice and provider behavior patterns will need to change in order to achieve your performance objectives for the contract.

   You may need some actuarially based data to answer the Golden Question, if the HMO will not provide the response. Specifically, you must first know historical utilization patterns for your geographic service area. Look first for inpatient utilization expressed in days per 1,000 population (both with and without skilled nursing days). Most actuaries can provide benchmarks (especially for Medicare historical utilization) regarding current inpatient utilization for the service area. They should also be able to tell you what a target utilization point is to breakeven financially based on the premium that the HMO is charging the employers, the percent of premium contributed to the hospital pool, the service matrix for hospital pool services, and the specific health benefit options for the plan. Once you have this information, you can begin to develop programs for changing utilization patterns as may be necessary.

5. **Determine the strategic value of the contract.** How important is this contract to you strategically? Does the health plan have a book of business (i.e., covered lives) that will be delivered upon signing the contract, or will it be starting from scratch? The greater the number of potential lives associated with the contract, the greater its strategic value. Primary care physicians should carefully assess the roles they will be required to fulfill, and determine an approximate number of additional covered lives they might be responsible for, especially if a gatekeeper model is used.

   As a rule of thumb, some HMOs expect to have approximately four physician visits per member per year, with approximately 75 percent of these visits going to primary care physicians—this is for a typical commercial population. For Medicare, HMOs expect nine to 11 physician visits per member per year in areas where managed care is new; then physician visits have dropped to seven to nine per member per year as the market matures over several years' time.

   A useful mathematical exercise is to multiply the estimated per patient office overhead cost times the projected number of patient visits per year, and compare this expense number with the total annual premium (revenue) that will be received under capitation. This calculation will show roughly whether or not you can expect any profit at year's end for these patients based on the proposed rates.

   How do the health plan's monthly premiums to employers compare with what exists in the community? Are their premiums significantly lower, about the same, or higher than other plans? What are the benefit options that are offered? How marketable will their options be? Does the plan currently offer other non-managed care options to employers? Will it seek to convert lives from one payment type to another? Will this contract shift patients from a currently profitable arrangement to one with lower reimbursement schedules? Will this plan offer Medicare or Medicaid options? Do it have a track record with these payer types in other markets? Is it good or bad?

   Many new entrants into emerging managed care markets are doing so because of opportunities for enrollment growth among the Medicare and Medicaid populations. Payment rates for Medicare are correlated to the per member per month premiums that the Health Care Financing Administration will pay to HMOs, referred to as the AAPCC rates. These AAPCC rates are determined on a county-by-county basis, and are often much higher than average commercial managed care premium rates (sometimes by factors of three, four or five times greater). Medicare rates are necessarily higher to cover the additional utilization for senior patients.

Medicaid rates are not correlated to either Medicare or commercial premium levels. Both the Medicare and Medicaid populations typically require more assertive utilization management, and careful financial and clinical due diligence should be done using actuarial analysis before signing these contracts.

6. **Request a copy of the health plan's Provider Policy Manual.** Obtain and review a copy of the provider policy manual before signing the provider services agreement. Many contracts will reference policy and procedure manuals, which outline in specific terms what you will be required to do in the service delivery process. Know what obligations you are agreeing to before signing. Also, watch for clauses in the provider agreement that automatically bind the providers to future changes made to the policy manual. Avoid these clauses, and obtain the right to review and approve any changes to these policies before their taking effect. When a provider contract refers to a provider manual for details, insist on a specific citation (i.e., section number, page number, paragraph).

7. **Review specific contract terms relative to the following:**

    a. Obligations to submit data to health plan—The health plan will probably require that encounter data be submitted by the providers on a regular basis, typically monthly. Make sure that you understand your obligations as an individual provider, as a medical group and through the IPA or PHO. Clarify timing, format (e.g., electronic, hard-copy) and extent of reporting required in order to assess your administrative burden and the capabilities you have to provide the data in a timely way.

    b. Access to annual financial statements—The HMO may also request access to provider financial information. Determine what statements are required, and make sure that the health plan agrees to review only information that is relevant, non-confidential and reasonable. Ask that confidentiality agreements be signed pertaining to this information. You should also request that reviews of financial statements be done on your premises, and that the reviewer be qualified to perform such tasks.

    c. Use of providers' names—The contract will likely have a section specifying that the HMO will have the right to use individual and/or group names in marketing materials, advertising media, Internet Websites, etc. You should request prior approval for use of names and likenesses in all media venues. However, it is reasonable for the HMO to use individual or group names without prior written approval in provider panel listings and health plan rosters.

    d. Universal product structures/enrollee population to be covered—Some health plans are writing "universal products" contracts. These contracts require that providers participate in all lines of business (e.g., Medicare, Medicaid, commercial, point-of-service, direct access, other) offered by the health plan under one agreement. A key negotiating point for these universal contracts is to get an allowance for terminating participation without cause in specific products without terminating the entire agreement. Also, pay close attention to the exhibits of these contracts, since the specific details, responsibilities and obligations pertaining to each product type are outlined there rather than in the body of the agreement.

e. Calculation of premium and accuracy of payment—There are often many problems with capitation calculations and eligibility tie-ins. The contract should precisely define how capitation is calculated. Percent-of-premium contracts should specify exactly what the percentage is applied to (e.g., where are broker commissions and other relevant expenses accounted for?)

   There are some health plans paying capitation that have a practice of not assigning enrollees to providers or groups until the member makes an initial visit to a physician as a patient. Thus, if an enrollee does not visit a physician for his or her first five months after enrolling as a subscriber, the health plan does not make any prospective payments to providers for that period. You should insist on mandatory assignment of enrollees if you encounter this type of arrangement. Members who are not assigned to a primary care provider should still be included in the IPA/group's capitation payment and calculation basis.

   Capitation payments should be made by the health plan by the 10th of the month. Member eligibility lists should be provided by the 25th of the month.

f. Risk sharing formulas—Many contracts will include risk sharing arrangements primarily for two purposes: first, to align provider incentives toward common objectives of providing quality, cost-effective care; and second, to allow the providers to share in the financial results of their performance. "Good" performance should ideally result in financial surpluses; "poor" performance mostly results in deficits.

   Look at your contract to determine whether or not there are provisions for you to participate in any risk pools, such as inpatient hospital, ancillary, pharmacy or others. An IPA should be participating in hospital pool surpluses, at a minimum. Initial risk sharing within the IPA, physician side of a PHO, or provider group should probably begin with a 50/50 formula between primary care and specialist physicians. With enrollment growth and experience, other formulas can be developed correlated to utilization performance, resource consumption benchmarks, patient volume, referral experience and others.

   Risk-sharing participation formulas for Medicare and Medicaid contracts should be evaluated very carefully, and be correlated to actuarial projections for these populations. There is typically significant financial risk associated with these groups.

The foregoing points are not comprehensive in scope. The selective list included herein is meant to provide an initial strategic framework for you to understand the managed care contracting process. Specific benchmarks, utilization and cost targets will vary from market to market, and contract to contract. Therefore, it is imperative that you seek competent legal, financial and strategic advice before signing any managed care contract. This article does not constitute that advice.

Managed care contracting offers opportunities, pitfalls, challenges and new inroads for providers to take more responsibility and financial control in the care delivery process. It is essential to understand that many capitation and risk-sharing arrangements transfer, to varying degrees, actual underwriting risk to providers. This is a good news/bad news situation. Each provider must evaluate his or her particular circumstances to determine how, when and under what conditions managed care contracting is appropriate. There are many examples of success and failure in the managed care arena to date, and due diligence should be conducted to learn the lessons that are available from these experiences as you determine how to respond to the dynamic forces impacting healthcare delivery.

About the Author

Mr. Masters is a vice president with the Camden Group. A co-author of the Healthcare Capitation & Risk Contracting Manual, Masters has also written numerous articles on managed care strategy and physician-hospital integration.

Risk Contracting

By Hara J. Schwartz, MD, Robin L. Smith, MD, and David B. Nash, MD, MBA

In Chinese the word "crisis" is composed of two characters: One represents danger and the other symbolizes opportunity. Danger and opportunity rolled into one package is also another way to define risk.

Managed care has been the catalyst for the formation of innovative healthcare delivery organizations and a new reimbursement mechanism—capitation. A hallmark of the new organizations and reimbursement mechanism is the shifting of risk from insurers or payers to medical providers. The organizations capable of assuming responsibility for some or all of the payer's administrative and financial risk will be able to control their destiny. In addition, these teams will win the market share. Many are skeptical of this positive outcome based on the unexpected fallout we have seen from risk assumption in the past several years. Risk offers the promise of improving the quality and containing the costs of care. But this will not occur until the concept of capitation matures in a delivery system guided by the right values, where doctors and organizations are committed to improvement and change.

To gain autonomy and revenue, providers must position themselves to "go at risk." This will require reorganizing and redefining their relationships with other members of the healthcare delivery system. Risk contracting is the means to this end. A contract delineates the terms of a relationship. The parties that may be involved in risk contracting are health plans, hospitals, providers and patients. The goal of each party is to maximize what it can gain from the relationship. This chapter will identify the fundamental knowledge and skills providers must acquire and hone to be successful at risk contracting. (We advise readers to consult an attorney for questions about the technicalities of contracting.)

◆ ◆ ◆

The term capitation refers to paying a provider a fixed sum of money to cover a different set of healthcare services for an individual enrollee for a defined period of time. Under fee-for-service reimbursement, providers are financially rewarded for increasing the amount of healthcare services provided to each patient. Under capitation, the financial incentives for providers are exactly the opposite. This reversal in traditional economics will have (and in some cases, already has had) a profound effect on the behavior of physicians.

A question commonly asked is: Can the healthcare problem be fixed under a system of pure capitation, where the provider takes the full risk for all healthcare services? Providers order the tests, do the procedures, prescribe the drugs and decide when to admit and when to discharge. Who, then, is in a better position to control the healthcare costs than providers?

Patient volume as a market force. Managed care, *if* properly conducted, brings healthcare costs under control and eliminates "unnecessary care. (*Unnecessary care* is defined here as care that does not affect health outcomes.) By containing costs and providing quality care, managed care plans have become popular among many purchasers and individual patients and have become a critical source of patient volume for the providers of healthcare.[1] This market force will drive more physicians into capitated contractual relationships with managed care organizations.

Under capitation, revenue does not increase with the number of services provided. To increase revenue, a provider must increase the patient population base by negotiating competitive, capitated contracts with managed care organizations. Such contracts transfer the risk of providing healthcare services from the insurer to the provider. Providers able to assume the responsibility of managing care and lowering utilization should be able to accept risk and share in the rewards of doing so.[2] The other option providers may choose is to step aside while intermediaries manage and prosper. Regardless of who manages care and governs utilization, accepting risk also means there's a risk of loss. In addition, it is critical that patients, the purchasers of healthcare, do not feel that rationing of service is occurring. If patients sense this, then everybody loses.

Integrated delivery systems. The ability to manage risk is one major reason why hospitals, physicians and insurers are forming integrated networks and systems.[3] Integrated healthcare refers to the banding together of healthcare providers (primary care physicians and specialists) and facilities (hospitals, ancillary sites) as a means to coordinate patient care, broaden the range of services, expand geographically and more successfully compete for managed care contracts. Initiatives that integrate organizations for the delivery, financing and management of healthcare will gain market share. Providers must align with organizations that can accept and profitably manage capitated risk for all healthcare services. Integrated delivery systems that provide quality care for a low price will win contracts and achieve a competitive advantage.

Risk Equals Opportunity Plus Danger

The assumption of risk affords the opportunity to providers to increase profits and maintain control. It is estimated that capitation, projected across the whole population, could result in billions of dollars of savings in annual healthcare costs.[4] Providers that assume risk and contain costs will be able to "pocket" some of these savings. In addition to potential profits, assuming risk offers providers the chance to regain control of clinical decision making. Physicians are slowly losing the authority to make autonomous clinical decisions. They are being second-guessed and overruled by doctors, nurses and administrators employed by managed care organizations. The critical question is, "To manage or to be managed?"

But beware—with risk there is always danger. The challenge is just beginning once the contract is won. Providers must effectively manage the cost of care, and those unable to will lose money and possibly, future viability. Another downside of risk capitation is being too restrictive, which can result in lack of quality and increased legal problems.

The premium dollar. Acquiring and managing risk contracts will require learning new skills and understanding how the premium dollar is allocated. We will trace the premium dollar from payer to provider to illustrate what the financial risk involves (*See Figure 1 below*). The purchaser (individual, employer or government) pays 100 percent as premium, for example $100 a month for healthcare. The managed care organization consumes anywhere from 17 percent-30 percent ($17-$30) of that premium.[5]

FIGURE 1: THE PREMIUM DOLLAR

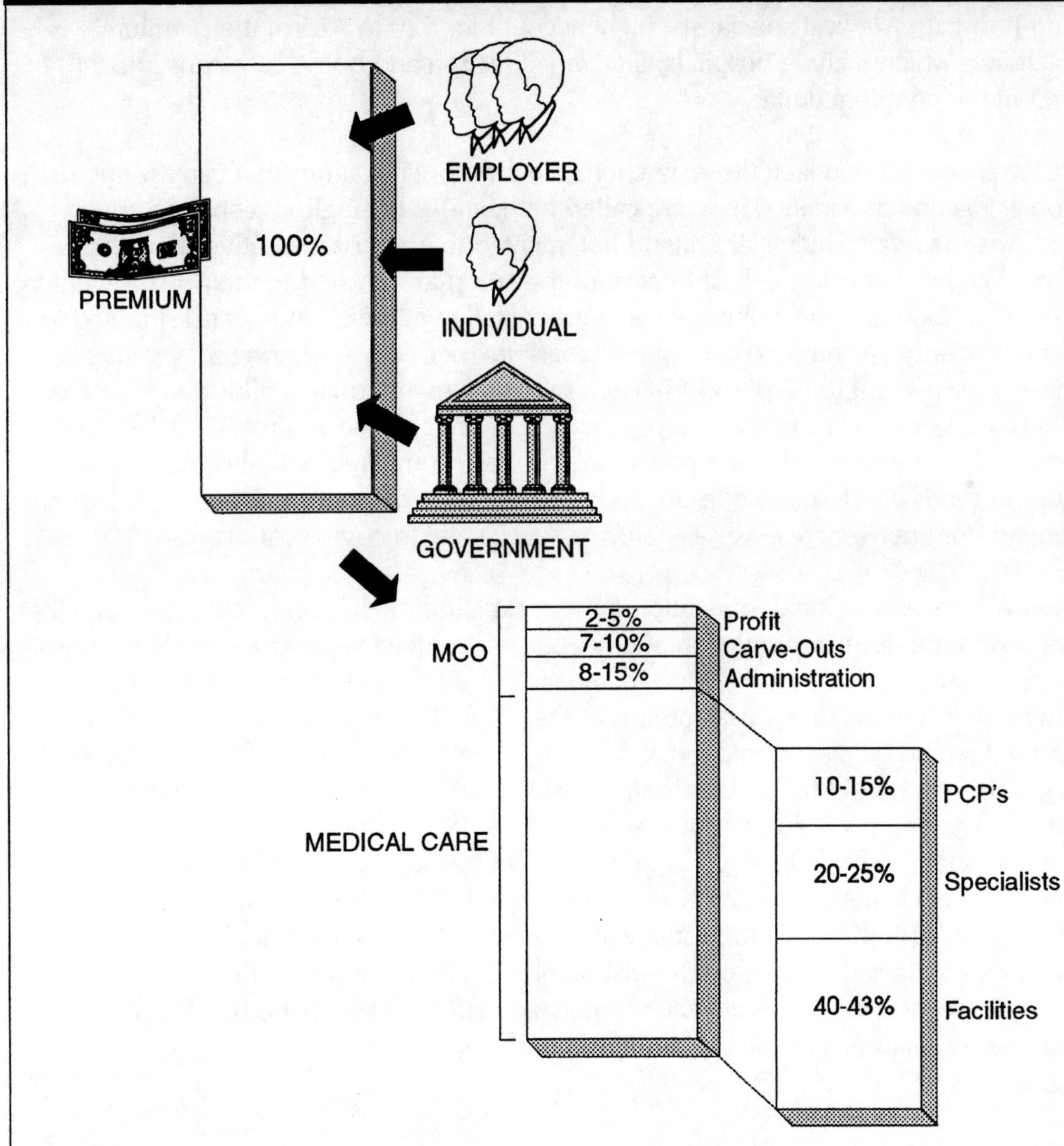

The breakdown of that percentage is as follows: Administrative costs of running a health plan range between 8 percent to 15 percent of the premium per member per month (PMPM). These costs include marketing, claims payments, contract negotiating, case management and credentialing providers. Carve-outs, such as formularies, laboratory tests, mental health and stop-loss coverage, account for 7 percent to 10 percent of the premium. Managed care company profits are 2 percent to 5 percent of the premium.

That leaves $70 to $83 of the initial $100 premium for medical care. How these remaining monies are divided among the primary care physicians (PCPs), specialists, hospitals and other healthcare facilities depends on the degree to which physician groups and hospitals have integrated to share risk. There are many different ways of paying physicians and hospitals, including discounted fee for service, capitation, per diem, per case and so forth.

This discussion is limited to capitated payments. PCPs may receive $10 to $15 PMPM to provide basic primary care and to control access to specialists, procedures and hospitals. Medical specialists might account for $20 to $25 of the premium. Facilities, which include hospitals, ERs, rehabilitation and home care consume $40 to $43 of the premium dollar.

PCPs, specialists and facilities may choose to form organizations that can assume risk and act as one provider. These are called foundations or single risk-sharing pools. Risk-sharing arrangements are often implemented to establish incentives that encourage providers to act in the best interest of the group as opposed to their own self-interest. Risk pools are pools of money that are initially withheld, and later distributed to providers only if certain predetermined goals are met. In risk-sharing arrangements, usually 10 percent to 20 percent of each reimbursement dollar is allocated to one or more risk pools. Throughout the year, expenses are charged against the respective pools. At the year's end, each pool's expenses are compared with those budgeted. Surplus funds are distributed to providers based on prearranged formulas. Deficits are funded from network reserves established specifically to cover cost overruns.[6]

We will create a fictional foundation to help explain how it works. Let's say 10 PCPs get together to form a foundation and negotiate a contract with a managed care organization for $13 PMPM for 11,000 members. To establish incentives that encourage the providers to act in the best interest of the group, 20 percent of the capitated amount would be placed into a risk pool. This would result in the foundation receiving a check for $143,000 each month (11,000 members X $13 PMPM) from the payer. The group would then put aside $28,600 each month (20% X $143,000) for the risk pool, leaving $114,400 a month ($143,000-$28,600) for physician compensation. If total claims to care for those 11,000 members are less than they had figured, the doctors split the risk pool, usually at the end of the year. But, if claims exceed what was budgeted, funds from the risk pool will be used to cover them. Risk pools can be designed to control utilization, manage performance—or both.[7] The specialists and the hospitals can create the same risk pools.

Now let's look at an integrated delivery system (IDS). Just as before, the "purchaser" pays $100 a month for healthcare, but this time the PCP's, specialists and facilities band together to form one integrated risk pool. The IDS negotiates a contract with the MCO to receive $82 PMPM for the 17,000 members in its panel (the MCO receives $18 PMPM). The group then decides to put 35 percent of their capitated payment into a risk pool. As a result, the group would receive a check for $1,394,000 each month (17,000 members X $82 PMPM) and set aside $487,900 (35 percent X $1,394,000) for the risk pool, leaving $906,100 ($1,394,000-$487,900) to pay the salaries of the PCPs and specialists and the PMPM for the hospitals. Again, if physicians and hospitals utilize more resources than estimated, dollars are deducted from the risk pool, decreasing what remains available for distribution among the team members; if they use fewer resources, all share in the rewards.

Therefore, it is in the team's best interests to keep patients healthy, because it will keep costs down. Ideally, this arrangement should also satisfy enrollees, who will theoretically stay healthier. By placing themselves at financial risk, providers have an incentive to work together as a team, sharing information and overseeing one another.

Some groups have decided to negotiate full risk contracts and have attempted to "manage" care. This would enable the providers to assume a greater portion of the premium at the expense of the managed care company's revenues. If the providers manage their own claims and utilization, they have the opportunity to extract an additional 8 percent to 15 percent of the premium that had been allotted to the administrative expenses of the MCO. If the providers additionally take on the responsibility for carve-outs, they can extract even more of the premium dollar. However, this also increases their risks.

The Skills

In order to successfully take on full risk contracting, providers must acquire new skills, skills that will enable them to create an infrastructure and control risk. Each organization must decide which risks it will manage and which risks it will delegate to someone else. It is the wise team that knows when to ask for help. The following skills will lay the groundwork for controlling risk:

- Financial;
- Informatics;
- Leadership;
- Marketing;
- Medical Management; and
- Operations Management.

A Hypothetical Case

To illustrate the tools providers need in order to assume and manage risk, we will discuss them in the context of a hypothetical organization, A&E Health Systems. A&E Health Systems is a physician hospital organization (PHO) formed by Glow Memorial Hospital and its affiliated physicians. A&E Health Systems has a contract to exclusively provide care to the 75,000 members of Effective Health Plans (EHP, just one more to add to the alphabet soup), a local managed care organization, on a discounted fee-for-service basis. Effective Health Plans has recently decided to fully capitate the PHO and made it clear that if the negotiations do not meet their terms, it will take its 75,000 members to another PHO.

Before entering into negotiations, the chief executive of the PHO, Dr. Dee quickly mobilized his forces to determine what is fundamental to successful captitation. Here's the list he came up with:

1. **Financial Skills.** Projecting healthcare costs and establishing an adequate captitation rate (this will require assessing the cost of providing care to the population served).
2. **Informatics.** An information system that monitors and interprets the administrative, financial and clinical data of the delivery team while simultaneously managing medical information.
3. **Leadership Skills.** Establishing and communicating a clear vision of the team's future (while providing direction and motivation for the providers and support staff).
4. **Marketing Skills.** Identifying and enrolling consumers for the goods and services your team provides.
5. **Medical Management.** Developing and implementing case management strategies leading to efficient inpatient and outpatient healthcare services.
6. **Operations Management Skills.** Ensuring that the day-to-day functioning of the team is operating effectively and in accordance with the team's mission.

Over the next year A&E Health systems gained more and more enrolled members, becoming the largest and most successful PHO in the nation. After taking the steps necessary to fully understand and implement the skills needed for managing risk, A&E became a winning team.

Let's take a closer look at each of the skills a practitioner can implement to achieve success.

Financial

Understanding the true cost of providing services will empower physicians to seek good contracts with payers that ensure sufficient reimbursement. Physicians must define and measure the health expenditure risk of the population for which they are considering "going at risk." This entails characterizing the enrolled members by age, sex and certain health status indicators such as smoking. In addition, physicians must calculate the expected volume by diagnoses as well as the costs for treating those diagnoses. Actuarial cost models can be used to estimate the costs of care, develop premium rates and evaluate the adequacy of capitation rates. It is fundamental to successful financial management to know what it costs to deliver a service to the market.

Informatics

The changes in the healthcare system that include the growth of knowledge, an emphasis on prevention, new technologies and new treatments, along with the reorganization of the delivery system, have led to a complex system of healthcare. The traditional one-to-one patient-physician relationship has blossomed into a one-to-many relationship involving patients with physicians, physician extenders and hospitals. This networked relationship requires a strategy for communicating and sharing information in order to ensure quality healthcare and cost control. An information system will be essential for facilitating the effective delivery of care and the assumption of risk. The ideal system would have the capacity to link all parties, merge clinical and financing information, integrate protocols and guidelines into patient data, measure the quality of care and outcomes and provide care givers with real-time data.

Leadership

Success will require a change in the traditional philosophy of medicine from treating disease to preventing disease. This will require a team leader capable of developing and communicating a clear vision for the team. While keeping the team inspired and motivated, the leadership must ensure that resources and support systems are available to bring the team's goals to fruition. The American health system is changing and has led to the adoption of quality initiatives, increased value and cooperative collaboration.[8] These changes will require the guidance of committed leaders. With a reputation of having a self-interest focus, physicians have generally avoided involvement in administration.[9, 10, 11] Without such participation the profession is sure to lose control of directing professional activities, and autonomy will continue to decrease. It is time for physicians to lead their peers in meeting the healthcare needs of the population.

Marketing

Providing quality care is not enough to ensure success. Success also depends on maintaining a sufficient volume of business with profits in order to pay the bills. So how do you acquire the patients? Marketing can be viewed as a service that provides the public with information on products and services. Providers must target their marketing techniques (public relations, direct mail and local advertising) to reach the consumers to whom their services are applicable and increase patient volume. To increase market share and better serve customers, providers must meet the needs of consumers. By meeting these needs, providers will gain customer loyalty and customer satisfaction. Those that plan to thrive in this revolution must be proactive in developing strategies to identify, address and fulfill the needs of the consumers.

Medical Management

Medical management refers to the methods used to achieve the efficient delivery of quality heathcare services. Ensuring this outcome will require management of how healthcare is delivered and by whom. The model of medical management has been described as having two components, clinical and administrative.[12] "The clinical management processes include provider credentialing and selection, utilization management (prior authorization, certification for claims adjudication, concurrent review, case and disease management, utilization review, second opinion and referral management), quality assurance, formulary management, health promotion and outcome measurement. The administrative components of medical management are relationship management, demand management (using clinical protocols and algorithms), and grievance abatement and resolution."[13] These activities offer an approach to improving clinical practice. Effectively managing physicians and patient care while appropriately using healthcare resources in order to deliver efficient, quality healthcare, leads to successful medical management.

Operations Management

Operations management creates the services and products guaranteed by an organization. Providing high quality services on a timely basis will give health consumers "value for their money." This task entails ensuring that the space, equipment and staffing of an office are appropriate and sufficient for the population being served. Physicians must address the day-to-day tasks of clinical practice, which technologies to choose and how to budget and control costs. Excellent operations management is a critical attribute of a winning team. Providers will be challenged with "make versus buy" decisions. These issues concern whether organizations will provide management and support services on their own (make) or turn to external consultants (buy). Many provider organizations would prefer to purchase expert external support in areas that they feel less equipped to handle so they may spend more time perfecting quality treatment of care, while others refuse to become dependent and prefer to address these issues from within. These decisions about whether an organization will be managed in a decentralized or tightly centralized fashion may have a great impact on the team's success.

Summary

Taking on risk is both a threat and an opportunity for all providers. Those providers who invest the time and energy to become part of an organization capable of delivering cost-effective quality healthcare and profitably managing risk will undoubtedly emerge as winners in today's healthcare market. Those providers who refuse to change in the midst of a new era of healthcare will have difficulty surviving into the 21st century.

◆ ◆ ◆

SUGGESTED READING

Boland, P. *Making Managed Healthcare Work: A Practical Guide to Strategies and Solutions*. Gaithersburg, MD: Aspen, 1993.

Conrad, D., Bonney, R., Sachs, M., et. al. *Managed Care Contracting: Concepts and Applications for the Health Care Executive*. Chicago, Il: Health Administration Press/ACHE, 1996.

Danzi, T. J. *Positioning Your Practice for the Managed Care Market*. Baltimore, MD: Williams & Wilkins, 1996.

Degoulet, P. and Fieschi, M. *Introduction to Clinical Informatics*. New York, NY: Springer-Verlag, 1997.

Eddy, D. *Clinical Decision Making: From Theory to Practice*. Sudbury, MA: Jones and Bartlett Publishers, 1996.

Kongstvedt, P. R. *Essentials of Managed Health Care*. 2nd ed. Gaithersburg, MD: Aspen, 1997.

Kongstvedt, P. R. *The Managed Health Care Handbook*. 3rd ed. Gaithersburg, MD: Aspen, 1997.

Miller, K. A. and Miller, E. K. *Making Sense of Managed Care*. vol. I, II, III. San Francisco, CA: ACPE, 1997.

Pyenson, B.S. *Calculated Risk: A Provider's Guide to Assessing and Controlling the Financial Risk of Managed Care*. Chicago, Il: American Hospital Publishing Inc., 1995.

References

[1]Iglehart, J.K. "Physicians and The Growth of Managed Care." *Health Policy Report, NEJM* 33(17):1167-1171, October 27,1994.

[2]Wolford, G.R., Brown M., McCool, B.P. "Getting To Go In Managed Care." *Health Care Manage Review,* 18(1), 7-19, 1993.

[3]Bader, B.S. and Matheny, M. "Understanding Capitation and At-Risk Contracting." *Health System Leader,* 4-16, March 1994.

[4]Advisory Board Company. *Vertical Integration Strategies for Physicians and Health Systems,* 1993.

[5]ibid., "Understanding Capitation and At-Risk Contracting."

[6]Gapenski, L.C. *Understanding Health Care Financial Management.* Chicago, IL: Health Administration Press/ACHE, Chapter 18. 1996.

[7]ibid.

[8]Wolford, G.R., Brown, M. and McCool, B.P. "Getting To Go In Managed Care." *Health Care Manage Rev,* 18(1), 7-19, 1993.

[9]Miller, R.H. and Luft, H.S. "Managed Care Plan Performance Since 1980: A Literature Analysis." *JAMA,* 271:1512-9, 1994.

[10]Freund, D.A., Rossiter, L.F., Fox, P.D., et al. "Evaluation of the Medicaid Competition Demonstrations." *Health Care Finance Review,* 11(2):81-97, 1989.

[11]Retchin, S.M., and Brown, B. "The Quality of Ambulatory Care in Medicare Health Maintenance Organizations." *American Journal of Public Health,* 80:411-5, 1990.

[12]Miller, K.A., and Miller, E.K. *Making Sense of Managed Care.* vol. I, page 4. San Francisco: CA/ACPE, 1997.

[13]ibid.

About the Authors

Hara J. Schwartz, MD, is currently a fellow in the U.S. Quality Algorithms Managed Care Fellowship between U.S. Healthcare and Thomas Jefferson Medical College. As a board certified Internist, she serves as a clinical attending physician in primary care at the Wilmington Veteran's Affairs Hospital in Delaware.

Robin L. Smith, MD, is a Specialist Project Consultant to the Department of Health Policy and Clinical Outcomes at Thomas Jefferson Medical College. She is a Primary Care Attending at the Wilmington Veteran's Affairs Hospital in Delaware and an Associate Medical Director at Aetna-U.S. Healthcare.

David B. Nash, MD, MBA, FACP is the founding Director of the Office of Health Policy and Clinical Outcomes at Thomas Jefferson University Hospital and Associate Professor of Medicine at Jefferson Medical College in Philadelphia. In December 1996, Dr. Nash assumed additional responsibilities as the first Associate Dean for Health Policy at Jefferson Medical College.

Physician Leaders Are Essential for Achieving Health Gain

By James A. Rice, PhD, Partner,
The Governance Institute

What will the future bring? A better question for America's physician leaders and their healthcare organizations is: Which future do you prefer? There are many possible futures. The challenge for physician leadership is to define the preferred one.

A physician leader's job is to set a direction, personally commit to it and then spread that vision throughout the local community and health-related organizations. This way, he or she can empower employees of health organizations to act and then listen and look for feedback. As we move into the 21st century, physicians need to join the effort to lead local communities toward a health orientation and to educate them in the prudent use of scarce healthcare resources. Physicians are uniquely positioned by training and disposition to champion health, not just healthcare, and to be active advocates for their patients and the public at large.

◆ ◆ ◆

As healthcare leaders, physicians first need to alter their perception of health status measurement and improvement or they will be ill prepared to lead organizations and communities to embrace an emphasis on health rather than sickness. Concurrent with a change in mindset, physician leaders must return to the basics of population-based health planning, not only acute service delivery planning.[1] To do so requires a shift from interventions that restore health person by person to an emphasis on efforts to protect and promote the health status—what the British call "health gain"—of entire communities. This article offers a guide for the journey "back to the future" of public health. Because the public health planning strategies of the late 1960s and 1970s were instrumental in fostering an understanding of factors that affect population health status, it is essential to revisit them when constructing a strategy for the next century.

No individual, organization or sector alone can improve the health status of a community. A variety of leaders must band together to form a "network of responsibility." Therefore, a good starting place for physician leaders would be to collaborate with such networks (where they exist) to help transform the health sector of today into a healthier community in the future, as shown in Figure 1 on page 130.

Figure 1: Moving From Today's Healthcare Organizations to Tomorrow's Healthier Communities

Healthcare Today	Leadership Transformed	Healthier Communities
Focus on illness	Old assumptions challenged	Personal health valued
Cloistered hospitals	Knowledge base expanded	Illnesses avoided
Red Tape	Collaborations forged	Safety at work and at home
Millions of people excluded	Creativity fostered	Injuries avoided
Facilities poorly used	New strategies explored	Mind/body/spirit integrated
Costs out of control	Systems thinking employed	Costs reduced while patient outcomes improved
Corporations crippled	National issues addressed	Children valued
Public eager for change	Healthcare redefined	Elderly valued
Leadership unprepared	Shared vision crated	Disabled valued
Values questioned	Wider community included	Differences respected
	New approaches tested	Businesses successful
	Change mastered	Employees educated, eager, involved
	Processes continuously improved	Art valued
		Environment valued
		Community/heathcare partnerships strong
		Health services integrated
	Process of change refined	Education value

Source: The Healthcare Forum, Community Health Action Kit, 1993

Building on the competencies identified by programs such as The Healthcare Forum's national study, *Bridging the Leadership Gap in Healthcare,*[2] and the Community Care Networks of the AHA and VHA, it is hoped that this chapter will spark ideas for physician leaders to develop healthier communities.

Community Health Services.[3] To leverage personal and organizational effectiveness, physician and healthcare leaders must acknowledge the pivotal role that local public health agencies and service providers have played and will continue to play in the transformation of communities' health status. Many states are forging a new public health system that represents a partnership among state and local governments and private healthcare organizations. Most of these public health agencies should be supported through collaboration with integrated health systems and HMOs to develop a multi-year community health plan that addresses locally determined public health problems. Unfortunately, most medical school curricula offer little by way of an understanding of public health or its leadership, so a review of basic concepts may be helpful.

According to public health epidemiologist C.E.A. Winslow, "Public health is the science and art of preventing disease, prolonging life, and promoting health and efficiency through organized community effort for the sanitation of the environment, the control of communicable disease, the education of the individual in personal hygiene, the organization of medical and nursing services for the early diagnosis and preventive treatment of disease, and the development of the social machinery to ensure everyone a standard of living adequate for the maintenance of health..."

Physician leaders in HMOs and integrated delivery systems should champion such basic concepts as:

- Focusing public health planning and interventions on the health needs of the aggregate;
- Giving primary prevention priority over secondary and tertiary prevention;
- Reorganizing community resources around local health needs;
- Providing interventions for the greatest good for the greatest number of people;
- Having public health interventions do what others cannot or will not do; and
- Basing the methods of public health inquiry on scientific principles and epidemiology.

Physicians' role in public health includes participating in community-wide health assessment, health policy development and assurance of service delivery; this role also entails outreach, advocacy, monitoring, education, evaluation and service coordination.

Use Scenarios to Predict Healthcare's Future

"The future of healthcare cannot be predicted with certainty," stated Clement Bezold of the Center for Alternative Futures. For instance, no one knows whether the trend of heightened consumer interest in health will continue. How will national healthcare policy and financing evolve? Scenarios—snapshots of what the future may bring—allow us to explore a variety of answers to these and other uncertainties. Through this exploration, scenarios should also spark the imagination and raise fundamental questions.

The following scenarios summarize the best thinking of a core of leading health futurists in the United States.[4] Whether they represent an accurate portrayal of the possible range of futures or are entirely off the mark, they provide a sense of the potential threats and opportunities. With those in mind, healthcare executives can then ask themselves: What do we want to create?

Physician leaders can start to use scenarios in local organizations by asking health planning committees and staff to review the three descriptions below.[5] Ask each group to focus on a different sketch but explore the same questions.

In this scene, how successful are the healthcare provider's current strategies?

What does this scenario imply for your healthcare organization? Poll participants on the scenario's likelihood and their preference for it. Announce the results and look for the gap between what is thought to be likely and what is preferred. Discuss what the gap means regarding how the organization is operating. Ask the group as a whole to rank all of the scenarios based on likelihood and preference.

The three scenarios presented here are excerpted from the Institute for Alternative Futures as part of the national study *Bridging the Leadership Gap,* which examined the differential between leadership practices today and the organizational demands that healthcare leaders will face in the next century. These capsules—set in the early 21st century—are thematic images developed to be learning tools; as such, they simplify a great deal of complexity. The actual future is likely to be some combination of these and others, yet they illuminate plausible futures for healthcare, posing key choices for healthcare leadership.

Figure 2: Scenario 1—Continued Growth

National healthcare reform never occurs, but costly advanced technology and therapeutics push healthcare's share of the gross national product (GNP) to 17 percent by 2001. Although providers shift to predicting and then managing illness far earlier, poverty and lack of access to healthcare persist.

The economy continues to grow, and so the United States holds its place in global competition. Technology advances on all fronts. The information revolution provides highly evolved tools for learning, entertainment, and personal/ home management (including health). But because the percentage of poor remains approximately constant, federal expenditures cannot keep pace with need. Most states follow Oregon in consciously setting priorities on availability of healthcare for the poor. Malpractice concerns are still not resolved, and so the practice of defensive medicine continues to add to costs.

A profound shift. Beyond 2000, major changes in healthcare, for those who can afford it, are achieved not through formulating new government policy but through execution of the "predict and manage" model. High-tech interventions become common—for those patients with adequate resources or insurance. Healthcare delivery becomes more effective and efficient, with most care directed by large, multispecialty physician groups. Expert systems constrain physicians' clinical discretion but improve outcomes.

Hospitals shrink, and their numbers decline. Hospitals with a large share of insured or private payers take advantage of evolving technology and accelerate diversification into ambulatory care.

The "predict and manage" paradigm ultimately lowers lifetime morbidity for most people, yet the failure to deal with poverty and the limitations of government subsidies keeps the poor and near-poor from benefiting fully.

Figure 3: Scenario 2—Healing

In this abstract, the integration of the human spirit with healthcare leads to a greater focus on healing. Healthcare leaders, particularly those running hospitals, take an early, active role in starting to address personal, community and environmental health, rather than continuing to treat individuals. Poverty, other social problems and environmental causes of poor health are systematically tackled.

Healthcare structures have changed dramatically, merging with a variety of other community organizations. Efforts to develop shared visions of healthcare's future should accelerate change.

People in the early 21st century witness a growing focus on spirituality and on healing the ills not only of Americans, but of the globe. Poverty, pain and unnecessary illness remain but are significantly reduced by 2010. Economic ups and downs occur, but the overall pattern is one of continued growth.

Access to healthcare is guaranteed through mandated, employer-sponsored health insurance for all working people, as well as expanded Medicaid and Medicare. This is a major advance, yet in the grand scheme it is overshadowed by the fact that health policy at all levels of government becomes coherent.

There is an awareness that both the causes and prevention of ills come from sectors beyond healthcare.

Local delivery systems become more consistent and effective in most communities. Many hospital leaders begin to perceive their organization's budget as an ethical account, which has a part to play in enhancing the health status of everyone in the community. Such thinking leads to "hospitals without walls."

Physician leaders in the early 21st century guide their hospitals to become the pinnacle of health design for their communities. In this setting, management takes on the task of declaring what ought to be, establishing shared visions and enhancing the organization's energy. One aspect of the CEO's job becomes the spiritual, mental and emotional development of every person in the organization.

Healthcare expenditures hover around 12% of the GNP because key forces are balanced: There are more elderly people, some expensive new therapies and an expanded number of health providers offering "healing touch" services—e.g., acupuncture, massage—yet morbidity is generally compressed, there is a greater acceptance of death, therapies are more effective as a result of decades of research and outcomes measurement.

While each scenario projects a singular image, one change is common to all—the "predict and manage" paradigm. This ideal refers to the ability to use new tools to forecast with some reliability which illnesses or diseases may afflict which individuals and then help those people take all available precautionary measures.

Being a Change Agent in an Increasingly Complex Society

The latter two conceptualizations are visionary scenarios that recognize the importance of creating healthier communities through local community collaborations. The future is not about people traveling to hospitals or medical clinics; it is about medicine meeting people where they are—homes, schools, businesses and so forth.

The challenge for physician leadership to contribute to communities' well-being will be complicated as the public shifts gears at the same time. American society and its dilemmas bear little resemblance to their counterparts in the 1960s and early 1970s. Thirty years ago, "the old boy network," a small group of influential businessmen (often including healthcare executives) and politicians controlled most major metropolitan areas. Today, with the prevalence of grassroots organizations, few groups hold enough power to act unilaterally, yet many have enough power to block action by others. Few hierarchies prevail in communities, meaning there is no single center to which people can appeal. Responsibility and accountability are blurred. Issues have become even more complex and interdependent, making any solution to them a difficult proposition.

Figure 4: Scenario 3—New Generation

Dramatic changes in science, technology, society and government hasten healthcare transformation. Healthcare broadens its scope to include the community and the environment. National healthcare reform favors managed care—particularly social HMOs, which are effective at predicting and often preventing various personal and community health problems. The community ambulatory centers of SHMOs perform most of the functions of the community hospital of the early 1990s. The remnants of 20th century hospitals are found in regional critical-care institutions at which the inpatient census is a fraction of an average hospital's census in 1990.

High-tech and alternative therapies are common. Healthcare consumes 12% of the GNP by 2001.

National healthcare reform takes place in the early 21st century. By that time, key positive trends, particularly the development of more effective managed care, are visible in healthcare. Leading HMOs increase their focus on prevention. These HMOs also facilitate and sometimes coordinate other community services.

National policy establishes an employer-based insurance program combined with enhanced Medicare and Medicaid for the unemployed. Both private insurance and public programs include incentives and regulations supporting more effective managed care, prevention and a community health emphasis. Heroic, life-saving measures for the elderly decrease as society in general becomes more accepting of death.

Consumers are empowered by government policies encouraging the development of outcomes measures and their application. Local healthcare markets become smarter and are quicker to reward cost-effective innovation.

State laws and regulations change so physician extenders can receive direct reimbursement for care they deliver. In addition, physicians, nurses and other clinical care providers are recertified on the basis of outcomes, a practice that has sharply reduced ineffective treatments. Malpractice reforms have lowered damage awards. Continuous improvement systems are fully operational in most healthcare systems.

A strong "predict and manage" approach evolves, based upon each person's unique biochemical, emotional and spiritual levels. The 20th-century healthcare paradigm had split body, mind, and spirit. This evolves as the role of the mind is rediscovered in healthcare.

Virtually all consumers are healthier and living longer, including those with low incomes. A majority express satisfaction with their local healthcare systems, but dissatisfaction surfaces in some local markets, where people feel that definition of community has turned healthcare into an overly restrictive "big brother."

In a culture of individualism, the interests and needs of the broader community can go unrecognized and unmet. The emerging task for physician leaders is to help unite the segments to address issues of shared concern.

But progress will not be accomplished by a person or even a group with a great idea. The process of change must also be well conceived.

In 1991, the MacArthur and Luce foundations funded an investigation of 52 cases of collaboration in American cities. The purpose of the research, conducted by the American Leadership Forum, was to pinpoint the characteristics of successful change efforts in communities. It identified five keys for collaboratively addressing complex public issues.

- Include stakeholders affected by the problem and essential to the solution. Responsibility for decisions and action must be accepted and taken by those who are committed to solving the problem.

- Sustain the group with relationships of trust and respect. Open relationships create the atmosphere necessary for innovations and risks that would be impossible in traditional settings.

- Make problem resolution a credible, public process. This way, group members will trust the process even when they don't get their way.

- Keep all members of the group well informed. They should have access to accurate, reliable information so they may reach a deep level of understanding about the substance of an issue.

- Nominate strong leaders, who will promote and safeguard the collaborative process rather than advocate for specific solutions.

Physician leaders who want to address complex public policy issues must first understand that success depends more on a well-designed process for constructively bringing stakeholders together than it does on substantive knowledge about a particular issue. Therefore, the best starting place is to comprehend the dynamics among stakeholders.

Setting the Stage to Improve a Community's Health

Physicians should keep in mind that there are myriad ways—not a single template—for launching a healthier community effort. Still, there are some similar strategies. Start with an analysis of past, current and planned initiatives to see how your group's effort will relate with others. Now is the time to ensure that interrelationships are clear and initiate communication among all players.

Timing is also a critical success factor. Think strategically about the appropriate month or season to kick off the project so as to maximize media support and avoid competition with other civic events. Meanwhile, someone should be investigating various possible starting points or intervention levels, which will be determined in part by the community's sophistication—or lack thereof—about population-based health improvement. And, because it bears repeating, make sure that stakeholders involved are politically, racially, geographically, ethnically and economically diverse.

Develop a community health profile. In order to measure progress, you will need to know where you started. A community health profile contains a set of key wellness indicators, which also will be useful in setting priorities for interventions. Which indicators are included in the profile will depend largely on the breadth of a community's definition of health. It's helpful if the county or city has readily available information upon which to base measures. Keep in mind, though, that these measures need not always be either standardized or quantifiable. While many health issues lend themselves to quantifiable measures, some aspects may not. Where they don't, qualitative and anecdotal yardsticks may be appropriate. Whatever combination is chosen, make sure it is what the community wants to use to evaluate the project.

Healthy People 2000. For traditional—or more medical—determinants of health, many standard measures are available. The U.S. Public Health Service's "Healthy

People 2000" initiative, for example, established a large set of measurable indicators and objectives. Examples of commonly available data include: infant mortality rate; incidence of death from coronary heart disease; rate of lung cancer death; death rate for alcohol-related motor vehicle accidents; rate of teen pregnancy; and rate of low-birth-weight infants.

There are indicators, however, for other factors such as housing, jobs and public safety that directly contribute to health and quality of life yet do not fall under a traditional medical service-delivery definition. In some areas, such as public safety, there may be a great deal of information available, but it may be sparse in others, such as housing. In addition, indicators of employment, education, recreation, environment and transportation are likely to be available yet perhaps not in an immediately useful format. See Figure 5, below, for assistance in selecting the most relevant and accurate data as they relate to your initiative's priority indicators.

Sources of data. In most states, relevant community health statistics can be obtained from a combination of public and private sources. Typically, the bulk of the work will involve conducting secondary research—gathering and formatting information from

Figure 5: How One Community Set Guidelines for Indicators

Florida's Duval County, which includes the major metropolitan area of Jacksonville, Fla., has had a quality of life project under continuous development since 1985. This effort, comprising 74 indicators in nine categories, developed the following questions to guide the selection of indicators of health and quality of life:[6]

Validity: Does the indicator measure a factor issue that is directly related to the quality of life? If the indicator moves, would a diverse group of people agree on how the movement affects the quality of life—positively or negatively?

Availability and Timelines: Is the indicator readily available annually? If not, are staff able to readily collect and compile the data on an annual basis?

Stability and Reliability: Can we be confident that the statistic will be compiled using a systematic and fair method, and that the same method will be used each year?

Understandability: Is the indicator simple enough to be interpreted by the general user and the public?

Responsiveness: Does the indicator respond quickly and noticeable to real changes?

General Considerations: Is the leading indicator coincident or lagging relative to the occurrence of a problem? Leading indicators are more valuable, because they facilitate an active rather than reactive response to a situation. Is it preferable to state the indicator as a rate or relative to population, rather than as an aggregate figure? If money is involved, is it preferable to state in terms of constant dollars, eliminating the effect of inflation?

[6]See "Healthy Community Handbook," The Healthcare Forum, San Francisco.

existing sources—although for some issues, indicators may need to be developed from primary sources. The latter is particularly useful when studying issues involving perception (e.g., neighborhood safety, access to service and so on). In addition, communities should not be constrained in defining or measuring health solely by available data. For instance, in developing its profile, Pennsylvania's Delaware County conducted 12 focus groups involving more than 100 people, as well as more than 50 open-ended interviews.

Models of community health profiles. There are a number of models that communities have used to create community health profiles. Physician leaders should also review the Healthy People 2000 indicators and objectives for comprehensive measures on traditional health issues. The indicators included in Figure 5 are intended to serve only as one example, not to define the categories or scope of the indicators that might be most relevant to another community. Many indicators can be developed within each category, both quantitative and qualitative. Each community must determine its need for and comfort with the use of various measures, as well as what are most appropriate for its health profile.

Develop an effective communication strategy. An effective communication strategy will be flexible and make use of an array of different tools depending on the purpose and desired outcome. Be prepared to use newsletters, facsimiles, columns in local newspapers, billboards, posters and Web sites. Further, the strategy will need to be tailored to respond to local realities and to build on key issues and perspectives that attract people's attention. You will also want to embrace the local leaders who influence:

- Education;
- Housing;
- Availability of meaningful employment;
- Access to job skills training and retraining;
- Access to efficient public transportation;
- Availability of recreational opportunities;
- Healthy and clean physical environments; and
- Access to health education and preventive services.

Relationships Among Community Assets. Part of an assets map for community health planning includes physical characteristics—land as well as intangibles. Map out the relationships that exist now. For help, see Figures 6 and 7 on pages 138 and 139, which are hospital-oriented examples of asset diagrams for a community. Discuss with a local team of citizens: How can we build new and better relationships? How can we be more active in leveraging existing strengths into greater assets and more health gain in the future?

As your local team discusses this model and maps these relationships, keep in mind that the most important ingredient for successful regeneration of the health status of your community is the time and talents of your neighbors in this community. Build a brighter future upon the pride and assets of the past and present.

FIGURE 6: COMMUNITY AND HOSPITAL PARTNERSHIPS

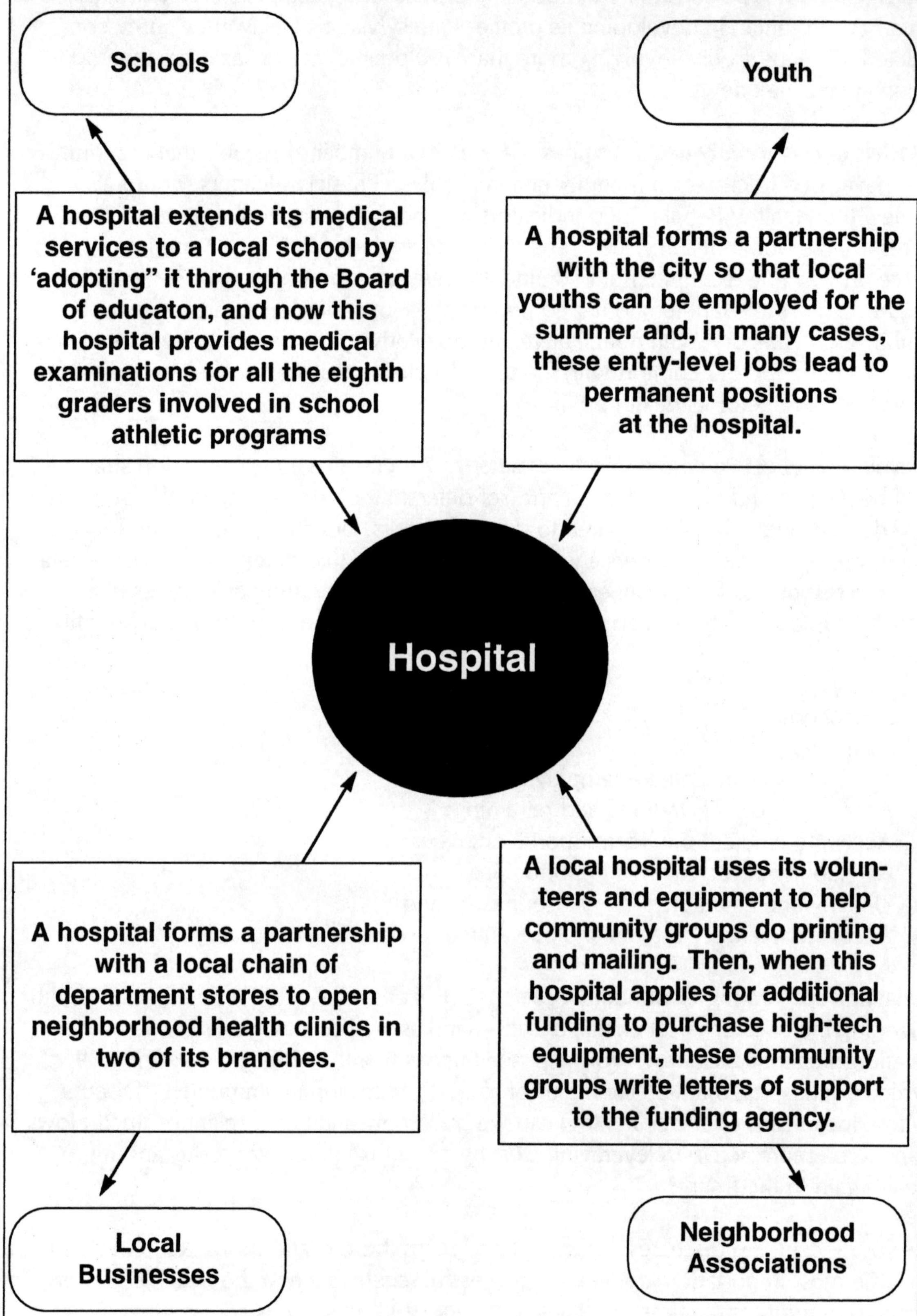

Source: Krotzman and McKnight, 1993

FIGURE 7: COMMUNITY AND HOSPITAL RELATIONSHIPS

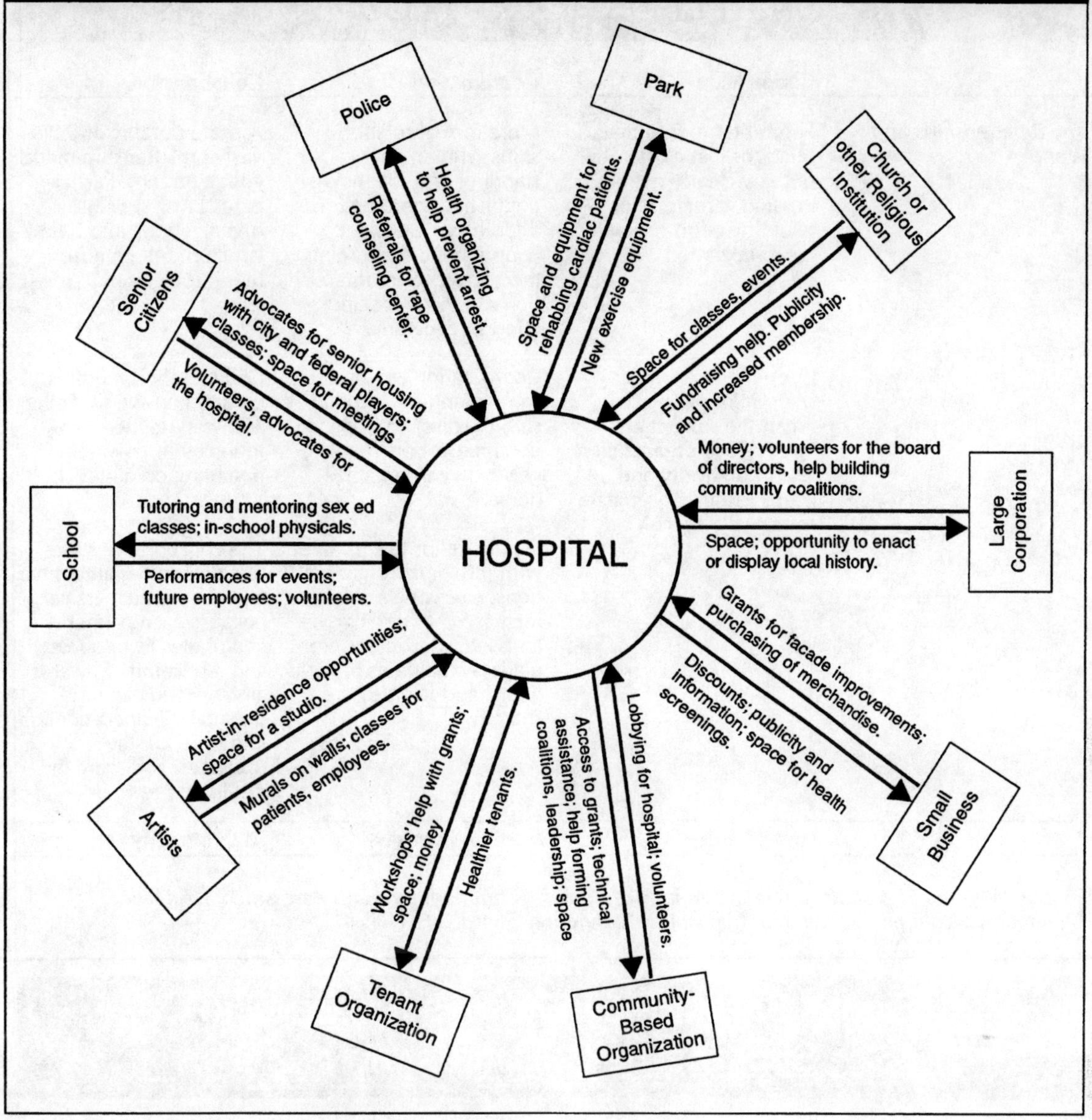

Cooperation, coordination and collaboration. Most healthcare leaders have never been trained and so are ill prepared to face the challenges of community partnering, which the health assessment process will require. To be effective, leaders must manage the exchange of ideas, energy and resources among individuals and institutions. To do so takes cooperation among individuals and institutions, coordination of efforts and collaboration.

These concepts—cooperation, coordination and collaboration—are subtly different. Figure 8 on page 140 presents definitions of each concept and the levels of intensity needed to bring the concept to fruition.

Gathered from a review of the literature, Figure 9 on page 140 summarizes 19 factors

FIGURE 8: DEFINING THE DIFFERENCES: COOPERATION, COORDINATION AND COLLABORATON

	Cooperation	Coordination	Collaboration
Key Relationships and Work	Shorter-term, informal relations that exist without any clearly defined mission, structure, or planning effort characterize **cooperation.**	More formal relationships with an understanding of missions distinguishes coordination. People involved in a coordinative effort focus their longer-term interaction around a specific effort or program.	A more durable and pervasive relationship marks **collaboration**. Participants bring separate organizations into a new structure full commitment to a common mission.
	Cooperative partners share information only about the subject at hand. Each organization retains authority and keeps resources separate so virtually no risk exists.	Coordination requires some planning and division of roles, and opens communication channgels between organizations.	Collaboration requires comprehensive planning and well-defined communication channels operating on all levels.
		While authority still rests with individual organizations, everyone's risk increases. Power can be an issue. Resources are made available to participants and rewards are shared.	The collaborative structure determines authority, and risk is much greater because each partner contributes its resources and reputation. Power is an issue and can be unequal. Partners pool or jointly secure the resources, and share the results and rewards
	Low Intensity	**Medium Intensity**	**High Intensity**

Source: Work on Sharon Kagan as shown in Rice, James, "Community Health Assessment: A New Generation," Volume 16, Number 4, Hospital Technology Series, AHA

FIGURE 9: NINETEEN FACTORS INFLUENCING SUCCESSFUL COLLABORATIONS

Environment	Communication
1. History of collaboration or cooperation in the community 2. Collaborative group seen as a leader in the community 3. Political/social climate favorable	13. Open and frequent communication 14. Established informal and formal communication
Membership Characteristics	**Purpose**
4. Mutual respect, understanding and trust 5. Appropriate cross-section of members 6. Members see collaboration as in their self-interest 7. Ability to compromise	15. Concentrate on attainable goals and objectives 16. Shared vision 17. Unique purpose
Process/Structure	**Resources**
8. Members share a stake in both process and outcome 9. Multiple layers of decision making 10. Flexibility 11. Development of clear roles and policy guidelines 12 Adaptability	18. Sufficent funds 19. Skilled convener

Source: Mattessich, P., and Monsey, B. Collaboration: What makes it work. St. Paul, MN: Wilder Research Center, 1992

that influence successful collaboration efforts. Use this list of characteristics as a checklist when monitoring your collaborative activity in the community. Any number of these factors can either fuel or jeopardize the success of joint efforts.

Common Obstacles on the Path to Health Status Improvement
Recent experiences suggest developing a successful health improvement plan for a community is even more difficult than it first appears. A number of practical realities block success. In fact, seven obstacles have proved to be particularly troublesome in various cities around the world. Physician leaders would do well to review these obstacles and the suggested strategies to remove or reduce them ahead of implementation, because forewarned is forearmed.

Through trial and error, three principal strategies to attack each of the seven obstacles have become evident. The 19 strategies below represent a positive but incomplete collection of actions your community can use to improve your chances for successful health status improvement. Carefully consider these ideas and add variations and refinements as you go along.

Strategy Cluster One: Leadership
Physician executives are more apt to reap positive contributions from others if they assume a strong but supportive role. This may initially mean orchestrating events from the edge rather than in the center spotlight.

1. **Select a Steering Committee Chair from Outside Your Organization.** The prospects for broader community understanding and participation can increase if the leadership for the initial planning and steering committee comes from outside the hospital or HMO or clinic. Of course, the ultimate key is to get the best leader—one who listens, is visionary, shares success, stimulates action and has a sense of humor. More progress is likely if the committee chair does not come from your hospital but rather from somewhere—the schools, business, social work, neighborhoods or the arts. Fewer people will complain about the hospital trying to run everything, and you may get more participation from various community agencies.

Conversely, it may be appropriate to tap the skills or resources of different individuals at various times in the process to serve as chair (including hospital leaders). A rotating chair could be useful, especially when a variety of issues or projects are being addressed.

2. **Hold meetings outside the hospital or health system.** Some folks may avoid trooping into a hospital, which is unfortunately often associated more with "sickness" than with "health." Also, broadening the number of meeting sites is more likely to broaden the base of participation. Meeting sites that contribute to the "democratization" of the health planning process include: libraries, city hall, churches, business boardrooms, recreation centers and apartment building party rooms. Site visits or mobile meetings in a bus can also loosen up the thinking and action process.

3. **Provide staff and resources for subcommittee work.** Like other well-established organizations and businesses in the community, hospitals have a large concentration

of human and technological resources that can help feed the process. The trick is not to usurp the process; leadership and support from the hospital should come in a variety of quiet ways. For example, it could provide: the executives on loan, as is done in United Way programs; survey volunteers; photocopy and fax machines; transportation; and so forth. Healthcare personnel should also be available to help implement a variety of interventions to enhance health, such as immunizations, Meals on Wheels, fitness and nutrition information, home care, smoking cessation and alcohol and drug abuse prevention.

Strategy Cluster Two: Visioning
The ability to envision what a healthier community could be and how to achieve it requires new methods and diverse participants.

4. Cast a wide net for participants. While a diversity of views, life experiences and organizations can be represented in the steering committee, the process probably needs to attract more folks from throughout the community into task forces and subcommittees.

5. Recycle early drafts, and then march under a single vision. Participation by multitudes will generate many ideas. Not all will be clear or realistic. The early versions of the vision crafted by the steering committee should be given one last blast of exposure to the media, local neighborhood groups, and social welfare organizations. This openness to ideas reinforces the need for broad-based input and ownership of the vision. The final, polished version should be celebrated and waved widely. Try to avoid the temptation to endlessly refine the vision's wording.

6. Use consultants cautiously. Rely on experienced advisors to help plan and execute the planning process, but do not become dependent on them. In fact, you may find such consultants among the stakeholder partners to engage in the planning process. These experts can be very desirable because they can offer a positive mix of expertise, local sensitivity and reasonable cost.

Strategy Cluster Three: Prioritizing
A good process yields multiple ideas, some more cost-effective and enduring than others. The key to success rests on three words: prioritize, prioritize, prioritize.

7. Transform obstacles into paths to solutions. Healthy community planning founders when it seeks to immediately answer the question, "What actions should we take to achieve a healthy community?" Either a deafening silence or a cacophony of ideas will be the reply. Communities may find it helpful to list obstacles to implementing and sustaining a healthier community, and then systematically conquer those judged the most important. For example, brainstorm about everything that could hinder success, and then agree on bite-sized actions that will remove, reduce or circumvent the most challenging obstacles. As in judo, the skillful planner will use the antagonist's own weight to overcome the problem.

8. Use brainstorming tools. Experienced planners and community organizers can harness the power of nominal-group techniques to promote participants' thinking, tap their experiences and engage them. Although adults are resistant to "games," sensible requests for people's ideas, which are then quickly recorded for others to see and react to, are essential tools in the health planning process. Be creative. Try new ideas to generate new strategies.

9. Use team voting tools. Large groups usually get something done only when they are mobilized to do bite-sized tasks. Mobilized action requires focused action. Focused action can occur only when directed at problems/solutions that have been prioritized by the majority as important enough to address. Possible voting tools include: rocks in baskets associated with each choice, voice votes, applause, electronic option polling and so forth.

Keep in mind: Voting may not be necessary if a comfortable consensus has been reached. In general, long-term sustainability is enhanced if a "super majority" (i.e., more than 75 percent) agree about how best to proceed.

Strategy Cluster Four: Scope of Work.
Work must be accomplished or the promise of healthier communities will be swept away by the "paralysis of analysis."

10. Create a work breakdown structure. Project management gurus advise that big projects are achieved by people accomplishing small tasks. Get your group to a consensus on a hierarchy of three to five subtasks, which may themselves have three to five subactivities. (See *Figure 10 on page 144.)*

11. Make Bite-Sized Pieces. The work must not only be organized into a hierarchy of subtasks, but each piece of work assigned to a group of volunteers must be "chewable." Too large a task can choke volunteers, wasting effort or producing burnout that pollutes others' enthusiasm.

12. Jump in, the Water's Fine. The group cannot sit on the sideline wringing its hands, wondering whether it has the best plan, whether the members are attacking the most significant problems, or whether they can get everything done on time and on budget. Start doing some small activities that can yield fast and visible results.

Strategy Cluster Five: Continuity
Many volunteers will stay with the process longer and be smarter if leaders move as quickly as possible to action, and if succession plans are in place to periodically rejuvenate or transfer task leaders. You should be prepared to accept that organizations and individuals will have different needs and capacities at different times. Long-term continuity is more likely when such leadership evolution can occur.

13. Minimize Participation Leakage. Volunteers will burn out and leave. You can minimize their leakage and loss by adapting the following tactics:

- Provide leaders with coaching, orientation and support;
- Invite local civic and business leaders to volunteer to do a weekend training session for your volunteer leaders; and

FIGURE 10: SIMPLE WORK BREAKDOWN STRUCTURE DESIGN

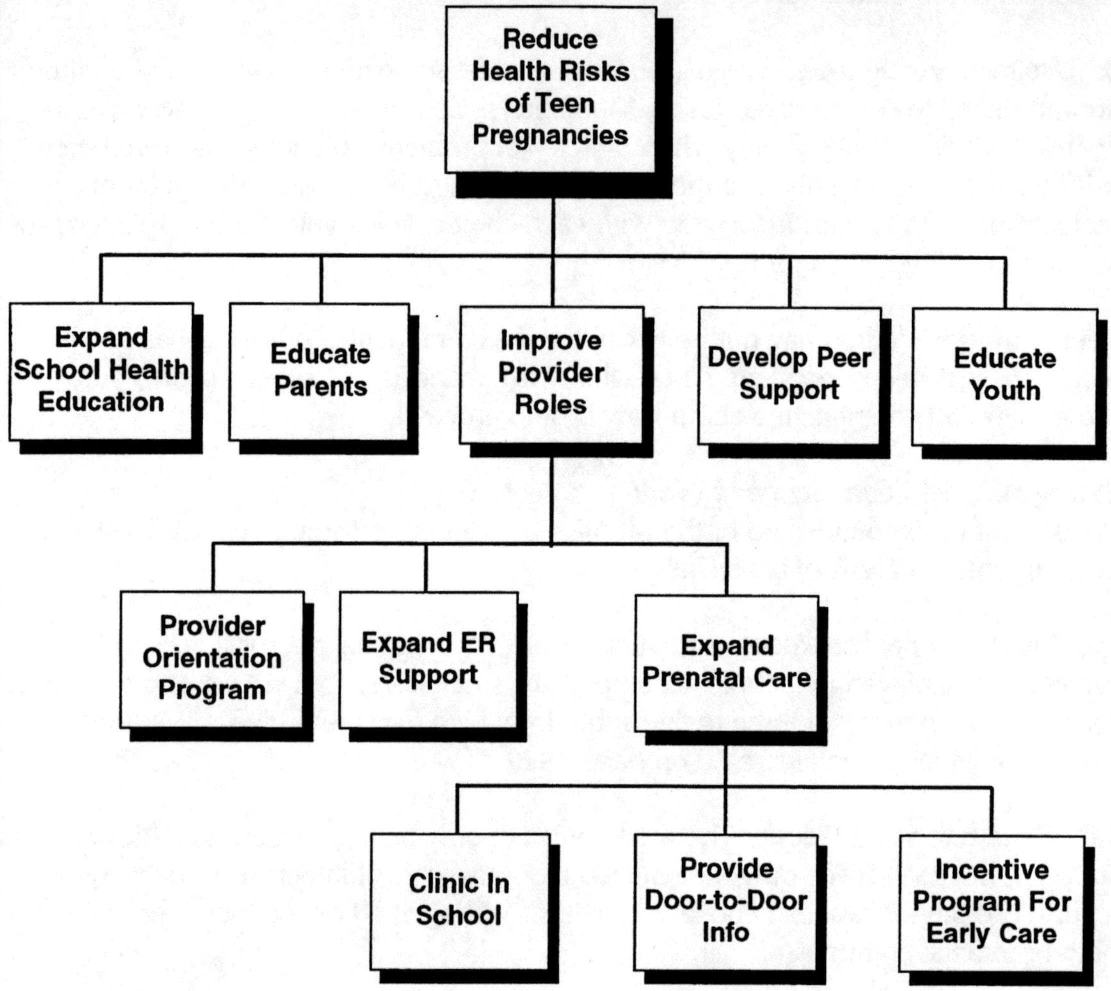

- Review and adapt the ideas available from United Way, the National Civic League, the Points of Light Foundation, and/or successful local ministries, Parent-Teacher Association officers and neighborhood organizers.

14. Provide Structure, Not Stricture. Mobilizing, and then sustaining the participation of volunteers in community health planning is a key to your success. Experiences gained frrm groups like the Points of Light Foundation suggest volunteers are more likely to get engaged if someone provides them with a clear definition of bite-sized and time-limited tasks. Remember, however, that too much prescription can dampen their enthusiasm. You will have to experiment with the right balance, but it is usually better to offer details and then indicate you are flexible about inviting their input and refinement.

Volunteers are generally smart and busy, and have probably burned out in prior volunteer endeavors. Their willingness to help provide continuity of support will be increased if you offer enough structure to their project or task so that they can see what is expected and how it is important to the overall goals of the program. The structure, however, must be flexible enough to invite their ideas and enhancements. Too much structure becomes a constraint not only to their creativity, but also to their willingness to stay with the task. Remember, structure, not stricture.

15. Partner with the Media. The media, if carefully informed and cultivated, can be a valuable partner in both attracting and then retaining volunteer participants to your planning and implementation process. Media announcements, discussions, progress reports and celebration of success can help create much needed awareness and credibility for your process.

Strategy Cluster Six: Impatience
Your participants' impatience to see demonstrable progress is the infamous double-edged sword. Impatience can spark a needed rush for action, but it can also create a sense of urgency that overlooks problems and opportunities.

16. Build in Milestones. Interim targets of accomplishment or "milestones along the journey" are essential to focus and sustain the interest and enthusiasm of planning participants. Such measures of progress help remind everyone of short-term objectives to be met if long-term goals are to be achieved. The interim targets also help nurture the participants' willingness to keep working as they see results.

17. Encourage Engagement. Participants are more likely to own the targets of opportunity (goals, objectives and milestones) if they help define them. The players are also more likely to keep their creativity and participation high if they are actively involved in specific tasks and projects (i.e., they are vested in the process). One person fully engaged also increases the chances that he or she will want to bring in a friend or colleague.

Strategy Cluster Seven: Sharing Success
Sustaining progress from community health planning to real health gain is difficult enough, but the chance of success erodes quickly if the leaders selfishly seek credit only for themselves.

18. Clarify Contributions. Shared success is more likely when all players see how they can make a contribution. Clear expectations about roles and interests can head off the confusion that obstructs shared enthusiasm for positive results.

19. Celebrate People and Institutions. The power of praise and compliments is too often forgotten in a group's rush to achieve results. Workers need positive recognition for their ideas, efforts and accomplishments. In addition, just as a plant needs small, periodic waterings to stay alive, a project requires praise dispensed frequently, as opposed to one big reward at the end of a long journey.

This chapter is too short to be exhaustive in its conclusions and recommendations about how physician leaders can champion and guide the move from community health assessment through planning to actions that yield health gain. There are numerous other resource texts, several of which have been referenced here. But, if you take nothing else from reading this chapter than a few proverbs to light your way, I will feel I have done my job as its author.

"Life by the yard is hard; life by the inch is a cinch"
Be neither immobilized nor infatuated by the importance or challenge of guiding a community to purse health gain. A big vision requires small steps, small successes well celebrated, and bite-sized pieces well chewed. Transforming the health of a community is a monumental undertaking. Try not to make it too hard.

"You can't pick up a potato with one finger"
Community health improvement is not the work of an individual, but of teams of individuals and organizations. Cooperation, coordination and collaboration are therefore essential processes to master if many stakeholders are to work together and move forward.

"Healthy communities are a journey, not a destination"
Even with success, the challenge of sustained health gain can be elusive. The process of establishing, nurturing and enhancing a community's health is unending. Healthy communities are a journey—plan well for it. Physician leaders should pack the right tools and books, arrange to be accompanied by fun and creative fellow travelers, marvel at the sights and stops along the way, and use the above scraps of ageless wisdom as eyeglasses through which you view your challenges and opportunities.

Good planning. Good luck. Good health.

◆ ◆ ◆

[1]See Rice, James, "Community Health Assessment: The First Step to Community Health Planning," 12(13), Hospital Technology Series (AHA Number 012875).

[2]For further information, see The Healthcare Forum's "Community Action Kit", Summer 1993 by contacting Kathryn E. Johnson, President, The Healthcare Forum, 830 Market Street, 8th Floor, San Francisco, CA 94102 (415) 421-2411; The National Clinic League, Denver, Colorado; and Dan Borque of VHA, Inc., Washington, DC, (202) 822-9750.

[3]Excerpted from materials prepared by The Minnesota Department of Health, provided by Linda Olson Keller, The Minnesota Department of Health.

[4]Roy, A., Clement, B., and Russell, C. et al. "Bridging the Leadership Gap."

[5]Materials excerpted from the work of The Healthcare Forum as captured in the various versions of their "Community Action Kits".

About the Author

Through The Governance Institute, Dr. Rice is working with physicians, leaders and boards throughout the country for leadership performance improvement. He remains active in international health policy reforms through Cambridge University in England and The World Bank. He previously served as a senior officer of one of the healthcare systems that founded Allina in Minnesota.

Continuous Improvement

The Evolution of Quality Assurance and an Overview of TQM

By Martin D. Merry, MD

The approaching millennium is witnessing a fundamental transformation of healthcare quality evaluation and improvement processes. Formalized standards and mechanisms to assess and improve patient care date to the American College of Surgeons' 1917 Hospital Standardization Program, which has since evolved into the accreditation process of the Joint Commission on Accreditation of Healthcare Organizations. Until the late 1980s, quality evaluation and risk management approaches fostered by accreditation and regulatory processes had relied upon a combination of peer case review and statistical monitoring techniques to define and assess quality. A patient might suffer an adverse clinical result, or monitoring might reflect a comparatively high hospital infection rate. But if case review or infection control analysis confirmed that correct care processes have been followed, the conclusion would have been that no "quality problem" was present. Of particular note, both the definition and determination of quality lay within the total control of "the professionals"—either the clinical providers of care, or the regulatory bodies that likewise relied wholly on still-active or semi-retired clinical professionals.

◆ ◆ ◆

The importation of modern quality science from manufacturing and other service industries to healthcare has changed this landscape forever. In particular, the evolution of this science, as it now combines with healthcare's quality heritage, has initiated what might be viewed as the third era of formalized healthcare quality assessment and management. Properly understood and implemented, the philosophy and practices that define total quality management (TQM) and continuous quality improvement (CQI) offer practitioners and managers unprecedented opportunities to improve healthcare processes. While CQI practices empower all members of the provider team, the most important beneficiaries must be the recipients of care. Future patients can expect better clinical outcomes, increased levels of functional capability following care and treatment, and greater satisfaction from a more service-conscious provider community.

The First Era: Nightingale, Codman and the American College of Surgeons

Noting that patients in some mid-19th century London hospitals fared better than others, Florence Nightingale in 1863 first called for systematic inquiry into the nature of care processes that might be related. This process would uncover what we now call outcome variability.[1] Boston surgeon Ernest Codman similarly noted such variation and called for systematic inquiry regarding the care processes.[2] Though his personal efforts met considerable resistance, the American College of Surgeons (ACS) in 1913 established quality of hospital care as a founding principle, subsequently formalizing this principle in the form of its 1917 Hospital Standardization Program.[3]

The quality evaluation "technology" of the 1917 "minimum standard" was retrospective case review and peer discussion. This method has peer clinicians reviewing the records of patients, most often those experiencing some adverse occurrence (death, complication, etc.), and considering whether alternative approaches might have led to a better outcome. Essential to the "quality assurance" (QA) aspect of this process is the group discussion surrounding the case. Implicit in this model is the notion that an individual maintains the "quality" of his/her practice through an ongoing personal and group learning process. The supportive educational context allows individuals to learn both from prior experience, and from the knowledge offered by colleagues.

The Hospital Standardization Program was notably successful in improving hospital quality of the era.[4] This success culminated in 1951, when the American Medical Association, American College of Physicians, the American Hospital Association and the Canadian Hospital Association joined ACS to form the Joint Commission on Accreditation of Hospitals. The subsequent departure of the Canadian Hospital Association to sponsor its own program, plus the addition of the American Dental Association and consumer representation completed the evolution to today's Joint Commission on Accreditation of Healthcare Organizations (JCAHO).

The Second Era: Donabedian and the JCAHO's Monitoring and Evaluation Process

Accreditation standards evolved slowly through the 1950s and early 1960s. At the academic level, the University of Michigan's Avedis Donabedian, MD, was bringing together what research existed, formulating a theoretical framework for patient care evaluation.[5] He is best recognized for his structure, process and outcome model of quality evaluation. (*See Figure 1, below.*) This model suggests the importance of relating healthcare structures (the qualifications of practitioners and facilities/technology avail-

Figure 1: Avedis Donabedian's Model

STRUCTURE →	PROCESS →	OUTCOME
Professionals	Diagnosis	Clinical
Facilities	Therapy	Functional
Technologies	Interaction	Perception
Organizations	Leadership	
Resources	Management	

able to them) and processes (the activities involved in prevention, diagnosis and treatment) to outcomes (how patients actually are faring as a result of their care). The 1990s emergence of "outcomes research" finds its origins in this model.

In the late 1960s, JCAHO progressively encouraged methods that moved beyond case review as the sole method of quality assessment and into analysis derived from data encompassing large numbers of patients. Infection control methods served as the model for data-based review methods. By the 1970s it had long been recognized that review of individual patients acquiring infections in the hospital was relatively unrewarding. On the other hand, tracking nosocomial (hospital acquired) infection rates, comparing them with statistical norms could prove helpful in detecting a possible infection "outbreak." Epidemiologic techniques could then focus investigators on potential causes and remedies. Based upon this model, JCAHO began to encourage criterion-based audit methodologies.[6] Clinical professionals establish written structure and process criteria defining "correct" practice, for example, for the diagnosis and treatment of bacterial pneumonia. Using these criteria, quality assurance personnel can systematically compare charts to determine the degree of compliance with these criteria. This move beyond isolated case review and toward larger groups of cases, in turn, allowed for statistical tallying of results. For example, the hospital QA process could now determine the rate at which an emergency room might be failing to obtain electrocardiograms for patients admitted with a complaint of chest pain. By focusing upon groups of patients, QA personnel could begin to assess how well a disease entity was being managed overall at a given facility. Most significantly, through the use of pre-established, professionally generated clinical criteria, the review process clinical criteria allowed these professionals to moved beyond the subjectivity of implicit case review. This innovation thus added a more objective data analysis element to overall quality evaluation methodology.

Both criterion-based audit and infection control, however, had specific weaknesses. The audit was a simple snapshot of care for a given time frame. A facility might "prove" through an audit that it had managed myocardial infarction patients well for a specified three-month period in the past. But this did not verify how well this disease state was being managed concurrently. For its part, infection control was too narrow in its focus. Obviously patients could suffer a much broader range of complications than infection, but similar monitoring for other clinical occurrences was atypical.

By 1980, JCAHO incorporated its cumulative learning of case and statistical methods into its Quality Assurance Standard. This emerged as the "umbrella standard" under which surveys would be conducted throughout the 1980s. The concept and practice of "monitoring and evaluation" (M&E) was developed to guide data-based approaches. (*See Figure 2 on page 152.*) M&E encompassed professionally derived quality indicators and clinical screening criteria to process large numbers of case records. Resulting data displays then depict observed results referenced against a pre-set standard or threshold. (*See Figure 3 on page 153.*) In the example depicted, the "quality" of medication administration is "assured" as long as the medication error rate does not exceed the threshold value of 0.5 percent. Should this threshold be exceeded, as in March and April, a more in-depth evaluation is needed. The figures for May and June reflect that the potential "problem" is no longer present. Whether this resulted from simple statistical variation, or a "quality improvement" effort is not clear from the data alone.[7]

Because hospitals have tended to use national averages as thresholds, such monitoring and evaluation states conceptually that "no problem" exists as long as the institutional rate is no worse than the average for peer facilities. While M&E complements case review in creating a richer quality assessment process, even the two together have a serious defect. By "justifying" cases simply because no obvious error was detected and by establishing numerical thresholds that represent "national averages," traditional healthcare quality assessment has had the unintended effect of establishing performance "no worse than average" as an implicit goal.

Figure 4 on page 154 illustrates this problem. This bell-shaped curve shows that in the total spectrum of quality there will be a small amount of true excellence and a small amount of actual negligence with much in the space between. Case review actually works best in the "A" (risk management) zone of Figure 4. That is, most physicians and other

FIGURE 2: THE MONITORING AND EVALUATION PROCESS

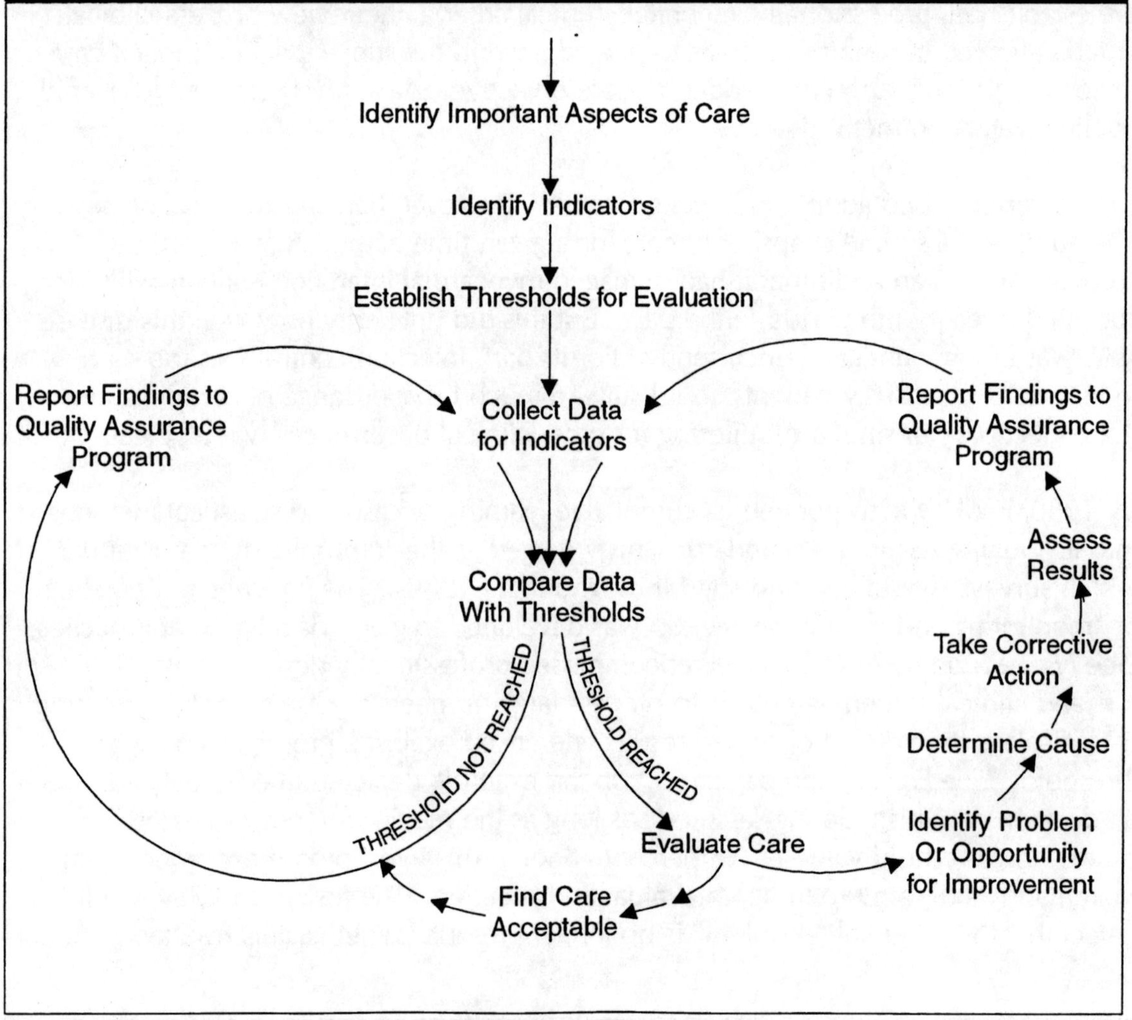

FIGURE 3: EXAMPLE OF MONITORING AND EVALUATION

Critical Care Indicators	Thresholds (%)
Medication errors	0.5%
Tracheostomy care	95%
Nosocomial infections	4%
Code success	70%
Patient/family satisfaction (surveys)	90%

Indicator	Jan	Feb	Mar	Apr	May	Jun	Jul	Aug	Sept	Oct	Nov	Dec
Medication errors	0.3	0.2	1.0	1.5	0.5	0.4						
Tracheostomy care	98	98	99		To semi-annual reporting							
Nosocomial Infections	5.3	6.1	4.9	4.0	3.8	4.8						
Code success	40	35	55	68	72	74						
Patient/family satisfaction	65	70	60	82	85	85						

FIGURE 4: THE TOTAL QUALITY SPECTRUM

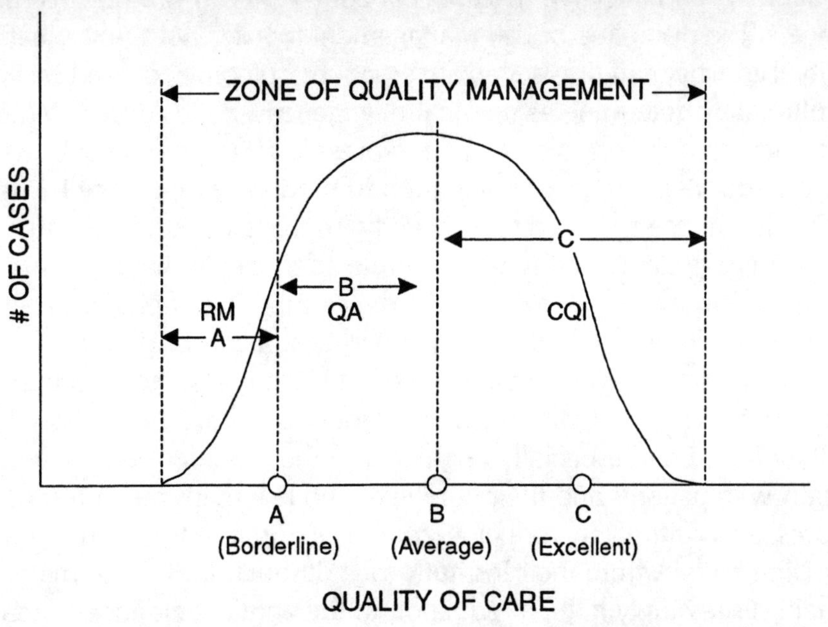

clinicians can agree when standards of care are seriously violated. There is, however, considerably less consensus in the "B" (quality assurance) zone. Here two peer physicians might have real disagreement over the adequacy of individual case management. In general, M&E has been more useful in demonstrating a graded "degree of quality" in this zone. For example, a nosocomial infection rate double that of the national average is likely to be further "down" the quality spectrum than one only 10% above. Indeed, the latter might simply represent normal fluctuation, and hence not be statistically significant.

But the real weakness of M&E was its failure to encourage providers to move toward excellence. It was essentially silent in the "C" (quality improvement) zone, which allowed providers to be comfortable by simply maintaining the "B" point of average. In short, a long and commendable history of development of healthcare quality standards failed to develop a process to systematically promote a continuos striving for excellence.

Perhaps the greatest handicap of JCAHO and other "inspection" processes has been the difficulty they have encountered in attempting to dispel the common perception that they chiefly focus on finding "violations of standards"—they zero in only on zones A and B of Figure 4. As a result of this focal point, practitioners and others tend to perceive such organizations as regulators, prone to imposing bureaucratic and/or punitive intrusions, which contribute little to improving patient care. In response to this perception, most review bodies, including JCAHO, the federal Professional Review Organizations (PROs), and the National Committee for Quality Assurance (NCQA), have tried to adopt more user-friendly approaches—"We're here to help you"—for the 1990s.

As Figure 4 suggests, quality management encompasses an entire spectrum, from negligence to excellence. Whether regulatory bodies can simultaneously "inspect" for zone A and B practice and "inspire" zone C, pursuit of excellence, remains a subject of debate.[8] What is certain is that highly publicized adverse clinical events continue to plague healthcare, and effective detection of zone A and B is a practice of continuing importance.[9] The discipline of risk management focuses not upon what produces highest quality, but what can prevent adverse patient outcomes caused by what a court might ultimately determine as medical negligence—zone A care. While negligence and its legal counterpart, malpractice, represent an unpopular subject among providers for obvious reasons, greater attention to medical malpractice by healthcare attorneys and risk managers has led to a recently improved risk management capability. Where risk management once implied simple adequacy of liability insurance, modern risk managers seek now to minimize exposure—first of patients to harm and ultimately of their institutions to patient-originated legal actions. Progressive risk managers use all review technologies—case review, M&E, surveys, etc. Recognizing that patient unhappiness is more commonly at the root of a malpractice action than is true negligence, they have been especially cognizant of the need for better care of and communication with patients and their families. The risk manager's present goal might be expressed as ultimately reducing zone B of Figure 4 to a minimum, while totally eliminating zone A from their institutions. Although individual malpractice settlements remain distressingly high, a reduction in the actual incidence of malpractice actions in the late 1980s and early 1990s may well reflect the early success of increasingly sophisticated risk management practices.

The Third Era: Deming, Juran and "Japan Inc." Enter Healthcare

CQI represents not an evolution of prior healthcare quality practice, but an "import" of both a philosophy and practice of quality from manufacturing industries. While case review and traditional M&E will continue as technical components of future comprehensive quality processes, their limitations have set the stage for engaging Figure 4's zone C. For example, it is revealing that healthcare never contemplated the notion of active quality improvement so long as information suggested care was (even minimally) "above average." In fact, prior healthcare QA systems unwittingly established "average" as a goal; if one was "no worse than average," no action was needed.

FIGURE 5: SHEWART'S PDCA CYCLE

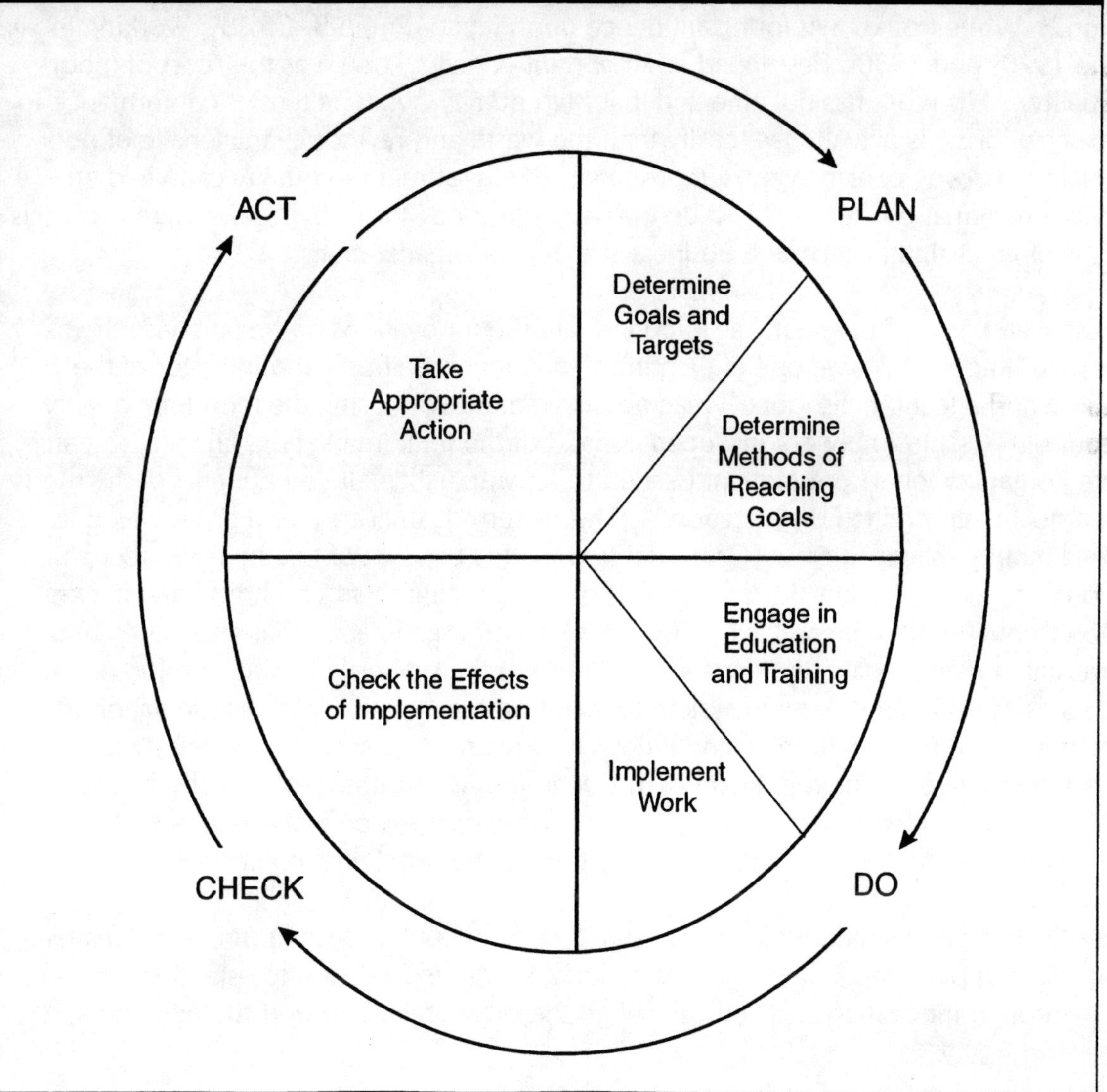

Interestingly, the origins of systematic quality processes in manufacturing coincided almost precisely with the early efforts of the American College of Surgeons. In 1917, G.S. Radford wrote a journal article calling for quality to become a distinct management responsibility.[10] During the 1920s, Walter Shewhart developed innovative statistical process control methodologies, and invented the famous "Plan–Do–Check–Act (PDCA) Cycle." (*See Figure 5 on page 155.*)[11] This endlessly recurring cycle, actually an adaptation of scientific method (hypothesis—experiment—measurement–conclusion/new knowledge), is at the core of the entire CQI process. Once initiated, PDCA never stops. It seeks after improved performance without cessation. Unlike traditional healthcare quality assurance, it offers no "zone of complacency." PDCA is a constantly running engine, fueled by leadership, internalized by everyone engaged in the enterprise and driving ultimately to Figure 4's "C" point of excellence.

Probably the most famous of the industrial quality "gurus" is W. Edwards Deming, PhD, a physicist, statistician, student of Shewhart's and ultimately philosopher of quality and the learning organization. The story of post-World War II America's rejection of Deming's quality exhortations, and of his subsequent excursions to a war–devastated but receptive Japan, is now legend.[12] In particular, the Japanese seized the PDCA Cycle. In 1952, Joseph M. Juran followed Deming to Japan, where he emphasized the key role of top leadership in firmly embedding quality processes in the organization.[13] While not known for his influence upon Japan, Philip B. Crosby, working in the 1970s and 1980s, developed an important concept known as the "cost of (poor) quality." His work has documented that high quality, what he terms "conformance to expectations," is actually less costly than the waste and rework characteristic of poor quality. Crosby conclusively demonstrated that investment in quality can yield an enormous financial return.[14] Aside from being "good" for its own sake, high quality is thus of great significance as a business strategy for organizations.

Less well known but equally as important are the innovations of the Japanese themselves. Kaoru Ishikawa, one of Deming's early Japanese hosts and inventor of the cause-and-effect (or "fishbone") diagram, is credited with using the term total quality control (TQC) to imply not just operational, but the total (marketing, finance, research, etc.) organizational commitment needed to fully actualize all components of the modern quality-committed organization.[15] (The preferred American term has evolved as total quality management—TQM). Implied by this concept of totality is the recognition of a need for sophisticated methods of vertical alignment and horizontal integration throughout the organization. GOAL/QPC, an organization that researched and translated many Japanese innovations built upon the work of Deming and Juran, defines TQM as "a structured system for creating organization-wide participation in planning and implementing a continuous improvement process to meet and exceed customer needs." The fulfillment of this definition is illustrated graphically by the TQM Wheel. (*See Figure 6 on page 157.*)[16] This conception features a central, customer-driven master plan, surrounded by three main functional components:

- Daily management, which works day by day to continuously improve processes,
- Hoshin planning, which uses institutional vision and mission to establish breakthrough innovation and vertically align the organization around strategic goals, and

- Cross-functional management, which creates the horizontal integration necessary for interdisciplinary groups to achieve synergistic teamwork.

FIGURE 6: GOAL/QPC'S TQM WHEEL

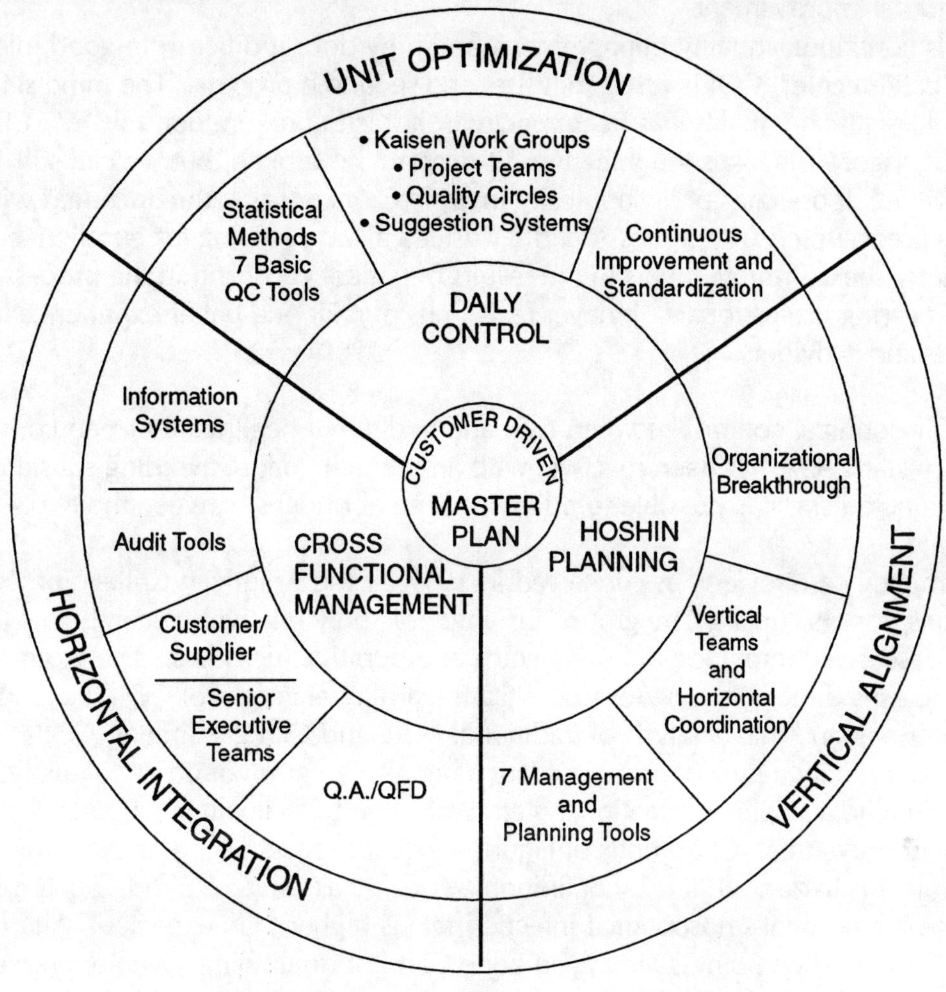

Source: Reprinted with permission from ©GOAL/QPC, 13 Branch Street, Methuen, MA 01844-1953. Tel: 508-685-3900.

Early in their experience, healthcare professionals often use the terms TQM and CQI interchangeably. Experienced quality experts, however, identify CQI primarily with the functions depicted under the daily management portion of the TQM wheel. While an attitude and practice of continuous improvement are indigenous to CQI, true TQM encompasses as well rigorous vertical and horizontal alignment practices necessary to set direction and to coordinate the energies of continuous improvement activities.

Pediatrician Donald Berwick, quality director of a Boston-based HMO in the 1982, heralded TQM's arrival in healthcare in a *New England Journal of Medicine* article now recognized as classic.[17] It conveyed insights Dr. Berwick gained from his research of industrial methods and their application to healthcare. The 1987 National Demonstration Project on Quality Improvement in Healthcare (NDP), a multi-year project involving 21 healthcare organizations, conclusively demonstrated the applicability of TQM processes in healthcare.[18]

Continuous Improvement

What is continuous quality improvement, and how does it differ from good, old-fashioned patient care? CQI is first a mind-set and second a process. The mind-set of traditional healthcare quality has been reactive: "If it isn't broken, don't fix it." CQI, by contrast, vigorously takes the initiative: "It may not be broken, but we can still improve it." It operates philosophically in zone C of Figure 4, unconcerned with regulators preoccupied with zones A and B, instead always striving for excellence. It constantly seeks improvements in the results of patient care, and in the processes that support caring professionals. It never rests in its pursuit of a better experience for both patients and providers.

The philosophical contrast between CQI and traditional healthcare QA could hardly be more stark. QA has been reactive, with an implicit goal of avoiding substandard care. Nonetheless, it is possible to build conceptual bridges between the two.

First, implicit case review, as conceived in 1917 by the American College of Surgeons, fosters "quality" by group learning. It is only relatively recently that this tradition descended into a fog of bureaucracy and punitive measures. The group learning process is directly analogous to the team learning elements of CQI. Second, the measurement and data analysis of traditional M&E and CQI are similar. CQI's contribution is not only a philosophy of initiative but also an array of powerful analytic tools. Finally, a single information system will serve both quality assurance (B) and quality improvement (C) portions of Figure 4's quality spectrum. If the starting point of a project is in zone B, it is by definition a "quality assurance" effort. Such might be the case if a hospital's nosocomial infection rate is higher than expected. Alternatively, if the starting point is already in zone C, it is a quality improvement project. Performance is already above average, but participants are not yet satisfied.

It is clear that the information needs of the QA and QI zones of the overall quality management spectrum require large databases. Because adverse outcomes occur in the face of truly excellent quality, and, conversely, satisfactory outcomes can occur despite poorly functioning structures and processes, single-outcome analysis is inadequate to assess quality in these zones of the quality spectrum. Especially for large systems, statistical approaches to measurement are essential to genuine quality management. While an individual bad outcome may be virtually meaningless from a quality assessment perspective, many adverse outcomes may well be significant. Likewise, an unusual number of "better-than-expected" outcomes— more than would be expected for a given provider entity (physician, hospital, HMO, etc.)—may indicate superior overall quality. An organization able to consistently achieve this status for a given quality measure might well become a "benchmark," a reference point for others seeking after excellence for this measure.

CQI is rigorous in its assessment of outcome. Healthcare professionals have traditionally conceived outcomes narrowly, in terms of clinical results: morbidity and mortality. The patient surviving his coronary bypass operation previously was adequate to define a "quality " outcome. Now, however, we must know of his subsequent functional status. Yes, the patient survived, but is he able to return to work? Finally, how did he perceive his overall experience? Was everything done to add comfort and caring to the curing?

To this scenario the payer increasingly adds, "Did this experience maximize value?" That is, was the outcome achieved at reasonable cost as compared with that achieved by alternative "quality" providers? The mathematical basis for value is quite simple:

Value = quality/cost.

The concept of value-purchasing—large-scale purchasers such as managed care plans and self-insured employers seeking to contract with integrated providers based upon information relating to quality and cost—increasingly dominates large, competitive healthcare markets.[19, 20, 21] Providers maximize value by minimizing care inputs through the elimination of waste and rework characteristic of pre-CQI healthcare settings. They "turbo-charge" the value equation by improving patient outcomes while at the same time reducing the costs of achieving those outcomes. They do this by constantly scanning for evidence of waste and rework and by steadily innovating toward more efficient processes.

The Future: Applying CQI to Population-Based Medicine

Her internist had read the mammogram report, and immediately telephoned her. Though conveyed with caring, her physician's words cut deep. Will it or will it not turn out to be cancer? The sleepless nights began.

The appointment with the surgeon was expeditious—only three days after the telephone call. Scheduling operating time for the biopsy required another five. Two days later the pathology lab had processed the biopsy and faxed the results to her physician.

The good news? Biopsy benign. The opportunity? Nine sleepless nights.

It was this scenario that motivated leaders of HealthSystem Minnesota to embark upon a large-scale quality improvement project.[22] HSM was not reacting to patient or third-party demand. As an original participant in the National Demonstration Project for TQM in healthcare, its leaders had the depth of patient focus to care about the "sleepless nights" (their term) their patients were experiencing in the "routine" mammography screening process.

HSM is focused upon success in Stage 3 of futurist Jeff Goldsmith's concept of healthcare systems integration. (See *Figure 7 on page 160.*)[23] As Dr. Goldsmith's model suggests, Stage 3 is a phase in which economic considerations generally, and value-purchasing specifically, might move the best health systems toward a true population-focused, value-centered (Stage 2) delivery system. In this "community health" stage, preventing breast cancer—as a "targeted intervention"—isn't just good for patients. It makes economic sense for the population as a whole.

FIGURE 7: EVOLUTION OF INTEGRATED HEATHCARE

Stage 1 Event Driven	End of Old	**Stage 2** Value
• Hospital Usage • Primary care networks • Compete on price		• Control resource intensity • Redesign system-patient interface • Total quality– clinical paths, outcomes monitoring, etc. • Evolve MD/DO networks

Source: Adapted from the work of Jeff Goldsmith, Ph.D.

So what did HSM actually do regarding its patients' sleepless nights?

- Its quality improvement team learned that stereotactic biopsy was both a more accurate approach to tissue analysis for most patients—and less costly than the surgical biopsy, its pre-project routine;
- But its surgeons earned considerable "incentive income" from the current practice and got "good results"; also
- System leaders decided that the overall goal of creating better systems from the patients' perspective was more important than the internal interests of specific group of clinicians.

The resulting system:

- Patients are asked to allow for possibly two hours delay following their mammogram;
- Radiologists do an immediate "wet read" of the films;
- If the reading is positive, an immediate stereotactic biopsy is done;
- Pathologists do an immediate "frozen section" biopsy reading; and
- The patient receives biopsy results within two hours of the mammogram.

Statistical summary:

Pre-project sleepless nights:	Average 9 (216 hours)	
* Post-project sleepless nights:	0 (2 hours)	
* Improvement percentage:	By hours (216 to 2)	10,800 (1)
	By nights (9 to 0)	Infinite

Patient perception:

> "Those patients, and there are quite a few of them, who have had both procedures—the old surgical biopsy and the newer stereotactic biopsy—have knelt down and kissed the feet of the people who are doing it the new way. It is so much better for them personally at a service level. Reducing sleepless nights turns out to be very important as a quality indicator."[24]

Beyond this patient perception, it is important to note that the deeper clinical objective of HealthSystem Minnesota is to detect virtually all breast cancer at a potentially curable stage. Stage 3 quality thus focuses both upon superb service to patients, and significant improvement in clinical outcomes for an entire population.

Total Quality Commitment

Quality must be measured to be managed. Quality measurement (comparison of observed results with reference values) is, in turn, inextricably linked to information systems and management. Excellence is defined as superior performance (outcomes) compared with that of comparable delivery entities. As indicated by Figure 1, superior outcomes must encompass not only clinical results, but longer term functional status of the patient, and his or her total satisfaction—even delight—about the care received.

As the HealthSystem Minnesota example suggests, current and future quality management depends upon the commitment of clinical and administrative professionals to:

- Focus relentlessly on meeting and exceeding the needs of those they serve;
- Strive always toward improving current practice;
- Create the valid, reliable information systems needed to support these pursuits; and
- Create true "learning organizations," i.e., systems of care in which the collective knowledge of all far exceeds that of even the most brilliant individuals.[25]

Finally, in a TQM environment, quality does not exist in a vacuum. It is inextricably linked to considerations of cost. That is to say value, the level of quality considered in the context of cost, is central to nature of a true TQM organization.

FIGURE 8: QUALITY: THE THREE CHANGE METHODS

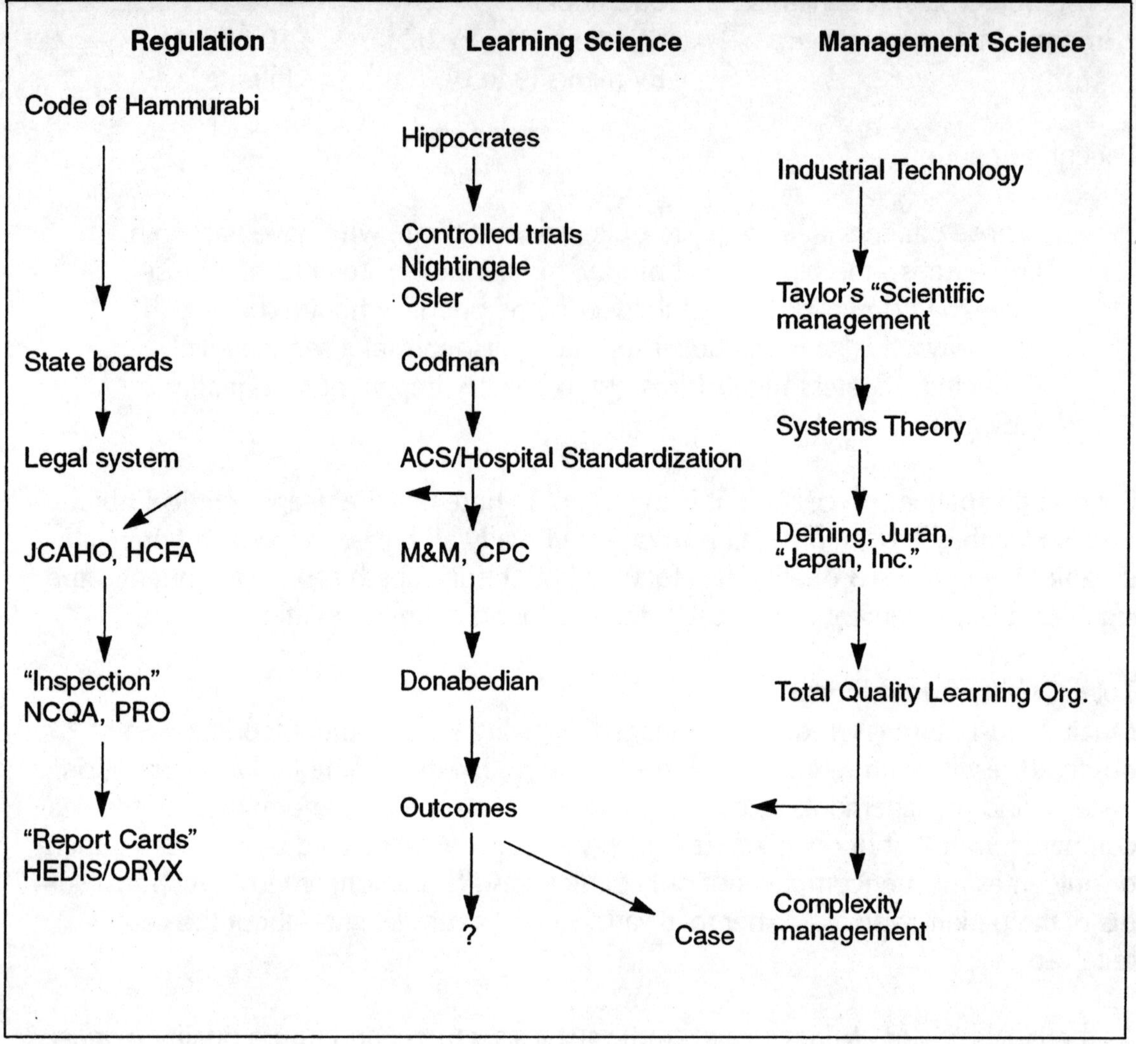

Figure 8 graphically depicts the three historical "tracks" of healthcare quality management. Regulation began with the Code of Hammurabi's (2100 B.C.) application of punitive measures to "errant practitioners." Because any large system will have its share of errant practitioners and because society can never "trust" the lowest end of the quality spectrum to self-correct, regulation will always be needed. Indeed, reality demonstrates that not simply poor quality but active criminal elements haunt this region, so regulators must command strong actions.

Beginning with Hippocrates in the third century B.C., and continuing through the 1980s, learning about science dominated healthcare's quality processes. This long has given us many excellent traditions and methods and ideally should remain a vibrant element of any healthcare system. Indeed, this learning tradition has "crossed over" into the management science column to create the concept of the "learning organization."[26]

But it is this third column that generates the enormous potential to improve healthcare quality and value in the modern era. This is the era not simply of professional excellence (a "pure" column 2 concept), but of organizational dominance and systems theory and practice. Management science generally, and quality science specifically, offer those coming out of a column 2 tradition to greatly leverage their knowledge in teamwork and the creation of new health systems. These systems, using the best of columns 2 and 3 can be expected to offer superb and unprecedented quality to individuals, and highest value to the society as a whole. Only committed and unwavering leadership—both clinical and administrative—can energize and sustain the effort toward such a vision.

◆ ◆ ◆

References

[1]Nightingale, F. *Notes on a Hospital* (3rd ed.). London: Longman, Green, Longman, Roberts and Green, 1863.

[2]Codman, E.A. *A Study in Hospital Efficiency (1916),* reproduced in 1972 by University Microfilms, Ann Arbor, Michigan.

[3]Roberts, J.S., Coale, J.G., and Redman, R.R. "A History of the Joint Commission on Accreditation of Hospitals." *JAMA* 258:936-40), 1987

[4]MacEachern, M.T. *Hospital Organization and Management.* Chicago: Physicians' Record Co., 1935.

[5]Donabedian, A. *Explorations in Quality Assessment and Monitoring.* Ann Arbor: Health Administration Press, 1980.

[6]Jacobs, C.M., et al. *Measuring Quality of Patient Care.* Cambridge: Ballinger, 1976.

[7]Merry, M.D. "Medical Staff Motivation and Peer Review." *Topics in Health Records Management,* December 1984.

[8]Merry, M.D. "Can an External Quality Review System Avoid the 'Inspection' Model?" *Quality Review Bulletin,* October, 1991.

[9]Brennan, T.A., et al. "Incidence of Adverse Events and Negligence in Hospitalized Patients." *NEJM* Vol. 324, No. 6. Feb. 7, 1991.

[10]Garvin, D.A. *Managing Quality: The Strategic and Competitive Edge.* New York: Free Press, 1988.

[11]Walton, M. *The Deming Management Method.* New York: Putnam Publishing Company, 1986.

[12]Deming, W.E. *Out of the Crisis.* Cambridge, Massachusetts: MIT, 1986.

[13]Juran, J. *Juan on Leadership for Quality: An Executive Handbook.* New York: The Free Press, 1989.

[14]Crosby, P. *Quality is Free: The Art of Making Quality Certain.* New York: McGraw-Hill, 1979.

[15]Ishikawa, K. *What Is Total Quality Control? The Japanese Way.* Englewood Cliffs, NJ: Prentice-Hall, 1985.

[16]King, B., Muir-Hutchinson, L., and Hotopp, D. *Total Quality Management Implementation Manual* (Healthcare Series) Methuen: GOAL/QPC, 1992.

[17]Berwick, D.M. "Continuous Improvement as an Ideal in Healthcare." *NEJM,* 320:53-56. 1989.

[18]Berwick, Donald M..A. Blanton Godfrey and Jane Roessner. *Curing Healthcare.* San Francisco: Jossey Bass, 1990.

[19]McClure, W. "Buying Right: The Consequences of Glut." *Physician Executive.* September-October, 1987.

[20]Reinertsen, J.E. "The Tyranny of Piecework." *The Healthcare Forum Journal*, Vol. 37, No. 4

[21]Goldsmith, J.C., et al. "Managed Care Comes of Age." *The Healthcare Forum Journal*, Vol. 38, No.5

[22]Op. cit., *The Tyranny of Piecework.*

[23]Op. cit., "Managed Care Comes of Age."

[24]Op. cit., *The Tyranny of Piecework.*

[25]Senge, P.M. *The Fifth Discipline: The Art and Practice of the Learning Organization.* New York: Doubleday/ Currency, 1990.

[26]Op. cit.

About the Author

Martin D. Merry, MD, is associate professor of health management and policy at the University of New Hampshire. Dr. Merry is a long-time consultant on quality of care issues and served as project director for the U.S. Department of Defense Civilian External Review Program.

Doctors and Patients: Breaking Down the Walls

By Thomas L. Delbanco, MD

There's a lot of unhappiness these days with relationships between doctors and patients. Doctors are accused of arrogance, even as we lament the assault on the human side of care that attracted most of us to medicine. We are justifiably proud of what technology helps us accomplish, but find that gadgets, tests and procedures get in the way, distancing us from our patients' experiences with healthcare and illness. Choked by fax machines, voice mail and an ever-accelerating rush, both doctors and patients suffocate in today's frantic world. Walls rise between us. The explosive quest for alternative herapies reflects both a yearning for the cherished (and affordable) aspects of the "good old days" and growing disenchantment with the mixed messages and unfulfilled promises of scientific medicine.[1]

◆ ◆ ◆

What can we do to improve the doctor-patient relationship, to move forward toward a more effective and satisfying therapeutic partnership? First, we need to study and understand the patient's perspective much more carefully. Second, we can incorporate into our practices a patient's review—an organized and systematic consideration of each patient as a unique individual that complements the organ-specific review of systems we learned in medical school. And finally, we can move beyond individual patients and invite patients collectively to report about their clinical experiences. Feedback of this sort can provide valid and reliable information about important aspects of our practices, thereby providing a benchmark for efforts to improve quality.

Understanding the Patient's Perspective

Since 1988, my colleagues at The Picker/Commonwealth Program for Patient-Centered Care (now The Picker Institute) and I have explored what patients consider important in their care, above and beyond the primarily biomedical aspects of their management. We have learned that patients do not focus on prettier waiting rooms, better hospital food, smiling office staff, or problems with parking. They turn first to issues of clinical significance that affect both the process and outcome of care. Patients want to trust the competence and efficiency of their caregivers. They want to navigate the healthcare system effectively and be treated with dignity and respect. They search for relief from pain and discomfort, and they worry about functional disabilities. They strive to understand how their illness or treatment will affect their lives, and they fear that doctors aren't telling them everything they know. They worry about caring for themselves away from the clinical setting and agonize over the impact their illness has on family, friends and finances. And they worry about the future.

Breaking Down the Walls As Doctors, We Need to

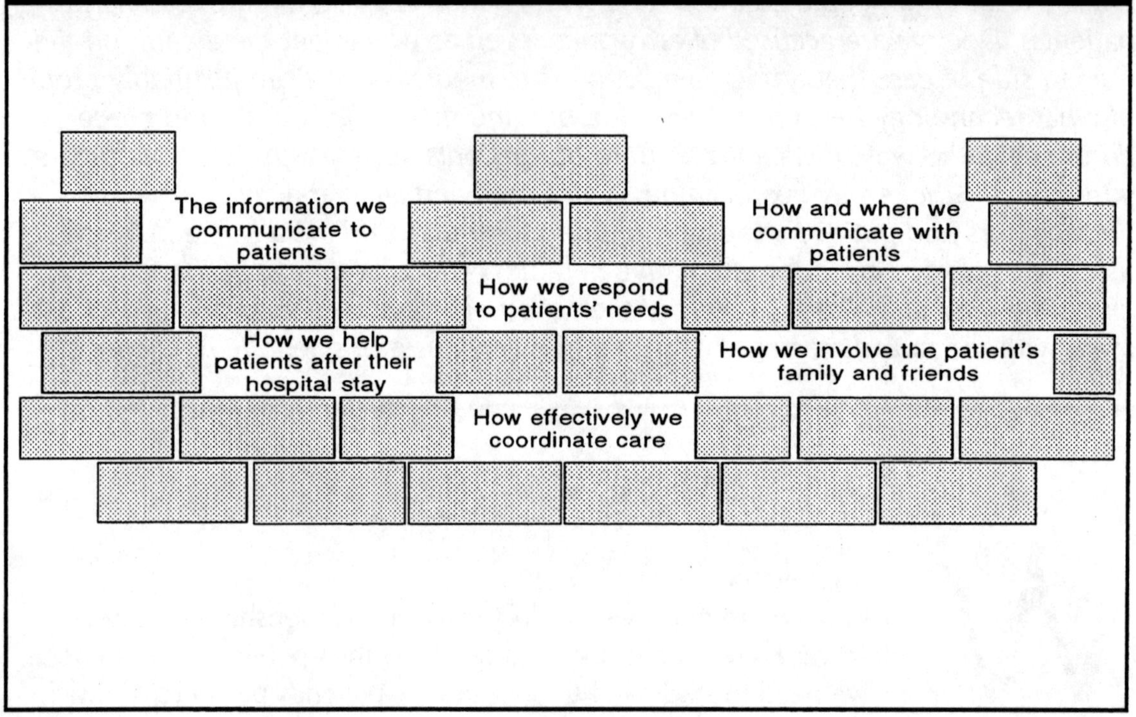

We have met with many patients—one on one and in focus groups—and they've helped us define seven broad dimensions of care that concern them the most.

Values, Preferences and Expressed Need

Some patients want me to tell them what to do. Others want to negotiate with me. Still others take my counsel under advisement and then make up their own minds. But whatever their approach, most patients want to know three things from me:

- My recommendation for preserving health and dealing with illness,
- My opinion of what is wrong with them, and
- What outcomes they can expect.

Although doctors still describe disease processes primarily in physiological terms, we understand increasingly that illness and the experience of illness are social and cultural phenomena. And culture—in the broad sense of the term that includes not only ethnicity but class, gender and other social attributes—affects how patients understand their illness, how they respond to and communicate about it, and how it changes their lives. We must remember that effective therapeutic strategies require a negotiated understanding, merging the culture of biomedicine within which doctors work and the patient's cultural experience of illness.

We are learning that doctors regularly underestimate how much their patients want to know or do. We are frightened about informing patients fully about treatment options, side effects, or outcomes, in part because we worry they will make a decision that is not in their best interest. But only the patient can define his or her best interest, what constitutes acceptable risk, tolerable side effects, or quality of life worth preserving.

Communication, Information and Education

I practice with a paperless medical record, surrounded by technologies that give me and my patients immediate access to overwhelming amounts of information. But this is not enough. How can we better transmit information and feelings so they are satisfactorily received and understood, even as the constraints of limited time seem to grow inexorably?

We have learned that patients seek more information than they get, although individual needs vary markedly with age, gender, past education and many cultural factors. Patients' desires also change over the course of an illness. Patients need time to hear, assimilate and process the information they are given. Perhaps paradoxically, the worst place to try to teach patients is on the hospital ward or in the doctor's office. Even with the brightest, most attentive patient and/or family, my words go in one ear and out the other. There is too much stress, sedation from medicines, too many inputs. We have to think very carefully about transmitting information and teaching *after* the encounter is over, and in this area, new technologies to enhance communication and education may prove invaluable. I'm already beginning to send patients home with transcripts of our visit, which I transcribe in collaboration with them. We also can print out on our computers informational material that accompanies many of their prescriptions. Many doctors around the country are sending patients home with ever-improving educational material, but this is all just a start.

Physical Comfort

Whatever criteria doctors, managed care gatekeepers, insurance companies, or government officials use to justify an office visit or hospital admission, patients still expect healthcare providers to alleviate discomfort. The symptom of pain may be critical to establishing a diagnosis or monitoring a patient's progress, but patients endure far more pain than is necessary. Individual thresholds, responses and communication about pain differ and make assessment difficult, but clinicians' attitudes toward pain also vary, and misplaced fears of addiction abound.

Well beyond pain, clinicians also often ignore or underestimate the impact of functional limitations of all types. All too often, we give relatively low priority to basic physical needs in favor of technically more sophisticated—or what we view as intellectually more challenging—therapies. For example, a patient at home with AIDS may benefit far more from attention to nutrition than to the latest, high-tech diagnostic evaluation for a rare and likely untreatable infection.

Fears and Anxieties

Illness imposes on patients and their families emotional and psychological burdens that often are as heavy as their physical ailments. How freely do we offer patients the chance to express their own beliefs, feelings, and fears, however extreme or irrational they may seem? How carefully do we consider what we can do to offer support or aggressive intervention in the psychosocial contributors to illness?

Involvement of Family and Friends

We give far too little attention to the family. Family members, close friends and significant others have a greater impact on a patient's experience of illness or long-term health than any healthcare professional. They take on the myriad responsibilities of daily life that a sick person cannot fulfill. They steer the patient through the receptionists, triage nurses, doctors, billing and insurance offices, and other hurdles of the healthcare system. They are often the eyes and ears that watch and then report to doctors and nurses. They are acutely aware of their role as advocates, finding themselves at times in an adversarial position with clinicians. And clinicians may dread encounters with family members, for fear that their demands will be overwhelming.

Serious illness throws a monkey wrench into any family. Adding to the physical demands of care is the emotional strain of not knowing if, when, or how the patient will recover. Family members worry that they will be unequal to the task of caring, that they will do the wrong thing, or that they will not have access to the resources they need. Many are woefully unprepared to take care of family members who have chronic ailments or long-term disabilities.

Transition From the Hospital Ward or Doctor's Office

Patients tell us, both anecdotally and through aggregate data we have gathered now from more than 30,000 patients in the United States, Canada and Great Britain, that this is where we fail most regularly.[2,3,4] Doctors and nurses all too often act as if responsibility ends at the moment of discharge. Patients go home with little information about what they can or cannot do and frequently are unaware of available resources, such as home health services. They find little proactive help in negotiating the complex system of health and social services.

Leaving the doctor's office can also be a difficult transition, although it has received less attention as a subject for inquiry. Many encounters are short, stressful and even traumatic, beautifully designed to ensure that the patient remembers little advice or information.

Coordination of Care and Integration of Services

Finally, patients and their families are expert witnesses. They can watch closely the processes of healthcare delivery. They judge instantly if the care they receive is effectively coordinated and cognizant of their individual needs and circumstances. On the other hand, care that appears uncoordinated or unintegrated instills little confidence or trust, no matter how "good" it is when measured by some other indicator of quality.

The Patient's Review

How can we incorporate these elements of care and each patient's unique perspective into our practices? One technique is to address them through a format similar to the review of systems that has focused traditionally on the heart, the skin and the psyche.[5] A "patient's review" that outlines the individual's unique perspective can be incorporated into the history that is the foundation of clinical practice. I use this in my practice and find it helps tailor care to the individual patient and forces me to make explicit what often has been implicit. Patients place their own stamp on such an interactive process. How much do *they* really want to know? What do *they* want to decide? What are *their* worries and fears? How well are *they* functioning?

During my first few encounters with a patient, I draw out and document important areas under the first six elements of care outlined above. I develop this review using information contained in a computerized history that the patient completes in our waiting room and responses to a few targeted questions that add little time to the encounter.

I have a few favorite questions. I ask patients about the three largest stresses in their life. I ask them what they want their doctor to be like, and I am struck by their eagerness to answer what, at first, may seem a strange question. Indeed, I am constantly fascinated by the range of responses I receive. I go on to assure patients (and family members, if they are present) that I plan to live up to their requests if I think I can, and I ask them to feel free to tell me when I am letting them down. The latter charge is often difficult for patients to accept, given the passive role they traditionally have taken, so I repeat and reinforce it during subsequent visits. I also raise the question of first versus last names, and we both agree to use the first or the last name.

To level the playing field further, I give patients copies of the transcript of their visit, if they so desire. If problems or issues were brought up during the visit, we negotiate how they will be handled. If the patient thinks obesity is not a problem, and I do, how should we compromise? In the future, recordings of the interchange will travel home via audiocassette or on transcripts generated by voice transcription, technologies that remain elusive today but which will mature sooner rather than later.

Limited time remains the greatest obstacle to such practice, and the pressures from managed care that compel the primary care practitioner to use time carefully are intense. But not everything has to be done at once, and efficiencies grow over time. Moreover, that extra time taken today may pay off handsomely in the long run. It is up to us, and our patients, to convince society that that is the case. Once we do, the rewards for clinicians' time will grow, at the expense perhaps of many tests and procedures that add little at the margin.

Using Patient Feedback to Evaluate our Practices

Ernest Avery Codman made the radical suggestion early in this century that we pursue our patients to learn from them the outcomes of their treatment—a notion that led to virtual ostracism by his surgeon colleagues at Massachusetts General Hospital. Avedis Donabedian took the next step by suggesting that patients are in a unique position to assess important aspects of the quality of care we deliver. These insights fuel the growing interest in gathering from patients aggregate feedback about our practices, using instruments that solicit explicit reports about their experiences.

Such reports should focus on clinically important issues about which we can take action and should ask:

- What happened?
- Did the doctor explain what you can or cannot do once home? and
- Did the surgeon address your anxieties or fears about the operation?

Answers to such questions prove much more helpful than those that focus on satisfaction with care, ratings easily confounded by subjective bias, low or high expectations, or differing cultural values. And, I believe doctors are apt to take reports from their patients seriously, indeed, more seriously than those offered by administrators, regulators, payers, or even peers.

Aggregate data from surveys using such questions serve as terrific "screening" tests, but they are rarely "diagnostic." They point us toward problem areas worthy of further inquiry. We learn, for example, that pain management is a problem in the intensive care unit. We then have to seek further evidence to determine the exact cause and therapy for the problem.

Above all, asking our patients in an organized, scientific and urgent way to respond to our questions reflects our desire to improve care, to take their perceptions seriously. It is a fitting prelude for what I believe is a logical next step: inviting patients to join us in developing solutions for systemic problems they have uncovered. What better way to break down walls between us and those we serve?

◆ ◆ ◆

References

[1]Eisenberg, D.M., et. al. "Unconventional Medicine in the United States: Prevalence, Costs, and Patterns of Use." *The New England Journal of Medicine.* 328:246: 252, 1993.

[2]Cleary, P.D., et. al. "The Relationship Between Reported Problems and Patient Summary Evaluations of Hospital Care." *Quality Review Bulletin.* 18:53, 59, 1992.

[3]Bruster, S., et. al. "The Patient's View: A National Survey of Hospital Patients." *British Medical Journal.* 309:1542,1546, 1994.

[4]Charles, C., et. al. "How Was Your Hospital Stay? Patients' Reports About Their Care in Canadian Hospitals." *Journal of the Canadian Medical Association.* 150:1813, 1821, 1994.

[5]Delbanco, T.L. "Enriching the Doctor-Patient Relationship by Inviting the Patient's Perspective." *Annals of Internal Medicine.* 116:414, 418, 1992.

ABOUT THE AUTHOR

Thomas Delbanco, M.D., is chief of the Division of General Medicine and Primary Care at Beth Israel Deaconess Medical Center, Professor of Medicine at Harvard Medical School, and Chairman of the Picker Institute, formerly the Picker/Commonwealth Program for Patient-Centered Care.

Dr. Delbanco created one of the first nationally-recognized hospital-based primary care practice and teaching programs, Healthcare Associates, which today provides for more than 65,000 patient visits annually and serves 500 patients with HIV infection.

The Application of Evidence-Based Guidelines to Clinical Practice

by Robert M. MacInnes, MD

In the first edition of The Physician Leader's Guide, a related chapter focused on the role of the physician leader in quality improvement. At the time of publication (November 1991), physicians were concerned about the emphasis being placed on review of aggregate data as opposed to single-case review. Practitioners and others were confused about how their clinical work could be linked with the process improvement team's work on complex hospital processes. Critical pathways appeared rigid, with no alternate protocols for coping with variation in the severity of clinical disease. Although it made conceptual sense, continuous quality improvement (CQI) seemed somehow divorced from the everyday practice of medicine.

Today, as a result of the publication of numerous articles and exchange of ideas and successes, CQI has gained general acceptance in medicine. Through the application of patterns of "best practice," evidence-based guidelines and tools to support clinical decision making, the concept of CQI has become an accepted part of the practice of medicine. The transition occured as clinicians developed their daily clinical practices for individual patients into vehicles that could be used for groups of patients. The development was made possible by the explosion in technology, particularly clinical information systems, that are able to capture valid data and analyze them for the support (or refutation) of conclusions. Conversely, until recently, such conclusions were based almost exclusively on "expert opinions."

◆ ◆ ◆

Best practices in the form of evidence-based guidelines bring resource utilization into the range of "appropriate"—providing no more nor less care than what is needed. In general, these practices can be codified and applied to approximately 80 percent of patients and as much as 95 percent of elective surgical patients in a hospital setting. Guidelines for ambulatory care based on evidence are also applicable to a significant majority of patients with acute and chronic conditions. "Outlier" cases—those that are unpredictable because of an intrinsic mix of pathology or unexpected events—and episodes of poor quality should be analyzed separately, through traditional peer review.

Therefore, have we not arrived at a point where best practices are observed by most physicians most of the time? The answer, unfortunately, is no. As many physician leaders will attest, guidelines, best practices and other tools are often not known or implemented and thus remain unused. The reasons are multiple, with several aspects masterfully covered in a recent article, "The Awareness to Adherence Model of the Steps to Clinical Guideline Compliance."[1] In this revealing study, two childhood immunizations endorsed by the American Academy of Pediatrics and American Academy of Family Practitioners are consistently used only 30 percent of the time. This pattern persists even though 98 percent of practitioners surveyed say they are aware of the expert recommendations.

Why Evidence-Based Guidelines Are Rarely Used

One reason evidence-based standard practices are underutilized is that many of the critical paths and protocols developed for elective surgical procedures had poor applicability to medical diagnoses. Aligning services with specific days of post-admission care was a model created for elective procedures, not for the care of patients admitted to the hospital with varying degrees of severity and acuity.

To understand and benefit from the clinical information available, physicians need to receive it in context and in a process that makes sense and provides value (e.g., better patient outcomes, less rework, reduced "hassle factor"). Agreeing upon a set of measurable clinical outcomes is a first step toward that goal. Note, though, that for hospitalized patients, achievable outcomes may be highly variable and dependent upon the clinical status of the individual patient.

Researching the efficacy of therapeutic interventions is a necessary second step. The clinical literature is replete with trials and analyses to assist with this goal. Unfortunately, a single, proven strategy rarely works for all. There usually are, however, a handful of strategies that yield best outcomes according to randomly controlled trials or meta-analyses of trials. Utilizing one or more of these strategies will be consistent with the practitioner's patient advocacy role. Getting a group of clinicians to review the current literature also helps bring everyone up to speed on their knowledge, something busy practitioners may not have time to pursue.

Once one or more likely strategies are chosen, the next step is to analyze resource utilization of the various clinical strategies and then compare costs. Decreasing variation and standardizing care, when appropriate, is cost effective. This is important to keep in mind because physician leaders are increasingly expected to be accountable for the quality and cost implications of the care they and their colleagues deliver. Indeed, success under managed care will elude all physicians who do not concern themselves with cost and quality issues.

Successful Guidelines are Flexible Guidelines

The foundation for clinical quality improvement rests on developing best practices and clinical guidelines as dynamic tools to be molded by improvements from current literature and clinical experience. By measuring variance in the use of any part of a given guideline, physicians are striving to produce a tool for continuous improvement, not one for discipline.

As mentioned earlier, guidelines vary in the degree of flexibility necessary for successful implementation. Without the ability to be customized to an individual patient's clinical state, a guideline's utility for practicing physicians declines precipitously. For medical diagnoses in both children and adults, guidelines should consist of evidence-based interventions such as pharmaceutical choices and supportive care elements (e.g. respiratory in neonates, COPD, pneumonia and asthma; laboratory in diabetes; cardiac monitoring in cardiovascular disease). The frequency and duration of use of these elements should be governed by each patient's response to the interventions, not by a schedule of daily change derived from a "guideline source book." When goals for an individual's care are set on or near the time of hospital admission (i.e., what physiologic parameters need to be met for this individual in order to move to a lower level of care setting) then daily monitoring and success of interventions provide the guidelines for that patient. By setting goals, utilizing guideline-driven elements in delivering care processes and communicating frequently, the physician and caregivers function as a team. As such, they help ensure that important parts of the process don't slip through the cracks. Of course, the physiologic parameters for elective surgical procedures are substantially more predictable and therefore, more easily codified into a daily plan.

To achieve success with guideline implementation, the method of development and data sources must be clear to practicing physicians and supported by current evidence from the literature. Because there is legitimate concern regarding the incentives underlying care delivery in managed care systems, the correct utilization on a per patient basis is the goal that physicians should honor. Both extremes—under and overutilization—can be avoided when "common cause" variation is the focus of guideline development. In other words, the resources, generally required in order to manage 75 percent to 80 percent of the care are predictable when processes of care implemented address the usual course of interventions.

Special cause variation. All that being said, "special cause" variation is important. Special causes of variation are a major contributor to many physicians' backlash against standardization of care. The attempt to codify steps in the care processes for special causes of variation has not been successful. Therefore, flexible, customized care plans for patients who should not be managed in a standardized way are essential for managed care to be quality care.

In addition, it is important to keep in mind that guidelines are not protocols or critical paths; they are a compilation of information regarding the diagnosis and treatment of specific medical conditions. The information is then arrayed in a chronological order supported by current medical literature. For example, let's examine the treatment of community-acquired pneumonia in hospitalized patients. Three elements in the care process have been shown to improve outcomes and shorten acute hospital length of stay: 1. Antibiotic provided intravenously within four hours of the patient's arrival; 2. Early mobilization or ambulation (when appropriate); and 3. Early, appropriate change from I.V. to oral antibiotic administration. Three elements of care lend themselves to standardization: 1. Antibiotic choice; 2. Use (or not) or respiratory therapy and oxygen; and 3. Use of laboratory (gram stain, cultures).

To codify these processes and elements into a daily pathway or care map is usually not possible. To set physiologic parameters for improvement and measure them daily, however, is possible. Thus, a clinical care team should be able to:

- Begin use of the appropriate antibiotic based on gram stain results, specific hospital bacteriology reports and clinical literature, within four hours;
- Assess the need for bronchodilator therapy and oxygen by frequently using a stethoscope and reviewing oxygen saturation results; and
- Monitor the patient's progress for fluid intake (and ability to swallow), vital signs and culture results and mobilize early for secretion management.

Surmounting the Roadblocks to Guideline Use

So if it's generally understood that dynamic guidelines are essential to delivering quality, cost-effective healthcare, why does such a high degree of practice variation persist? Issues of autonomy, conflicting literature sources, powerful advertising and detailing by the pharmaceutical industry and the acceptance of unproven, new technologies all play a role. Combine these factors with those already operative in small-area variation and you have a daunting set of roadblocks to the use of guidelines for physician leaders. What's necessary is to continue moving forward rather than allowing ourselves to be paralyzed by variation.

Physician leaders can maintain a forward impetus by first recognizing that physicians must embrace the method of a guideline's development and implementation before they can wholeheartedly accept the guideline. Evidence-based guidelines as developed and tested by Scott Weingarten, MD, at Cedars-Sinai Medical Center in Los Angeles and the Episode of Care Model developed by Neal Friedman, MD and others at Lovelace Medical Center in Albuquerque, N.M., provide just two examples of how clinical leaders can help ensure that guidelines are integrated into the care process rather than rejected.

First, the need for some degree of standardization should be documented with data on variation in outcomes and costs. If variation exists and is accepted as a determinant of quality by a majority of physicians, only one step has been taken. Historically, the variation has been provided to showcase perceived overutilization patterns without any or, at best minimal, severity adjustment. This approach has not met with physician approval, and when pathways or guidelines are developed utilizing these data, they are soundly rejected or simply never used. When the existence of variation is accepted and outcomes and costs analyzed to highlight the most efficient practices, a second step has been taken. Evaluating all aspects of the most efficient data is essential to gaining broad physician support. The data should include readmission rates, patient satisfaction and, in the best of all worlds, functional health status of the patients. When these practices are analyzed, supportive evidence from the current medical literature should be added to reduce the effect of individual opinions.

Evidence comes in many forms, but all of us learned that random, controlled trials (RTCs) supply the best evidence. In the absence of data from an RTCs, meta-analyses of studies and observational studies are the next best thing, followed by expert opinions after that.

Many organizations decided to simply adopt guidelines developed by national specialty societies or the Agency for Healthcare Policy and Research (AHCPR). But these guidelines are often viewed as too complex to follow, too costly to execute and measure and not applicable to the local practice of medicine. In many instances these guidelines are adopted at the local level by a committee voting process, but the actual use versus expected use is found to be less than 30 percent. When these same guidelines are carefully examined and supportive evidence from the literature is attached to specific elements, they can be *modified for local use* while upholding a comparable standard of care.

"Modified for local use" is emphasized because without engaging the expertise of practicing physicians in an organization or group, a guideline usually goes nowhere. In addition, there needs to be a leader or champion of the process, which is where physician leaders often come in. They may fill this role or facilitate the acceptance of this role by a colleague.

Educate staff. But don't forget staff training and support, because even with a leader and physician's engagement, an excellent guideline will have a low use rate (e.g., "the doctor didn't ask for it"; "we were too busy"; "they (doctors) don't want them or really use them anyway") without all the necessary infrastructure in place. Order sets must accompany each guideline, and the guideline should be offered as the management tool for all patients admitted with the specific diagnosis the guideline addresses.

Still, physicians will opt out of using the guideline for some patients, and some physicians will initially elect not to use any guidelines. That's to be expected. Typically, use rates over the first few months are less than 50% of eligible patients. The exception to this is a guideline for an elective surgical or invasive procedure performed, in large part, by a single group of physicians. The use rate in this case often approaches 90% shortly after implementation. Use of the guidelines should be voluntary. But doing a profile on patient outcomes per doctor may encourage those physicians who don't use guidelines (and have poorer outcomes) to change their management.

Meanwhile, data should be stratified by patients managed with the guidelines and those managed without so that variance can be recorded and periodically collated. These variances will be used to further improve the guideline. If broad acceptance is gained, the guideline has improved care, and the process for continually improving the guideline is in place and working, then the "Act" element in the CQI cycle of Plan-Do-Check-Act is achieved and use rates increase, often to the 85 percent range. (For an example of the Plan-Do-Check-Act, see Dr. Merry's chapter on page 755.)

Because these efforts are specifically designed to continually enhance the quality of care, physician leaders find themselves on very solid ground with respect to their colleagues. But if the process outlined is not followed and shortcuts based on personal opinions replace solid evidence, the outcome of this process will unlikely be positive.

Two specific components of the development and use phases that deserve special attention are:

Assessment of new technology and methodology, including pharmaceuticals. These variables are introduced at a particularly rapid rate and deserve validation before insertion into an existing guideline. The pressure to adopt changes is often significantly ahead of the appearance of substantive evidence of efficacy in the literature.[2] Committees that deal with technology assessment and pharmacy and therapeutics, in particular, require strong physician leadership to be effective and to resist rapid change unsupported by reliable evidence.

Data validity. Outcomes data for an illness or procedure are not easy to obtain. With short hospital stays physicians can document only one phase of an illness or procedure. If satisfaction and functional status data are available it is very helpful. Follow-up data are available in staff-model HMO settings and where electronic medical records are in use. Also, large surgical databases that contain follow-up elements (e.g., STS/summit database for cardiac surgery and invasive procedures) are useful if available. In their absence, literature-based outcomes information is our best surrogate. Cost information is best reported to physicians as total costs and direct, variable costs. Direct variable costs are the only costs over which physicians feel they have any control.

Traditional Case Review's Place in 1998

If the foundation for clinical CQI is defining best practices and developing clinical guidelines, where do peer review and the definition of poor quality belong? In the first edition of this guide an effort was made to move toward the evaluation of aggregate data and away from single-case review. The exception to this was (and still is) the sentinel event, where much can be learned about the quality of processes that we use in care delivery. We also emphasized the analysis of trends of lesser-impact events. For both categories of event, an educational rather than a disciplinary approach was suggested. Because the most such events result from the lack of processes and procedures or the faulty application of existing procedures, analysis—not discipline—is the action step. When "special cause" variation exists or there is a poor outcome, confidential review by true peers should be the rule. Analysis should focus on care processes (including communication) where the answers to causation usually reside. Improvement efforts that address processes, as opposed to singular disciplinary actions, are usually effective. The physician leader's role is to facilitate discussions among peers and move toward process redesign and away from attempts to fix blame. Creating a systemic change should be the goal. Tracking results to document improvement and disseminating that information to physicians in a user-friendly format completes the peer review-based CQI effort.

By comparison with 1992, clinical applications of CQI have shifted from exclusively addressing hospital processes to the delivery of most clinical care. Where it was simple five years ago, there is abundant literature addressing the best methods of diagnosis and treatment for many common diseases. There is also plentiful literature detailing procedure rates and outcomes, as well as the application of CQI methodology to the operational aspects of the procedure iself (e.g., the New England Cardiovascular Surgery CQI initiative). Furthermore, evidence- based guidelines are becoming plentiful for a variety of diagnoses.

Unfortunately, the methods for implementing guidelines continue to vary widely and often do not address the necessary elements in right chronological sequence. This is why, although abundant, guidelines have failed to achieve broad physician acceptance and result in necessary behavior change.

There are now ample tools available for data-driven decision making and multiple examples of evidence-based practices to support physician learning and, ultimately, behavior change. The methodology is clearer and expressed in terms physicians have been using for decades. The huge task all physician leaders face is to facilitate physician learning with data and evidence so that practicing physicians either create and use or adopt and adhere to proven guidelines and best practices.

◆ ◆ ◆

[1]Pathman, D.E. "The Awareness to Adherence Model of the Steps to Clinical Guideline Compliance." *Medical Care,* (34) 9: 873-89.

[2]Grimes, D.A. *JAMA.* (269)23.

About the Author

Robert M. MacInnes, MD is director of quality improvement for Blue Shield of California in San Francisco.

Counseling a Physician With a Clinical Performance Problem

by Steven Landgarten, MD

How do you deal with a physician who has a clinical performance problem? The author offers six specific ways to handle this situation as well as strategies for:

- *Laying the groundwork for successful interaction, and*
- *Preparing for the actual encounter.*

◆ ◆ ◆

One of the most important and sensitive aspects of medical staff leadership is dealing with other physicians on issues related to their individual performance. From time to time, a medical staff leader will face an encounter with a peer whose care does not appear to conform with the standards of good medicine. But medical staff leaders can take steps to approach these difficult situations in a positive manner consistent with the goal of continuous improvement of the quality of patient care.

Laying the Foundation

The successful outcome of an individual encounter with a physician over a quality of care issue is heavily determined by the QI culture established by the medical staff leadership. If quality improvement activities are viewed by leaders as an important joint effort—an obligation of all physicians to continuously improve the quality of care of all the patients within the organization—then individual encounters are more likely to be perceived as educational, supportive and beneficial to physicians and patients alike.

If, on the other hand, quality improvement activities are performed only because they are externally mandated; if they are regulatory, hostile and punitive in intent; and if the only scorecard for QA activities is the number of corrective action letters sent to physicians, then interactions between physician leaders and individual members of the medical staff are doomed to failure, as is the QI program.

I have never met a physician who wanted to practice bad medicine. Nevertheless, there are a number of physicians who do not realize that their patient care is substandard. If, as a result of our monitoring and evaluation studies or even anecdotal observation, a physician with a potential quality problem is identified, this situation is best approached from a remedial rather than a punitive perspective.

Too many medical staffs rely on an exchange of letters to resolve issues raised by generic screens, anecdotal reports, or monitoring and evaluation activities. While it is important to document quality of care interactions, I am aware of no Joint Commission standard that requires us to "send nasty letters to doctors." For this reason, quality assurance inquiries should be initiated by direct contact with the physician involved whenever possible. While written documentation is important, it is better to notify an individual firsthand that an inquiry is being made than to send a letter that may be perceived as threatening or hostile.

If the organizational culture is one of improvement through education, a discussion between the individual physician and the chief of service, chief of staff, or medical director will most often achieve the indicated change in the pattern of care. This change, and the agreement with the physician that leads to it, should be documented through the appropriate medical staff mechanism.

One other point is important: A medical staff that is committed to QI will elect as its leaders clinically respected members of the staff. Leadership positions are far too important to simply pass on, like a baton, to the next person in line. Effective physician leaders need not be perfect. However, they must be good clinicians with strong communication and counseling skills.

The Encounter

Now, on to the core question: How do you deal with a peer involved in a serious performance issue? The assumption here is that a duly authorized peer review committee or individual reviewer has serious concerns over a case or trend of patient care events.

A private meeting often is a far more "user friendly" approach than a "kangaroo court" at which a physician must defend before a group of peers an issue that he or she may already understand could have been handled better. It generally is better to reach an agreement privately with the physician on what can be done better and then bring that consensus forward.

While the style and content of conversations regarding clinical performance will vary with the nature of the event and the personalities involved, there are some helpful guidelines. Although these are presented below as a step-by-step process, leaders should recognize that each encounter is different, and none are easy. Use judgment and common sense in applying these ideas.

1. Choose an appropriate setting. Do not attempt to have a conversation over a serious quality issue casually in the hospital hallway. Not only does this threaten the confidentiality of the conversation, it also sends the wrong message regarding the importance of the conversation. Always inform the physician in advance that a meeting is needed to discuss a problem of clinical performance, then set up an appointment in an appropriate office in the hospital.

2. Don't go alone. Although the conversation is frequently collegial, it is nonetheless official. It may be useful to arrange to have a second individual present to participate in the conversation. The chief of the appropriate medical staff department, an officer of the medical staff, or the chairman of the appropriate medical staff committee are likely candidates. Always inform the physician in advance if other individuals will be present.

3. Keep the discussion objective. It is important to open the conversation with a reminder that, as physicians, our objective is to deliver the highest possible level of care to patients within our organization. The incident or data in question should be discussed in a fashion that is objective rather than judgmental, collegial rather than hierarchical. If the issue regards deviation from established clinical guidelines or variation from anticipated patterns of care based on the monitoring and evaluation program, the supportive documentation should be available. This objective approach serves to diffuse concerns that "you are doing this to me because you don't like me." Many physicians' first reaction to this type of discussion is a variant of "my patients are sicker than the established standard assumes." However, most come to recognize the importance of the variation and, because most physicians are sincerely concerned with quality of care, they are very willing to accept remedial help if offered.

4. Choose the right remedy. The range of remedial steps available is quite broad. It includes voluntary agreement to change future practice patterns, recommendations for consultation in similar cases, formal educational programs, proctoring and (at the extreme) modification or loss of privileges.

If the problem is simply a variation from an established clinical guideline, often a formal request for compliance with this guideline will resolve the issue. Where a gap in skills or knowledge appears, requiring consultation for a limited number of cases or a limited period of time is sometimes a very successful strategy. On one hand, it protects or improves the quality of care in the area of deficiency. On the other hand, it provides an educational resource to the physician requesting the consultation.

5. Close the loop. Once agreement is reached, it should be documented, usually in the form of a letter or memo. If problems recur, a documentary file is available.

While the need for medical staff follow-up to ensure compliance is apparent, in many cases the process needs to proceed no further. There are exceptions, however. *If* there has been an agreement on a voluntary change in privileges, this must go through the formal medical staff credentials process and ultimately to the board for confirmation.

6. Counsel difficult physicians. Unfortunately, leaders occasionally encounter a physician who either lacks insight into the issue at hand or is totally committed to the conceit that "my patients are sicker" or "my way is better," but is unable to support either contention with documentation from medical literature or available statistical analysis. Unfortunately, these disputes will have to be dealt with through formal mechanisms. Even in these cases, however, differences of opinion must be kept at a professional, rather than personal, level. If a formal hearing or "judicial review" is held, conduct it in a manner that fully complies with the medical staff bylaws' requirements for procedural and substantive due process. Assume that the record will be subject to legal scrutiny at some time in the future.

Healthcare organizations engaging in continuous improvement activities are learning to focus attention on systems and processes rather than on individuals. At the same time, however, medical staffs must still monitor the clinical competence of each physician who cares for patients within the organization. While on the surface these activities may appear diametric, both are centered on improving patient care.

QI is taking root in healthcare because it stresses improvement through education and avoids assigning blame. Conducting peer review and peer counseling in the same manner will, in most cases, lead to improved patient care. At the same time, this approach will earn the respect and support of the medical staff.

About the Author

Steven Landgarten, MD, is medical director at Hillcrest Medical Center in Tulsa, OK.

How to Work With a Physician Who Is Having Interpersonal Problems

by A. Charles Massaro, MD

Physicians who don't get along well with others can be very disruptive to the care delivery environment. In this article, the author lays out a three-pronged strategy for working with a disruptive physician to improve his or her interpersonal style. It involves:

- *Identifying the problem;*
- *Considering the possible causes; and*
- *Deciding what kind of remedial action to take.*

◆ ◆ ◆

One of the difficult challenges facing physician leaders involves dealing with a colleague who is having interpersonal problems. Such problems can manifest themselves in a variety of ways. It could be the physician who is rude, patronizing, or verbally abusive toward staff and patients; the surgeon who storms out of the operating suite protesting inadequate patient preparation; or the physician whose language or actions are considered by some to be sexually harassing.

Such situations are not new, nor are they unique to healthcare. Society, in fact, has come to expect and, to a great extent, to tolerate erratic, egocentric and eccentric behavior from its "superstars," be they gifted artists, whose creativity inspires others, or scientific wizards, whose determined pursuit of knowledge opens new vistas. Physicians, whose talents combine the arts and sciences, traditionally have been afforded great deference by society in general, by their patients and by colleagues and staff in many healthcare organizations.

Society, however, is reaching for a new paradigm, or behavioral view of the world, characterized by personal accountability, equal opportunity, empowerment and teamwork. In the work place, the now popular and all prevailing TQM movement is a byproduct of this paradigm shift. In this new environment, all staff must be able to collaborate and work cooperatively to produce a system that provides value to the customer. Clearly, disruptive behavior has no place in this setting. To function in the new paradigm, the disruptive physician will have to modify his or her behavior to reflect the characteristics of the changing world view.

The Role of Physician Leaders

Physician leaders can use their positions within the organization to positively influence the attitudes and behaviors of the medical staff.

The physician leaders' key roles are to *define, model* and *enforce* expected standards of behavior for the medical staff. In their training, physicians may have observed senior faculty and attendings whose egos were tolerated and abuses condoned. In later practice, similar behavior may have been excused with rationalizations like "He's a good doctor; he just gets a little rude sometimes." It is neither easy nor pleasant for physician leaders to counsel their peers that such behavior is not acceptable, but that is precisely their leadership role.

Standards for physician behavior must be clearly articulated in the medical staff bylaws and in the credentialing policies and procedures. Mechanisms must be put in place to continually reinforce appropriate behavior and also to monitor variations that are considered to be potentially unacceptable.

Physicians can be made aware of the necessity and value of appropriate behavior during medical staff orientations and at annual general medical staff meetings. If the organization publishes a periodic newsletter for the medical staff, articles that focus on awareness of appropriate behavior may be included. If a rise in the number of interpersonal problems occurs at any specific time, special presentations to various levels of the medical staff can be made.

Monitoring variations in behavior can be implemented in the same manner as other quality issues. Indicators and criteria can be developed and communicated to all members of the organization. Instructions to all should clearly define and describe the process for documenting alleged incidents and collecting information, and the system for communicating the findings to department chairs and the medical director. The physician leader's role is to analyze these data and identify serious isolated events and trends.

For such a system to be effective, the organizational environment must be nonthreatening and encourage complete and objective reporting of unacceptable behavior.

Identifying a Problem

A physician leader may become aware of a problem informally, through written information provided by anyone in the organization, or from patients or families. In addition, formal monitoring mechanisms may identify a problem. Information also may come from an outside source, including a hospital, an insurance company, or a regulatory agency such as the state health department or local peer review organization.

Any source of information must be encouraged to be specific regarding the complaint and provide needed details that give credence to the complaint and allow for appropriate investigation.

When a physician with a real or a potential interpersonal problem is identified, the physician leader should first establish the validity of the allegation. Conflicts of interest or other personal reasons must be eliminated as possible motives for such a report. On the other hand, a competitor or disgruntled associate or former friend may bring forth a legitimate problem. Reports from such individuals can't be summarily dismissed. It is critical that the physician leader expeditiously investigate the sources and scope of the information and establish whether it is a real problem and, if so, if it is new or ongoing.

There are many subtle differences between the significance of a new or an ongoing problem. A newly developed behavioral problem may signal the onset of what could become a habit of abnormal behavior. In such cases, early intervention may well preclude further problems. On the other hand, it may be an isolated event precipitated by a specific problem such as a system support failure. If this is the case, it will present an opportunity to improve the process. In either case, the physician leader's investigation should include discussion with the physician and other individuals who were involved in order to collect enough data to analyze and reach a decision as to the true nature of the problem.

If the identified event represents an ongoing interpersonal problem that has become well established and allowed to continue, a more intense remedial process will be required. If a particular physician persistently has been rude, verbally abusive and noncooperative with colleagues and staff, or continuously harasses staff in the operating room, a greater effort will be required to solve the problem.

The physician leader's investigation includes the collection of information from all staff involved and witnesses to the events. Oral and written documentation should be assessed and documented. An expeditious interview should occur with each of the persons bringing the allegations and the physician involved. The allegations, analysis and possible conclusions should be discussed with the physician. The physician should be told to refrain from all behavior that may be perceived to be a problem even if he or she is convinced that the behavior is appropriate. Following such a discussion, written documentation of the meeting should be entered into the file and copied to the physician. All people involved should be informed of the results of the investigation.

Consider the Possible Causes

If the allegation proves true, the physician leader must then determine if there are any systemic causes for the physician's interpersonal problems, for example, uncontrolled diabetes mellitus, electrolyte disturbances, anemia, or a brain tumor. If a systemic cause is present, it may be correctable and thus resolve the issue. Failing this, the physician leader must privately meet with, and present the facts to, the physician in question. The process must be frank, objective and complete, and carried out in the spirit of continuous improvement rather than punishment. The physician must have an opportunity to explain his or her behavior and any possible underlying systemic causes of the problem.

Remedial Action

As a physician leader, you may be reluctant to take formal remedial action. However, this is your job, and the organization is depending upon you to do it well.

Initial action should include informal discussions with the involved physician. In the event a systemic or medical problem is suspected, the physician may be advised to seek medical help. Counseling may be recommended for the physician and/or for family members. Counseling could be arranged through an employee assistance program or private individuals or organizations. During informal meetings, the physician leader may be able to advise the physician regarding changes in behavior to deter further perceived or real problems by the staff.

When the investigation concludes that the physician has a significant and unacceptable interpersonal problem, more formal remedial action must be initiated, including counseling, education, monitoring, outcome evaluation and, if required, disciplinary action. These actions should clearly focus on helping the physician change rather than punishing him or her.

- **Counseling.** Counseling should be initiated with the goal of reaching agreement on a change in the attitudes and behavior of the physician in question.
- **Education.** Formal programs, seminars, or reading material can be offered to assist the physician in understanding and resolving the behavioral problem.
- **Monitoring and evaluation.** Depending upon the seriousness of the problem and how long it's been going on, the physician's progress toward meeting agreed-upon self-improvement goals will need to be formally monitored.
- **Outcome evaluation.** A physician's progress in modifying his or her behavior can be measured by the number or type of events that are still considered problematic. This should be assessed at periodic meetings with the physician and staff during the monitoring period. In addition, input from the physician regarding his or her perception of the progress being made should be solicited.
- **Formal disciplinary action.** As a last resort, formal disciplinary action must be taken in the event the physician's behavior does not improve. The action taken, which can range from reprimand to loss of clinical privileges and medical staff membership, must be proportionate to the seriousness of the problem.

Whichever intervention strategy is selected, it is critical that objective, valid and complete documentation be made of the entire process of investigation, monitoring, evaluation, outcome analysis and disciplinary action.

As healthcare organizations progress further with total quality initiatives that focus on organizational development, customer-centeredness and continuous improvement, aberrant and disruptive physician behavior will no longer be tolerated. If these problems are not addressed and resolved by senior physician leaders, the results can be devastating to staff morale, the organization's ability to compete and, most important, the quality of patient care.

About the Author

A. Charles Massaro, MD, is vice president for medical affairs at Sisters of Charity Hospital, Buffalo, NY.

Disease Management: Clinical Practice Improvement in Action

by Derick P. Pasternak, MD, MBA

In the late 1990s, healthcare organizations are feeling increasingly accountable for quality as well as price. Although few private payers make network decisions primarily on the basis of quality of care, they and the U.S. Health Care Financing Administration—which is establishing Centers of Excellence in cardiology and orthopaedics—are harbingers of imminent market share loss for those who do not make the cut.

◆ ◆ ◆

As healthcare has fragmented over the past half century, practically all groups of providers have wrapped themselves in the quality mantle. Specialty care promised better outcomes through superior knowledge of the disease process, wiser use of resources and better access to high technology. Primary care made the same promise, claiming superior knowledge of patients and their environments, use of care processes with lower risk and continuity of care. Nursing care management claimed more efficient inpatient care along with superior outcomes through coordination of caregivers' services, optimal sequencing of clinical activities and early involvement of social services. To apply the ubiquitous sports analogy, constituencies throughout healthcare act like members of a well-constituted but poorly coached football team. The runners run; the receivers catch; everyone does his job well and is convinced of his own critical role in the success of the team. But coordination is lacking, and the team consistently falls short of its own superior expectations.

The trend of holding entire institutions, rather than individuals, responsible for quality in healthcare probably gladdens those who have labored during the past decade to measure and improve quality. Logically, this trend should also place those who have implemented extensive practice guidelines and continuous quality improvement in an advantageous position. Yet some of the most progressive physician executives have found that overall quality of care hardly budged after all those initiatives in the late 1980s and early '90s. They have been actively searching for better approaches to measurably improve quality of care within their organizations.

The Quality-Value Equation

With businesses and other healthcare purchasers increasingly making purchasing decisions based on value instead of on price, reexamination of the components of value in healthcare has intensified. Certainly the V(alue) = Q(uality)/C(ost) equation has been appearing on more and more overheads at meetings. While we can measure costs rather readily in dollars (most institutions have recognized that true cost measures, as opposed to crude approximations from charges, have great management value), we continue to founder on the question of how to measure quality.

Again, the purchasers have come to our aid. First, they correctly pointed out that without access to care, all reference to quality is specious. The degree of access is a multiplier of all other factors entering quality because if a = 0, then Q = 0 (where a = degree of access to care and Q = overall quality of healthcare). Secondly, these purchasers made us pay attention to patients' and patient surrogates' perception of the quality of care, expressed as patient satisfaction. Finally, some purchasers—including the government—noted that even universal access and expert performance cannot add up to quality care when care is inappropriate. Appropriateness of care is, therefore, another multiplier. Mathematically, if A = 0 or a negative number, Q = 0 or negative as well (where A = degree of appropriateness of the medical procedure and Q = overall quality of care). Thus, for healthcare purposes the traditional equation for value should be redefined as a slight modification of Tarlov et. al's formulation[1]:

V = Q/$ = A*a(css+ (ciqi)/$C
where
V = value
A = appropriateness of the care provided
a = access to care
s = patient satisfaction
cs = efficient of patient satisfaction
qi = various components of clinical quality (such as mortality, physiologic outcomes, functional outcomes, etc.)
ci = coefficients related to the individual components of quality, and
$C = actual cost of providing the care (for the buyer, replaced by P = price).

(*Editorial note: $C represents actual cost of services, whereas $, above, is simply the author's way of representing general costs, sometimes also expressed as "C"*).

Assuming continuing attention to the cost and price of care (by providers and buyers, respectively), quality can be maximized by increasing access, patient satisfaction, various components of clinical quality and attention to the appropriateness of care.

The continuous quality improvement (CQI) movement in healthcare addressed these very issues. Why, then, did it have such modest effect, and what could be done to enhance CQI's effectiveness? One possible explanation is the lack of coordination that has typified the still-fragmented U.S. healthcare system, the ever-accelerating trend toward consolidation notwithstanding.

Where Quality and Disease Management Intersect

Though the movement to improve quality dates back to the early 20th century, its popularity started increasing in the middle to late 1970s. The correlation between managed care participation and the expansion of quality-related activity (which assumed massive proportions in some organizations) has been the subject of reviews elsewhere.

The box below summarizes quality-related activities for 1990 in an organization that pioneered the concept of integrated healthcare delivery.

Medical Practice Board (MDs):	Practice guideline algorithms Monitoring "bad apple" physicians
Nursing service:	CareMaps™
Pharmacy:	Drug interaction and toxicity monitoring
Administration:	Continuous Quality Improvement
Quality Assurance:	Sentinel events JCAHO indicators
Risk Management:	Adverse outcomes and incident reports
Surgical Departments:	Tissue review
Medical Departments:	Mortality and complications

For individual physicians and other professionals all this frenetic activity often led to bewilderment and lack of confidence in the process. Recognizing this, a number of organizations—often those that integrated provision and financing of care—independently developed methods to focus their clinically related CQI activities. These integrated systems then gave their systems names that reflected their intensely clinical orientation: "clinical decision support," "clinical effectiveness," "clinical roadmaps," "episodes of care." No matter what they were called, these systems invariably set up coordinated programs to address improvement of care in a defined clinical sphere, cutting across traditional barriers such as inpatient versus outpatient care, primary versus specialty care, medical versus nursing versus physical therapy services and so forth.

Having evolved, in part, from these efforts, disease management has a very impressive pedigree, indeed. The other side of disease management's ancestry is rooted in the commercial world of pharmaceutical manufacturers and consulting firms, which detected an opportunity to help healthcare providers reduce the fragmentation of care without necessarily forcing an organizational realignment. This side, in fact, gave "disease management" its name and, thereby, its commercial connotation. The question facing physician executives is whether disease management is a "solution of the month" or a valid approach to organizing patient care.

Disease management was recently defined as "the systematic approach to a health condition (e.g., asthma, congestive heart failure) or a healthcare intervention (e.g., coronary artery bypass graft, smoking cessation) that organizes preventive, interventional and care approaches throughout the continuum of care and that measures outcomes in terms of populations, not individuals."[2] As we'll see, a well-designed disease management program addresses every component of the value equation and institutes a condition-specific feedback loop (i.e., utilizes a condition-specific application of the Deming-Shewhart cycle) to ensure improvements, once made and demonstrated, are not abandoned.

Beginning the Process

The first activity in the disease management process is identification of clinical areas that need it. Because disease management is costly in actual dollars spent, time and effort of staff and opportunity costs, its application is necessarily limited to "important" clinical entities. Different organizations may define importance differently, but those that have assumed responsibility for care of significant populations of patients—either through contracting, capitation, or legislative mandate—understand that multiple criteria play a role in the decision of whether to invest in the process.

Choosing a clinical process and team. Selection of clinical processes is a leadership function. While it is important to solicit input from professional and support staff, medical and administrative leadership are best positioned to prioritize reviews of coronary artery bypass grafts, pregnancy care, care of children with asthma, care of depressed patients and so forth. Scenarios throughout the rest of the chapter will convey more concretely how others have followed the process.

> **Scenario A.** Senior management of an integrated system consists of an equal number of physician executives and administrators. After the decision is made to embark on disease management, senior managers decide to apply the following criteria to selection of disease management topics:

Population related criteria	Institutional criteria	Economic criteria
Prevalence of condition	Institutional mission	Cost of care
Incidence of condition	Interest by leadership	Impact on employers
Impact on population health	Known quality problems	Cost of the process
Morbidity	Availability of data	Availability of funding

Applying these criteria through a process that involves multiple rounds of voting, senior managers choose the following topics for the first set of disease management projects:

- Pregnancy and childbirth;
- Low back pain;

- Asthma in children;
- Coronary artery bypass graft; or
- Depression.

Once a medical condition, surgical process or other clinical entity is chosen for review, a team must be formed to coordinate all quality improvement activities in the area. This team must include physicians, preferably in leadership roles, who represent every specialty or department with a significant role in the care process (e.g., family practice, internal medicine and cardiology for congestive heart failure; family practice, pediatrics and allergy—or pediatric pulmonary—for children with asthma). The team must also include nurses and other prominent caregivers in the particular clinical process to be improved (e.g., physical therapists for low back pain and stroke, or exercise professionals for coronary artery disease).

Administration must be represented by a manager with sufficient control and visibility in the organization to lend the project credibility, and to make things happen if they get stuck. Other members of the team should at least include representatives of pharmacy, social services and patient education. The team needs support from individuals familiar with team dynamics, statistical process control and information technology, as utilized in the setting. Excluding any of these specialists from the meeting table will significantly hamper the team's efforts.

Establishing a mission and goals. Teams function best when they have a clear mission that gives members a common frame of reference. The mission can be defined in a written charge to the team, or the team may take on the definition itself as a valuable team-building activity. Even in the latter case a written charge from top management, preferably signed by the lead physician executive, is an important first step. The charge documents management's expectations for the team's activities and the participation of individual members. Individuals who are unable to agree with the goals set out in the charge will either express their opposition or withdraw, thereby signaling to the team and to management that the team's recommendations may encounter obstacles. Dealing with the anticipated opposition can then be incorporated in the roll-out plan. The following scenario—an actual event, that resulted in significant noncompliance and major rework of a team's efforts—underscores the danger of ignoring internal opposition early on.

> **Scenario B.** Even before the Chronic Anticoagulation Team was called into being, there was known disagreement within the multispecialty group. One subspecialty, composed of three physicians, unanimously dissented from all internally published guidelines for the use of chronic heparin therapy. The team chosen did not include any of these physicians, who were regarded as obstructionists, and no plans were made to understand and accommodate their objections. Medical management and the chosen team leader counted on the weight of high-level support to bring the dissenting doctors in line. After publication of the team's recommendations, the three physicians continued their opposition and cited their specialty literature, which indeed dissented from other published guidelines. Partly

as a result of this controversy one of the three physicians resigned from the group on short notice, creating a major void in a specialty whose coverage was essential for critically ill patients. The team's work also had to be repeated, and 18 months later the members are still unable to agree on new recommendations.

Setting boundaries. The mission of the team is used primarily to erect boundaries around the team's work. Even definition of a disease entity, such as "depression," leaves too large a field. The team might set as its mission "improvement of outcomes of care of patients managed mainly in primary care settings," or "improvement of hospital and post-hospital care of severely depressed patients," resulting in entirely different processes to be measured, and different process improvements. For disease management to be optimally effective, its perimeter must remain broad enough to encompass inpatient and outpatient care.

With the team agreed on the mission, members should direct their attention to the indicators of quality to be measured. Given the extensive literature available on quality management, it will not be necessary always to be original in goal setting. On the other hand, if some aspect of care is known or strongly suspected to be in need of improvement, this is an opportunity to address that area. Referring to the value equation, the team ought to be encouraged to define *at least one indicator* in each of the following domains: appropriateness, access, patient satisfaction, clinical outcomes (this may be further subdivided into physiologic and functional outcomes) and cost of care. This encouragement can take the form of a mandate and can be incorporated in the charge.

One important attribute of these indicators will be their measurability within the healthcare system. On this point the information system experts can make their most significant contributions, either providing the team with critical knowledge or receiving its mandate. Two scenarios illustrate these general possibilities.

> **Scenario C.** The depression team of a multispecialty group/hospital consortium is convinced that the best way to track the cost of care of patients with clinical depression is to compile all of the patients' healthcare costs over a given time, because studies have shown that inadequately treated patients with depression develop somatic complaints at significantly greater rate than those adequately treated. A member of the team read that measuring the cost of a patient's total care, both retrospectively over 12 months before the team's intervention and prospectively over 12 months after the change in processes, will provide a particularly useful case control method in this regard. The team is enthusiastic about adding this indicator to its list. However, the IS representative points out that given the open nature of the system, there is no way to know when a patient accesses a professional outside the system; although the system is capitated, the patient may choose unconventional practitioners, particularly for non-specific symptoms such as aches and pains. When challenged to develop a system that can track these costs, IS responds that even

if that were possible, there is no reliable way to reconstruct past expenditures for the control period. The team reluctantly looks for another cost of care indicator.

Scenario D. The Pediatric Preventive Care Team of a staff-model HMO chooses "completion of all recommended immunizations by age 2" as an indicator. The IS member of the team objects, saying that tracking this variable is extremely difficult, given that childhood vaccinations are administered in variable settings, including state-run public health clinics for Medicaid recipients who are now under managed care. The objections are noted, but the pediatricians and the quality manager point out that under NCQA's HEDIS 3.0 criteria, tracking and reporting these immunizations is mandatory in order to achieve and maintain accreditation. The quality indicator stands as chosen by the team; administration promises to provide the resources IS needs to set up a reliable reporting system.

Moving to Action

Before defining specific processes of care for a condition or procedure and choosing the critical processes to improve, there must be objective evidence that improvement is needed and possible. There are multiple reasons for taking the time this early in the team's life to collect such evidence. The following scenarios should illustrate some of these reasons.

Scenario E. The Breast Cancer Care Improvement Team chooses "percent of patients diagnosed with Stage III and Stage IV tumor" as an indicator of the effectiveness of screening, because the surgeons on the team are concerned that with the controversy surrounding proper mammography criteria, there may be changes in the frequency of screening mammograms in the near future. The excellent records of the tumor board are used to establish the baseline. These show an overall Stage III rate of 7 percent and a Stage IV rate of 4 percent of all patients initially diagnosed with breast cancer within the past 12 months. However, in women over age 70, the Stage III rate is 3 percent and Stage IV rate is 0 percent over this same period. The team concludes that while there is room for improvement in every age group, it will concentrate its efforts on the population under age 70 (in large part the non-Medicare population).

Scenario F. The Coronary Artery Bypass Graft Team chooses "unplanned return to the emergency room within 72 hours after discharge" as an indicator of meeting proper hospital discharge criteria while keeping length of stay short. During the 12 baseline months under study, only one patient of 465 discharged returned with a complication that was unforeseen at the time of discharge. The team, therefore, considers this indicator to be of too low incidence to yield statistically meaningful results for comparison. While it will remain under monitoring as a sentinel event, it must be replaced by another indicator in the team's work.

Scenario G. The Diabetes Mellitus Care Improvement Team chooses "percent of patients who have Hemoglobin A1c measured within the past 12 months" as an indicator of the adequacy of the chronic care process. Pre-improvement testing shows compliance rates significantly below those published in the literature. Internists and endocrinologists on the team protest that this value must be erroneous, because they consider themselves highly compliant with published guidelines, which recommend measuring this parameter every six months. Investigation reveals that about 15% of all diabetic patients had the test done in the endocrinologists' office and the results entered manually in the record. Neither the results nor the performance of the test was noted in the laboratory's electronic record system, which was the basis for the performance report. The report is corrected, and a process established to generate reports correctly in the future.

Defining the Processes of Clinical Care

Flowcharts and other tools defining clinical and service processes have been used almost universally for a decade now. But teams should be aware that while flowcharts documenting every possible branch point and every reference to subsidiary flowcharts may be useful to those concentrating on an abstract process, they will be of limited value to the practitioner as a guideline for patient management. While under daily pressure to increase productivity, practitioners must not only use these charts; they must also promptly return all patient telephone calls, communicate well with colleagues and support staff, complete increasing paperwork for care as well as other documentation, attend meetings and keep current with advances in their specialties.

Scenario H. The chair of the Low Back Pain Team was first exposed to a patient care guideline by a meticulously drawn 17-page flowchart on how to respond to an abnormal Pap smear. Being a successfully compulsive physician, and having studied the U.S. Department of Health and Human Services' five-page algorithm on management of acute low back pain,[3] he insists on completeness in anything that the team publishes. Pre-improvement testing of compliance rates with previously drawn guidelines indicates 63 percent compliance by family practitioners with the criteria for referral to magnetic resonance imaging (MRI). After the new guideline is published and publicized, compliance apparently drops to 59 percent. In a meeting with the family practice department, it becomes clear that the two results do not really differ; the practitioners simply agreed among themselves that they will do nothing to implement new ways of treating patients with low back pain until an algorithm they consider user-friendly is published. After two more revisions, the team publishes a one-page version of the algorithm. Twelve months after publication, use of MRI by family practitioners for low back pain drops 25 percent, and is substantially in compliance with the new guideline.

Locating the Focal Point of Care and Putting Ideas Into Action

Healthcare in the United States is fragmented into primary care, multiple providers of specialty care, alternative care and self care, without much coordination. The disease management paradigm gives teams or organizations an opportunity to use a more rational system to decide where the optimal locus of care may be.

Scenario I. The Pediatric Asthma Team of a managed care plan arrives at the patient flow documented in Figure 1, below.

FIGURE 1: PATIENT REFERRALS IN TREATMENT OF CHILDREN WITH ASTHMA

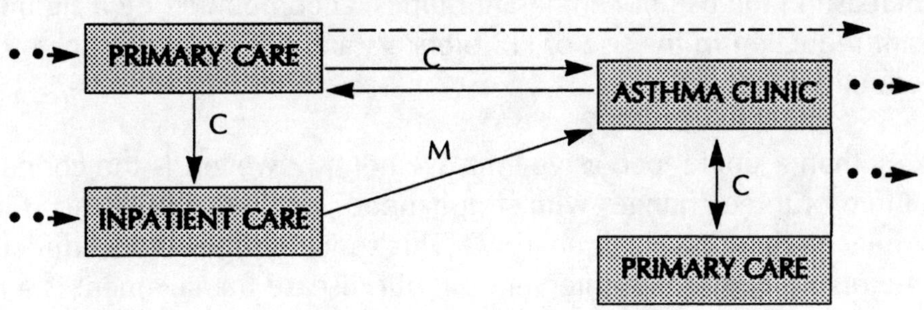

In this figure, *M* represents a mandatory referral—any patient who enters the system requiring hospital care for asthma, or any patient already in the system who requires hospital admission, is automatically referred to the asthma clinic following discharge. Under all other circumstances, referral criteria (represented by C) exist in both directions: from primary care to asthma clinic, and from asthma clinic back to primary care. The criteria in question are derived from the National Institutes of Health's criteria for specialist versus generalist care for children with asthma.[4] Implementation of this patient flow, along with other changes (including outreach into the community), results in sustained decreases in hospitalization rates and in hospital days per 1,000 enrollees in the plan.

Designing process improvements. The team exists primarily to design clinical practice improvements. At times the team will merely endorse improvements already conceived, but not yet implemented. But often, the interaction of the patient care professionals and managers on the team will create an environment in which healthcare process improvements can be fundamentally redesigned. Teams are constituted so that "solutions" that merely create problems for someone else can be readily identified and weeded out, while changes that have a good chance of yielding true improvement in patient outcomes, in access, in reduced cost, etc., will gain approval. It is not necessary to design one improvement for each of the agreed-upon indicators. A single improvement in patient flow or improved access can yield results in multiple domains, as can the dissemination of new knowledge about new treatments.

> **Scenario J**. The Peptic Ulcer Care Improvement Team designs an education program for primary care physicians on diagnosis and treatment of *Helicobacter pylori* infections. Financed externally, the program has excellent attendance and results in the following clinical improvements: 1. Reduction by 45 percent in the number of hospital admissions due because of complications of and surgery for peptic ulcer (clinical outcome and cost reduction); 2. Significant increase in patient satisfaction with the treatment of peptic ulcer (patient satisfaction); 3. Reduction by 22 percent in the number of endoscopies for indications other than hemorrhage (cost reduction); and 4. Increase in the use of certain antibiotics, accompanied by a significant reduction in the use of H2 blockers and other drugs (slight cost reduction).

More likely than a single, pervasive improvement, however, is the concurrent design of two or three changes with simultaneous or closely sequenced implementation, similar to that cited in Scenario I. This sequencing makes it difficult to ascribe the results to any one intervention, but disease management is a management tool, not a research protocol. Designing one or more improvements corresponds to the "P" phase of the Deming/Shewhart cycle.

Completing the designed improvement. Implementation is the "D" phase of the Deming-Shewhart cycle. Implementation of a plan, no matter how carefully designed, is the riskiest phase of the process. In the worst-case scenario, the entire investment in the process is at stake, as it was in Scenario B. An unsuccessful implementation early in the course of adopting disease management may doom the entire effort. This phase is frequently the domain of educators, whose advice is needed to create the most favorable environment for change in behavior. There may be education for patients, physicians, other providers and support staff alike. These may have to take place separately; certainly the content of patient education will be different from that provided to other customers of the process. Education for change in behavior should occur early and often; intervention at a single instance is rarely successful (although it was in Scenario J).

> **Scenario K.** The Pediatric Asthma Team organizes the proposed changes in patient flow, establishment of a new asthma clinic, and separation of the outreach program into two educational packages. The two physicians who co-chaired the team deliver the package for providers at a meeting of the family practice department. Physicians will receive continuing education credit for attending this meeting. The same program is repeated at various remote sites so physicians and nurses who could not attend the department meeting also have an opportunity to ask questions. The asthma clinic case manager, a

nurse with special credentials in respiratory disease, prepares patient education materials in English and Spanish and distributes them to patients.

Who needs to be on the team?

Education must be accompanied by management action, whether that be reorganizing a department, approving all expenditures, enforcing changes in IS support for clinical activities or generally lending credence to the team's recommendations. Without executive-level support, changes—especially those calling for an investment of funds—will be delayed or never carried out. This support is also the primary reason for the presence of a high-level administrator on the team. She or he has to champion the team's mission in organizational competition for the elusive dollar.

Having clinicians on the team is also essential to move improvements from ideas to actions. Physicians and other clinical personnel need to act as coaches and cheerleaders in their respective spheres, because such people are best positioned to explain why unsettling and sometimes troublesome changes must be made. They can also inform the team as soon as an unforeseen problem develops, so that they or management can promptly make any necessary adjustment.

Measure the results of changes.

In performing the "C" or "S" phase of the cycle, the measurement process should take care to reproduce the same measures reported for the baseline period. This is a phase that requires foresight and statistical expertise. The reported results must stand up to scrutiny by a highly critical and usually statistically sophisticated audience.

Communication of the results to all constituencies is important, even if improvement is less than anticipated. Some of the disenchantment with quality management programs in the past has resulted from a tendency to celebrate successes and ignore failures. If the subject of a disease management project was appropriately chosen, it will be critical to evaluate and present the results, even if less than stellar, and proceed with a second effort at crafting an improvement.

The measurement of healthcare outcomes is in considerable flux. The recent implementation of the ORYX program of mandatory clinical performance measurement by the Joint Commission on Accreditation for Healthcare Organizations (JCAHO) may lead institutions to abandon previously used measures. (*Editorial note: ORYX is the name of JCAHO's new initiative requiring every accredited entity to contract with an "accepted" third-party vendor for the independent analysis of its quality indicators*). These changes will accelerate. JCAHO has already announced that today's measurements will not be sufficient in the future; ORYX requirements will multiply, notably to include valid risk or severity adjustment for patient populations under care. The new measures may well be relevant to one or another disease management project. It will always be important, however, to produce post-improvement measures that allow valid conclusions about whether improvement has occurred.

Integrate the Improvements

Those versed in continuous quality improvement know the "A" phase of the cycle is the one most often taken for granted. After demonstration of successful improvement, why would the new procedures not be followed? The well-known Hawthorne Effect holds the answer: A system's improved performance while under scrutiny will relapse when management or other outside attention is directed elsewhere. (*Editorial note: For more explanation of this phenomenon, see Dr. MacInnes's chapter on implementing evidence-based guidelines, page xx*).

It may be appropriate for management to craft incentives for continuing compliance, or disincentives for lack of compliance. New policies may need to be put in place once improvement is demonstrated. The continuing importance of superior outcomes of care in the selected clinical areas must remain visible to the entire staff. Inevitably, new challenges will distract management from clinical care in areas where quality improvement seems to work. Therefore, it will fall to the team to coordinate efforts to hold the gain.

At this point we return to the question posed earlier, "Does disease management work?" There is little point in learning how to implement an elaborate and costly program if its benefits are nonexistent or evanescent.

Some questions that come readily come to mind are:

Q. Is there evidence that this approach works?

A. As with all things new in healthcare, disease management now has user groups, newsletters and, above all, continuing education seminars. Information about successful improvements is easy to come by. But the critical observer will note that as generous as these reports are with charts and tables, few of them meet the rigorous criteria of proof that a biomedical scientist or epidemiologist would demand. In large part, that situation has persisted because the proponents of disease management have been managers, not scientists. In many settings, reported improvements and cost reductions have been deemed positive enough to justify the continued investment of relatively large sums.

Q. If it works in selected settings, is it transportable to all settings?

A. Organizations in which inpatient and outpatient care are integrated under one management team and supported by one information system are most favorable for disease management. Integrated systems such as Henry Ford in Detroit, Group Health Cooperative of Puget Sound, Harvard Pilgrim Health Care, New Mexico's Lovelace Health System, and Kaiser Permanente originated the concept among providers. Among these providers, those without inpatient facilities tend to have excellent information system support and close relationships with participating hospitals. As a result of the costs involved (see below), hospitals are likely to take the lead in less-integrated systems simply because they have the resources. Still, to be effective, any disease management program needs ready access to information about patients' care outside the hospital. If a hospital is unable to obtain data about outpatient care, it is not going to be able to support an extensive disease management program. In a few areas, such as pregnancy care, cancer or trauma, where information is available through registries and similar sources, even these hospitals may embark on a program.

Q. What is the cost of a successful disease management program?

A. There are multiple classes of costs of disease management programs. Out-of-pocket costs vary widely, depending partially on whether the institution builds its own system or purchases one from a vendor. Consultants may be engaged. There also will be opportunity costs when team members are taken from other tasks, such as patient care and administrative work. There will be variable overhead and travel. All told, internally developed programs may cost $200,000 per year per condition. Purchasing or licensing computer-based platforms may cost considerably more than that, even without factoring in opportunity costs. This degree of required investment will limit the viability of disease management in small and mid-size organizations.

Q. Will it last?

A. In a recent article, disease management was called "new wine in new bottles."[5] One has to wonder, though, if it is really new. Admittedly, its focus on population shifts the general practitioner's or primary care doctor's focus on individual patients. But care of some conditions has become so complicated that a support mechanism is necessary to organize care, reduce variation in the care process, consistently evaluate the outcomes of care, and provide feedback to practitioners.[6] If this were not done by disease management teams, someone else would have to do it.

In fact, someone else is already managing disease in some settings. The managed care trend empowers primary care providers at the expense of other physicians; the integration trend tends to put hospitals in leading roles in consolidating healthcare; the Medicare reimbursement trend is harshest with non-surgical specialists. All together, these trends have elicited a reaction from specialists: They are beginning to present themselves as uniquely qualified to fill the role of care organizers and managers.[7] If groups of specialists—the huge single-specialty groups already active in some parts of the country—acquire access to reliable and comprehensive information system support, and if they are able to exert significant local influence, they will indeed be able to fulfill the role envisioned for disease management teams. However, they will lack the inherent advantages of having their primary care colleagues and senior health system managers with them at the table.

Expansion of disease management in other directions is also likely. It has always been suspected in clinical circles that pharmaceutical manufacturers' interest in this and other "value-added services" is aimed at increasing demand for the manufacturers' drugs. Some of the commercially available platforms are perceived as designed to prompt the use of certain products when there is a choice, much like the airlines' proprietary scheduling systems. Others will likely attempt to use the non-proprietary disease management term to promote their individual commercial interests, which eventually will result in the modification or abandonment of the term by healthcare providers. It is likely, however, that the concepts of population-based medicine and cross-functional care coordination teams are here to stay.

Disease management is similar to the establishment of a coaching staff to support the performance of the outstanding players of that less-than-stellar football team. It is designed to improve collaboration and coordination. Its success is measured in the overall product of the system, not in individual performance statistics. And, since it assists in designing long-term outcomes to be measured in a variety of clinical conditions, it broadens the healthcare playbook, potentially to championship levels.

◆ ◆ ◆

References

[1]Tarlov, A.R., Ware, J.E., Greenfield, S., et al. "The Medical Outcomes Study: An Application of Methods for Monitoring the Results of Medical Care." *JAMA,* 262(7):925-930, 1989.

[2]Pasternak, D.P. and Harris, J.M. "Does Disease Management Work?" *Physician Executive*, 22:28-31, December 1996.

[3]U.S. Agency for Health Care Policy and Research: Clinical Practice Guideline Number 14: Acute Low Back Pain in Adults. AHCPR Publication 95-0642. Attachment A: Algorithms, 137-141, December 1994.

[4]National Heart, Lung and Blood Institute. National Asthma Education Program Expert Panel (Sheffer, chair) "Guidelines for the Diagnosis and Management of Asthma." *Journal Allergy Clinical Immunology* 33(No.3, part 2):433, 480, 489, 1991.

[5]Harris, J.M., Jr. "Disease Management: New Wine in New Bottles?" *Annuals of Internal Medicine and 1,* 124(9): 838-842, May 1996.

[6]Epstein, R.S. and Sherwood, L.M "From Outcomes Research to Disease Management: A Guide for the Perplexed." *Annuals of Internal Medicine and 1,* 124(9): 832-837, May 1996.

[7]Vollmer, W.M., O'Hollaren, M., Ettinger, K. et al. "Specialty Differences in the Management of Asthma," *Arch Int Med 9,* 157(11):1201-1208, June 1997.

About The Author

Derick P. Pasternak, MD, MBA, FACPE, is a senior quality of care consultant with the Chicago firm of Michael Pine and Associates. He is also a clinical associate professor of medicine at the University of Illinois in Chicago School of Medicine. Dr. Pasternak served as medical director and chief executive officer of Lovelace Health System, an integrated delivery system in Albuquerque, N.M., for 14 years. During his tenure there, he lent heavy support to the implementation of disease management.

Developing And Using Clinical Paths

By Kathleen A. Bower, DNSc, RN, Principal and Co-owner, The Center for Case Management

The impetus to balance the quality-cost equation continues to build. Pressures resulting from patients with increasingly complex situations, rapidly changing payment methodologies and heightened competition have contributed to this momentum. These pressures and changes have stimulated the evolution of new partnerships, tools and operating strategies in many healthcare organizations. The clinical path is one such development, and it has gained increasing acceptance and use since its inception in 1986. In this article, the author describes clinical paths, their development and their application in the clinical setting.

◆ ◆ ◆

The clinical path is a clinical mechanism for achieving better quality and cost outcomes by outlining and sequencing the usual and/or desired care for specific populations of patients. It facilitates communication between and among care providers, sites and the patient/family. Clinical paths have demonstrated their effectiveness in supporting the management of patient care in acute care (e.g., hospitals) and are increasingly being used in a wide variety of care sites, including subacute care, physician offices, home health and ambulatory settings.

Clinical paths create a matrix that profiles interventions on one axis and time (or other indicators of progress such as phases) on the other. Second generation clinical paths, or CareMap™ tools, incorporate usual patient problems, desired clinical outcomes and intermediate goals into the matrix. In a CareMap™ tool, the relationship between quality (as reflected in the clinical outcomes) and cost (as reflected in the length of stay and resource utilization) is clearly evident. (CareMap™ tools are a registered trademark of The Center for Case Management).

Clinical paths are important tools for physicians. (*See Figure 1 on page 204.*) They serve as implements of communication among the physician, other clinicians, the patient and healthcare organizations. By reducing unnecessary variations in care processes and by creating a forum in which care practices can be thoughtfully examined, clinical paths make a major contribution to managing and improving quality. In addition, because they are used by all care providers, they increase the likelihood that needed care is provided in a timely manner. This is essential for quality. It is also important to physicians who operate under clinical and financial risk agreements, as increasing numbers of physicians do.

FIGURE 1: CAREMAP™ TOOLS: CONGRESTIVE HEART FAILURE

	Day 1	Day 1	Day 2	Day 3	Day 4	Day 5	Day 6
	Benchmark Quality Criteria						
Location	**ER 1–4 hours**	**Floor Telemetry or CCU 6–24 hours**	**Floor**	**Floor**	**Floor**	**Floor**	**Floor**
Problem							
1) Alteration in gas exchange/profusion and fluid balance due to decreased cardiac output, excess fluid volume	Reduced pain from admission or pain free Uses pain scale O_2 sat. improved over admission baseline on O_2 therapy	Respirations equal to or less than on admission	O_2 sat = 90 Resp 20–22 Vital signs stable Crackles at lung bases Mild shortness of breath with activity	Does not require O_2 Vital signs stable Crackles at base Respirations 20–22 Mild shortness of breath with activity	Does not require O_2 (O_2 sat. on room air 90%) Vital signs stable Crackles at base Respirations 20–22 Completes activities with no increase in respirations No edema	Can lie in bed at baseline position Chest X-ray clear or at baseline	No dyspnea
2) Potential for shock	No signs/symptoms of shock	No signs/symptoms of shock	No signs/symptoms of shock	No signs/symptoms of shock Normal lab values	No signs/symptoms of shock	No signs/symptoms of shock	No signs/symptoms of shock
3) Potential for consequences of immobility and decreased activity: skin breakdown, DVT	No redness at pressure points No falls	No redness at pressure points No falls	Tolerates chair, washing, eating, and toileting	Has bowel movement Up in room and bathroom with assist	Up ad lib for short periods	Activity increased to level used at home without shortness of breath	Activity increased to level used at home without shortness of breath
4) Alteration in nutritional intake due to nausea and vomiting, labored		No c/o nausea No vomiting Taking liquids as offered	Eating solids Takes in 50% each meal	Taking 50% each meal	Taking 50% each meal Weight 2 lbs from patient's normal baseline	Taking 75% each meal	Taking 75% each meal
5) Potential for arrhythmias due to decreased cardiac output: decreased irritable foci, valve problems, decreased gas exchange	No evidence of life-threatening dysrhythmias	Normal sinus rhythm with benign ectopy	K(WNL) Benign or no arrhythmias	Digoxin level DNL Benign or no arrhythmias	Digoxin level WNL Benign or no arrhythmias	Digoxin level WNL Benign or no arrhythmias	Digoxin level WNL Benign or no arrhythmias
6) Patient/family response to future treatment & hospitalization	Patient/family expressing concerns Following directions of staff	Patient/family expressing concerns Following directions of staff	Patient/family expressing concerns Following directions of staff	States reasons for and cooperates with rest periods Patient begins to assess own knowledge and ability to care for CHF at home	Patient decides whether he/she wants discussion with physician about advanced directives	States plan for 1–2 days postdischarge as to meds., diet, activity, follow-up appointments Expresses reaction to having CHF	Repeats plans States signs and symptoms to notify physician/ER Signs discharge consent
7) Individual problem:							
Staff Tasks							
Assessments/Consults	Vital signs q 15 min Nursing assessments focus on lung sounds, edema, color, skin integrity, jugular vein distention Cardiac monitor Arterial line if needed Swan Ganz Intake & output	Vital signs q 15 min–1 hr Repeat nursing assessments Cardiac monitor Arterial line Swan Ganz Daily weight Intake & output	Vital signs q 4 hrs Repeat nursing assessments D/C cardiac monitor 24 hr D/C arterial and Swan Ganz Daily weight Intake & output	Vital signs q 6 hrs Repeat nursing assessments Daily weight Intake & output	Vital signs q 6 hrs Repeat nursing assessments Daily weight Intake & output Nutrition consult	Vital signs q 6 hrs Repeat nursing assessments Daily weight Intake & output	Vital signs q 6 hrs Repeat nursing assessments Daily weight Intake & output
Specimens/Tests	Consider TSH studies Chest X-ray EKG CPK q 8 hr x 3 ABG if pulse Ox: (range) Lytes, Na, K, Cl, CO_2 Glucose, BUN, Creatinine Digoxin: (range)	B/G	Evaluate for ECHO Lytes, BUN, Creatinine			Chest X-ray Lytes, BUN, Creatinine	
Treatments	O_2 or intubate IV or Heparin lock	O_2 IV or Heparin lock	IV or Heparin lock	DC pulse Ox if stable D/C IV or Heparin lock			
Medications	Evaluate for Digoxin Nitrodrip or paste Diuretics IV Evaluate for antiemetics Evaluate for antiarrhythmics	Evaluate for Digoxin Nitrodrip or paste Diuretics IV Evaluate for pre-load/after-load reducers K supplements Stool softeners	D/C Nitrodrip or paste Diuretics IV or PO K supplements Stool softeners Evaluate for nicotine patch	Change to PO Digoxin PO diuretics K supplements Stool softeners Nicotine patch if consent	PO diuretics K supplement Stool softeners Nicotine patch if consent	PO diuretics K supplement Stool softeners Nicotine patch if consent	PO diuretics K supplement Stool softeners Nicotine patch if consent
Nutrition	None	Clear liquids	Cardiac, low-salt diet	Cardiac, low-salt diet	Cardiac, low-salt diet	Cardiac, low salt-diet	
Safety Activity	Commode Bedrest with head elevated Reposition patient q 2 hrs Bedrails up Call light available	Commode Bedrest with head elevated Dangle Reposition patient q 2 hrs Enforce rest periods Bedrails up Call light available	Commode Enforce rest periods Chair with assist 1/2 hr with feet elevated Bedrails up Call light available	Bathroom privileges Chair x 3 Bedrails up Call light available	Ambulate in hall x 2 Up ad lib between rest periods Bedrails up Call light available	Encourage ADLs that approximate activities at home Bedrails up Call light available	Encourage ADLs that approximate activities at home Bedrails up Call light available
Teaching	Explain procedures Teach chest pain scale and importance of reporting	Explain course, need for energy conservation Orient to unit and routine	Clarify CHF Dx and future teaching needs Orient to unit and routine Schedule rest periods Begin medication teaching	Importance of weighing self every day Provide smoking cessation information Review energy conservation schedule	Cardiac rehab level as indicated by consult Provide smoking cessation support Dietary teaching	Review CHF education material with patient	Reinforce CHF teaching
Transfer/Discharge Coordination	Assess home situation: notify significant other If no arrhythmias or chest pain, transfer to floor Otherwise transfer to ICU	Screen for discharge needs Transfer to floor	Consider Home Health Care referral		Evaluate needs for diet and anti-smoking classes Physician offers discussion opportunities for advanced directives	Appointment and arrangement for follow-up care with Home Health Care nurses Contact VNA	Reinforce follow-up appointments

Source: The Center for Case Management, South Natick, MA. CareMap is a registered trademark of the Center for Case Management.

Developing Clinical Paths

Clinical paths are developed for specific patient populations. The patient populations can be defined by diagnosis (e.g., myocardial infarction), procedure (e.g., total hip replacement) or condition (e.g., failure to wean from the ventilator or neutropenia). Selecting populations for clinical path development is based on an examination of the usual mix of patients served by the physicians and the system. Patients who represent the high volume and high interest populations are most often selected initially. Earlier in the history of clinical path technology, high cost and high risk were also cited as desired case types for clinical path development. Ongoing experience suggests that, rather than high cost case types, case types demonstrating high variability in costs should be selected. This is because high cost and high risk patient populations often present with high individual variability in their care needs as a result of multiple pathophysiology and socioeconomic issues.

The most effective clinical paths are developed by multidisciplinary teams representing the disciplines and departments usually involved in the care of the identified patients. In the case of myocardial infarction patients, for example, physicians, nurses, respiratory therapists, pharmacists, discharge planners and others form the team that writes the clinical path content. In addition, the team should represent the various sites across the episode in which patient care will be provided. Again, using myocardial infarction patients as an example, the team would, ideally, represent emergency transport, the emergency department, ICU/CCU, step down, cardiac rehabilitation, physician office staff and home health.

Team meetings should be scheduled to be as convenient for the team members as possible. In addition, the team needs an identified leader and a facilitator to enhance its efficiency. The leader and facilitator organize details between meetings and enable the team to focus directly on writing the content. They also keep the team moving and assist members in finding ways to resolve disagreements.

Defining the patient population is an important first step in clinical path content development. When the population is defined too broadly (using "cerebral vascular accident"—or CVA—as the identified patient group, for example), the clinical path is difficult to write and becomes either too general to be useful in the management of patient care or too narrow, generating numerous variances from the path. Alternatively, the patient population can be defined too narrowly, leading to the need to develop multiple clinical paths for similar groups of patients. The authoring team translates this discussion into inclusion (and/or exclusion) criteria. This process focuses all the team members on the same profile for the patient population and, ultimately, makes the process of writing content go more smoothly. It also assists all clinicians who will use the path to determine whether the individual patient at hand matches the profile of the patient for whom the path was written.

As the writing process progresses, the team integrates information about current practices and care protocols, preferred practice patterns, clinical practice guidelines, "best practice" patterns and clinical research findings into the discussion. The resulting clinical path summarizes the essentials within a clinical practice guideline in a timeline format that incorporates interdisciplinary documentation. This format increases the likelihood that guidelines will be consistently applied to patient care. Some clinical paths have algorithms embedded in them. In other situations, such as the diagnostic process, algorithms lead to the identification of the case type and a clinical path then outlines the care involved with that population.

It may be useful for the authoring team to review clinical paths from other organizations. However, using a clinical path developed by an external organization without seriously considering internal systems and issues can lead to unrealistic content that will not be used as a care management tool. The output of clinical path content is important but the process of negotiation and discussion that leads to the content is equally (and sometimes more) important. The final product must strike a balance between current practice and best practice that is realistic, yet moves practice forward. For example, clinical path content may be based on availability of physical therapy seven days a week, which may not be currently available; this may have an effect on the expected length of stay for orthopedic patients. In addition, the team should consider quality and/or utilization indicators for the case type under development. Including these indicators in the clinical path provides an efficient way to collect data about them and also educates a wide variety of staff about these issues.

Clinical paths are always "works in progress." They need to be revisited, as do care practices, at least annually, to ensure the most current information is available to clinicians. As a result, obsessing over many of the details will not be productive, although the authoring team should do a thorough job in writing content. Instead, the clinical path should be a dynamic learning tool that allows the team to hypothesize about and test different approaches to caring for a population of patients. In addition, during the authoring process, many excellent and creative ideas about improving care emerge, some of which will not be immediately applicable to the current clinical path. Those ideas should be captured and maintained on a list that is revisited and prioritized with the quality improvement staff or other staff at a later stage of the writing.

Participation in a clinical path authoring session is exciting. The process of writing a clinical path is one of exploration, discussion and negotiation with a great deal of discovery about how care is provided by different staff and in various areas. Team members bring diverse experiences and knowledge, making the ensuing discussions vigorous. As a result, practice changes are often added before the clinical path content is completed. Questions can send the team to the literature to seek research findings. Ultimately, patients and clinical staff alike benefit from clinical path development.

When writing clinical path content, the team should take into consideration the entire episode of care for the identified patient population. Using total hip replacements as an example, the clinical path ideally will outline interventions needed pre-, intra-, and post-hospitalization. This is particularly important as increasing numbers of patients are same day admissions and as pressure builds to shorten lengths of stay. An experienced, facilitated team can often draft a clinical path for straightforward cases in about three to four hours. For instance, the pre-hospital phase of the total hip replacement clinical path developed at Anne Arundel Medical Center in Annapolis, MD., reflects the need to orient and educate patients, encouraging them to:

- Become participants in their care processes;
- Begin upper-body exercises and gait training;
- Assess whether extended care is likely to be needed after hospitalization (and if so, to make the necessary arrangements for it); and,
- Complete preoperative testing and assessments.

Several considerations will make the clinical path more useful to all clinicians. For physicians, the development of order sets that parallel clinical path content will make their work more efficient while maintaining their control of patient care. Although somewhat controversial, clinical paths designed to be included as a key component of patient documentation are useful and supply very clear information about the patient's status and previous course. This improvement markedly reduces documentation time for nurses and other clinicians. In addition, patient education materials often complement the clinical path, increasing the standardization of content provided to patients and their families and equipping them to manage their care more independently.

Physician involvement. The active participation of physicians in writing, using and analyzing the results of clinical paths is vital to the success of the process. The exact nature of physician involvement in writing clinical paths varies, usually as a result of physician preference and availability. Some physicians prefer to be involved in each stage of clinical path development and participate in all related discussions. Others prefer to participate in the first meeting where the case type is clearly defined and the care patterns are broadly defined. They then review and revise the details developed by the team. Although the first option is more time consuming, it leads to important interdisciplinary discussions about the most effective and efficient ways to provide care to the patients.

As Melum Zander notes, "Clinical paths reflect the practice patterns of the clinicians who develop them. Practice patterns are extremely important to clinicians and are deeply rooted in knowledge, algorithms, culture, tradition, ethics, available resources, preferences, intuition, research, and hope." They can also reflect standards of care, practice guidelines, clinical algorithms and other established work. The clinical path format and process is an important link to all of these tools because it makes the information available to caregivers *as they are interacting with patients*. Thus, the caregiver becomes a powerful force in patient care management.

In many settings, a number of physicians provide care to similar groups of patients. In these cases, the physicians may decide to collaborate on writing a clinical path for the diagnoses they share. This may be particularly appropriate within a partnership or group practice. Conversely, physician groups may elect a colleague to represent them during authoring sessions. In this scenario, the representative physician must actually be a conduit of information and communication between the

How Clinical Paths Affect Physician Practice

1. Patients express higher levels of satisfaction.
2. Clinical paths increase the likelihood that patients will receive the care desired no matter where they are in the institution or whether the nurse for that shift is full time or part time. Clinical paths keep all other providers "in sync" with the physician's plan of care.
3. The physician retains control over patient care. Activities that currently require a physician's order continue to do so. Physicians are actively involved in the development of clinical paths, reflecting the care they have determined their patients need.
4. Clinical paths facilitate the resolution of system issues that are often annoying and/or frustrating to the physician.
5. Physician's time requirements are minimal.
6. Clinical paths decrease the number of phone calls to the physician's office because the team has a clearer picture of the plan of care and because utilization management staff have better information about the patient and the plan of care.
7. Clinical paths allow research findings to be readily incorporated into practice.
8. In academic settings, clinical paths convey the attending physicians' care preferences to the resident staff concretely, consistently and efficiently.
9. Communication between the physician, the nursing staff and other members of the patient care team is enhanced. Collegiality is strengthened.
10. In some cases, the greater organizational efficiency of clinical paths can enhance the physicians' revenue, such as by reducing lost operating room time.
11. Clinical paths are patient focused quality improvement processes leading to improvements in the systems and processes of care that create benefits and efficiencies for physicians and other staff as well.
12. In a competitive market, clinical paths provide a system to effectively manage care and data to demonstrate that efficiency to third-party payers and others.

team and his or her peers. Without this link, acceptance of the path content by the larger physician group is likely to be more difficult. Alternatively, clinical paths can be customized to the practice patterns of individual physicians, creating more than one clinical path for a topic. Some organizations list all of the physicians who have adopted the content on the finalized clinical path. The important consideration is to reflect physicians' desired practice preferences so that the organization's support systems can be more effectively synchronized with them.

Clinical Paths in Practice

Once written, clinical paths are made available to the clinicians involved in direct care of the patients. They are guidelines for what care is needed and when. In addition, they provide sign posts or road maps for assessing the status of individual patients. The clinical path synchronizes the activities of every member of the patient care team so they occur at the most effective time and location. Mapping these activities on a clinical path enhances the probability that the required care will be provided on a timely basis, minimizing delays and cancellations.

Using clinical paths is a dynamic process; they become a blueprint or template for the care of individual patients. One physician likened clinical paths to the pilot's preflight checklist, a process designed to ensure that nothing is overlooked. Clinical paths are initiated as early in the patient's care as possible. They may be started in the physician's office or in the pre-admission testing area for elective admissions. They may also be used for patients who are managed in the ambulatory setting or through home health.

Clinical paths are never a substitute for excellence in clinical and critical thinking. Although they can provide suggestions and reminders, it is the clinician's knowledge and relationship with the patient/family that directs care. Clinical paths must always be a support and never a mandate. This means that the clinical path is tailored to fit the needs of an individual patient based on initial and ongoing assessments.

The clinical path becomes the core of a system designed to more effectively coordinate patient care. Nurses and other team members use clinical paths as a checkpoint, continually evaluating where the patient is along the trajectory. The clinical path becomes the cornerstone for intershift nursing reports and team communications such as discharge planning rounds, ensuring that all care providers are familiar with the plan and the patient's current status. This is particularly valuable in an age in which increasing numbers of healthcare employees work part time or per diem (part-time nurses, for example, or weekend physical therapists). It can also be an excellent reference for physicians who are providing coverage to colleagues' patients on weekends or during vacations. The clinical path provides a quick reference to any care provider regarding the treatment and its current status *vis* a *vis* the patient.

Clinical paths provide a vehicle for creating partnerships between clinicians and patients/families. Depending on their comfort level, clinicians share clinical paths verbally and/or visually with patients and their families. Some organizations develop "patient language" clinical paths to provide to patients and their families. Patients are less anxious when they know in advance what to expect at each stage of treatment. Initiating communication with patients and enlisting their participation in the pre-admission stage is generally easier than during their hospital stay, when they may be dealing with distractions such as postoperative pain. For example, when a mother anticipates a three-day hospital stay to be followed by a restriction on heavy lifting for an additional week, she can make advance arrangements for help with her two small children. This reduces the crisis modality that commonly surfaces upon patient transfer or discharge. As a result, patients feel adequately informed, are more satisfied and experience fewer feelings of "being pushed out."

Variances from Clinical Paths

Flexibility is the key in using clinical paths; they are guidelines and maps, not inflexible dictates for care. Because clinical paths reflect the care needed by most but not all patients within a population, situations arise in which there are variances from the anticipated plan. Deviations from a clinical path are to be expected and are a cueing mechanism. Variances can be positive (the congestive heart failure patient who is discharged a day earlier than expected) or negative (the myocardial infarction patient who remains in CCU an extra day). Many variances reflect very necessary adjustments to the plan in response to clinical judgment about the patient's responses to treatment or his or her condition. Some variances illustrate bottlenecks or weak points in the system that need to be retooled to enhance the coordination of patient care.

Variances and other data (such as cost per case, etc.) must be assessed in light of clinical outcomes. Clinical outcomes are the final arbiter of whether clinical practice has been effective and efficient. Variance and other case type data must be assessed in conjunction with mortality, morbidity, readmissions, patient satisfaction, functionality, return to work, etc. This data may not be immediately available but will ultimately be needed to assure clinicians, managers and administrators that more aggressive management of care processes results in improved patient status.

Variance data are used most effectively as a means of educating clinicians and enabling them to make considered changes in their practice based on emerging trends and the results of that care. Variance data are also an educational tool for managers and administrators, highlighting internal systems that need to be redesigned to make care processes more efficient and effective. The physicians and the clinical path development team work closely together to determine whether changes are needed in the clinical path itself or whether other changes are required.

Addressing Variances: Two phases

Variance is addressed in two phases: Concurrently for individual patients and retrospectively for aggregate groups of patients. Concurrently, clinicians identify variances as they interact with the patient. This facilitates immediate problem solving and reduces unnecessary delays in care. Retrospectively, individual patient variances are aggregated by case type and then analyzed for patterns and trends. The most significant patterns and trends are incorporated into the organization's quality improvement process.

For example, clinicians on the myocardial infarction team may discover that they need to cue orders for exercise tolerance tests on day two of a patient's stay to ensure the test is done in a timely manner. Similarly, variance data from the pediatric asthma clinical path may lead the team to provide family members with instructions about home respiratory treatments a day earlier than originally profiled.

Organizational involvement stems from the need to resolve issues that are identified across case types and areas. In one hospital, delays in obtaining laboratory test results may be identified in the aggregate variance patterns. Here, the most efficient approach is to deal with the generic problem. Administrative staff become involved when resources must be allocated to extend the available departments or services to meet clinical and financial goals. Administrative staff are also essential when devising strategies for transitioning patients from acute care to other levels such as subacute, long term and/or home healthcare. In some situations, formal agreements are needed to make this more efficient and effective. Variance data demonstrate the quality and cost impact of these situations and encourage reasoned decision making.

Analyzing variance data is essential to using a clinical path system effectively. It is, in essence, the clinical application of the continuous quality improvement process. In the pre-computer era, however, it was necessary to prioritize the components of the clinical path that will be subjected to retrospective, aggregate analysis. Attempting to analyze variances from all of the elements of a clinical path was overwhelming and bring the entire process to a halt. Prioritization was accomplished by asking the authoring team to identify a limited number of key elements within the clinical path that are important indicators or mileposts. In this scenario, only variances from those key elements are aggregated and then analyzed by the team.

Variance data often confirm the observations and long-held suspicions of clinicians and managers. The difference is that, by using clinical paths and other quality improvement tools, the suspicions are quantified and there is, implicitly or explicitly, an institutional commitment and mechanism to address them. At times, variance data can only suggest areas where additional information is needed. For example, a variance trend may be observed but identifying why it is occurring requires more data and analysis. This process then folds into the quality improvement process, using many CQI techniques and strategies.

Clinical Paths and Their Effects

Clinical paths have demonstrated their effectiveness in strengthening the cost-quality link both quantitatively and qualitatively. Ongoing measurement and evaluation of the clinical path process and outcomes is important as a continuous learning vehicle. It is also essential to provide feedback related to the findings and results of clinical paths to physicians and other staff. Feedback gives the process credibility. It also enhances participation in the quality improvement process.

Implementation of a clinical path system has been consistently associated with reduced length of stay and cost per case. For example, Providence Medical Center, in Portland, Oreg., reduced average length of stay by more than four days and increased total charges for total joint replacement patients by $1.8 million.

Baystate Medical Center reported several pertinent findings in a study of the use of a stroke clinical path. Using a control group of patients not on a clinical path and a study group on a clinical path, there was a highly statistically significant reduction in length of stay during the first year the clinical path was in use. That decrease was reported to have statistically exceeded the expected natural decline in length of stay. In addition, after controlling for length of stay, charges for patients who were not on the clinical path varied much more than the charges of the pathway patients. The authors also noted that "there were fewer complications, less steroid usage, fewer transfusions and lower readmission rates for patients who has the critical pathway tools applied."

In an unpublished report, St. Luke's Hospital in Chesterfield, Mo., demonstrated a sustained decrease in average charges and length of stay for clinical pathway patients. This was the result of changes in a number of case types, including COPD, pneumonia, myocardial infarction, coronary artery bypass graft, congestive heart failure and major joint replacement.

These trends reflect the enhanced coordination and communication that stem from using clinical paths. As a tool, they keep all clinicians, departments and sites "tuned in" to the patient's progress while allowing for immediate action as variances are identified. Day-to-day variability is reduced as all caregivers follow an agreed-upon checklist of activities. Lengths of stay drop and patient satisfaction levels increase. At Anne Arundel Medical Center, for example, patient outcome scores improved 100% in the two years following implementation of the clinical path for total hip replacement. Patients in the 80 to 85 year age group showed the most improvement.

At the institutional level, clinical paths provide a vehicle for efficiently identifying systems issues that interfere with, rather than support, effective patient care. Teamwork becomes the organizational norm, and staff better understand clinical resource management—the allocation of staff work processes, policies and organizational resources needed to produce clinical services. As these issues are addressed, care becomes more efficient for patients and less frustrating for physicians and other clinicians.

By including desired clinical outcomes on the clinical path and expanding them to a CareMap™ tool, the quality component is also included the process. This assures physicians and other clinicians that patients are not being "rushed through the system" and discharged before they have reached an appropriate clinical status. Physicians are more satisfied because care progresses smoothly and patient outcomes improve. Nurses feel their capabilities are better utilized, and they feel ownership of the care process. Patients enter the healthcare delivery process with realistic expectations for their treatment and a degree of personal responsibility for its outcome.

Clinical Paths as a Tool in the Future

The healthcare environment is likely to continue evolving at the same (or even increased) pace. Cost will be a driving force for the foreseeable future. Careful attention to both the quality and cost of care by clinicians and others, along with well crafted integration of providers and sites within the continuum will be essential. Ongoing development and evolution of the technique also will be needed to ensure clinical paths maintain their effectiveness as a care management tool. Although many clinical paths are currently site specific (to the acute care environment, for example) the future will demand clinical paths that represent the entire episode of care. These clinical paths will outline the care provided in the many sites from onset of the episode until conclusion. As such, they may begin in the physician's office and continue through acute care, subacute and/or rehabilitation care, into home care. Clinical paths will be one component of the glue that holds clinically integrated delivery systems together in a functional way.

The influence of managed care is rapidly expanding into the ambulatory area and other settings, too. While most clinical paths are in the acute care area, it is realistic to predict their development will increase in the ambulatory setting (including physician office practices), home health, rehabilitation and the subacute setting as well.

It is likely that many of the clinical paths of the future will deal with patient care exclusively in the ambulatory or community setting, including those patient populations who are never admitted to the inpatient area.

Another influence on the healthcare environment of the future is the dramatic growth in the information technology arena. This exciting development will facilitate and augment many aspects of the clinical path system. Data that support writing clinical path content, particularly that related to current practice, will be increasingly available in an automated world. Likewise, automation will make the process of documenting care via a clinical path much more streamlined. This, in turn, will make the variance documentation process easier. Automation is likely to have one of its most dramatic effects on aggregating variance data, currently a labor intensive, retrospective process. Perhaps the most exciting contribution of automation will be its ability to link sites within an integrated delivery system. This will allow information to be transported without transporting paper or people. Clinical paths are likely to be one of the components of that integrated system.

Clinical paths are effective tools for coordinating patient care. They emphasize quality while simultaneously attending to length of stay and resource utilization. The process of writing clinical paths provides a forum for interdisciplinary planning and problem solving, reflecting the highly interdependent nature of today's patient care environment. In addition, they can bring new research and clinical findings to bear on patient care in an efficient way.

Clinical paths are only one approach to the coordination and management of patient care. They will always need to be an adjunct to the expertise and critical thinking of the clinicians who use them in practice.

◆ ◆ ◆

References

Zander, K. Melum, M, and M. Sinioris, eds."Clinical Pathways." *Total Quality Management: The Health Care Pioneers.* Chicago: American Hospital Publishing Inc., 1992.

Selbovitz, L. Pleet, S., Scott, S., Wittner, D., et al. "Baystate Medical Center Stroke Clinical Pathway." *Measuring and Managing Health Care Quality*, 323-340, August 1995.

Miller, D., and Durbin, S. "Improving Patient Recover Following Total Joint Replacement." *The Quality Letter for Healthcare Leaders*, 22-26, February, 1992.

About the Author

Kathleen A. Bower, DNSc, RN, is a principal and co-owner of The Center for Case Management, South Natick, Mass.

A Primer on Statistical Tools and Concepts

by Vahé A. Kazandjian, PhD, MPH

"Statistics." Even the simple word can strike fear to a grown physician's heart. This article makes statistical concepts understandable and applicable through metaphor and example. It explains:

- *The importance of variation (or the lack of it);*
- *How to analyze distribution as an aspect of variation;*
- *How to apply an analysis of variation to healthcare; and*
- *How to use the results of this analysis.*

◆ ◆ ◆

Variation in the use of health services has been documented for centuries. Perhaps the most provocative statement was by a physician to Britain's King's College Hospital and one of the honorary secretaries of the Statistical Society who, in 1856, reported that "annual per capita rates for hospitalization in King's Hospital varied from 325 per 1,000 population in the parish of St. Mary-Le-Strand to 1 per 1,000 in the District of Marylebone." Dr. William A. Guy concluded that charitable medical care was being consumed in such parishes as St. Mary-Le-Strand by an "increasing class of working men in receipt of good wages who are in the habit of applying to hospitals as a matter of course, even for trifling attacks of illness, to say nothing of those which sometimes follow immediately on expensive acts of self-indulgence."[1]

One may be surprised at the lack of variation between today's definition and interpretation of regional differences in the utilization of health services and the one presented by Dr. Guy.

The rediscovery of variation analysis was popularized by a number of health services researchers several decades ago, according to Wennberg, Chassin, Roos. The impetus behind these studies was to investigate the possibility of demonstrating that cost, utilization and appropriateness of healthcare services are related in a quantifiable way. Today, the analysis of variation in utilization rates is an integral part of initial efforts to identify the types of services that may be rendered "much differently" than in other hospitals, integrated systems or within larger geographic areas.

But the interest of the healthcare field has evolved further. Increasingly, healthcare organizations are embracing the principles and methodologies of W. Edwards Deming, Joseph Juran, Kaoru Ishikawa and other quality management visionaries. Among these organizations, there is a growing realization that understanding variation should not be limited to a macro level analysis, but should become part of a hospital's ongoing internal performance assessment, evaluation, improvement and monitoring activities. There seems little debate, albeit much more confusion, about the need to continuously measure, evaluate and improve performance.

The purpose of this chapter is to provide healthcare leaders with a systematic and ongoing method for:

- Understanding variation;
- Explaining its causes; and
- Instituting a plan for monitoring and minimizing variation.

The careful application of this method will increase knowledge and have a positive effect on the quality of patient care.

Understanding Performance and Variation

At the center of the difference between industrial models and healthcare initiatives is the definition of "performance." Indeed, the term "quality assurance" has disappeared from the healthcare lexicon. From the Joint Commission for the Accreditation of Healthcare Organizations (JCAHO) to sole community hospitals, performance has replaced "QA." The reason is that providers and recipients of care have come to realize that it is not only important to do what is thought appropriate but to factually ascertain the impact of actions. Hence the increasing popularity of "outcomes research," or impact analysis. Was the performance of an organization appropriate after financial, utilization and clinical dimensions have been balanced? Is it possible that variation across institutions denotes difference in utilization without connoting differences in quality or in value?

That variation exists is an observation. As such, there is nothing "good" or "bad" about variation. In fact, variation is the "stuff of statistics." In every observation we make about a group (e.g., people or events), we will see variation. Just as two groups of patients are not clinically exactly the same, one should expect that the healthcare needs of these two groups will also be variable. Thus the quantification of variation is an objective method of measurement.

What makes variation undesirable is its adverse effect on the systematic flow of a well-defined process. The key word is systematic. When a product is produced and delivered through a "system," that systematic process should be predictable. Variation hits at the heart of predictability. A highly variable process reduces predictability and, therefore, has an impact on evaluation, forecasting and strategic planning. That is why the analysis of variation becomes crucial.

What Is Important in Analyzing Variation?

The opposite of variation is consistency. Therefore, the analysis of variation is the assessment (measurement/quantification) and the evaluation (decision making/

qualification) of how an observation differs from other observations. But, what other observations? Should these observations be an institution's own past experiences or profile (monitoring), or that of comparable peer groups (reference analysis)?

The answer is: Both. If data are available from external sources about comparable groups' performance profiles, the comparative analysis will be much more robust (i.e., somewhat insensitive to error). However, at the least, a hospital should be able to retrospectively trace its previous performance profile, as well as prospectively follow up on its progress. There are a few statistical tools and concepts to assist in that search, including:

Trend analysis. How can the various points in time be graphically displayed? (It's important to know, because the best way to predict your future is to know your past.) Line charts are more than adequate for such analysis.

Limits of acceptability. What are these limits? Are they defined statistically? Based on experience? Defined according to societal norms? The statistical limits of acceptability are often depicted in a control chart. Both tools will be presented later in this section.

What Is a Distribution?

Consider shooting at a target once with a shotgun and another time with a rifle. The shotgun will fire a large number of pellets, all of which will, hopefully, be distributed around the target. Thus, we have a distribution of the outcomes of that process. In contrast, the rifle ammunition contains only one slug, which will hit the target at only one point. There is no distribution of outcomes when the rifle is used.

Now consider the scenario when two shotguns are tested for their hit capability "goodness." Figure 1 below shows the distribution of both shotgun pellets around

FIGURE 1: DISTRIBUTION OF TWO SEPARATE SHOTGUNS' PELLETS AROUND THE BULL'S EYE

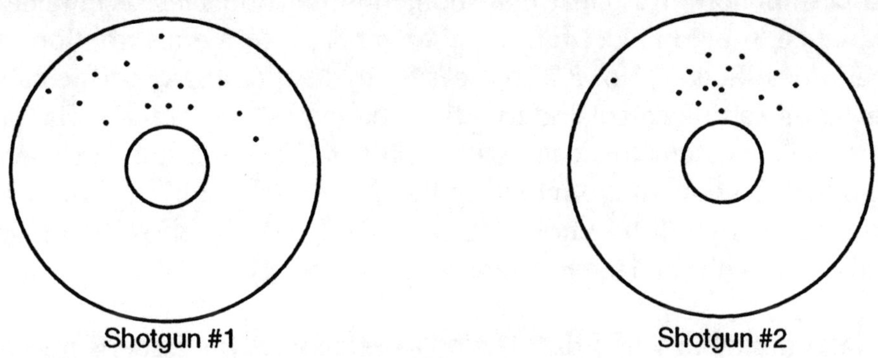

Note: 15 pellets in each round of ammunition. Same person shooting the two shotguns. Same ammunition.

Kazandjian, 1992

the target. From a common sense viewpoint, it seems quite obvious that shotgun #1 hits more of the target, although it seems less accurate than shotgun #2. If the object of the exercise were to hit the target, one would probably choose shotgun #1. How does the "common sense approach" translate into more sophisticated statistical tools and reasoning?

The 15 pellets hit the target according to a certain distribution. One may visualize the distribution as a normal bell-shaped curve (*See Figure 2 below*). Assuming that the "acceptable" area for the distribution is the target itself, any pellets that totally missed the target would be the statistical outliers and are described as falling in the outlier zone.

FIGURE 2: DECISION MAKING ABOUT THE "BETTER" SHOTGUN

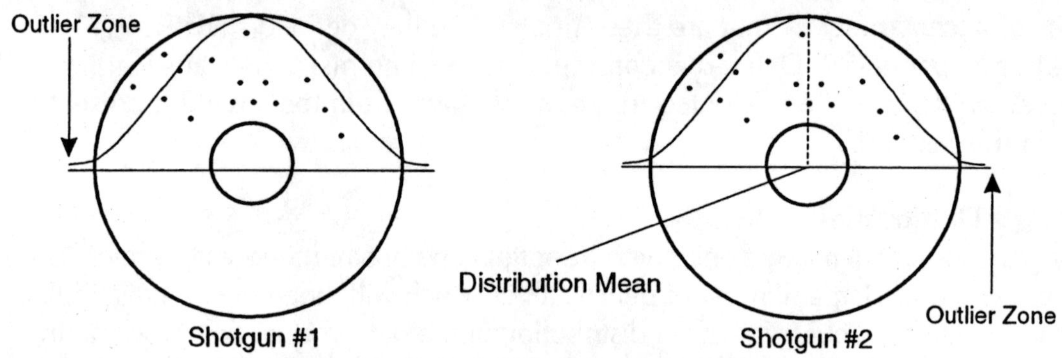

Decision-Making Criteria

Shotgun #1	Shotgun #2
Observation: Pellets widely spread .. High variation distribution .. Large SD value	Observation: Pellets Narrowly distributed .. Low variation distribution .. Small SD value
Objective: Hitting the target	Objective: Hitting the target

Decision: Shotgun #1 is less accurate but maximizes the chance of hitting the target – therefore choose Shotgun #1

Kazandjian, 1992

Analyzing a Distribution. It is clear that shotgun No.1 shoots less accurately. In statistical parlance, shotgun No.1 has a higher variation in the distribution of its outcome than does shotgun No. 2. To measure that variation, a statistic called standard deviation can be calculated to reflect the magnitude of the variation. Because most pocket calculators can compute the value of the standard deviation, it is not important to know the formula nor the theory behind it. It should suffice to know that: When two distributions are compared, the one showing the larger variation is the one with the larger standard deviation.

Deciding on the desirability of a distribution's outcomes. The issue is not that there is variation, but how much of it is appropriate and acceptable. In the case of the two shotguns, it is clear that the one with a higher distribution of pellets (high variation in outcome) is the more desirable. In the analysis of healthcare utiliza-

variation in outcome) is the more desirable. In the analysis of healthcare utilization and outcomes, the decision is often to opt for the methods and processes that minimize variation.

The above example is presented not only to describe the concepts of variation and decisionmaking but to also stress that high variation is not always undesirable. Depending on the nature of the question, decision making about the variation may differ.

The Analysis of Variation in Healthcare

It is commonly accepted that variation among patients and their health conditions (hence, need for care) is expected. However, variation in the delivery of health services is often undesirable. The reason for the pursuit of uniformity stems from the belief that the science of medicine should be quantifiable, predictable and always improving, like any other scientific discipline. It is, therefore, the science and not the art of medicine that any analysis of variation is aimed at documenting and studying.

The scientific approach to variation analysis is aimed at answering two questions:

- Where is our institution compared to *xxx*? and
- Why is our institution where it is?

Where is our Institution Compared to xxx?

To answer this question, one needs a reference point to compare performances. The availability of comparative data—regional or national—is essential for objective position assessment. For example, if Anywhere Hospital knows its cesarean section rate, the regional or national average rate for hospitals within Anywhere Hospital's peer group becomes the needed reference point.

The commonly used reference point is the mean outcome rate. (*See Figure 3 on page 220.*) For purposes of this discussion, the mean is assumed to be identical to the distribution average. Thus, the rate of cesarean sections at Anywhere Hospital can be:

- Identical to the mean,
- Higher than the mean, or
- Lower than the mean.

If Anywhere Hospital's CEO decides to assess the hospital's cesarean section rate compared with other hospitals' rates, he or she may use Anywhere's rate relative to the mean as a "yardstick for quality."

This is the wrong approach. What the chief may be missing is the fact that, over time, there will be differences (variation) between Anywhere's rate and the mean of the reference distribution (regional or national). Therefore, the chief executive should continuously monitor the position of Anywhere's cesarean section rates over time and determine its profile. In order to do that, the CEO should refresh his

FIGURE 3:

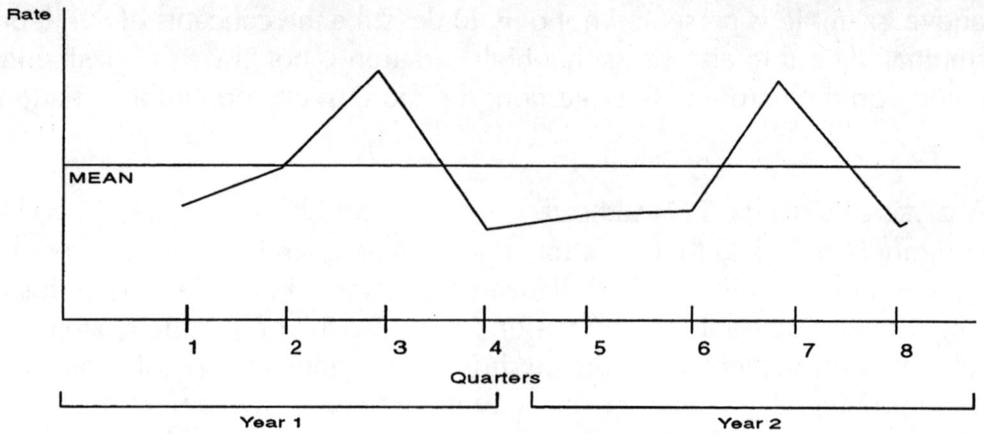

Note: The above line chart suggests a cyclical pattern of increase over two years.

Kazandjian, 1992

or her memory about the three most important aspects of distribution.

1. Anywhere's rate may be outside a statistical range. The range, called a confidence interval, implies the range within which Anywhere's rate, although not exactly at the mean of the distribution, is not different from the majority of other hospital's rates. If the rate is outside that statistical range, Anywhere will be an outlier hospital (*See Figure 4 below*). This is the now well-known logic behind HCFA's annual *Medicare Mortality Report*.

FIGURE 4:

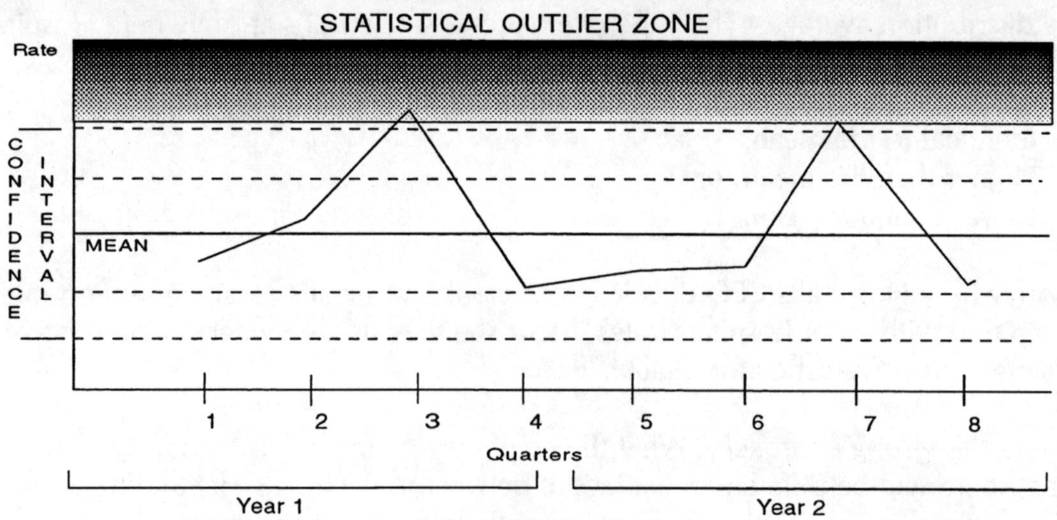

Note: The reference point mean is the average cesarean section rate among Anywhere General Hospital's national peer group.

Kazandjian, 1992

2. Anywhere's rate may be within the statistical range. In this case Anywhere Hospital will be a statistical inlier.

3. Anywhere's rate may be identical to the mean. If, time after time, Anywhere's rate is identical to the distribution's mean, the profile could be false. The concept is simple: It is practically impossible for a hospital's rate to longitudinally (time after time) be exactly the same as the reference point. There should be natural variation.

Why is Our Hospital Where It is?

Finding the answer to this question necessitates an analysis of the process of care. For example, the CEO should ask for a clinical, administrative and patient characteristic analysis to understand why the cesarean section rate is higher or lower than the reference point. It is imperative that, during this search, no subjective attribution be made to the high or low rate, since neither magnitude may reliably represent "good" or "not so good" care. (*See Figure 5 below.*)

FIGURE 5: THE STEP-WISE DIAGNOSTIC TOOL FOR DEALING WITH VARIATION

A. **Position Analysis**
("Where are we compared with <u>xxx</u>?")
- Comparative temporal analysis
- Comparison to my own performance over time
- Comparison to a reference/peer group over time
- Understanding the basics of variation analysis

B. **Reason Analysis** ("Why are we there?")
- Clinical
- Administrative
- Patient characteristics (*e.g.,* preferences)
- Provider characteristics (*e.g.,* job satisfaction)
- System characteristics (*e.g.,* incentives/ disincentives

C. **Objectives Analysis**
("Where do we want to be?")
- Performance targets
- Strategic quality management plan and positioning
- Societal expectations

D. **Trajectory Analysis**
("What path have our efforts taken?")
- Middle-of-trajectory measurement (*eg,* frequent evaluation of current efforts)
- Revisiting previous steps as better understanding accumulates

©1992, Kazandjian

Next Steps

When the above two questions have been addressed and answered, the CEO needs to concentrate on three additional questions.

- Where do we want to be?
- What have we done to pursue these objectives?
- What has been accomplished?

These three questions pertain to the analysis of objectives and trajectory. It is not the purpose of this chapter to discuss the underpinnings of these two inquiries. Once variation analysis has been conducted and understood, however, it should be placed within the hospital's strategic quality management plan. If not, variation analysis remains an esoteric exercise destined to shed more shadows on the already dim area of hospital continuous performance analysis.

The ultimate test of goodness is the impact analysis. Because it is difficult to accept that any science-based discipline can apply the seemingly appropriate protocols and approaches to issues management (i.e., treating a disease; or population screening for early detection of asymptomatic maladies) and yet be unable to show an attributable impact upon the health of the individual or that of the community, it is necessary to do an impact analysis. Without such a "proof of goodness" the analysis of variation will not help providers demonstrate accountability to society through improvements in cost, quality and access.

There is nothing inherently good or bad about variation. When the performance of a group of hospitals or people is contrasted and analyzed, some are likely to be within the "expected" range, others are not. This is the nature of distributions. What is important is the interpretation of the variation. The interpretation of variation (differences in performance) can be performed using statistical techniques, subjective thresholds, or arbitrary cut-off points. No matter what the approach, one should not lose sight of the fact that an outlier may be a sub-par performer as well as an innovator.

. . . After all, Galileo, Einstein, Pasteur and, perhaps, Deming were all outliers in their thinking.

◆ ◆ ◆

Reference

[1]Barnes, B.A. "Population-Based Small Unit Analysis of Health Care" *Regional Variations in Hospital Use*. Rothberg (editor), Lexington Books, page 188, 1982.

ABOUT THE AUTHOR

Vahé A. Kazandjian, PhD, MPH, is president of The Center For Performance Sciences Inc. in Lutherville, Maryland. Performance Sciences conducts research and provides consulting services on quality of care evaluation and health informatics. Dr. Kazandjian is also vice president for research of the Maryland Hospital Association, Inc.; and an adjunct associate professor at the School of Public Health, Johns Hopkins University, Baltimore.

HEDIS Measures and the Physician

By Craig P. Tanio, MD, MBA

There are a great number of formal models and systems that measure the quality of managed care. The most widely known and used of these systems is HEDIS—the Health Plan Employer Data and Information Set. HEDIS is a set of performance measures designed to evaluate managed care organizations or health plans that has been developed by the National Committee for Quality Assurance (NCQA). More than 300 health plans are currently producing some of the HEDIS statistics, which are used to compare plans to each other.

◆ ◆ ◆

Measurements such as HEDIS are quite useful for physicians as they strive to become adept not only with providing high quality care to each patient, but to care for an entire population of patients. A different mindset and structures are necessary to manage a population, because doing so shifts emphasis from care of sick patients to preventive care, including education, facilitating patient behavioral changes, early detection and screening and other preventive services. Physicians need to become proficient at working within a system of care and utilizing other members of the healthcare team in delivering care. Different structures are needed to measure success in this system. Physicians cannot judge success on a one-patient-at-a-time basis, but require measures on the outcomes of the global population they are managing. Using these tools requires a basic understanding of statistics and epidemiology. HEDIS measures help to provide physicians with a tool set that provides them with crucial data on clinical and process outcomes of care delivered to the population of patients served by a health plan. The standard methods used in the HEDIS set allow physicians to compare plans to each other.

NCQA is a not-for-profit agency whose mission is to evaluate and report on the quality of managed care organizations. It was founded in 1979 by a coalition of managed care trade organizations, which decided in 1987 to establish itself as an independent organization for credibility reasons. NCQA accreditation is usually a voluntary process, but several states mandate NCQA review. NCQA usually conducts a three-day site review organized around standards in six functional domains:

- Quality Management and Improvement;
- Utilization Management;
- Credentialing;
- Preventive Health;

- Members Rights and Responsibilities; and
- Medical Records.

This accreditation process helps to provide consumers with information about the health plan's capability and control, but it does not provide them with information about the plan's clinical performance. The HEDIS data set provides this complementary information. Similar to software upgrades, HEDIS has evolved from version 1.0 in 1989 to v2.0 in November 1993, v2.5 in 1995 and v 3.0 in 1996.

NCQA did not assume management of the HEDIS project until 1992 when it published version 2.0. At the time, HEDIS 2.0 represented a major step forward in report cards that contained performance measurements in five major sections:

- Quality of care—in four categories, preventive medicine, prenatal care, acute and chronic diseases and mental health;
- Member access and patient satisfaction;
- Membership and utilization;
- Finance; and
- Descriptive information on health plan management.

Because of these improvements, HEDIS 2.0 achieved rapid dissemination in the managed care industry and became accepted as one of the industry standards in performance measurement.

Soon after HEDIS 2.0, a separate work group began to develop a HEDIS for Medicaid populations that was released in early 1996. At that point, it became clear that there was a need to develop similar measures for the Medicare risk population. Discussions between NCQA, the Health Care Financing Administration and the Kaiser Family Foundation ultimately led to the planning of HEDIS 3.0. This next step was planned as a performance measurement set that could measure performance in all payers, including Medicare, Medicaid and the commercial sector. A basic philosophical tenet underlaid NCQA's planning for this work: "High quality care should be the same no matter who is paying for the care."[1]

A committee known as the Committee on Performance Measurement included collaborators from multiple sectors of the healthcare industry. This committee developed an open process for developing measures beginning with a public call for proposals and suggestions in December 1995. It laid out criteria that it felt was important for future HEDIS measures to possess including:

Relevance—Measures needed to be relevant to the extent that they addressed issues known to significantly affect health outcomes, be controllable or influenced by the plan and were important to purchasers and consumers;

Scientific soundness—Measures needed to be reproducible, valid and accurate. They also needed to have sufficient statistical power to detect differences between health plans and to contain risk adjustments; and

Feasibility—Measures needed to be relatively easy to produce, precisely defined, and capable of being produced at a reasonable cost, and collection of data could not threaten patient confidentiality.

HEDIS 3.0 was officially released in October 1996 and health plans were required to report 1996 data in the HEDIS 3.0 set by June 1997. HEDIS 3.0 represented some major evolutionary developments from prior efforts such as:

- More outcomes measurements—HEDIS 3.0 includes a mixture of both outcome and process measures while in the past more of the measures were process measures;
- Wider diversity of measures—New measures had been developed for age groups for children through seniors and including more conditions such as AIDS and smoking;
- Same measurement standards—HEDIS 3.0 applies the same standards to care regardless of payer. This should allow the possibility of comparing care across populations in the future;
- Development of a testing set of measures—HEDIS 3.0 contains a set of measures for which all plans seeking NCQA accreditation must report. In addition, it contains an additional set of measurements that are acknowledged to be in development. NCQA hopes that plans will begin to utilize these measures and plans to work with researchers, purchasers, consumers and health plans to refine the methodological issues in the next two years; and
- Development of new measurement domains—HEDIS 3.0 contains new measures in the effectiveness of care, accessibility/availability of care, satisfaction with the experience of care, cost of care, stability of the health plan, informed health care choices, use of services and health plan descriptive information.

NCQA is moving to broaden the dissemination of HEDIS through "Quality Compass," a national database that includes HEDIS data and NCQA accreditation status information. NCQA's plans are to update the database at least twice a year. Interested physicians should access NCQA's World Wide Web site (www.ncqa.org) to review national and regional benchmark information that is freely available. The full details of the database are available for purchase in CD-ROM and print format from the NCQA.

The full set of the HEDIS 3.0 measures is listed in the accompanying tables.

HEDIS 3.0 (r) Reporting Measures[2]

I. Effectiveness of Care

All measures are on members who were continuously enrolled in the health plan for a certain period of time

- **Childhood immunization status**
  Percentage of children who have received appropriate immunizations by their second birthday
- **Adolescent immunization status**
  Percentage of 13 year olds who received all of their appropriate immunizations by their 13th birthday
- **Advising smokers to quit**
  Percentage of adult smokers or recent quitters who received advice to quit smoking from a health professional as measured in the Member Satisfaction Survey

(more)

HEDIS 3.0 (r) Reporting Measures[2]

- **Flu shots for older adults**
  Percentage of adults over 65 years who have received the influenza vaccine during the past year, collected through patient survey data

- **Breast cancer screening**
  Percentage of females between ages 52 to 69 who had at least one mammogram during the past two years

- **Cervical cancer screening**
  Percentage of women ages 21 to 64 who had at least one Pap smear during the past three years

- **Prenatal care in the first trimester**
  Percentage of pregnant women who began prenatal care during the first 13 weeks of pregnancy

- **Low birth-weight babies**
  Percentage of babies born who were underweight

- **Checkups after delivery**
  Percentage of women with live births who had a postpartum visit within six weeks after delivery

- **Treating children's ear infections**
  Percentage of children with uncomplicated acute otitis media who do not receive amoxicillin or trimethoprim-sulfamethoxazole (i.e., broad-spectrum antibiotics)

- **Beta blocker treatment after a heart attack**
  Percentage of members discharged from the hospital after a heart attack without contraindications who received a prescription for beta blockers within seven days of discharge

- **Eye exams for people with diabetes**
  Percentage of diabetics who had at least one eye exam in the past year

- **The health of seniors**
  Utilization of functional status survey in elderly patients

- **Follow up after hospitalization for mental illness**
  Percentage of members over age six hospitalized for mental disorders who were seen on an outpatient basis by a mental health provider within 30 days

II. Access/Availability of Care

- **Availability of primary care providers**
  How many primary care providers are accepting new patients

- **Availability of mental health/chemical dependency providers**
  How many mental health and chemical dependency providers are accepting new patients

- **Availability of obstetrical/prenatal care providers**
  How many obstetricians and prenatal care providers are accepting new patients

- **Adults' access to preventive/ambulatory health services**
  Number of adults getting preventive and ambulatory services

- **Children's access to primary care providers**
  Number of children who visit pediatricians, family physicians and other health care providers.

- **Initiation of prenatal care**
  Proportion of women who enroll in the health plan during pregnancy for whom prenatal care begins within six weeks after they enroll

- **Low birth-weight deliveries at facilities for high-risk deliveries and neonates**
  Percentage of low-birth-weight infants born at special facilities for high-risk deliveries and newborns (deferred until 1997 reporting year)

- **Annual dental visit**
  Percentage of plan members between ages of 4 to 21 with dental coverage who had a dental checkup during the past year

- **Availability of dentists**
  The number of dentists accepting new patients

- **Availability of language interpretation services**
  Number of healthcare providers and member services personnel who can speak languages other than English, as well as out-of-plan interpreter availability

III. Satisfaction with the Experience of Care

- **The Member Satisfaction Survey (numerous measures)**
  Utilization of NCQA's Annual Member Health Care Survey for commercial populations

- **Survey descriptive information**
  Information on all member and disenrollee surveys conducted during the past five years, and actions they have taken to improve member satisfaction

(more)

HEDIS 3.0 (r) Reporting Measures[2]

IV. Health Plan Stability

- **Disenrollment**
  Numbers of members who left a plan within a given year (Medicare and commercial patients only)

- **Provider turnover**
  Number of providers who leave the plan within a period of time

- **Indicators of financial stability**
  Years in business; total membership; total revenue; net income; net worth; debt-to-service ratio; overall loss ratio; administrative loss ratio; medical loss ratio; profit margin; days cash on hand; ratio of cash to claims payable; days in receivables; days in unpaid claims; admitted reserves; and state minimum reserve requirements.

- **Narrative information on rate trends, financial stability and insolvency protection**
  Narrative information on rate trends, financial stability and insolvency protection

V. Use of Services

All measures are on members who were continuously enrolled in the health plan for a certain period of time

- **Well-child visits in the first 15 months of life**
  Percentage of children who had one, two, three, four, five, or six well-child visits by the time they turned 15 months of age

- **Well-child visits in the third, fourth, fifth and sixth year of life**
  Percentage of children who are three, four, five and six years of age who received at least one well-child visit with a primary care physician during the past year

- **Adolescent well-care visit**
  Percentage of members 12 to 21 who had one or more well-care visit with a primary care provider during the past year

- **Frequency of selected procedures**
  Several, mostly surgical procedures that are frequently performed where considerable variation has been observed and that contribute substantially to expenses. These procedures are coronary artery bypass graft, angioplasty, prostatectomy, cholecystectomy, reduction of fracture of femur, total knee replacement, partial excision of large intestine, carotid endarterectomy, total hip replacement and hysterectomy.

- **Inpatient utilization—non-acute care**
  Number of stays in institutions for nonacute care in the reporting year, and how long patients stayed in these institutions on average.

- **Inpatient utilization—general hospital/ acute care**
  How many hospital days and how long patients stayed in the hospital for inpatient hospital treatment because of pregnancy, childbirth, surgery, or non-surgical medical treatment.

- **Ambulatory care**
  Use of outpatient visits, emergency room visits, ambulatory surgery and observation stays

- **Discharge and average length of stay for females in maternity care**
  How many women gave birth and how long these women remained in the hospital on average after vaginal births or cesarean sections

- **Cesarean section and vaginal birth after cesarean rate**

- **Cesarean section and vaginal birth after cesarean rate**

- **Births and average length of stay, newborns**
  How many infants were born and how long these newborns remained hospitalized reported by well newborns and those with medical problems

- **Frequency of ongoing prenatal care**
  Percentage of recommended prenatal visits (ACOG standards) by members who had live births during the past year

- **Mental health utilization—percentage of members receiving inpatient, day/night care and ambulatory services**
  Percentage of members who received mental health services broken down by these intensity levels

- **Mental health utilization—inpatient discharges and average length of stay**
  How many hospitalizations and how long patients stay in the hospital on average

- **Readmission for specified mental health disorders**
  Readmission to a hospital or to day/night treatment for disorders such as schizophrenia and depression within three months and up to a year after the first hospitalization.

- **Chemical dependency utilization—inpatient discharges and average length of stay**

- **Chemical dependency utilization—percentage of members receiving inpatient, day/night care and ambulatory services**
  Percentage of members who received chemical dependency services broken down by these intensity levels

(more)

HEDIS 3.0 (r) Reporting Measures[2]

- **Readmission for chemical dependency**
  Readmission to a hospital or to day/night treatment for chemical dependency within three months and up to a year after the first hospitalization.
- **Outpatient drug utilization**
  Total prescription costs, average prescription costs per member, and average number of prescriptions per member within a year

VI. Cost of Care

- **High-occurrence/high-cost DRGs**
  Cost per Diagnosis Related Groups primarily cardiovascular diseases, lung diseases and joint replacements
- **Rate trends**
  Long-term average premium rate trends

VII. Informed Health Care Choices

- **Language translation services**
  An inventory of all non-English language member materials
- **New member orientation/education**
  Description of a plan's procedures to orient and educate new members on how to use its services

VIII. Health Plan Descriptive Information

- **Board certification/residency completion**
  Proportion of plan physicians who have obtained board certification and have completed their residency training
- **Provider compensation**
  Description of the physician compensation plan to understand the type of financial incentives that may exist
- **Physicians under capitation**
  Exact descriptions of how capitated physicians are paid including payments to individual physicians or groups and what services the capitation payments are meant to cover
- **Recredentialing**
  How plans monitor ongoing credentialing requirements
- **Case management**
  How a plan utilizes case management to manage catastrophic, acute, or complex illnesses including methods of identifying cases and creating disease management and education programs.
- **Utilization management**
  Plan's policies and procedures regarding pre-authorization of services and provider and patient appeals.
- **Risk management**
  Description of a plan's risk management policies.
- **Quality assessment and improvement**
  Reports on any strategies or programs plans are using to improve care.
- **Preventive care and health promotion**
  Programs that encourage members to seek early detection of health problems and appropriate treatment.
- **Arrangements with public health, educational and social service organizations**
  Description of mechanism to provide and coordinate services from public health, education and social service agencies.
- **Pediatric mental health network**
  Description of mental health network including whether subcontracted or internally developed.
- **Chemical dependency services**
  Description of provisions for chemical dependency services including whether subcontracted or internally developed.
- **Family planning services**
  How a plan establishes this service and how it evaluates whether it meets family planning needs of its members.
- **Total Enrollment**
  Overview of plan's enrolled population
- **Enrollment by payer (member years/months)**
  Age and gender characteristics of persons covered by different payers.
- **Unduplicated Count of Medicaid members**
  How many Medicaid members enrolled at any time during a given year
- **Diversity of Medicaid membership**
  Number and percent of Medicaid members who belong to different racial and ethnic groups and percent of those who speak languages other than English
- **Weeks of pregnancy at time of enrollment**
  Stage of pregnancy at the date of enrollment for all Medicaid women who give birth to a child during the reporting year

HEDIS 3.0 (r) Testing Set Measures

I. Effectiveness of Care

- Number of people in the plan who smoke
- Smokers who quit
- Flu shots for high-risk adults
- Cholesterol management of patients hospitalized after coronary artery disease
- Aspirin treatment after a heart attack
- Outpatient care of patients hospitalized for heart failure
- Controlling high blood pressure
- Prevention of stroke in people with atrial fibrillation
- Colorectal cancer screening
- Follow-up after an abnormal Pap smear
- Follow-up after an abnormal mammogram
- Stage at which breast cancer was detected
- Assessment of how breast cancer therapy affects the patient's ability to function
- Continuity of care for substance abuse patients
- Substance counseling for adolescents
- Availability of medication management and psychotherapy for patients with schizophrenia
- Patient satisfaction with mental healthcare
- Family visits for children 12 years of age or younger
- Failure of substance abuse treatment
- Screening for chemical dependency
- Appropriate use of psychotherapeutic medications
- Continuation of depression treatment
- Monitoring diabetes patients
- Chlamydia screening
- Prescription of antibiotics for the prevention of HIV-related pneumonia
- Use of appropriate medications for people with asthma

II. Access/Availability of Care

- Problems with obtaining care

III. Satisfaction with the Experience of Care

- Satisfaction with breast cancer treatment
- Disenrollment survey
- Consumer Assessments of Health Plans Study (CAHPS)

IV. Health Plan Stability (none)

V. Use of Services

- Use of behavioral services

VI. Cost of Care

- Health plan costs per member per month

VII. Informed Health Care Choices

- Counseling women about hormone replacement therapy

VIII. Health Plan Descriptive Information (none)

What Does HEDIS Mean for the Practicing Physician?

In the late '90s, one can hear a consistent theme in the healthcare industry: A call for accountability. Physicians, hospitals and health plans are being asked by consumers and employers to become accountable for their quality. Report cards, such as HEDIS, are an attempt to provide systems that can result in such accountability. Such systems usually measure clinical performance in the three areas of quality initially defined by Donabedian:[3] structure, process and outcome.

An ideal report card would:

- Be universally reliable,;
- Adopt standards that are accepted by all;
- Provide a set of rules that can be unambiguously interpreted and consistently applied across health plans;
- Account for differences in data systems and in population risk that might affect results independent of performance;
- Provide meaningful information about the value of healthcare; and
- Allow systems to benchmark performance.

No report card has yet achieved this ideal state. Indeed, it is important for the physician leader to distinguish the rhetoric from the reality when examining the current state of report cards. Report cards have been around for more than a decade with the movement beginning in earnest in 1986 when the Health Care Financing Administration launched its hospital mortality report. The HCFA ultimately disbanded its dissemination of such data because of several problems with reporting mortality data. These problems are inherent in any system that attempts to measure quality through clinical outcomes. Such problems include:

- **Clinical constraints on timeliness of outcome measures.** The natural course of disease processes limit the utility of certain outcomes such as disease-related morbidity and mortality. For example, it may take 10 or 15 years before the consequences of untreated diabetes becomes manifested in terms of kidney or eye complications. Furthermore, an issue of accountability is raised from these clinical constraints. If an individual with diabetes changes health systems frequently over this period of time, which system is ultimately accountable for the clinical outcome measured?

- **Risk adjustment.** There are many other characteristics besides the quality of care that result in a clinical outcome. Most clinical outcomes depend on the clinical risks and characteristics of the individual patient. Therefore, such outcomes need to be adjusted for these clinical characteristics. The science of risk adjustment is ever-developing, but many of these issues have not been completely resolved.

- **Statistical issues.** Many clinically relevant outcomes occur relatively rarely. As a result, there are limitations on the statistical power of such measurements to delineate meaningful differences between health plans. A measure of a clinical outcome may be completely valid, but because of the problem of small numbers, it may not be useful in distinguishing one plan from another in that clinical outcome.

- **Quality of the data.** Many health plans are constrained in their ability to collect meaningful clinical data. The best data is in the paper medical record but the cost of getting such data is high. Most health plans do not have electronic medical records yet. As a result, many systems collect data through administrative data for HEDIS and other report cards. However, administrative data contains limited clinical information and their credibility is often in question because of their link to financial payment and their inability to identify the timing of comorbid conditions. Reliability of such information creates some limitations on the accuracy of risk adjustment and of the performance measure in general. Meeting HEDIS standards will put more pressure on health plans efforts to upgrade their information systems to accurately and reliably capture the necessary information to report the measures.

While it is important to recognize the limitations of clinical outcomes, outcomes measurement is a rapidly evolving area. The HEDIS system recognizes these limitations as it continues to rely a great deal on measurements of clinical processes and organizational structure for which these issues are less worrisome. The creation of a "test set" of outcome measures should help to accelerate the improvement in the science of outcome measurements.

Data quality is one area in which rapid progress can and should be made in report cards. Many of the report cards in the market place are developed by individual health plans without peer review or an auditing process and utilize disparate measures and different means of collecting, processing and defining the data.[4] NCQA is taking steps toward developing a data auditing process to ensure credibility of the data. One future possibility is that clinical quality data measures would be audited by an external third party in a similar manner to financial data being audited by a financial auditing firm. This would help to prevent current variation in how data is being collected and reported.

Where do Report Cards Fit in Today's Healthcare Marketplace?

Ideally, the purchasing of healthcare should be a decision that balances cost and quality. To the degree that one can quantify value in healthcare, the concept is fairly straightforward: Value=Quality/Cost.

In most healthcare markets today, the purchase of healthcare is done by a different entity than the user of healthcare. The standard purchaser of healthcare is a large employer. The benefits purchaser for a large employer usually has long experience in quantifying costs and judging their impact on an organization's bottom line. Even with improvements in systems such as HEDIS, the value of quality is still not as readily apparent on an employer's bottom line. As a result, the cost factor still outweighs the quality factor in many decisions.

Indeed, some purchasers are not even aware of the availability of performance data in their regions. A survey by Judith Hibbard of large employers in California, New York State, Pennsylvania and metropolitan Cleveland showed that awareness of hospital performance data in the region ranged from 25 percent to 93 percent. Most purchasers did not use hospital outcomes data and were more likely to consider consumer satisfaction data and accreditation status.[5] In a recent essay, Enthoven concludes that "so far it appears that published comparative quality data are not driving large changes in market shares; this perhaps reflects unfamiliarity with the data or uncertainty about their validity.[6]

The immediate relevance of HEDIS measures for the individual consumer can come into question. In a recent review of focus groups with consumers, Edgman-Leviatan concludes that consumers are "interested in knowing about other consumers' evaluation of healthcare providers or systems.[7] Focus group work suggests that consumers are primarily interested in information about technical competence, information and communication provided by physicians, coordination of care, access and the costs of coverage. However, she points out that "no one has distinguished the information needs of the general consumer from those of the healthcare decisionmaker in a family—that is, the person responsible for choosing the healthcare benefits." Indeed, most consumers have limited or no choice with respects to health plans because their employers offer just one or a few options.

While consumers may be interested in HEDIS data, their ability to use it to make an open choice may be constrained by the current marketplace. Once they are in a plan, consumers do seek data about treatment at the doctor and hospital level. While such data is not in the current scope of HEDIS measures, the issues of risk-adjustment and faulty comparisons become even more greater at this level of measurement because of the small numbers involved.

Future of HEDIS Measures

Availability of HEDIS data may allow physicians to better determine the quality of the managed care organizations with which they work. HEDIS measures of a plan's utilization management and quality improvement plan, financial data, disenrollment surveys and access measurements of patients problems with obtaining care will give physicians useful information to help them better determine the plans with which they wish to be affiliated.

The HEDIS data has made important strides in expanding the set of clinical quality measures. Most measures are still focused on processes rather than outcomes, although evolution of the data set promised by the existence of new measures in the testing set promise a continuous evolution toward better measures and better resolution of technical issues such as population risk adjustment.

The selection of certain measures in the HEDIS data set will likely create more impetus toward improvement on those clinical processes. Public display of such clinical measures such as the percentage of patients with flu shots will put pressure on the plan and the physician to collaborate on systemic approaches to improving these outcomes and demonstrate that they are adding value in healthcare. Ultimately, we should expect to see data on the connection between process measures and outcome measures, such as seeing the relationship between a successful flu immunization program and a drop in the rate of hospitalization of older adults for flu and pneumonia.

Most measures of clinical processes have focused on preventive measures that are readily quantifiable such as flu shots, cervical cancer screening and eye exams for diabetics. The new HEDIS measures continue the attempt to develop more relevant clinical outcomes as well as measures that are complementary. For example, there are measures for the stage at which breast cancer was detected, follow-up after an abnormal mammogram and an assessment of how breast cancer therapy affects the patient's ability to function. All of these measures attempt to quantify important aspects of how a system treats breast cancer. While each of those measures may have methodologic issues, when looked at as a whole they begin to paint a more complete picture of the system of care.

As measures are developed, it will be crucial for systems to develop applications and methods to improve the actual outcomes of care. Future study of the application of quality improvement efforts on the results of specific HEDIS measures will be critical in continuing efforts for system improvement. These types of studies will be attempting to developing better methods for translating information on efficacy that is known in the scientific literature into effective intervention methods that work in reality in a defined population. The research will not be studying the efficacy of treatments but evaluating the effectiveness of organizational strategies that implement these interventions. For example, the effectiveness of breast cancer screening programs on decreasing the amount of stage III and IV breast cancer may be dependent on a system's ability to know that a patient needs to be screened, to ensure that a screening mammogram is performed in the optimal manner and to followup appropriately and in a timely manner.

Health plans and physicians may improve their performance through a variety of means, including better information and tracking systems, dissemination of practice guidelines, development of patient education programs, financial incentives, development of internal practice profiling and outreach programs to underserved populations. Which method or combination of methods result in the greatest success will become a larger area for research and study. An example of this is the Robert Wood Johnson Foundation's new program for 1998, Addressing Tobacco in Managed Care, which seeks to fund a series of grants to evaluate systems changes aimed at reducing rates of tobacco use among managed care subscribers. Development of a standardized measure set such as HEDIS should help to define areas for quality improvement and help to disseminate information on improvement methods more readily through the entire health system.

The physician leader must understand that the evolution of quality measures such as HEDIS is as important, if not more so, than the current state. Comparing the current state of the HEDIS measures with the late '80s demonstrates a rapid development in the technology of outcomes measures that is bound to continue. Wide dissemination of these standardized measures will serve only to accelerate performance improvement efforts such as the national, collaborative work groups launched by the Institute for Healthcare Improvement that has allowed organizations to work together to improve patient outcomes. Improvement areas targeted have included cesarean section rates, physicians' prescribing practices, low back pain and outpatient asthma care. While individual measures may be fraught with technical difficulty and the interpretation of such measures still may be open to questions, the evolution of such measures represents a quantifiable good for the healthcare system. "One cannot manage what one cannot measure" is an old saying in the quality improvement trade. Continuing the incremental steps toward better measurement systems such as HEDIS leads the healthcare system toward continuous improvement.

◆ ◆ ◆

References

[1]*HEDIS 3.0 Draft for Public Comment.* July 9, 1996.

[2]NCQA. *HEDIS Reporting and Data Set.* 1997.

[3]Donabedian, Avedis. "The Definition of Quality and Approaches to its Assessment." Ann Arbor, MI: Health Administration Press, 164: 1980.

[4]"How good is your health plan?" *Consumer Reports*, 28-42: August 1996.

[5]Center for Studying Health System Change. Issue Brief, July 1997.

[6]Enthoven, A.C., and Vorhaus, C.B. "A Vision of Quality in Health Care Delivery." *Health Affairs*, 16:1, 44-57, 1997.
[7]Edgman-Levitan, S. and Cleary, P.D. "What Information Do Consumers Want and Need." *Health Affairs*, 15:4, 42-56, 1996.

About the Author

Craig P. Tanio, MD, MBA is chief operating officer and chief financial officer for Baltimore Medical System, a group of urban community health centers serving 32,000 patients, and an assistant professor of medicine at the Johns Hopkins School of Medicine.

Appointment, Reappointment and Clinical Privileges

The Role of the Physician Executive in Orchestrating Credentialing and Privileging

By Raymond Fabius, MD

Years ago, physician practices and hospitals accepted doctors who practiced within their domains based on an interview and a copy of an existing license. Subsequent to that minimal, initial credentialing, little effort was exerted for periodic review of the physician's credentials and/or performance. This approach allowed physicians to operate with less oversight or interference, but denied them an opportunity for evaluation and feedback.

◆ ◆ ◆

Those who gravitate to the medical field are by nature competitive and, therefore usually driven by performance feedback. Once in medical school, physicians-to-be strive for excellence because the goal is to obtain the best residence training programs. Once medical students graduate from their residency program and enter practice, however, they are often met with a dearth of performance feedback. As a consequence, I used to joke when I was a network medical director of a health plan that, 90 percent of the doctors I visited told me they were in the top 10 percent in their field. Without much by the way of comparison, these physicians had little to support their contention. On the other hand, there was little information to dispute it, either.

Physician executives have a tremendous opportunity to convert the credentialing and recredentialing process into one that contributes greatly toward improving clinical care, clinical services and efficiencies of care.

Credentialing and Recredentialing Standards

Any physician executive involved in credentialing physicians needs to be intimately aware of the credentialing standards established by the National Committee for Quality Assurance (NCQA). The Standards Committee of NCQA, on which I have served for the past several years, has strived to develop a dozen of standards that can be applied to all credentialing and recredentialing processes to some extent. These credentials were originally written for HMOs. More recently, these credentials have been used with some modification to certify physician organizations' credentialing processes. These standards may be applied to all arenas where physician credentialing and recredentialing takes place. Therefore, even if you are a medical director of a group practice or a department head at a hospital, this resource can help you develop your own appointment and reappointment process.

Highlights of the NCQA Standards for Credentialing and Recredentialing

When developing a mechanism for credentialing and recredentialing, the process and scope should be well delineated. Written policies should include responsible parties and the appropriate actions to be taken. Documentation of the credentialing process should describe its criteria, verification sources and decision-making process, as well as any agents of delegation.

The process should include peer review. As such, a credentialing committee should have the ability to make recommendations regarding credentialing decisions to the responsible authority. At a minimum, the credentialing process should verify a physician's:

- Current medical license;
- Status of clinical privileges at the hospital designated as his or her primary admitting facility;
- Valid DEA or CDS certificate;
- Evidence of education and training in the field of practice;
- Board certification where appropriate;
- A review of work history;
- Adequate and current malpractice insurance policy; and
- Any medical liability claims that resulted in judgments or settlements paid by or on behalf of the practitioner.

As part of the application process, it is also important to seek a statement from the applicant regarding any inability to perform the essential functions of the position, a lack of present illegal drug use within the confines of the applicable law, any history of loss of license or felony conviction, any history of loss or limitation of privileges or disciplinary activity and, finally, an attestation of the correctness and completeness of the application. External sources of information regarding a potential applicant should include inquiring to the National Practitioner Data Bank, the state Board of Medical Examiners, the Federation of State Medical Boards and/or the Department of Professional Regulations, if available. In addition, the process should review previous sanction activity by Medicare and Medicaid. It is also appropriate to visit the office or offices of all potential primary care physicians and obstetrics/gynecology specialists at a minimum Benchmark efforts with regard to credentialing and recredentialing include initial office visits for all providers. As part of the office visit, there should be an evaluation of the medical record-keeping practices. This should include evaluating the care taken to keep office records secure and confidential.

NCQA recommends that recredentialing should occur at least every two years. At that time, similar licensure and certification should be verified, and physicians should be given the opportunity to report any disability to perform essential functions that they may have acquired since the last credentialing or recredentialing effort. The recredentialing decision-making processes should include elements of performance that have been collected by the organization in regard to that practitioner since the point of initial appointment or participation. Internally generated elements to consider during recredentialing include member complaints, information from quality improvement activities, utilization management, member satisfaction surveys, medical record reviews and a recent site visit.

Effective credentialing and recredentialing processes should be able to document policies, procedures and efforts extended to alter the conditions of a practitioner's participation within his or her organization. This should include suspension or termination of privileges, where appropriate. The organization should also be able to demonstrate its responsibility for reporting serious quality deficiencies to the appropriate state and federal authorities. Such efforts to alter the conditions of the practitioner's participation in the organization should be subject to appeal. If the organization delegates any credentialing and recredentialing activities, that organization is still responsible for effective oversight of the delegated activities. All delegated agents need to follow similar guidelines as highlighted above. Physician leaders involved in the appointment and reappointment process need to master the credentialing and recredentialing standards the NCQA established.

Credentialing Verification Sources

Fraud is a side of medicine that most physicians would prefer not to discuss, but the fact is that the rare submission of fraudulent credentialing certificates creates a sensational front page and embarrasses everyone involved in healthcare. At a minimum, the credentialing process needs to document its efforts in verifying the veracity of credentials submitted by potential healthcare providers. The NCQA, *1997 Surveyor Guidelines for the Accreditation of Managed Care Organizations,* provides a list of credentialing verification sources. For example, the American Board of Medical Specialties Compendium provides an excellent source of verifying board certification status. The American Medical Association Master File is also an excellent source of verifying residency training completion. Similarly, the Joint Commission on Accreditation of Health Care Organizations (JCAHO) is one of the best places for verifying the approval status of hospitals and skilled nursing facilities.

Two exciting technology advancements are making the credentialing verification process considerably easier for physician executives. One is that these sources of credentialing verification are now organized databases. The second is that most of these databases are now available for electronic connectivity. As recently as five years ago, it was necessary to either write or call these sources in order to receive verification of credentials. Today, batch submission is possible through an electronic link, with turn-around times of as little as 48 to 72 hours.

Credentialing, Certification, Recredentialing and Recertification

To allow for a better understanding of the process of appointment, reappointment and clinical privileges, it is important to appreciate the difference between credentialing and certification, as well as recredentialing and recertification. While not all physician executives agree, I like to think of credentialing and recredentialing as the review of externally generated information, and the certification and recertification process as the review of all credentialing information sought from internal and external sources. Externally generated information refers to credentialing elements that need to be primarily verified from external sources, such as current state medical licenses and board certification status. An example of internally-generated information is the inspection of the facility by a site visit from a representative of the medical care organization. At the time of initial certification, most of the information obtained on a prospective candidate to join a staff or network is derived from external sources. At the time of recertification, most of the substantive information that is available concerning the performance of an existing participant within a network is internally generated.

Some of the elements from the wealth of data generated related to the physician's performance within a hospital or health plan include: member survey information, transfer rates out of the practice, grievance and complaint rates, utilization of resources, prescription trends and within some organizations, direct medical chart evaluations. Physician executives should utilize the recertification process to identify opportunities for improvement and implement efforts to enhance care.

Peer Review

Peer review is a generally accepted and essential element of the process of credentialing, certifying and privileging physicians. It is up to physician executives to ensure the peer review process provides meaningful input from practitioners within the organization, because this is how the process garners expertise on current practices within the medical community. Although doing so can be quite expensive and labor intensive, it is ideal to have "like" physicians reviewing the performance of their peers. For example, an Obstetrics and Gynecology Committee of peers would evaluate the credentials of OB/Gyn applicants and the recertification of OB/Gyn specialist peers.

At the same time, physician executives should recognize and remove conflicts of interest. All of us in medical management are concerned when there is a potential financial impact on the reviewers caused by the decision to either approve or deny privileges to a candidate. Therefore, physicians who compete directly with a physician being reviewed must remove themselves from the decision-making process.

Physician executive participants on a credentialing committee need to be guaranteed that they are covered from a liability standpoint for what is called "E&Os," or errors and omissions. At a minimum, any healthcare organization that seeks active and robust participation from practicing doctors needs to provide assurance that they can be protected against any legal claims of unfairness.

Good record-keeping is an essential part of the peer review process. It is not necessary to note who said what in the minutes, but it is important to document that there was substantive discussion. In addition, there needs to be documentation that the advice generated by the peer review process is weighted heavily in the final decision concerning participation, privileging or hiring of the physicians presented to the committee of peers.

Benchmark Efforts

All physician leaders involved in credentialing, certification, privileging and hiring of staff need to dedicate themselves to improving the effectiveness and efficiency of their staff. The benchmark efforts in this process seek to identify opportunities to improve their network. More than 20 years ago, a medical director from US Healthcare came to my office to tell me that my member satisfaction survey was average. Despite the fact that the managed care organization liked the practice in every other way, the score was just average because the MCO perceived our waiting times, both in the office and for appointments, as being three times worse than the HMO average. To assess whether the rest of my patients felt the same way, I instituted a self-administered patient satisfaction survey from the Pennsylvania Medical Society. The results were the same. Once this was brought to the attention of everyone else in my pediatric practice, they devoted great effort to changing the way our patient flow was conducted, and the waiting time problem was resolved. We found this out through another medical director who visited me on behalf of the peer review committee while the MCO was recertifying my office. Benchmark recertification efforts provide the physicians reviewed with feedback on their performance as compared with peers, which helps them improve.

Indeed, a wealth of data has shown that simply providing information to physicians about their performance as compared with colleagues can improve the quality of care they deliver. Benchmark efforts abound. Within large provider groups, for example, weaker performers can be paired with successful clinicians so they can get better. In fact, tying poor performers with benchmark ones in a "buddy system" can be very effective in improving the performance of the network in general.

Quality of Care

Physician executives should create recredentialing programs that emphasize the elements that most closely relate to the doctor's quality of care. Using the Donabedian model, we can look at quality of care indicators as being either structural in nature, process components or outcome measurements. A structural indicator could relate to the evaluation of the physical site. If, for example, a geriatrician had an office on the third floor of a three-story walk-up, this would be a structural problem. Process indicators, in the realm of quality of care, are increasingly being recorded through administrative data. For example, screening rates of appropriate preventive services are increasingly tracked through claims and encounter data. The ability to evaluate the performance of physicians through the use of administrative data is a huge step forward in recertification and privileging. Largely based on the measurement of indicators established by HEDIS, (the Health Plan Employer Data Information Set), healthcare organizations are now able to report on such things as the primary doctor's panel of patients' rate of mammography screening for appropriate women, or the immunization rate of children in the practice. Outcome indicators have been somewhat more elusive. While systems are being built to deliver administrative outcome data, often chart review is required for this form of assessment. While it may be easier to measure the rate of annual eye examinations within a diabetic population, it may be much more difficult to discern the actual incidence of blindness within the same diabetic population. The latter measurement is an outcome measurement, while the former is a process indicator that correlates with the outcome incidence of blindness. Chart review requires knowledge-based experts to evaluate the performance of physicians based on what has been documented in the medical record. Issues of legibility, interviewer liability, and personal biases need to be minimized in this assessment. An experiential chart review can ask questions that are more process-related, such as, "Was the care delivered adequate?" or it can approach outcome indicators by answering the question, "Could better care have improved the outcome of the patient?" Lastly, a chart review can ask questions that relate to both process and outcome, such as, "Considering both the process and outcome, was the overall quality of care acceptable in this patient?"

Quality of Service

Quality of service indicators should be weighed, not as heavily as quality of care measures, yet more significantly than efficiency measures. Again, we can look at quality of service indicators from a structural, process or outcome perspective. Structurally, a doctor is providing greater quality of service if he or she has more office hours and daily access. Concepts of access and availability are extremely important components of quality.

Process indicators relate to the patients' perception of the ease with which they can make an appointment, or with the practice's ability to minimize waiting times.

Outcome indicators relate most closely to the perception that patients have with regard to concepts such as the overall care they receive from the doctor or practice, or ultimately, whether or not they would recommend the doctor to friends and family. Most service indicators can be measured by facility site visits and member satisfaction surveys. Specialty physicians not only serve their patient population, but also the primary physicians who refer to them. It is, therefore, intriguing to survey the primary physicians with regard to the service they receive from specialty physicians, and to incorporate this into any recertification or privileging process.

Efficiencies of Care

Of all the indicators, it often easiest for healthcare organizations to obtain information about an individual provider's use of healthcare resources. Through information largely obtained from claims-driven administrative data, it is possible to identify physicians who utilize hospital, specialty care or emergency room services much differently than peers. Those doctors who greatly underutilize services need to be reviewed from a quality of care perspective; those markedly overutilizing services need to be evaluated by physician leaders who are expert in the field of utilization and patient management.

Talking with a physician about over- or under-utilization is taken seriously because doctors have come to fear, to a remarkable degree, discussion about being "outliers." This is largely based on concern that hospitals and health plans might engage in what has been called "economic credentialing." Their fear is not unfounded. Such entities may and have actually terminated relationships or reduced the privileges of physicians not generating satisfactory margins for the parent company. For such assessments to be fair, it is necessary to engage in severity adjustments.

The first response of a doctor who has been identified overutilizing services usually is "My patients are older and sicker." With the increasing sophistication of information systems, it is possible to evaluate the veracity of such a statement. In my experience, most physicians who have been identified as being remarkably high utilizers of services do not have patient populations that can justify such remarkable expenditure of medical resources. Providing information in terms of both utilization and severity adjustment can spark an epiphany for a physician overutilizing services. Once overutilizers are presented with fair and credible data, most will make great efforts to adjust their treatment process.

Issues that Relate to Privileging

A wealth of literature supports the notion that outcomes are better for almost any given malady when treatment is handled by providers who see a high volume of similar cases. In other words, doctors who administer a certain therapy frequently do it better than doctors who provide that service occasionally. Privileging relates to this concept. On one hand, our capitalistic system allows for remarkable free enterprise. Once a doctor receives a state license to practice medicine, he or she theoretically can do brain surgery. All the physician needs is an institution that will provide privileges. While this example may be on the ludicrous side, it is not far from reality.

Healthcare organizations and health plans are increasingly challenged about which treatments, procedures and services an individual physician should be privileged to perform. Should a hospital restrict the use of the intensive care unit to physicians who are board certified intensivists? Does it make sense to allow cardiologists, pulmonologists and even internists to care for patients in that setting? Should colposcopy be performed only by OB/Gyn specialists, or should family physicians who are trained to perform this procedure in their residencies be privileged to perform this procedure as well?

Privileging is an area where a peer review body of like specialists is particularly important. They can draw on their experiential knowledge base, as well as on their understanding of the delivery of healthcare within their medical community. To some extent, privileging has to relate to the extent of available medical resources. For example, an internist in a small town may be required to handle all patients, even those who require intensive care at the local hospital. At the same time, the likely outcome of such medical care may be better if the patient is transferred to a metropolitan center that can offer providers who have conducted this treatment on a regular basis.

Integrated delivery systems and hospitals are frequently challenged to make decisions about privileging. And it gets more complex. While outcome is perhaps the key component for such decisions, patient preference must be a factor, too. Many patients still prefer to have their care delivered by local doctors in a community hospital, even though outcomes may not be as good statistically.

Delegation and Risk Relationships

Hospitals, large medical groups, IPAs and integrated delivery systems are increasingly willing to accept the responsibilities of credentialing, recredentialing and privileging their physician base. Over time, health plans have begun to delegate this responsibility to willing provider groups. In fact, NCQA has developed standards to allow for the delegation of credentialing and recredentialing. At the same time, these entities are increasingly receiving prepayment or case rates for the care their networks of physicians provide. This situation has increased pressure on provider systems and health plans to maintain a network of efficient physicians. But particularly when payment is rendered on a capitated or some other form of at-risk basis, physician executives must protect the providers from being credentialed on a purely economic basis.

The role of the physician executive in credentialing is significant. By understanding accepted industry standards and applying them with finesse and conviction, the healthcare delivery system can benefit. When a patient joins a health plan or is admitted to the hospital, he or she is dependent upon the provider network there. One of the best ways to improve the care that patient will receive is through a process that accepts the best applicants and works with all accepted providers to improve their performance over time. There is no greater opportunity for physician executives than to cultivate a provider network to better compete in the marketplace.

About the Author

Dr. Raymond Fabius is the corporate medical director for National Accounts AETNA U.S. Healthcare (AUSHC). Dr. Fabius also plays an active role within the National Committee for Quality Assurance (NCQA), and the American College of Physicians (ACPE).

Delineating Clinical Privileges for New and Cross-Specialty Procedures

By J. Edward McEachern, MD, Jonathan T. Lord, MD, and David Tropauer, MBA

Delineating privileges for new and cross-specialty procedures poses challenges for physician leaders. What criteria should the medical staff use to assess a physician's competency to perform a new procedure? Who should establish privileging criteria for procedures that physicians in two or more departments perform? In this article, the authors raise key issues to consider when making credentialing decisions such as these, including focusing on competence and clinical skills rather than economics and establishing fair credentialing requirements for different specialties.

◆ ◆ ◆

The delineation of clinical privileges is based on a seemingly simple premise: The education, training and current clinical competence of a practitioner should be matched to the support capabilities of the institution. Thus, the world-famous cardiothoracic surgeon would not be granted clinical privileges for coronary artery bypass surgery at a 50-bed rural hospital. By the same token, a thoracic surgeon without specific additional training and experience performing coronary artery bypasses would not be granted such privileges in a 1,000-bed cardiac center.

Furthermore, as the Joint Commission's standards indicate, credentialing decisions should also take into account an individual's current health status and risk management-related issues, such as liability claims history. For reappointment, performance measures such as quality improvement (QI) data and clinical activity statistics should be reviewed before privileges are renewed.

However, in today's rapidly changing healthcare environment, where technological advances are introduced almost every day, delineating clinical privileges becomes more complex. Four credentialing situations pose specific problems:

- Physicians requesting cross-specialty or "crossover" privileges;
- Physicians requesting privileges to perform new procedures;
- Network (PHO, IPA, etc.) delegated credentialing; and
- Recredentialing.

In these situations, many of the criteria routinely used by department heads, the credentials committee and the governing board to make decisions regarding appointment or reappointment offer little insight into the physician's competence. To resolve these issues see Figure 1 below.

Figure 1: Tips for Credentialing New and Cross-Specialty Procedures

- Develop a generic policy and protocol for delineating privileges for new and cross-specialty procedures.
- Clearly identify who has responsibility for what in these credentialing decisions.
- Identify the training and experience needed to perform the procedure.
- Keep economic issues out of the decision-making process.
- Apply the policy uniformly.
- Use national standards when able.

Physician leaders need to work with administration and the board to develop privileging guidelines for new and cross-specialty procedures based on the best interests of the patients served by the organization.

Crossover Privileges

Crossover privileges refer to privileges for procedures or technologies for which more than one specialty claims to be qualified. Credentialing decisions for crossover privileges, such as cardiac catheterization, colonoscopy and bronchoscopy, "force hospitals to examine the philosophical underpinnings of the credentialing process," says Steven Landgarten, MD, medical director at Hillcrest Medical Center, Tulsa, Okla. "Consider the following scenario: Two physicians request cystoscopy privileges. One is a urologist who learned how to do cystoscopies during a four-year residency program. The other is a pediatrician who had a three-month urological rotation during his residency and did a few of the procedures. Do we give privileges to both? If not, where do we draw the line? And does the department of urology or the department of pediatrics get to decide?"

Physicians are increasingly being held to regional and national standards of care. Because crossover privileges are requested by local providers, it is in the best interests of both the providers and hospital to quickly scan the regional and national credentialing practices for a procedure. Added liability could result if a provider has a bad outcome for a procedure for which he or she has been credentialed and for which the credentialing criteria fall outside of regionally or nationally accepted norms.

New procedures/technologies

When the first physician applies for privileges to perform a new procedure, a hospital needs to determine if it will offer this procedure at all, based on whether it has, or is willing to add, necessary equipment space, and staff; whether the new procedure fills a perceived community need; and whether the procedure is aligned with the organization's mission and overall goals. *(For more on the technology assessment process, see* "The Physician Leader's Role in Medical Technology Assessment" *by Kathleen Ciccone*). Second, the hospital needs to establish the requirements for clinical privileges as well as QI criteria for monitoring the procedure.

In the past few years, a classic example of rapidly emerging technology has been laparoscopic cholecystectomy. Estimates are that 80 percent—or 600,000—laparoscopic cholecystectomies are performed annually in the United States.[1] One manufacturer of surgical supplies, including laparoscopic equipment, estimates it has trained more than 19,000 of the nation's 32,000 general surgeons to perform the procedure.[2] Training courses generally run from one to three days. Some students practice the procedure on live animals; others do not. If a physician attends a course, does completion mean he or she should automatically have privileges to perform the procedure? Many courses are unaccredited by any educational authority and don't even grade participating doctors.

There are no clear-cut guidelines for making credentialing decisions for crossover or new procedures that will be applicable at all institutions or be embraced by all physicians. Serious discussion and consideration of the following four points, however, will aid the medical staff, administration and governing board in reaching consensus.

- Has the medical staff formally adopted a generic policy for delineating privileges for new procedures or technologies?
- Should the criteria for delineating privileges be exactly the same for all departments performing the same procedure, or are differences acceptable?
- Who has responsibility for ensuring that the criteria for delineating privileges are comparable, reasonable and fair across specialties?
- Is the governing board convinced that the criteria reflect clinically valid parameters? and
- Keeping in mind that economics can be the real motivating factor, is the board confident that the criteria are free of economically motivated restraints?

Responsibilities for Privileging

Each hospital needs to establish a general policy and protocol for granting privileges for new and cross-specialty procedures. Such a policy must be based on an understanding of some basic principles with regard to who has responsibility for clinical privileging.

Only the governing board has the prerogative to:

1. Grant appointments to the medical staff;

- Establish which services will be provided in or by the institution; and
- Grant clinical privileges for those services.

2. The medical staff, usually through the credentials committee and the executive committee, has the responsibility to:

- Make recommendations on the services provided by the medical staff at the institution;
- Evaluate requests of individuals applying for medical staff membership or clinical privileges; and
- Ensure compliance with medical staff bylaws pertinent to credentialing, including due process requirements.

3. Clinical department chairs (in hospitals with such positions) have the responsibility to:

- Develop criteria for the delineation of clinical privileges;
- Make recommendations concerning applications for appointment to the medical staff and delineation of clinical privileges; and
- Provide ongoing surveillance of the clinical practice of each department member who has clinical privileges.

Privileging Physicians for New Procedures

Using these basic principles as a framework, the medical staff at Anne Arundel Medical Center in Annapolis, MD., developed a policy and protocol for delineating clinical privileges for new procedures or technologies. (*See Figure below.*) The intent is that any time a new procedure comes along, from laparoscopic cholecystectomy to

FIGURE 2: SAMPLE POLICY AND PROTOCOL FOR ESTABLISHING OF PRIVILEGES FOR NEW PROCEDURES OR EXPANDED SCOPE OF CARE

The medical staff shall use the mechanism described below to make recommendations to the board of directors for adding privileges for significant new procedures and/or to significantly expand the scope of care of the medical center.

1. Upon application or request from one or more members of the staff for privileges that involve one or more services, the president of the medical staff may appoint an ad hoc committee to:

(a) Make a recommendation to the board of directors through the medical board (executive committee of the medical staff) of the advisability, efficiency and cost of the new procedure or expanded scope of care;

(b) Provide the medical board with proposed criteria for granting privileges for the new procedure or expanded scope of care;

(c) Propose a mechanism for enhanced monitoring and evaluation of clinical performance and outcomes; and

(d) Make an individual recommendation on the practitioner requesting the privileges.

2. If a chief of service fails to make any recommendation, the application will be referred to the medical board.

Figure 3: Policy and Procedures for Laparoscopic Cholecystectomy

Background

Gallbladder disease continues to be one of the most common digestive disorders seen by physicians in this country. Approximately 500,000 cholecystectomies are performed annually in the United States. Due to the magnitude of the disease, the discomfort of major abdominal surgery, the prolonged recovery interval, and the enormous costs in total healthcare dollars, many alternatives to operative cholecystectomy have been pursued in recent years. Procedures such as lithotripsy, percutaneous stone extraction, and stone dissolution are now being offered to an increasing number of patients. The indications for using these other therapeutic modalities are still limited. In addition, there is a significant recurrence rate of cholelithiasis following successful nonoperative therapy, and it remains unproved that such approaches will have any major impact on reducing healthcare expenditures.

A recently developed alternative to formal laparotomy and open cholecystectomy is laparoscopic cholecystectomy. This procedure, developed almost simultaneously in the United States and Europe, offers many advantages over standard open cholecystectomy. Hospital stay and the postoperative recovery period are greatly reduced. Approximately one-third of patients are discharged on the day of surgery with the remaining hospitalized for only one night. Most patients return to moderate activity within three to five days.

Patient Selection

In contrast to other, nonoperative alternatives for cholelithiasis, there are few absolute and relative contraindications to laparoscopic cholecystectomy. This is because the surgeon can, at the time of laparoscopic evaluation of the gallbladder and surround structures, choose to convert the procedure to open cholecystectomy. Situations that may render the laparoscopic approach difficult or impossible include extensive adhesion from prior surgery or recurrent attacks of cholecystitis, unusual vascular or ductal anatomy, discovery of unsuspected pathology, acute inflammation distorting the normal tissue planes, presence of excessive bleeding, and inability to safely identify the ductal and vascular anatomy.

Criteria for Clinical Privileges

In order to appropriately privilege individuals to perform this procedure, the following criteria will be considered:

- Existing privileges for cholecystectomy and for laparoscopic surgery, and
- Completion of a formal course that includes hands-on training using laparoscopic equipment (human or animal model); or
- Completion of a formal course (without hands-on experience) plus satisfactory performance of 10 laparoscopic cholecystectomy procedures under the direct supervision of an appropriately privileged surgeon; or
- Satisfactory performance of 25 laparoscopic cholecystectomy procedures under the direct supervision of an appropriately privileged surgeon.

Monitoring

The plan is to intensively monitor a physician's performance of this procedure for three months using the following screening criteria:

- Patients converted from a planned laparoscopic cholecystectomy procedure to the standard open cholecystectomy;
- Surgical wound or nosocomial infection;
- Any length of stay in excess of three days postop; and
- Any procedure requiring more than two hours of anesthesia.

Results of these reviews will be handled through the QA Program of the surgery department and reported to the QA committee, surgical case review committee, and medical board (executive committee) for review and follow-up action as needed. Summaries and trend reports will be included in the physician's performance profile. At the end of the monitoring period, the medical board will make a recommendation to the governing board regarding whether to grant or deny a physician privileges for this procedure, or extend the monitoring period.

Similar criteria, coupled with the hospital's financial statements, will enable the governing Board to assess whether the hospital should continue to offer this new procedure to patients.

balloon catheterization of the fallopian tubes or other procedures in the future, these generic guidelines will help develop appropriate privileging and QI procedures, avoid turf wars and protect the interest of patients. An example of how we applied this generic policy to laparoscopic cholecystectomy appears in Figure 3 on page 249.

The difficult process of delineating clinical privileges for new procedures or technologies can be accomplished by establishing policies and procedures that are based on the central tenets of privileging. These include:

- The appropriate involvement of department chairs, the credentials committee, the executive committee, and the governing board;
- Fairness in specifying similar requirements for different specialties;
- Focusing on current competence and clinical skills, not economic issues;
- Ensuring that criteria for delineating privileges for different services are comparable when delineating "crossover" privileges; and
- Comparison with national or regional standards of care, where applicable.

Figure 4: A Credentialing Checklist

1. Valid state license
2. Valid DEA registration
3. Current, valid and adequate professional liability
4. Certificate of graduation from AAAMC accredited medical school
5. ECFMG certificate for international medical graduates
6. Documentation of completion of an approved residency
7. Board and subspecialty board certification
8. Past and current practice employment (including explanation of any gaps in practice)
9. Professional liability claims history for the past 10 years
10. Clinical privileges in good standing at the hospital(s) designated by the physician as the primary admitting facility and other hospitals
11. Medicare and Medicaid sanctioned activity
12. Queries of practice patterns
    - State medical board(s)
    - National Practitioner Data Bank
13. Personal information
    - Current mental and physical health status
    - Lack of present drug impairment/substance abuse
    - Any history of loss of license and/or felony convictions
    - Any history of loss or limitation of privileges or disciplinary actions
    - Any reason why applicant cannot perform the essential functions of the position, with or without assistance
    - Attestation that the information is accurate and complete
14. Site visit and score
15. Reappointment data
    - Patient complaint
    - Internal investigations from QM/QI committee
    - UM data
    - Patient satisfaction surveys
16. Comments
17. Signatures and log of persons reviewing file, as well as reasons for review
18. Log of actions taken by the credentialing committee
19. Discrepancy and "out-of-date document" check sheet

Figure 5: Linking Credentialing to Process Improvement

1. Physician performance is process dependent. Many physicians will revolt if credentialing is coupled with performance without a good mechanism for improvement not only of their performance but also of the performance of the system in which they work. Despite the inclination to pair physician performance only with activities under doctors' control, a growing body of evidence supports the hypothesis that many are subject to larger, systemic causes for performance. Adequate process improvement systems need to be place for faulty systems to be examined and improved. Moreover, excellent process improvement systems help all physicians improve. Even the "best in class" doctors can use data on systems performance to improve their personal performance. This is a conceptual change from traditional credentialing mechanisms, whereby minimum standards are solely used.

2. Improve systems of care when performance is inadequate. HEDIS measures are proxy for quality care, or so asserts the NCQA. Typical performance data run about 60 percent to 70 percent for routine items such as childhood immunizations, cholesterol screening and mammograms. Why isn't that number much closer to 100 percent? It's not because physicians think immunizations, mammograms or cholesterol screening are insignificant. It is because the systems that support the timely acquisition of these valuable procedures are limited. Increasingly, data about poor performance can lead to knowledge about how and where to focus improvement efforts.

3. Improve efficiency and outcomes by reducing undesirable variation. Gain physician cooperation by focusing on systems of care that can decrease variation and improve clinical outcomes. Often, systems will focus first on cost, an error in our opinion. Efficient and productive medicine is doing the right thing right the first (and only) time.

4. Use valid data for comparisons. Data from billing (UB 92 and HCFA 1500) provide limited information upon which to make comparisons of quality. These data are useful for starting process improvement projects and seeing where variation occurs, but small denominators and sample sizes make comparisons with other enumerative data sets difficult. (For more information on this topic, see Dr. Barry Chaiken's chapter starting on page 85.)

5. Work with clinicians to link practice profile data to improvement efforts. Physicians want good information that will help them optimize their practices. A goal of a credentialing process linked to process improvement is shared responsibility for the improvement of clinical outcomes with a clinical and operational data set that focuses each physician's improvement efforts within efforts by the organization to improve the systems. Data presented in the proper way helps both the clinician and the system conduct a reality check.

6. The current system has limitations, so help doctors build a better one. Eventually physicians will earn the right to compete in the marketplace based on performance data. The present system all too often examines binary data about board certification, medical licensing and so on, with little information on process, outcomes and performance.

Credentialing "Delegated" Networks

Managed care organizations are increasingly delegating credentialing to IPAs, PHOs and other organizational structures able to perform primary source verification and credentialing. For most health plans to receive NCQA accreditation, all of the delegated physician groups must submit to the health plan's credentialing criteria and oversight mechanism. Often, these vary from plan to plan but roughly align with the NCQA guidelines for credentialing and data gathering. A typical credentialing check list appears as Figure 4 on page 250. Most insurers demand that credentialing be "primary source" so networks are seldom able to use the hospital's credentialing unless both hospital and network use a CVO or credentialing process outside the boundaries of both the network and hospital. A CVO must have its own policies, procedures and oversight board.

Recredentialing: Linking Quality Improvement to Credentialing

More and more, physician performance on multiple measures is used to recredential physicians for networks and hospitals. While credentialing is intended to ensure that physicians meet minimum requirements, many organizations are finding that just meeting the minimum is not enough. In a competitive market, physicians need to meet and exceed personal and organizational performance standards. *(See Figure 5 on page 251.)*

Linking credentialing to process improvement is a long-term process that seeks to realign the focus of credentialing. *(For more information on linking credentialing and CQI, see Raymond Fabius' article on page 237.)* It starts with a few realizations and small steps. Providers at West Paces Ferry Hospital in Atlanta have developed a system that links process improvement and recredentialing. *(See Figure 6 below.)*

FIGURE 6: QUALITY ALARMS

Mortality

Treatment failures

- Readmission within 33 days
- Unplanned return to OR
- Unplanned admission after outpatient procedure
- Unplanned OR procedure
- Laparoscopic procedure converted to open
- Unplanned transfer to critical care within 24 hours after surgery

Treatment issues—WPMC staff

- Treatment error
- Medication error
- Missed/delayed treatments
- Extravasation of IV agent
- Central line occlusion
- Response time >30 minutes to stat test request
- Positive dialysis equipment cultures

Treatment issues—physicians

- Patients not seen in ER by physician within 30 minutes
- Patients not seen in critical care within 4 hours of admission
- COBRA transfer requirements not met
- Time expired on legal forms in psychiatry
- Delivery missed by primary caregiver
- Pharmacy consultation
- Code 2 and 3 tissue specimens
- Crossmatch to transfused ratio

Adverse patient occurrences

- Traumatic events
- Pneumothora after procedure
- Transfusion reaction
- Adverse reaction to ECT
- Re-intubation
- MI or stroke post anesthesia
- Significant bleeding after procedure
- Adverse drug reaction
- Infection rates

Patient noncompliance

- AMA
- Elopement
- Drug use in outpatient A&D treatment
- Suicide attempt/overdose while inpatient

References
[1]Ubell, E. "It Could Be Called a Miracle." *Parade Magazine*, 5, January 12, 1992.
[2]Appleby, C.R. "Are Laparoscopy Docs Properly Credentialed?" *HealthWeek*, 5(15):1, 36, August 12, 1991.

ABOUT THE AUTHORS

J. Edward McEachern, MD is the vice president for medical affairs at St. Alphonsus Regional Medical Center in Boise, Idaho. Previously, Dr. McEachern was Vice president for medical affairs at Hospital Corporation of America (HCA)'s West Paces Ferry Hospital in Atlanta, and quality improvement consultant for direct patient care to HCA's corporate office in Nashville, Tenn. HE is the author of four books and numerous articles on quality improvement, and is on the editorial review board of three newsletters.

Jonathan T. Lord, MD, is the AHA's chief operating officer. Previously Dr. Lord was the director for quality assurance for the Department of the Navy and served as an advisor to the secretary of the navy during a major reorganization of navy medicine. He is a member of the American College of Physician Executives and the American Medical Association.

Using Physician Profiles in the Reappointment Process

By John S. Coldiron, MD, MPH, FACPE

All too often, medical staff reappointment tends to be viewed as less important than initial appointment. While the background of new applicants is closely scrutinized, reappointment may be perceived as an administrative routine, not an occasion for thorough reappraisal. In this article, the author argues that objective information about clinical performance, summarized in a readable profile, can be the basis for informed reappointment and privileging decisions.

◆ ◆ ◆

Medical staff reappointment should be an extremely important element of continuous quality improvement, an opportunity to reaffirm a practitioner's competence and identify any areas needing improvement. Unless a physician has been involved in a serious quality assurance matter, behavioral problem or other unusual circumstance, it is likely his or her reappointment file contains little more than a completed reapplication form and routine verification of licensure, CME, staff meeting attendance and so forth. If clinical performance information is available, it probably is not summarized in a format that allows quick analysis and comparison. This is not much help to a department chair or credentials committee asked to make a judgment regarding a practitioner's continuing clinical competence. And it's not terribly helpful to the practitioner either.

Development of a process for biennial reappointment has been an activity driven by the JCAHO in many accredited healthcare organizations. The medical staff task force of the JCAHO's Professional and Technical Advisory Committee, however, will be considering the recommendation proposed by the National Association of Medical Staff Services to drop the reappointment requirement.[1] Even if such a recommendation is eventually implemented, the need remains for a process that gives feedback to staff at regular intervals and provides timely evaluation of performance. The real importance of the profiling and performance review and feedback lies in performance improvement—not the fulfillment of a JCAHO requirement. A formal, biennial reevaluation of medical staff members' performance can provide the opportunity for a critical but constructive examination of current clinical and behavioral competence. The department chair or other physician leader can use this occasion to share with the practitioner objective performance information, as well as informal observations. Information that compares an individual's practice characteristics with aggregate information regarding peers can reinforce the practitioner's understanding of personal strengths and identify areas for improvement. The reappointment can focus on the future in other ways, too. The physician executive can discuss the physician's plans for the future at the hospital, group or managed care organization and hear any problems the physician is encountering within the organization that may interfere with optimal patient care.

The Value of Practice Profiles

In years past, it was often assumed that a department chair knew the competence of the other doctors in the department simply by proximity of practice and by passively listening for informal input. This subjective approach was prone to serious flaws, often complicated by the politics of proprietary and competing interests, and is no longer acceptable in any setting.

Physician practice profiles, particularly those that include comparative data, can be very useful in assisting physician leaders to make informed decisions about reappointing staff members and renewing clinical privileges. Practice profiles consist of locally relevant data elements measuring various aspects of a physician's practice at the institution, including results of peer review. This approach to evaluation of physician performance, also called practice pattern analysis (PPA), is emerging as an effective method for providing meaningful information to further decision making regarding reappointment. Several variations of PPA, including the use of aggregate data by practitioners, are successfully being used.[2] Almost 60 percent of hospitals surveyed in 1992 for a *Hospitals* magazine poll indicated that prepared physician-specific, comparative profiles.[3] It can be assumed that this practice has increased in hospitals, as well as having expanded into ambulatory care and group practice settings.[4,5]

Elements of a Physician Profile

As a physician leader, you should expect your organization (within its resources) to provide a profile of information that will help you assess the performance of practitioners for whom you must make a recommendation. You, in turn, have a responsibility to:

- Review the data carefully and use them judiciously;
- Discuss the information with the practitioner in an educational vein, if necessary;
- Use it as one — but not the sole — source of information for your credentialing decision; and
- Make clear to the organization the types of information you require so that data collection and profile development can be improved over time.

What should go into a profile? With the help of physician leaders, each institution can develop relevant parameters. In general, a profile may include information in four categories:

- Participation in medical staff activities;
- Clinical activity levels;
- Peer review results; and, in some organizations,
- Resource use/cost comparison data.

The profile is not the only information assembled. The practitioner completes a reapplication form, and the appropriate parties verify information on current licensure, liability insurance, National Practitioner Data Bank, health status, etc. The profile adds objective performance information not usually assembled in the past. Before discussing profile use, let's examine three of the major categories of profile information. (*Resource use/cost data are discussed in a separate chapter on economic credentialing.*)

Participation in medical staff functions. Few physicians enjoy taking part in required medical staff functions, but most recognize their significance. One portion of the profile summarizes how well practitioners are fulfilling these responsibilities. Although this is probably the least important aspect of the profile, it cannot be disregarded. The essential community service and quality improvement activities of the medical staff cannot be fulfilled without physician involvement.

FIGURE 1: REQUIRED MEDICAL STAFF ACTIVITIES

1. Orientation completion
2. Staff meeting attendance
3. Departmental meeting attendance
4. Committee attendance
5. Medical staff leadership role participation
6. Peer review participation
7. Fulfillment of service obligations
8. Participation in CME and teaching activities
9. Scholarly activity

Figure 1 lists common medical staff activities. Some are straightforward, such as attendance at department and committee meetings, participation in peer review activities and (for new members) participation in medical staff orientation. Other activities may include providing care for indigent and uninsured patients, contributing to continuing education activities and, as appropriate, participating in scholarly activity.

Information on participation in required activities can be summarized in a simple reporting format that reflects the local standards and preferences. For instance, the profile could show meeting attendance in percentages, a total of CME hours, and a list of participation on committees and other activities inside and outside the organization.

Depending upon the value placed upon these activities versus the contribution that the staff member makes through his or her clinical practice, the reviewer must make a judgment as to the relative importance of these activities. An applicant's failure to meet these obligations may not have any direct impact on the quality of patient care, but it can have a large impact on the fairness of the distribution of required medical staff clinical and administrative activities. Judgments in this regard must be based on policy. The judgment of the reviewer should follow the expectation guidelines set by the medical staff or departmental policy. In the absence of such policy, the reviewer should request guidance from the appropriate departmental or medical executive committee. Otherwise, lack of uniformity of treatment is likely to result among medical staff members and will, sooner or later, cause disharmony.

Characteristics of clinical practice activities. The next section of a profile is designed to describe, in numerical terms, the volumes and types of care involved in the physician's practice. There are no right and wrong numbers here, unless a facility has established minimum activity levels to ensure proficiency for certain procedures or for other reasons.

Comparative data for the various items included under the rubric of clinical activities (*See Figure below*) must also be based upon medical staff and departmental standards (e.g., standards for medical record and progress note completion) that are approved, promulgated and then monitored uniformly with timely feedback. Utilization data can be compared both internally and externally with properly adjusted case mix groupings. Numbers of admissions, procedures and consultations can be compared intra-institutionally to specialty-specific groups. The concept of "comparative data" will not apply to such items as professional liability cases, however, because the specifics of each situation must be reviewed to determine if a significant pattern exists.

Figure 2: Clinical Activities

1. Inpatient and day care/ambulatory admissions
2. Inpatient and day care/ambulatory procedures
3. Consultations
4. Utilization data, e.g.,
   Length of day
   Ancillary use
   Percent denied admissions
   Percent denied days
5. Compliance with administrative requirements
   Medical records completion
   Progress notes
   Response to UR inquiries
6. Patient compliments and complaints
7. Professional liability claim record
8. Potential liability occurrences

Again, these data can be presented in a simple reporting format that reflects the preferences of the individuals who will be expected to use the data.

Peer review results. Perhaps the most critical area in terms of quality is analyzing the peer review results that have accrued in the biennium since the last appointment or reappointment. Typically, this section of the profile includes information obtained from both internal and external formal peer review processes such as traditional quality assurance review activities, utilization review, issues identified through risk management occurrence screening, findings of focus case review, indicator monitoring and internally confirmed findings reported by external reviewers.

It is important to remember that the peer review information in the profile is only as good as the system that performs data collection and peer review in the first place.

FIGURE 3: FLOW CHART OF THE PEER REVIEW PROCESS

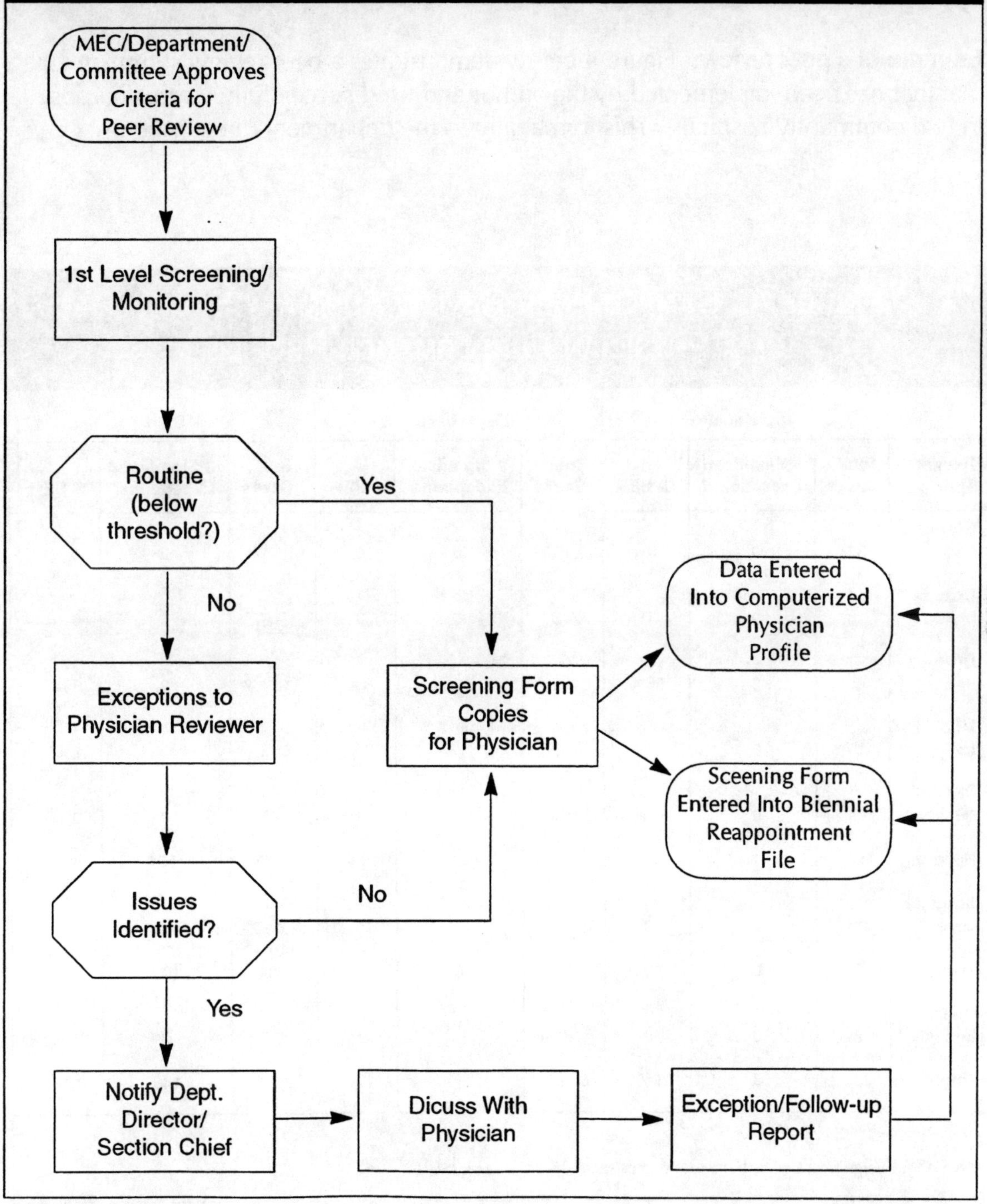

This system must allow the retrieval of both "numerator" and "denominator" data so that percentages can be developed. Saying Dr. A. and Dr. B. both had two preventable, serious complications is misleading without knowing their respective patient volumes.

In addition, the peer review system must be constructed appropriately. Such a system is based on an information flow that incorporates concurrent interaction with and feedback to the practitioner during the review process. *(See Figure 3 on page 259.)* The system summarizes the findings regarding the individual physician compared with a peer group. Such a system can be used to provide a summary report that can be easily reviewed by department directors, credentials committees, executive committees or other bodies involved in the reappointment process and, if necessary, used to prompt further investigation of specific cases or issues.

Example of a peer review. Figure 4 below demonstrates a peer review summary format that has been implemented by the author and used successfully for this purpose in two community hospitals. This format allows the department director or other

FIGURE 4: SAMPLE PEER REVIEW SUMMARY SECTION OF A PHYSICIAN PERFORMANCE PROFILE

	Individual			Department			Staff		
Review Type	Total Cases	# Significant Exceptions*	% SER	Total Cases	# Significant Exceptions	% SER	Toal Cases	# Significant Exceptions*	% SER
Blood use	34	0	0	1,160	3	0	1,547	3	0
Criteria based	18	0	0	773	0	0	1,127	0	0
Drug use	3	2	66%	109	9	8%	129	9	6%
Mor-tality	19	0	0	452	13	2%	503	14	2%
PRO quality	6	0	0	153	0	0	192	0	0
Record	17	1	5%	485	53	10%	1,032	83	8%
Surgical case	23	0	0	3,146	39	1%	7,412	40	0
Tissue	5	0	0	152	0	0	266	0	0
Utiliza-tion	6	0	0	151	0	0	187	0	0
Totals	**131**	**3**	**2%**	**6,581**	**117**	**1%**	**12,395**	**149**	**1%**

*Number of significant exceptions found after second-level review (SER)

reviewer to quickly compare an individual practitioner with others in his or her department and with the medical staff as a whole in terms of the number of cases that show a significant exception to the established standard following secondary review. The profile must provide an adequate representation of volume of cases treated by the individual practitioner.

Making the Data Useful

Physician profiles can be a very effective tool in maintaining a medical staff that uniformly meets established practice parameters, and they provide one avenue for continually improving practice through feedback. However, providing physician profile data to the department director, the credentials committee and other reviewers certainly does not ensure the desired result. For example, it is very important to establish forms and report formats that are straightforward and easily interpreted. Reappointment applications must be presented to the reviewer in sufficiently low numbers and on a timely basis to allow adequate time to assess each reappointment. "Batch" processing reappointment applications is unlikely to result in a thorough review process. Finally, experience shows that it is very important to orient—and, from time to time, reeducate—chiefs and committee members regarding the importance and proper use of all of the information that is contained in the reappointment materials— including the "physician profile."

"Weighting" Data Elements

As mentioned earlier, not all elements of the physician practice profile are of equal importance in the reappointment consideration. Each of the medical staff and clinical activities needs to be "weighted" in a manner agreed upon by the medical staff as a whole. A point system based upon aggregated scores of the physician profile items can be used to produce "scores" that, in turn, can be used to facilitate the reappointment review process.[6]

Avoiding Unnecessary Issues

Often the review of an application for reappointment is "hung up" because the applicant has not met the expected standard for meeting attendance, has had an unacceptable number of medical records problems, or has fallen below expected hospital use rates. Each of these issues is important in the total profile of the physician's relationship to the institution—but not for patient care-related reasons.

In the instance of poor meeting attendance, the solution may rest in having more than one active staff category. For those who are clinically active at the institution but do not participate in medical staff meetings and other kinds of medical staff activities, a failure to reappoint would seem inappropriate as long as they adequately participate in quality assurance activities of the institution. On the other hand, physicians who do fulfill all of their staff obligations could be given a staff category that entitles them to such things as lower dues, free parking and other incentives that would reward them for the work they perform on behalf of the other less active members. The "scores" obtained through the weighting system can be successfully used to differentiate staff members into such categories. (*See Figure 5 on page 262.*)

FIGURE 5: SAMPLE CRITERIA FOR SENIOR ACTIVE STAFF

	Weight
* Board certified — Does not apply to individuals who achieved this level	3.0
* Meets departmental, sectional, committee, and staff meeting attendance requirements	3.0
* No major disciplinary actions in past 5 years	3.0
* Staff member ≥ 5 years	3.0
* Has served successfully as a committee member	3.0
Admits ≥ 75 percent of expected admissions by specialty	2.5
Number of day care admissions ≥ 85 percent pf of expected for specialty	2.5
Proven teaching ability and participates as requested in medical education, graduate medical education, and continuing medical education	2.5
Number of consultations ≥ 75 percent of expected for specialty	2.5
Fulfills "service" obligations as requested	2.5
Satisfactorily complies with medical record, audit, and utilization review requirements of the hospital	2.0
Has served successfully as medical staff committee chair or on medical executive committee	2.0
Number of suspensions for incomplete records has not exceeded 6/year during past 2 years	1.5
Maintains academic appointment as appropriate	1.5
Number of notifications for "no progress notes" has not exceeded 8 times/year in past 2 years	1.0
Total	35.5

*=Absolute requirement
Eligibility total ≥ 30

In the situation of the staff member who has frequent lapses in medical records completion, one is well advised to handle this as an administrative matter (with possible disciplinary consequences). The department chief can take a very useful role in discussing medical records issues with the practitioner as they occur and conveying on a personal level the importance of complete and timely medical records to good patient care. Such discussion also provides the opportunity to review the medical staff and departmental standards for record completion. If such standards do not exist, the department chief should work with the executive committee or departmental membership to establish them. Otherwise, medical record discussions with staff members can become very subjective and argumentative.

If the department chief's intervention is unsuccessful, the physician may be asked to appear at a medical executive committee to discuss corrective action. Only in the very unlikely event that this level of intervention should fail would medical records issues become an important reappointment consideration.

In the case of the physician who has relatively low volume at the institution, the categories of staff membership should include criteria for the volume of cases that the attending physician should care for at the institution. The "low volume" staff member is of particular difficulty in the reappointment process, because the organization has little basis on which to judge current competence. It becomes very important to seek adequate reference and peer review information from other institutions where the practitioner has staff membership. In those situations where it is not possible to satisfactorily confirm current competence, special measures such as might be used during the initial observation period of provisional membership should be reinstituted or, if the volume has fallen below set criteria standards, then staff membership should be discontinued.

Reappointment as an Opportunity for Communication

The occasion of application for reappointment should be viewed as an opportunity by the department director to perform the equivalent of a performance evaluation with the staff member. In addition to the very important role of providing feedback to staff members regarding their "practice profile," such a meeting provides a formal occasion to review with the staff their future practice, plans and goals—and for the department director to set new goals and objectives and to discuss future departmental plans with staff members.

Physician practice profiles codify medical staff participation expectations and standards for practice within the institution and are an essential tool in the reappointment process.

Department directors, credentials committees and executive committees being asked to make reappointment decisions need objective bases for making judgments in a uniform manner. Internal and external comparative data, as appropriate, should be a part of the physician profile information that is developed. The profile must be presented in a format that is easily comprehended and interpreted so as to encourage careful consideration by the reappointment reviewers.

In addition, carefully prepared and easily readable profiles can be used as a centerpiece for discussion between the individual practitioner and the department chief at their biennial reappointment "performance review." Careful attention to the preparation of physician profiles and adherence to a procedure that encourages communication of the materials and good discussion between department director and the individual practitioner will enhance the quality of medical practice within an institution or organization.

◆ ◆ ◆

References

[1]"News briefs." *Briefings on JCAHO*, 2, June 1997.

[2]American Hospital Association. *Practice Pattern Analysis: A Tool for Continuous Improvement of Patient Care Quality*. Chicago: American Hospital Association.

[3]"HCFA: New Committees to Address Physician Medicare Hassles." *Medical Staff Leader*, 7, June 7.

[4]Newman, C., White, S., and Burman D. "Physician profiling: applications for the Robert Wood Johnson Profiling Project Database." *Journal of Ambulatory Care Management*. 19(4): 49-57.

5"Physician Profiling in Group Practices" *Journal of Ambulatory Care Management* 19(4): 28- 39).

6Op. Cit., "Physician Profiling: Applications for the Robert Wood Johnson Profiling Project Database"

About the Author

John S. Coldiron, MD, MPH, FACPE, is senior vice president of the Massachusetts Hospital Association's Clinical Affairs Division. He formerly was vice president for medical affairs at Carney Hospital, Boston.

Demystifying Economic Credentialing: The Myths and the Realities

by Barry S. Bader and Reggi Veatch

In this article, the authors offer an orientation to what is called economic credentialing. While describing how economically related factors are entering the credentialing process, they suggest that:

- *The term economic credentialing has been overused and misused, and it can lead to unnecessary conflict;*
- *Credentialing should be based on a comprehensive assessment of a practitioner's performance, not any single factor; and*
- *Physician, board and management leaders need to address economically related aspects of credentialing issues in a collaborative manner that serves the interests of patients, the organization and the community.*

◆ ◆ ◆

When people use the term "economic credentialing," they usually are referring to the incorporation of economic or business-related factors, criteria and data into decisions regarding physician appointment, reappointment and clinical privileges. Few phrases trigger more emotion among physicians. Much of the furor, however, is needless, because it's based on myths and misperceptions. This article endeavors to objectively discuss the topic and help leaders avoid unnecessary conflict and work toward collaborative solutions.

Myths and Realities

Myth No. 1: Economic data, such as resource utilization patterns, have no relationship to quality and, therefore, no place in the credentialing process.

Reality: Herein lies the fundamental flaw in arguments against using economic data in the credentials review and privileging processes. Economic data are not used alone, but rather to point to potential quality of care problems that also have economic impact. Data on the economic impact of a physician's practice typically employ such measures as overall financial gain/loss, average length of stay, average resource use and average charges or costs, often categorized by major diagnostic category (MDC) or diagnosis-related group (DRG). When these data identify physicians whose resource use is very different from colleagues who treat similar patients, the next step is not an adverse credentialing decision but, rather, peer review and analysis.

Peer review often indicates an underlying quality of care problem, such as inappropriate or redundant diagnostic testing, inappropriate drug prescribing, or inappropriate invasive procedures. For example, the financial table above shows a hospital is breaking even or earning a profit on patients of four physicians but is losing money on physician E.'s respiratory care patients. Note that patient severity does not explain the difference, as Dr. E.'s patients are no sicker, on average, than the patients of his peers.

The data show only the physicians' economic impact; they don't explain the cause. Subsequent peer review found that Dr. E. was inappropriately admitting patients to intensive care, using the costliest antibiotics when less expensive alternatives were equally effective and keeping patients hospitalized after they were ready for discharge. After being shown how his patient management differed from his peers and from current medical standards, Dr. E. voluntarily altered his practice patterns.

The lesson is this: Economic data alone almost never justify termination of privileges. Typically, economic impact data would be used to deny privileges only if:

- Peer review documented an underlying quality of care problem that caused the financial losses; and
- The physician had been given an opportunity to review the data and change his or her practice patterns but refused to cooperate.

Most of the time, education and counseling, including sharing objective data, result in physicians adopting more cost-effective practice patterns.

Myth No. 2: Doctors don't care how much money the hospital spends.

Reality: No physician wants to practice bad or unnecessarily expensive medicine; many, however, are unaware of their practice patterns. For example: One physician routinely ordered a $150 dollar IV solution for his patients when they could have been receiving oral medication for $5. The physician said he didn't know the cost of the drugs.[1] After he'd been shown the data, the physician changed his practice.

Myth No. 3: Economic credentialing means only economic criteria will be used to determine staff appointment.

Reality: Physician credentialing should be based on a comprehensive evaluative profile of a physician's qualifications and performance, including training, experience, clinical activity, clinical outcomes, peer recommendations, quality assurance reviews and so on. If an economic profile is included, it would be only one factor, used as described above.

Myth No. 4: Hospitals are extensively using economic criteria to remove expensive doctors from the medical staff.

Reality: Most hospitals do not formally examine economic factors at all in credentialing decisions. A 1989 AHA survey found just 4.7 percent of 3,400 hospitals reportedly tied economic profiles to credentialing. On the other hand, a 1991 survey for *Hospitals* magazine found more than 40 percent of 500 hospital CEOs believed they might consider economic factors in credentialing in the next five years.[2] So, physician leaders need to be ready to deal with this topic should it arise, but based on facts, not myths. Consideration of economic impact is likely to take the form of using economic profiles as an initial screen subject to peer review, not as the sole criterion for clinical privileges. The idea that hospitals are planning to use economic data as a club to remove physicians who adversely affect hospital finances is unsubstantiated.

Myth No. 5: Economic credentialing is a battleground for physician autonomy.

Reality: Many trustees and executives do not understand why many physicians are concerned about the possible misuse of economic data in the credentialing process. Physician leaders can play a vital education role here.

Most physicians have come to recognize the need for cost-effective resource use. They are quick to point out, however, that *overutilization* is not the same as *expensive* utilization. By their very nature, certain specialties are resource intensive, even when practiced with the highest degree of efficiency. Physicians in these specialties fear that they may be denied privileges based solely on the cost of their services. In the worst case, they argue, this may mean whole communities will lose access to certain expensive services.

Physicians are also concerned that hospitals will cherry pick doctors who treat only profitable, well-insured patients, abandoning sick or underinsured patients. Some practitioners worry that, despite promises to the contrary, economic data alone could be used to deny privileges to formerly open medical staffs. Hospital privileges are essential to the livelihood and professional practice of most physicians. Physician leaders can help boards and executives understand why talk of economic credentialing arouses such visceral feelings.

Hospitals and medical staffs are not as far apart on the use of economic factors as it might appear. For example, Duane Dauner of the California Association of Hospitals and Health Systems writes: Establishing parameters for quality patient care, acceptable patient outcomes and cost effectiveness lies within each hospital governing board's responsibility to patients and the community. And Jack S. Rotenberg, MD, an internist and activist against some forms of economic credentialing, writes: In most hospitals, the adverse economic impact of some physicians can be minimized or reversed by the cooperation of an enlightened administration and a knowledgeable medical staff willing to act responsibly. Most doctors are aware that closure of their hospital would not be good for them or their patients and would do almost anything to avoid that occurrence. Clearly, there's common ground here for those leaders who seek it.

Other Situations Involving Economically Related Factors

From the healthcare trade press and the legal system, there have come reports of other manifestations of economic factors having an impact on credentialing. Although these situations are not widespread and often can be avoided, physician leaders should be aware of them.

Channeling of unprofitable patients. Dr. Z. admits almost all his healthier, profitable patients to Hospital A, while admitting mainly sicker patients requiring more intensive resources to Hospital B. In today's current payment system, Hospital B loses money on this physician's sicker patients, who require more intensive resources.

Such situations require very careful handling. Physicians are often unaware of the financial impact of their admissions patterns on a hospital. In addition, physicians may admit sicker patients to a particular hospital because they believe it is better equipped to handle them, or because of patient preference.

One way to address this situation is for the medical director or a physician leader to objectively discuss the situation with the practitioner, present pertinent data and ask for the physician's input and help. Does the physician, in fact, admit less acutely ill patients elsewhere? Why? (There may be good reasons.) Was he or she aware of the financial impact on the hospital? Would the practitioner be willing and able to admit a fairer share of less seriously ill (and more profitable) patients to Hospital B?

Obviously, it is not in the interests of either the physician or the community if one hospital bears a disproportionate share of unreimbursed expenses and, therefore, must cut back necessary services or even close. However, this is best addressed through education and voluntary behavior change, not formal credentialing action. Ideally, payment reform would rectify the problem, but that is beyond the scope of this article.

Competitive situations. An even more sensitive and controversial scenario involves physicians who compete directly with a hospital. For example, an ophthalmologist operates an eye surgery center across the street from the hospital and performs all her routine ambulatory cases at the eye surgery center. She admits only serious cases and complications of outpatient procedures to the hospital, which posts significant losses on these sick patients.

Very few hospitals have even thought of removing privileges in such situations, but as hospitals face increasingly stringent economic pressures, more may do so. For example, a Florida hospital denied a physician privileges for cardiac surgery because it believed he posed a financial threat to the hospital. The physician's clinical qualifications were never an issue, but he directed the cardiac surgery unit at a nearby hospital. The governing board felt its $10 million investment in equipment would be compromised by credentialing a competitor, and, therefore, it voted to deny the physician cardiac surgery privileges. However, he was granted medical staff membership and granted thoracic (but not cardiac) surgery privileges. The physician sued, but a Florida court upheld the hospital's decision.[3]

Along the same lines, courts in California upheld two hospitals' decisions to close membership in, respectively, a cardiac surgery department (Redding v. St. Francis) and an anesthesiology department (Matteo Woodburn v. Fresno) on what the hospitals contended were quality and business grounds.[4]

Contractual situations. Similarly, economic factors are becoming enmeshed in disputes over exclusive contracts for physician services. Exclusive contracts are well established. In areas such as radiology, pathology, emergency services and anesthesiology, many hospitals have determined that giving an exclusive contract to a physician or group practice promotes administrative efficiency, cost effectiveness and quality of care.

Problems have arisen when the hospital wants to change contract terms or change the physicians under contract. For example, some hospitals have asserted the right to terminate contracts (and, in so doing, hospital privileges) for purely economic or administrative reasons, not quality of care grounds. An example of this allegedly occurred in a hospital in Culpepper, Va., where a group of radiologists contend the hospital demanded 36 percent of their fees in return for billing and management services and then removed their privileges when negotiations failed.[5]

Similarly, a hospital in Tallahassee, Fla. terminated a radiation oncologist's privileges because of what it said were administrative problems, including unwillingness to add a physician to an overly busy practice, failure to keep good records, and failure to arrange for adequate coverage. The physician sued and won on the grounds the hospital hadn't followed its own due process rules to remove his privileges.[6]

Ideally, situations such as these can be resolved without resorting to litigation. What is certain is that contracts for hospital-based services present controversial issues in which economic and quality of care factors are closely intertwined.

Leadership Role in Forging Collaboration

The foregoing discussion shows how the term economic credentialing is applied to a variety of different situations. Physician leaders can promote collaboration by educating themselves, the board, management and their peers about the complexity of the issue and by pursuing responsible and informed discussion on a very volatile topic.

Foundation: Trust and common values. An organization's ability to address and resolve these issues is directly related to whether a climate of mutual respect and trust has been created and whether the organization and its physicians have developed a common sense of mission and values. Education and communication, as discussed already, can provide a common foundation for rational exploration of the issue and the search for alternative solutions.

In addition, physician leaders can apply a number of practical strategies for collaborating, including:

- **Careful bylaws development and observance.** Avoid conflicts by developing bylaws provisions that reflect common values with regard to economic credentialing. For example, the bylaws might state that cost-effective use of clinical resources is one of the criteria for medical staff privileges. The bylaws should also be explicit as to the relationships between privileges and exclusive contracts. Once written, the bylaws must be observed in any due process proceedings.

- **Continuous quality improvement.** Address resource utilization issues through quality improvement and peer review mechanisms. Help all physicians develop more cost-effective practice patterns. Periodically share comparative resource use data, including at the time of reappointment, but take adverse action only if a practitioner refuses to follow the recommendations of the peer review process.

- **Medical practice guidelines.** As part of CQI efforts, practice guidelines can help physicians study and develop more cost-effective approaches to clinical care. According to J. Jarret Clinton, MD, administrator of the federal agency charged with promoting practice guidelines, "It is reasonable to expect" that practice variations and the associated resource utilization and costs will decrease once physicians have access to reliable, objective data on the most effective treatment choices.[7]

- **Medical staff development plans.** In cooperation with the medical staff, develop a plan that determines the number and types of physicians the organization needs, based on its current and future resources and community needs. The plan may serve as the basis for physician recruitment and credentialing efforts and the acquisition of new technology and facilities. Such plans should have medical staff input, but to avoid antitrust they must be based on objective criteria and approved by the governing board.

Clearly, economic factors have entered the credentialing arena. To avoid needless conflict, leaders should build their credentials policy making and decision making on four fundamental values:

- The best interests of patients and the quality of patient care;
- Cost effectiveness, availability and affordability of needed services;
- A recognition of the changing economic environment and the need for cooperative working relationships between hospitals and physicians; and
- Preservation of community and organizational assets and resources.

◆ ◆ ◆

References

[1]Greene, J., "System Pioneers Credentialing." *Modern Healthcare.* p. 1, April 29, 1991.

[2]Larkin, H., and McCormick, B. "The Many Faces of Economic Credentialing." *American Medical News.* pp. 3, 28, July 20, 1992.

[3]Larkin, *ibid*

[4]Bader, B.S. Economic Factors and Credentialing. *The Quality Letter for Healthcare Leaders.* p. 26, April 1991.

[5]Greeson, T.W. "Exclusive Contracts: Should Hospitals Substitute Financial Interests for Quality Considerations?" *The Quality Letter for Healthcare Leaders.* pp. 12-15, April 1991.

[6]*Bilek v. Tallahassee Memorial Regional Medical Center.* Reported in McCormick, B. "Suing Over Exclusivity: Courts Grappling With Economic Credentialing." *American Medical News.* p. 1, January 13, 1992.

[7]Clinton, J.J. "Overview." *Research News.* p. 6, March 1992.

ABOUT THE AUTHOR

Barry S. Bader is a governance consultant and speaker based in Potomac, Md. He has advised many hospitals, health systems and physician groups on improving board performance.

Medical Staff Responsibility for Physician Health

by Daniel A. Lang, MD

What is the medical staff's responsibility for physician health? How does a medical staff help members who become impaired while still ensuring the quality and safety of patient care? This article addresses these and other questions by looking at the evolving role of the physician well-being committee in identifying a disabled or impaired physician; developing appropriate intervention strategies; and establishing monitoring programs to support the physician's reentry into hospital practice.

◆ ◆ ◆

Much has been written about the hospital medical staff's responsibility to monitor care for the valid goal of ensuring adherence to professional standards. Physicians have grudgingly become accustomed to the need to monitor the performance of their peers and to having their own proficiency and even productivity reviewed. The modern focus on performance improvement of systems still identifies circumstances in which clinical error or adverse outcome is the result of individual action or omission. Thus, at various times, reviews will identify a physician whose performance, as demonstrated by quality assessment and peer review, has begun to decline, or who has had a sentinel event that forced corrective action.

Both circumstances will lead to an in-depth review to find the cause. In some cases, the cause will not be lack of knowledge or refusal to follow accepted protocols but rather the loss of physical or mental skills. The loss may be due to alcohol, drugs, psychiatric disease, physical illness or simply "wearing down" in response to age or the demands of modern medical practice. From time to time, a physician will voluntarily come forward because of a self-perceived problem with alcohol, drugs or a declining capacity to practice. When such a physician comes forward, the medical staff may need to respond with more urgency than it would under normal circumstances so as to seize the moment and to avoid patient harm.

Peer Review Responsibilities

What's a medical staff to do? Does it have an obligation to do anything? If so, should the action be supportive, punitive, or protective of the physician? Where is the border between protecting the patient and showing compassion for a colleague? In reality, the border is artificial. The best protection for the patient is a hospital medical staff program that ensures physical and mental fitness for the privileges all physicians enjoy.

The program starts with a provision in the medical staff bylaws requiring physicians to prove, to the satisfaction of the medical staff, physical and mental fitness to exercise the privileges requested. While broad latitude exists in the application of this principle, it provides the medical staff with the authority to deal with the blind radiologist and the totally deaf psychiatrist, as well as less extreme cases of disability affecting performance. It also provides a basis for developing policies and mechanisms for evaluating a physician's fitness to practice. Evaluation might follow a disabling illness or be part of the intensive assessment of a serious clinical performance failure in which fitness may have been a factor.

This evaluation is now virtually mandated by new provisions of California law that require the medical staff to determine the presence of mental or physical disability or substance abuse as factors in a clinical performance failure that has led to a formal investigation. Medical staffs are obliged to report those cases to the diversion program of the state medical board, which oversees the findings and actions of the medical staff. In the event of failure of the medical staff to address the problem of physician disability endangering patient safety, the diversion director is authorized to turn the matter over to the chief enforcement officer of the board for formal investigation and action.

Many medical staffs have recognized that a mechanism should be in place to assist with matters related to physician health at all levels. The California Medical Association (CMA) has been a leader in advocating the medical staff's creation of a physician well-being committee. With CMA's support, California hospitals now are required, as a condition of licensure, to have a medical staff program to support physicians who become disabled as a result of alcohol, drugs or mental illness. Although the state mandate contains a provision that preserves confidentiality within the medical staff, it requires the well-being committee to make quarterly reports to the hospital's medical executive committee and the governing board regarding physician support activities. According to the law, the reports to the board are general and statistical in nature, not physician-specific. In California now, if a physician comes forward voluntarily and is placed in a treatment program or in the state's diversion program, no report must be made to the disciplinary arm of the state licensure authority.

On the other hand, if the physician is referred to the well-being committee after there has been a performance failure and an associated disciplinary process, then that disciplinary process is reportable both to the state and to the National Practitioner Data Bank. Unfortunately, the medical board now holds that if a physician agrees to a monitoring agreement and random drug and alcohol testing as a condition of return to practice after treatment, it is reportable to the state as a disciplinary limitation of physician privileges. If that interpretation is allowed to stand, voluntary entry into structured rehabilitation programs is likely to be substantially limited.

The success of the California physician well-being committee concept has led hospitals around the country to establish similar mechanisms themselves or in a collaborative way with medical societies. Although there are no specific accreditation standards relating to physician well-being committees in any of the national programs, the emphasis on physician health in the JCAHO, NCQA and other similar assessments incudes an expectation that the hospital or medical group under review has an effective program for addressing issues related to physician health or disability.

Physician Well-Being Committees

The operative word in dealing with the disabled physician is "support."

Identifying physicians with problems. The well-being committee is most successful when it is able to interact with a physician before there has been substantial performance failure or the need for disciplinary action. The committee must, therefore, operate in a manner that permits and encourages confidential reports for physician behavior, even outside the hospital.

A well-being committee chairman would be receptive, for example, to hearing the observation that a member of the medical staff was seen drunk going down a ski slope. Even though this occurred outside the hospital, the fact that the physician would engage in dangerous activity while intoxicated raises serious questions about his or her health. Based on this and other reports that the physician was seen drinking to excess socially, the chair of the committee would be justified in initiating a confidential discussion with the doctor.

Supporting the physician. The goal of this discussion would be to apprise the physician of the observations and to offer the assistance of the committee. The offer of assistance may be spurned, but this encounter is the first step in the recovery process of an alcoholic or drug-dependent physician—namely, the knowledge that his or her behavior has been noted by peers. Acceptance of the offer of assistance could lead to the physician's voluntary entry into a treatment program. That early response is the ideal, although, realistically, physicians, like others, seek treatment when the internal or external pressures on them become unbearable.

Interventions. Whether a physician should be required to relinquish medical staff privileges upon entering a treatment program depends upon the severity of the problem at the time treatment began. Most treatment authorities would say that some interruption of practice is desirable. There are infrequent instances in which a physician recognizes that he or she has a problem before experiencing any significant social decline and well before showing any signs of professional decline. In those circumstances, a judgment could be made allowing the physician to retain privileges while entering ambulatory treatment and a 12-step program. In situations where a physician denies impairment in the face of strong evidence, the physician well-being committee can organize an intervention to confront the physician with all of the factors in his or her personal and professional life that mandate the need for treatment. An intervention of this sort is a highly skilled professional action, best handled by specialists who can be engaged to work with the well-being committee.

Figure 1: Confidential Agreement for Physician's Return to Practice*

Dr. Mac A. Newstart acknowledges that he is in the early stages of recovery from the use of controlled substances. Dr. Newstart has resumed the clinical practice of obstetrics/gynecology and wishes to resume those privileges at Anywhere General Hospital.

Anywhere General Hospital wishes to provide Dr. Newstart the opportunity to practice his specialty under controlled and structured circumstances as follows:

1. Dr. Newstart agrees to comply with the bylaws, rules and regulations, and policies of Anywhere General Hospital and its medical staff. He will also comply with any limitations on his privileges as approved by the Board of Trustees.
2. The length of this contract will extend for five years with periodic reviews.
3. Total abstinence from all psychoactive substances is required.
4. Dr. Newstart agrees that the following individuals will be informed of his problem and may function as monitors as well as members of his support group. These individuals are:
   a. Dr. Dee Livery, Chairman, OB/GYN
   b. Dr. Guy Necology, obstetrician
   c. Dr. Paul Patient, psychiatrist
   d. Dr. Sherman Potter, President, Medical Staff
   e. Dr. William Walters, obstetrician

   Dr. Newstart agrees to contact one of the above support group members when he is attending a patient at Anywhere General Hospital. For his first 10 deliveries and 10 outpatient surgeries, Dr. Newstart will be proctored by one of the obstetricians named above. The proctor will submit a report within 24 hours to the chair of the Credentials Committee.

   Thereafter, and for a period of two years, the support group may require such continual monitoring and personal observations as it deems appropriate.
5. Periodically, Dr. Newstart may be asked to donate body fluids for analysis for the presence of chemical substances. He agrees to submit to that examination. Such requests will not be unreasonably made. Tests will be performed through the hospital clinical laboratory at cost, to be paid by Dr. Newstart.
6. Dr. Newstart agrees to participate in the Impairment Program conducted by the State Medical Society. He agrees that Anywhere General Hospital may communicate with representatives of the program for purposes of monitoring and review of the progress.
7. Dr. Newstart agrees to participate in frequent meetings of Alcoholics Anonymous (AA), at least three to four times weekly. Dr. Newstart agrees that his AA sponsor will give Anywhere General Hospital periodic confirmatory reports on request and will inform it immediately if he misses two consecutive meetings or more than one meeting a week.
8. From time to time there may be monitoring of Dr. Newstart's patient care. He agrees to cooperate with monitoring physicians in that process.
9. Response to relapse: Any instance of noncompliance with any of the terms of this contract will result in an immediate re-evaluation of this agreement. The physician may be required to take leave from clinical responsibilities while the situation and this agreement are re-evaluated. A revised agreement may include requirements for additional treatment, additional monitoring, and/or an extended leave. Noncompliance could lead to loss of medical staff privileges.
10. Dr. Newstart agrees that the contents of this agreement and the circumstances surrounding it may be made known in a confidential manner to the chief of staff.

Upon acceptance of this agreement and approval by the Board of Trustees, Dr. Newstart will be permitted to continue his practice at Anywhere General Hospital. Should Dr. Newstart fail to live up to the terms of the agreement, those privileges will be terminated and appropriate reports will be filed with the state medical board.

I fully understand the above terms and agree to comply with them.

Signed:

Mac. A. Newstart, MD	*Sherman T. Potter, MD*
	For Anywhere General Hospital
July 1, 1992	*July 1, 1992*

*Adapted, with permission, from *The Disabled Physician: Problem-Solving Strategies for the Medical Staff*, published by American Hospital Publishing, Inc., © 1989.

Monitoring the physician. Well-being committees usually remain in touch with the progress of physicians who have entered treatment, in part to assist in developing a specific monitoring program to support the physician's reentry into hospital practice. The elements of a monitoring program are quite straightforward and are usually documented in a written agreement. *(See Figure 1.)* In return for the restoration of medical staff privileges, the physician agrees to restrain from using alcohol or recreational drugs. The medical staff is authorized to conduct random neurophysiologic testing and examination of body fluids anytime the physician is in the hospital. Usually, the physician is also required to participate faithfully in a 12-step or other outpatient recovery model during the course of the agreement, which usually lasts two to five years. Failure to pass the random tests or examinations or to continue the treatment program could lead to a summary loss of medical staff privileges. In California, the diversion program would be notified as well.

Other types of disability or impairment. This model of identification, support, intervention and monitoring is applicable to other clinical circumstances, as well. For example, a physician with a bipolar disorder may be required to agree to random behavior evaluation along with mandatory measurement of serumlithium levels. Similarly, a physician exhibiting bizarre or abusive behavior as a result of erratic control of diabetes could be required to participate in the same type of monitoring program.

The physician well-being committee is authorized by the medical staff to receive information from anyone who chooses to bring it forward. Nurses, particularly, have an opportunity to observe physician behavior, but other hospital professional personnel or a physician's family members also can provide useful observations. Through the well-being committee, physician support can extend in additional directions. The stress of modern medical practice takes its toll in divorce, suicides and chronic dissatisfaction. Medical staffs have recognized that physicians need an opportunity to ventilate constructively. The aim is not to merely blow off steam but, rather, to develop reality and coping skills that permit physicians to adjust to an environment that promises increasing stress and tension. Health promotion and wellness are also within the scope of the support activities of the well-being committee.

Formal Disciplinary Action

The physician well-being committee plays no direct role in medical staff QA activities, peer review, or disciplinary actions, other than in its involvement in the monitoring program. Referring a physician to the well-being committee to avoid other appropriate corrective action is improper in cases where the physician's action has led to patient injury. Consideration of physical or mental impairment is part of the work-up of a physician who has exhibited a negligent practice pattern; it is also an essential component of the physician's corrective action plan. Limiting the clinical privileges of physicians who have lost skills is the first step in their possible restoration. In addition to the alcoholic or drug impaired physician, the older or neurologically disabled physician must accept a reduction in privileges and may benefit from an honest and compassionate analysis of his or her current physical and professional condition. Supporting a physician in that circumstance is within the responsibility of the well-being committee and, indeed, is a true measure of the quality of the medical staff.

Future Directions for Well-Being Committees

Physician health is a potentially controllable factor in the reduction of clinical error or adverse outcome variation. The profession has the obligation to develop effective mechanisms for accomplishing that end. The requirements in California discussed above are likely to lead to the insistence that physician health be part of the root cause analysis of clinical performance failure. The voluntary well-being committee has given way to a mandated function that now must demonstrate its real effectiveness. If the California model is successful in protecting patient safety while returning physicians to useful practice, look for its equivalent nationally in accreditation requirements, if not licensure and regulation.

About the Author

Daniel A. Lang, MD, is medical director of the HealthCare Association of Southern California and a senior physician consultant to COHR INC. Dr. Lang is the author of The Disabled Physician: Problem Solving Strategies for the Medical Staff, published by the American Hospital Association. He is a consultant to the Committee on Wellbeing of Physicians of the California Medical Association.

Recredentialing the Impaired Physician: Considerations for Continuing or Granting Privileges

by David L. Breithaupt, MD, FACD

Physician impairment and disability, caused by disease or addiction, are two of the most difficult issues that a physician leader must face. In this article, the author suggests the key issues that must be addressed when recredentialing the impaired physician, including:

- *The nature of impairment;*
- *Common beliefs and attitudes toward physician impairment; and*
- *Conditions for re-entry into institutional practice, particularly hospital privileges.*

◆ ◆ ◆

Most clinical privileging decisions are fairly objective and straightforward. Applicants either have the training and experience required or they don't. Few emotional biases or myths affect privileging decisions. Credentialing and privileging decisions involving impaired or disabled physicians, on the other hand, pose special challenges for healthcare organizations.

At the outset, it's important to differentiate between impairment and disability. While the terms are often used interchangeably, physician leaders should be aware of the subtle and significant differences between them. Impairment is a medical term that refers to the *diminution of an individual's capacity or potential* to perform various tasks. Alcoholism, drug abuse and certain physical illnesses alter—or limit—a physician's capacity to use his or her clinical skills. Impaired individuals may, in fact, perform required tasks perfectly well at some or even never display disability.

Disability is a legal term, rooted partly in workers' compensation, that refers to the *inability—not the incapacity—to perform a specific task.* Thus the disabled physician is one who cannot perform, such as the surgeon with Parkinson's disease.

Diseases of impairment often can lead to disability. Therefore, organizations that credential physicians have a responsibility to address suspected physician impairment as a matter of patient protection and liability prevention. They also have a responsibility—morally, if not legally—to help the impaired physician enter treatment and to give due consideration to the physician's request to re-enter practice.

Addressing the issue of physicians re-entering practice first requires an understanding of the diseases leading to impairment. *(See Figure below.)* There are four major categories of impairment.

- Physical;
- Psychiatric;
- Addictive; and
- A combination of the three.

FIGURE 1: MAJOR DISEASES OF IMPAIRMENT

I. Physical
- Aging
- Neurological degenerative
- Cardiovascular

II. Psychiatric
- Depressions
- Dementias
- Psychoses

III. Addictive
- Sedatives: alcohol, benzodiazopine, marijuana
- Opiates: Demerol, Fentanyl, morphine, heroin
- Stimulants: cocaine, amphetamines

(Sources: prescribed, self-prescribed, stolen, purchased, legal, illegal

IV. Combinations of the above

It should be noted that addictive disorders and depressions have favorable prognoses. Nonreversible dementias alone or in combination with any of the others render a very poor prognosis.

Attitudes Toward Physician Impairment

When an impaired physician is under consideration for medical staff privileges, a number of beliefs and attitudes—some true, some conflicting and unresolved and some false—come into play. For example, some physicians have problems accepting addiction and many psychiatric syndromes as treatable diseases. They may dismiss completely the concept of reversible dementia. Some accuse the treatment community of overstating recovery rates. In these situations, the impaired physician isn't given a fair hearing on the request to resume medical practice.

A common but erroneous belief is that behavioral warning signs of addiction, such as irrational outbursts or chronic and unexplained lateness or absences, aren't significant unless they are accompanied by professional mistakes. In fact, the addicted physician usually displays disability last of all in the hospital setting—after the home, community and office, generally in that order.

Some unwarranted, but commonly held, beliefs include:

- Recovering addicts are at high risk to commit negligent actions;
- Individuals and hospitals are liable for negligent actions if they knowingly work with a *recovering* addict; and
- Malpractice carriers will not let physicians work with recovering physician addicts.

Education can help shed some light on the erroneous beliefs and also encourage constructive dialogue over legitimate differences of opinion.

Conditions for Re-entry

Physicians value their work and careers no less than other humans. They want and need to work. But an addictive disorder is a complex disease to treat. Granting privileges to a physician with a treatable disease of impairment can be considered only if the physician meets a set of basic requirements.

- It is critical that the physician-patient has been accurately diagnosed and has not suffered irreversible brain damage;
- The physician must be receiving treatment under the direction of a competent and qualified physician, be motivated to change and have responded to or be responding to treatment;
- The physician's family should be involved in treatment; and
- The physician must be feeling and functioning normally (i.e., thinking, reasoning, remembering and acting) and having normal relationships with people, things and concepts.

The physician must agree to allow his or her confidentiality to be breached by the treating physician when necessary, i.e., to inform those on a hospital staff with a need to know (such as the department chair) of his or her progress. The physician must remain fully licensed and able to maintain insurance or become insured against professional liability.

Re-entry Process

When re-entering practice, an impaired physician initially must agree to abide by a generic treatment plan, or re-entry contract. Such a plan is signed by both the physician-patient and the treating physician. It has do's, don'ts, and contingencies (*See "Confidential Agreement for Physician's Return to Practice" in Daniel Lang, MD's, article on page 276*).

The treatment plan or contract might require attendance at three to five self-help meetings per week; weekly physician support group meetings; individualized psychotherapy; couples and/or family counseling; chemotherapies such as naltrexone, Antabuse, and antidepressants (given in front of a witness); and regular and/or random analysis of body fluid. The plan also designates a primary monitor.

The physician's primary monitor may or may not provide primary medical care, but will coordinate all treatments (e.g., a migraine won't be treated independently of the addictive treatment process; elective plastic surgery won't be done in early sobriety). The primary monitor accepts the role of patient advocate with licensing authorities, office associates, hospital staff officers and malpractice carriers. A designated workplace monitor (a colleague, supervisor, or, occasionally, a nurse) is assigned who will report to the primary monitor as necessary and at designated intervals.

Fentanyl and Its Derivatives

Physician and hospital leaders should be knowledgeable about a particular class of addictive opiate drugs being used — fentanyl and its derivatives. An epidemic of abuse by anesthesiologists is still occurring. Overdose deaths and comas are all too common. Fentanyl and its derivatives are being used more and more in ambulatory surgical settings as "come and go" procedures increase. These drugs are extremely potent and detectable in urine only by special tests. Fentanyl addiction is treatable, but it is an extremely serious problem, and societies of anesthesiology are greatly concerned.

Organizational Support Systems

The re-entry program requires a number of support systems and inherent beliefs within the organization. The organization must persist in its belief that addiction is a treatable disease—not curable, but remittable. The hospital hierarchy must believe that the primary monitor will report setbacks, relapses, violations of the contract or discontinuation of treatment.

Patient rights—those of the impaired physician and his or her patients—must be honored. However, the physician-patient has a responsibility to colleagues, the governing board and society and must accept the legal consequences of personal acts when previously disabled.

A complex treatment/re-entry plan won't work if the organization has a poor quality management program and a weak credentialing process. (It should also be noted that new laws have made peer review a less confidential process.) If treatment is to work, the organization must be able to judge competence and the quality of care. It must have a clear and orderly drug record-keeping system. Drug security and good prescriptive and distribution systems must be a high priority in any hospital, clinic or surgicenter.

Some types of healthcare organizations face special challenges in treating the addicted physician. Small and/or rural hospitals that have trouble recruiting and retaining physicians may be reluctant to confront an impaired physician. When they do act, they may find that treatment and support facilities are not easily accessible or available for family members.

Physician Well-Being Committees

One method of dealing with impaired physicians is the physician well-being committee. Such committees have advantages but also major limitations.

Well-being committees function well in a resource capacity. They are effective in identifying available treatment facilities, primary monitors and caregivers, self-help resources and support systems. Well-being committees receive reports from staff offices and administrators, and they provide individual committee members to investigate, interview and confront impaired physicians. They also make good referrals and are effective in explaining staff orthodoxy and legal realities to anxious or resistant physicians. Additionally, well-being committee members can educate each other, provide peer review protection for members, and inspire awe and fear in the physician-patient. *(For a further discussion of how well-being committees function to help an impaired physician, see "Medical Staff Responsibility for Physician Health," by Daniel A. Lang, MD on page 273.)*

On the down side, well-being committees cannot assume total responsibility because they must distance themselves from the administrative, legal and quality management functions of the medical staff and governing board. This has become even more complex with changes in peer review law. Well-being committees can compound the confidentiality dilemma. They may take an inappropriate advocacy role on behalf of a physician with problems relating to staff privileges, licensure, or insurability by resisting appropriate disclosure of information to those who are responsible for credentialing and quality assurance functions. Well-being committees also can quickly "burn out" their most effective members.

Separating human behavior characteristics from syndromes and disease symptoms is a doctor's daily task. The same professional effort we take with our patients should be taken when one of our colleagues shows symptoms of disease and impairment. Relegating treatment of an impaired physician to a state licensing board is not the answer. State boards are too slow and overworked and frequently are too treatment-oriented for most medical staffs' liking. Nor should a healthcare organization's legal counsel (i.e., the hospital's; attorney) serve as the institutional authority on impairment treatment and disability management. It is the medical staff that must determine if the physician can practice at all, or practice with monitoring and/or preceptoring, and so recommend to the board.

Impaired physicians can successfully re-enter practice. The physician-patient's and primary monitor's commitment and motivation must be very high. The primary monitor must have specialized skills and experience. Patience, energy and the passage of extended healing time are fundamental. A sense of humor and a little luck seem to help a lot, too.

About the Author

David L. Breithaupt, MD, FACP, is an internist and a member of the physician well-being committee at O'Connor Hospital in San Jose, Calif.

Management and Leadership Techniques

Medical Group Governance: Keys to Success

By Barry S. Bader

Until recently, most physicians in group practice viewed governance as an administrative nuisance minimally related to running a successful clinical practice. That perception is changing.

Like so much else in medicine today, economic shifts require medical practices to be run in a businesslike fashion in order to secure managed care contracts, control expenses, navigate complex billing and utilization rules and address myriad other challenges. John McDonald, the retired executive director of Mullikin Medical Centers, credits much of the group's growth to the willingness of its physician members to entrust significant governance decisions to a board of directors chosen from its own ranks. At the time of the group's merger with MedPartners in 1996, Mullikin was composed of approximately 400 physicians serving 300,000 lives.

◆ ◆ ◆

Under the fee-for-service payment system, most medical groups weren't truly integrated economic units. While group members shared overhead and consulted one another on clinical matters, each physician was a separate revenue-generating enterprise in which the performance of one minimally affected other members of the group. Today, a physician's economic welfare is integrally tied to other members of the group and to the group's performance as a whole. For example, an individual physician's ability to join HMO panels or to prosper under risk contracts that reward appropriate utilization depends on the efficiency and the effectiveness of other physicians and allied health practitioners in the group, as well as on the group's infrastructure for billing, information systems, customer relations and other administrative mechanisms.

Consequently, medical groups need a few leaders who, as board members, spend time on planning, budgeting and other group management matters. There are a number of key elements for successful governance of a medical group practice.

1. Redefine the role of the board to focus on the group's long-term viability. In the past, the primary role of the group practice board was to protect the economic interests of individual group physicians by overseeing management affairs and divvying up compensation. The board's primary focus was on current operations, such as last month's financial performance and whether to give the office staff a raise.

Figure 1: Changing Views of the Role of Medical Group Governance

Old	New
◆ Protect the economic interests of individual group physicians	◆ Plan for the long-term economic viability of the group
◆ Oversee management of the group	◆ Select, evaluate, compensate and work collaboratively with highly competent professional management
◆ Develop compensation scheme to divide revenues among individual physicians annually based on productivity	◆ Approve a compensation mechanism that rewards individual physicians for productivity, patient satisfaction and contributions to group activities such as committee service, utilization review and quality improvement
◆ Monitor economic changes, e.g. proposed Medicare changes, that could affect the group	◆ Make strategic decisions that position the group for a changing economic environment
◆ Elect members for one-year terms	◆ Elect members for longer periods to allow them time to learn and to promote continuity of leadership
◆ Review cases for quality assurance purposes	◆ Ensure the group has an effective quality improvement and assurance process
◆ Allow meetings to be long, loosely organized and focused on operational details	◆ Keep meetings crisp and focused on major issues
◆ View governance as a nuisance	◆ View governance as important to group success

In today's more competitive, managed care environment, the board's focus shifts to the long-term economic viability of the group practice. Rather than trying to oversee management details, the board establishes goals and policies but invests significant authority in a competent, professional medical group executive. The board then holds management accountable for finance, facility, personnel and other administrative affairs by carefully reviewing performance reports.

2. Define a vision for the group. The single most valuable action a group practice board can take is to develop mission and vision statements. A mission succinctly states an organization's purpose. A vision describes the organization's desired future state in a way that guides decision making and inspires exemplary performance.

Mission and vision statements are an established element of successful organizational performance. The Henry Ford Health System in Detroit has developed statements of mission, vision and core values that include such concepts as integrated service delivery, meeting patient and community needs and continuous improvement (*See Figure 2 below*). The vision of Merck pharmaceutical company links the company's goals with measurement: "We are in the business of preserving and improving human life. All of our actions must be measured by our success in achieving this."

Figure 2: Mission, Vision and Values of the Henry Ford Health System

Mission—Henry Ford Health System is a national leader in healthcare. Our essential priority is to provide exceptional quality, cost-effective care, strengthened by excellence in education and research. We work together to improve health and the quality of life in the communities of Southeastern Michigan and the neighboring regions.

Vision—We are expanding the healthcare delivery system concept through our pioneering vision and leadership's commitment to innovation, always striving to improve access, cost effectiveness and quality of care:

- We are designing our services and programs around the needs of our patients and the communities we serve.
- We are integrating our services to provide complete, lifelong healthcare in ways our customers find easy to use.
- We are enhancing the value of our services through innovative partnerships, managed care and health education programs.
- To continually improve our services, we measure patient satisfaction and community health.

Values—The following values are fundamental to us:

- Patients come first. We exist to serve those who need our services. Our patients deserve our best work delivered in ways respectful of community diversity.
- People are our strength. Our work defines our success and determines our reputation. As each of us is perceived, so is Henry Ford Health System.
- We practice continuous improvement. We are each responsible for maintaining an environment that encourages learning and creative thinking, and helps us to develop and apply new knowledge and skills to everything we do.
- We support our communities. We advocate improved community health by getting involved. We volunteer our time, expertise and facilities as a responsible corporate citizen and a good neighbor.
- We are all in this together. We embrace the dignity of our diverse workforce as one of our greatest human assets. We respect the people of our communities as ourselves, and we welcome their volunteer activities in supplementing our services.
- We serve with compassion. To build trust and understanding, we listen. To help, we act on our understanding, we listen. To help, we act on our understanding.
- We have a social conscience. Our presence counts. We want our doors to be open to everyone.

Source: HFHS Annual Report, 1994

Similarly, a medical group might adopt a vision such as:

- The XYZ Medical Group will be the premier orthopedic practice in the metropolitan area, recognized for its clinical excellence and patient-centered care, and offering a complete range of surgical, rehabilitation and physical therapy services; or

- The ABC Medical Group is a highly integrated primary group practice of internists, family practitioners, pediatricians, nurse practitioners, physician assistants and health educators who emphasize disease prevention and health promotion and who actively seek responsibility to manage the care of patients under capitated contracts through partnerships with other physician organizations, hospitals and managed care plans.

A clear and compelling vision lays the basis for a board to agree on major strategic initiatives designed to achieve the vision. For example, the board of the ABC Medical Group might put a priority on:

- Strategic affiliations with other physician organizations, hospitals and managed care plans;
- Investing in an infrastructure to manage care and risk, including a managed care information system, an internal utilization management program and a continuous quality improvement program; or
- A physician compensation mechanism in which individual physicians are rewarded for appropriate, high-quality care, good patient communications, productivity and contributions to the group's management, governance and quality assurance programs.

3. Build a partnership with the group's executive. The second most important responsibility of a board, after defining the mission and vision of the organization, is to select, support, evaluate and provide compensation for a competent and visionary executive.

Effective boards resist the temptation to meddle in management. They work in partnership with the executive, holding him or her accountable for defining measurable goals for group operations and for reporting on performance. The board focuses its attention on major variances from targets, such as income shortfalls, poor collections or expenditures that are significantly above budget.

The board looks to its executive not merely to administer current operations but also to engage in strategic management. If, for example, the board has established a policy of growth and active solicitation of at-risk contracts, it would expect its executive to draft plans for strategic partnerships, information systems, managed care contracting, patient education and human resource management designed to achieve the board's goals.

4. Choose board members based on their governance skills. In the past, board members may have been chosen based on whose "turn" it was or which members were willing to put up with mundane board business. For a practice to have effective leadership, however, board members should be chosen on the basis of more objective criteria, including:

- Being respected and trusted by members of the group;
- Being interested in or willing to learn about medical economics, management methods, organizational theory, systems thinking, and other subjects related to successful group performance;
- Possessing good communication skills;
- Willing to put in the time necessary; and
- Having enthusiasm and ability to work as a member of a team with other board members, management and the group's business and clinical partners.

Board members should serve specific terms of one, two or three years, with no more than one-third of board members rotating off in any one year. Placing such limits balances turnover with continuity.

5. Build effective mechanisms for utilization management and quality improvement. Under fee-for-service payment, a group's profitability was driven by patient service volumes, including office visits, tests and procedures. Under managed care, a group may be financially penalized for inappropriate utilization of resources and, alternatively, it maybe rewarded for keeping patients healthy or for health promotion practices, such as childhood immunizations. (A group could be rewarded for denying necessary care, but no group could reconcile such shortsightedness with professional values.)

Consequently, it is in a group's self-interest to establish physician-directed programs to closely review utilization and referral patterns and to educate group members in cost-effective practice patterns. In addition, many groups are emulating hospitals and private industry by instituting continuous quality improvement initiatives. The board's responsibility is to establish and monitor these programs to ensure they contribute to the group's success.

6. Communicate with group members. Most practicing physicians accept the need to respond to the demands of payers, external regulation and competitors, but their primary interest lies with patient care. They want someone else to be concerned with business and management matters, namely the group's board and executive. Still, the average physician's apathy toward administration does not convey a *carte blanche* to the board.

To achieve the long-term vision of the group, a board may have to take many actions that trade off individuals' autonomy or their current incomes for the benefit of the entire group. For example, a multispecialty group practice board may adopt a compensation program to reward primary care physicians at the expense of subspecialists because the group's vision requires that it recruit and retain a core of primary care practitioners for its managed care contracts. Similarly, the board may vote to invest capital in information systems or joint ventures, in effect reducing each physician's current income with the goal of enhancing the group's future performance.

Physicians' characteristic indifference toward governance may be jarred when their incomes or professional freedom appear to be threatened, even by their peers on the group's governing board. Thus, board members have an important responsibility to communicate to the group as a whole the objective rationale for their actions and to seek support from the membership. Boards that get too far out in front risk recall and reversal, even if their proposed course of action is in the group's best interest.

7. Run meetings in a businesslike fashion. Many group practice leaders describe board meetings as rather informal gatherings with no fixed agendas, ambiguous starting and ending times and few rules of conduct. The meetings typically start late in the day when physicians finish seeing patients and run into the night with a few vocal members dominating.

By contrast, effective meetings reflect the following characteristics:

A. Written agendas that lay out the major work to be done by the board;
B. Written materials such as financial statements, utilization summaries and strategic planning proposals circulated in advance for the board's review;
C. Leadership from the board chairman to keep the discussion flowing and focused on the agenda, with all board members encouraged to participate but none allowed to dominate;
D. Written minutes that provide an accurate, ongoing chronicle of the board's work; and
E. A commitment from all members to start and end meetings on time.

Group practice boards can also take a page from effective governance practices of hospitals and publicly owned corporations to engage in such practices as annual planning retreats, incorporating education on major trends into board meetings and compensating board leaders to participate in outside education.

8. Periodically evaluate and improve board performance. All boards benefit by periodically reflecting on how well they are working and how they might improve. Board self evaluation involves an assessment by either a questionnaire or group discussion of such governance elements as:

- The board's definition and understanding of its roles and responsibilities;
- The appropriateness of the organization's mission, values and vision;
- The relationship between the board and management;
- The structure of the board, including the board's size, composition, use of committees and task forces, terms of office and selection methods, etc.;
- Communication between the board and the group as a whole; and
- The adequacy of information provided to the board on organizational performance, including finances, personnel, utilization, patient and customer satisfaction, etc.

A good basis for evaluation of a medical group can be found in *An Assessment Manual for Medical Groups*, published by the Medical Group Management Association.

A Change in Culture

Empowering a select group of physicians to make major decisions on behalf of the group will be, for many group practices, a major change in their traditional manner of doing things. It requires some physicians to accept leadership responsibility and then invest in learning organizational skills that were not part of their medical background or formal training. It also requires members of the group to trust their leaders and recognize that all group members share responsibility for the group's success.

For example, when the physicians of the Harvard Pilgrim Health Plan reengineered their entire group structure in 1996, moving away from a salaried, staff-model HMO to a more entrepreneurial group practice, a key concept—according to group leaders—was to "achieve commitment from clinicians to accept accountability for (the group's) performance." At the same time, the group's physicians empowered group leaders to make critical decisions and be accountable to the membership for the group's success.

Physician groups need to engage in something of a cultural transformation to develop their leaders, including their board members and other physicians who serve in key roles such as chairing committees or co-managing facilities with administrators. Recently, the Medical Leadership Forum of The Governance Institute identified the major areas of knowledge, skills and attitudes needed by physician leaders. Topping the list are knowledge of "how organizations (as opposed to organisms) function and thrive" and "how to achieve simplicity and better efficiency without sacrificing quality." Physician leaders also need to build skills in such areas as systems thinking, continuous quality improvement, risk sharing and risk management mechanisms, business management and communications. Finally, physician leaders need to nurture such attitudes as "a willingness to respect others as colleagues in a team setting; a positive, can-do outlook; pride in the medical profession; a sense of humor; and a willingness to make time to continuously develop leadership knowledge and skills."

Developing of an effective group practice board is one element of building strong physician leadership. While such efforts will differ depending on the size of the group, its culture and the local marketplace, the investment in effective leadership is one that will pay dividends for the group as well as for its patients and the quality of its care.

◆ ◆ ◆

References

Bader, B.S. "Physician Involvement in the Governance of Integrated Systems." *Health System Leader,* 4-14, May 1994.

Rhomberg, M. and Dreyfus, P. "Establishing Harvard Pilgrim Health Care's Health Centers Division as a New Medical Group Practice." *Group Practice Journal,* 12-14, March\April 1997.

Rice, J.A. "A New Era of Power." *Modern Physician,* May 1997: reprint.

Williams, S.J., Sanchez, J.P. and Melton, V.L. *An Assessment Manual for Medical Groups*. Denver, CO.: Center for Research in Ambulatory Health Care Administration, a division of the Medical Group Management Association, 1994.

ABOUT THE AUTHOR

Barry S. Bader is a governance consultant and speaker based in Potomac, Md. He has advised many hospitals, health systems and physician groups on improving board performance.

Physician Effectiveness in Teams

by James A. Rice, PhD.
and John H. Kleinman, MD, F.A.C.D.

Perhaps the greatest change of role for senior physician executives in today's healthcare provider and payer organizations is the way in which they view themselves. Five years ago, in a national survey, 80 percent reported seeing themselves as physicians first, 13 percent as leaders first and 6 percent as managers first. Today, 47 percent view themselves first as leaders, 42 percent as physicians, and 10 percent as managers. That is a remarkable transformation in perception to have been accomplished in such a short time—a virtual revolution.[1]

◆ ◆ ◆

Despite the diversity of opinions regarding future physician leadership development strategies, consensus has emerged: A new type of physician leader is needed to steer healthcare systems into the uncertain future. The authors of an article from the July/August 1993 issue of *Healthcare Forum Journal* state:

> As hospitals and physicians join together to form meaningful clinical and economic partnerships, the kind of physician leadership that worked well in the past....will no longer be adequate. New competencies will be required, both to guide in the journey toward highly complex integrated systems and, once there, to assume new roles. Unless they can develop such competencies, leaders...will lose the support—and potentially the respect—of their peers.[2]

Much of this new leadership role will be exercised in multidisciplinary and multifunctional teams in which one of the most important competencies must be the ability to make decisions. To be effective, these decision-making teams must:

- Be driven by results;
- Encourage multidisciplinary composition;
- Build consensus;
- Value each member's participation;
- Follow explicit work plans;
- Clearly delineate individual responsibilities; and
- Frequently recognize team wins as well as individual contributions.

Physicians have no choice but to participate in—if not lead—such teams.

A Typology of Teams

"Teamness" refers to the process of connecting people who come together to build a shared vision through developing and implementing strategies. Teamness is based upon trust and mutual respect for the talents and competencies of each person, as well as developing collaborative and interdependent relationships. Members of such a team often describe feeling that they are "making a difference," even though they may not always be able to define what that difference is.[3] In the health sector, teams can increase the quality of results from decision making in three interrelated arenas:

- Clinical (patient care);
- Administrative (strategy, finance, human resources); and
- Community health (population-based health status improvement).

Clinical teams are dedicated to enhancing the outcomes, quality and cost effectiveness of care processes. They seek to achieve such goals by engaging groups that represent as many of the perspectives, experiences and skills needed to enhance the health and well-being of patients. Doctors, nurses, technicians, social workers and others all play meaningful roles first, during a period of several weeks, when they design ideal guidelines for clinical care and second, during a several-day period, in which they apply the guidelines to care for a specific patient.

Administrative teams are generally focused on maximizing the cost effectiveness of multiple support processes. They concentrate on such areas as analysis of markets and competitors, strategic planning, financial planning and budgeting, staffing, inventory control and the maximizing of efficiency. Members tend to represent a wide mix of managers, technicians, analysts and, increasingly, care deliverers. Their time horizon is usually a mix of multi-day or multi-month cycles of planning, doing, controlling and assessing.

Community health teams involve many players outside the healthcare organization and concentrate on demonstrable improvement in the health and well being for large population groups in the regional market. The cycle of work for these teams is often multi-month and multi-year. Team players may include representatives not only from the hospital, health plan, or clinic, but also schools, social service agencies, local government, churches, police, fire and other agencies.

Physicians are increasingly being asked to join or lead this exploding array of teams.

As suggested in Figure 1 on page 297, the teams perform several functions and operate in contexts of varying complexity.

Are physicians ready to assume these roles? Are they prepared to consciously enhance the knowledge, skills and attitudes they need to maximize their effective-

Figure 1: Expanded View of Physician Team Settings

Team Type	Sample Settings	Illustrative Challenges
Clinical	Clinics Surgery Centers Emergency Rooms Hospitals Nursing Homes Hospital Systems Health Plans	Continuous Quality Improvement Care Pathways Clinical Guidelines Disease Management Systems Quality Assurance Standards Credentialing Standards Pharmacy Formulary
Administrative	Outpatient Care Sites Hospital Departments Long-term Care Sites Home Health Agencies Health Plan Enrollee Relations Office MIS Department	Continuing Education Systems Marketing Research into Targeted Populations Patient-Life-Safety Systems Customer Registration and Discharge Planning Computer Information Systems Long-term Care Placement Plans Home Care Referral Regional EMS Transport Systems Primary Care Office Network Process Improvement per Department
Community Health	Social Service Agencies County or City Health Departments Schools Police and Fire Department Highway Department Television and Radio Stations	Teenage Pregnancy Reduction Enhanced Immunizations Maternal Child Health Domestic Abuse Reduction Substance Abuse Reduction Weight Loss Nutrition Workplace Safety Hazardous Waste

Source: Jim Rice and John Kleinman

ness in such roles? If so, how can physicians best prepare for these roles, and what are obstacles to their effectiveness in such roles?

Answering these questions requires further insight into the nature of teams, teamwork and team leadership.

The Team Process

Today, there is significant pressure to manage better by using fewer resources and still respond to external pressures from healthcare reform initiatives. One way to do this is to bring more people into the management process—to create an environment in which teams of people from different levels of the organization can work together to improve service outcomes.

A vice president of managed care observes:

> As a person responsible for designing managed care contracts, I am concerned with how to produce positive service outcomes that can reduce future utilization of inpatient care while reducing the overall cost of care, particularly if capitation is the next generation of payment. I am only one person with a defined set of knowledge; I need others to help me manage smarter. I need people with different views and ways of thinking, people who can ask questions—the "what ifs"—and I need people who think with a systems perspective, including thinking about the long-term future, not just today or two years from now.[4]

For a team to function effectively, its members must utilize the concepts and tools associated with interactive planning, systems thinking, reengineering and quality improvement. These are learned through systematic, institution-wide education programs initiated by top leadership and carried out to the unit level and support areas.

Guidelines for Building Teams

Many leaders describe similar guidelines when they discuss the importance of relationships in team development, particularly in terms of joining members to do innovative work that will deliver improved value. Leaders' aggregate guidelines include:

- Pay attention to processes and systems in an effort to understand the organization's capabilities;
- Encourage ideas from people throughout the organization and replace fear with recognition of ideas and appropriate follow-up;
- Continually emphasize that moving toward the intended outcome is a priority, because members will be more productive when they know what is expected;
- Base decisions on shared data as opposed to guesswork to improve how work gets done;
- Advocate strategic thinking and allow creative use of informal learning to gain new insights;
- Focus on value through the use of systems improvement processes; productivity and efficiencies will follow; and
- Engage trained facilitators in the process to ensure a systematic approach; cross-functional teamwork is crucial to speed improvements and increase organizational quality.

Physicians tend to agree that teamwork is vitally important. While working as part of a team is the ideal, physicians also recognize that sometimes there are self-imposed barriers to their participation. William Manahan, medical director of quality assurance, Immanuel-St. Joseph's Hospital; Stephen Entman, professor/vice-chair, obstetrics and gynecology, Vanderbilt University Hospital; and Richard Lindsay, head, Division of Geriatric Medicine, School of Medicine, University of Virginia, explain:

Physicians benefit from one-to-one contacts with people they respect and work with side-by-side in the clinical area. Informal hallway conversations between caregivers can be very effective when in the early stages of changing practice patterns, such as through the development of clinical pathways. Physicians may feel, rightly or wrongly, they have more insight into clinical issues, therefore, they find it difficult to participate in team meetings to discuss such issues. It is extremely hard for them to take time to sit comfortably at a meeting and truly be a part of the team, not just physically, but emotionally and mentally. This may be one of the largest barriers for physicians becoming team players. Teamwork requires collaboration, and collaboration requires process, and process requires sitting down and spending time with each other discussing and talking. The intensity and acuity of patient care often takes the physician away or prevents concentration on the discussion. Physicians need to understand what is in it for them and their patients before they can commit to a process. Once they get hooked on what can improve and how the effort matches the needs of health reform, they will be enthusiastic.[5]

Healthcare teams also assume increasing importance as employers hold health plans and their providers accountable for performance. Accreditation by the National Committee for Quality Assurance (NCQA) requires evidence of measurable quality improvement through programs such as disease management. Many of the disease management programs currently being developed and implemented by managed care organizations rely on providers' use of clinical guidelines to standardize the management of targeted conditions.

But clinical guidelines will be successful only if physicians work to implement them on well organized and managed teams. Chronic diseases are complex and multidisciplinary, involving many processes and multiple "hand-offs." Many current efforts focus on high-cost chronic diseases such as diabetes, asthma and cancer, most of which include patient education to stress the importance of lifestyle choices, self-management and -testing and drug compliance.[6]

Importance of Teams

"The only sustainable competitive advantage is the ability to continue to learn faster than your competition....the long term winners are those who have learned how to learn and who can adapt and evolve more quickly and more effectively to the constantly changing market and competitive realities...."[7]

In today's increasingly competitive health market, where the pace of change is ever accelerating, the learning agenda has become even more challenging. It is no longer adequate for each piece of an organization to become more informed only about its own activities, and no organization can simply deep-discount its way to increased market share. Customers demand "complete service solutions," which means that engineering must actively associate with manufacturing and marketing; finance needs to understand what customer service and sales are doing (and vice-versa). The functional pieces within the organizations truly have to make music "that's pleasant to the ear."[8]

As physician leaders explore strategies to exercise their new roles in integrated systems, multi-specialty groups and community health improvement initiatives, they will find that teams and teamwork can offer essential leverage to their time and talents. Teams have become central vehicles for both the design and implementation of such strategically significant initiatives as:

- Strategic planning for market growth;
- Acquiring political and economic assets through mergers and acquisitions;
- Developing clinical care guidelines;
- Achieving new efficiencies from process reengineering;
- Enhancing satisfaction of health plan enrollees; and
- Maximizing health gain for the community.

Trends that will call for greater physician teaming include:

1. Increased focus on credentialing and privileging in order to:
   a. Protect the patient/member;
   b. Enhance quality by assuring providers have sufficient quantity of procedures to maintain competency; and
   c. Guard against restraint of trade associated with protecting physician income.

2. Discussing physician reimbursement per unit of service, which will:
   a. Have a direct impact on physician compensation;
   b. Ignite greater tension within the group;
   c. Put pressure on the balance sheet of practices; and
   d. Reduce growth in a period of contracting

3. Physician groups will become more interdependent with:
   a. HMOs;
   b. Corporate offices; and
   c. Bigger systems.

4. Focus on utilization is a must to be competitive, but it will generate:
   a. Tension within the group;
   b. Need for more support personnel and greater cognitive skills;
   c. A decrease in procedural and technical revenues; and
   d. A need for performance standards.

Effective teamwork is an essential ingredient for the new style of health organizations to thrive. These organizations are defined by their flattened organizational structure, an orientation toward outcomes rather than functions, subcontracted components and, most importantly, a refocus on the core business—caring for patients.[9]

The complexities of the current healthcare environment will not permit any single leader to wrap his or her mind around all the issues that these redesigned organizations are facing. Therefore, the successful healthcare organization of the future will be filled with people able to synergistically learn and effectively apply their learning. It will be filled, in short, with learning teams.[10]

Well managed learning teams harness a positive synergy from multiple members. With learning teams, good ideas can be generated faster, implemented more cost effectively and yield larger and more sustainable gains than an action launched by two or three physicians or allied health personnel. The value from teams, however, can be optimized only by embracing modern concepts of learning organizations and systems thinking.

"Just-in-time learning"—to borrow a phrase from manufacturing—can be an essential resource for building learning teams. Physician and healthcare leaders find that canned programs and a list of scheduled courses published a few times a year are no longer adequate to meet their complex educational needs.[11] The new levels of skill and knowledge needed to move through the formidable challenges they face today require new approaches to learning. One of the most valuable of these is "just-in-time" learning, which has as its goal the application of new knowledge and skills to improve processes and outcomes. Integrating team learning with real-time organizational issues enhances both the meaningfulness of the lessons and the quality of the results. This type of education addresses an immediate need, but its lessons create a cascading effect that carries over into longer-term needs.[12]

Physician Roles in Teams

Physician leaders accustomed to operating as "captain of the ship" must now employ group leadership skills to inspire a shared vision, facilitate consensus and ease the transition to integrated systems. The competencies needed for leadership of these integrated systems rest on effective group work and team decisionmaking. Figure 2 on page 302 summarizes conclusions from Farrell and Robbins' work on competencies needed for physician leadership development.

Physicians, therefore, need to be flexible enough to play both leader and follower roles on today's teams. Embracing both roles requires physicians to develop insight into the nature of effective teams and effective leaders. Consequently, the principles of continuous quality improvement can enhance team effectiveness.[13]

But the challenges facing a physician leader are no different from that of any other leader. Continual improvement will result when everyone in the organization understands the aim and works collaboratively to build new knowledge that will lead to change. It's the role of the organization's leaders to foster a shared sense of purpose and to promote learning throughout the organization.

Physician leaders can transform themselves in order to facilitate the transformation of others. They can move from operating in a dominance model that emphasizes hierarchical roles to a partnership model that stresses teamwork roles.

Figure 2: New Physician Leadership Competencies

Changes in healthcare trends require ...	New physician leadership roles and ...	New competencies
Increased governmental regulation through public-private partnerships	Strategic business partner	Strategic business orientation
Accelerated development of organized physician practices	Enabling/empowering manager	Empowering/developing others
Increased formation of physician-hospital economic and clinical alignments	Culture developer/mission implementer	Mission articulation
Emphasis on cost-effectiveness, not revenue enhancement	Group/team effort leader	Group leadership
Focus on vertically integrated healthcare organizations	Influence strategies user	Negotiation skills
Continuous redefinition and documentation of quality standards and outcomes	Consensus developer	Stakeholder relationship building
Increased use of protocols, guidelines, parameters for efficiency and payment[15]	Organizational systems aligner	Organizational awareness

Deborah Shilan, MD, who operates a Los Angeles-based physician recruiting firm, believes recruiters are looking for physicians who have experience "interacting with the non-physician side" of medicine.[14] In a letter to the editor of the *Journal of the American Medical Association*, Dr. Shilan wrote, "there is a growing realization that, as the traditional separation of administrative and clinical matters becomes obsolete, the new physician executive must be a manager first and a clinician second. Bringing a clinical background to the new role of manager enriches the job but does not substitute for specific management skills and training."

Change Facilitator

In addition to abilities to bridge gaps among various people, design clinical processes and manage the balance sheet, the new physician leader also will be responsible for helping physician organizations migrate from unstructured, loosely affiliated physician groups to tightly knit, integrated organizations. To expedite this transformation, physician leaders must assume the role of "change agent."[15] Only those physicians who exhibit the following attributes should be considered for leadership positions.

- Group leadership—As physicians move toward interdependence, their leaders will need the ability to work well with groups and facilitate group decision making.
- Direct persuasion—New leaders will need to marshal interpersonal relationships and logical arguments to convince clinicians to accept the "new order."
- Organizational awareness—New leaders will need the ability to navigate increasingly complex paths and interconnections within organizations.
- Initiative—"Change agent" physicians will have to be proactive in relationships with peers and seize opportunities to align with hospitals through either the sale of key assets or an outright sale of the total practice. In addition, leaders must be able to drive strategic partnerships. and
- Planning/Organizing—New leaders will be required to develop comprehensive long-range plans to track the intricacies involved in a wide variety of changes, including the shifting emphasis from office administration to operational management and from informal to formal performance reviews and the creation of clinical protocols and outcome measures.

Obstacles to Physician Effectiveness in Teams

At the dawn of the new century, healthcare and its delivery will likely be unrecognizable to those who ended their practices only a decade ago. Traditional management will wither and be replaced by self-managed, self-trained and self-motivated teams working through processes, projects and assignments in integrated systems. Becoming an effective physician leader, therefore, will be an active and arduous process that can no longer be approached haphazardly. To be effective, the physician must plot a course with clear and calculated intent and effort, which requires acquiring organizational tools and administrative skills to innovatively alter medical care for the good of all. This journey, however, will be fraught with a variety of obstacles.

A survey of physician executives found several areas of difficulty in the transition from clinical to managerial medicine including: psychological adjustment; shifting from an independent to a dependent role; change in focus from patient to organization; naiveté about organization dynamics; new skill requirements; and change from a controlling role to one of persuasion; from a comfortable relationship with colleagues to one based on authority; and from medical to business competencies.[16]

Key obstacles to minimize or avoid are:

1. Most physicians entering management are inadequately prepared to use standard management techniques.
2. The skills required in good management often contradict the skills learned in good patient care.
3. Physician executives tend to overestimate their management capabilities but underestimate their management value.
4. Physician executives tend to avoid conflict rather than manage it.
5. Appropriate management requires as much concerted effort as direct medical care.

6. The risks of failure for physicians entering management are greater than for their non-physician counterparts.[17]

Perhaps one of the most complex problems facing physicians in management is role confusion between authority and leadership.[18] This problem is a product of physician training and the assumption that physicians must and can "fix" problems. For example, in a team managing a cardiac arrest patient, the leadership role comes from the team's need for an authority who knows how to respond to and takes responsibility for the process.

But in the ER, the problem definition—"cardiac arrest"—and the problem solution—"resuscitate"—are clear. Outside it, leaders face problems that lack clear answers or problems that require education just to be understood. The solution to such problems is to be "adaptive."[19] Adaptive problems require changes in peoples attitude, habits and behaviors. Understanding the differences between technical and adaptive work and between authority and leadership are key to physician managerial success.

Strategies for Enhanced Physician Team Roles

As physician leaders seek to harness the power of teamwork—whether for clinical or managerial purposes—they will be well served by considering a series of practical concepts and strategies. One of the most important concepts is an ancient piece of team leadership wisdom. Today's movement away from authoritarian leadership and toward team development was really envisioned by the Chinese philosopher Lao Tzu more than 2,000 years ago: "Leaders are best when people barely know they exist, not so good when people obey and acclaim them, worse when people despise them. But of good leaders, who talk little, when their work is finished, their aim fulfilled, the others will say, 'We did it ourselves.'"[20]

The whole issue of creating teamness by assembling people from multiple disciplines is paramount. Everyone must feel he or she is part of the process in order to contribute meaningfully. To achieve an environment of such candor, consider the following guidelines for interdisciplinary groups:

- *All are equal.* Individuals leave their organizational status and functional titles at the door (see discussion below).
- *No "tech-speak."* No technical terms or systems terminology are used during group discussions.
- *No assumed answers.* Automation, particularly, is not assumed to be the answer.
- *Value all opinions and ideas.* Answer all questions or find a reason why a question cannot be answered.
- *Equal opportunity leadership.* The role of chairperson rotates among all team members, including front-line staff.
- *Achieve an overview of the process.* Some members will be specifically trained in interactive planning.

- *Don't get hooked on consensus.* While consensus building is a desirable method of decision making, it is not mandatory.
- *Dare to dream.* Encourage everyone to use his or her imagination.[21]

Physician executives sometimes find it difficult to work in this new capacity with their clinical colleagues—those who consider them "just one of us." This is similar to the phenomenon of prophets often not being heard by their own countrypersons. One way to help colleagues hear is to listen to them first. This shows respect and also helps the physician executive position him- or herself in the leader's role, capable of supporting colleagues. Listening first is a leader's ticket to cooperation and consensus. As a successful entrepreneur once remarked, "Everyone loves hearing a good listener."[22]

Similarly, a *Harvard Business Review* article about how to manage people stresses that the best leaders are "doers;" they are not a collection of particular personality characteristics.[23] Leadership does not need to be a popularity contest, nor does it need to be charismatic. Good leaders act and by so doing, they help others do more.

Identifying a Dysfunctional Management Team

Most healthcare organizations would have little trouble finding one or more of the following profiles somewhere in their workforce:

Turf protectors: If the members of a team distrust one another, it often results in "turf-guarding" behaviors. Although individuals may espouse an "all-for-one-and-one-for-all" philosophy, their closest colleagues see no evidence in behavior of what these team members claim to believe. Instead, the members of such a team often find themselves playing chess with the hospital's resources when they

Weak links: Some team members lack the critical competencies necessary to effectively lead and manage their areas, so they fail to contribute to overall team performance. Essential tasks do not get done or are done poorly. "Buck passing"" may occur. Effective team members become frustrated, decreasing morale and team unity.

Good intentions: Members of the team may be well-intentioned but unschooled in the activities and processes required to accomplish quality results, such as conducting meetings, strategic and tactical planning, creative group problem solving, decisionmaking, and/or communication. The result is unproductive meetings and unclear direction. They allow many opportunities to pass without taking definitive action.

Limitations: This team is composed of managers or executives, all competent but who lack a leader who gives them the vision and direction, freedom, or support necessary for them to function at their best. A caveat: Make sure the leader is not blamed for problems that should be owned by the team.

Misaligned: A team suffers from misalignment when the roles of individuals overlap and the interrelationship of accountabilities among team members is unclear. Team members spend a great deal of time on parallel courses of action—doing what others already have done. They also have trouble setting priorities, reaching decisions and taking action. Lack of alignment may also occur when the team does not hold a common vision for the organization, and so its members move in different directions according to their interpretations of the vision.[24]

Although different jobs will require different configurations of competencies, the sum of competencies of all team members together should ideally result in an overall balance, including capability in each key area.

Figure 3: Teams Requiring a Balance of Competency for All Key Areas

Key Area	Competency Examples
Achievement	Excellence orientation Initiative
Leading/managing others	Developing others Directing others Group facilitation
Problem solving	Analytical thinking Conceptual thinking
Relationship-building	Interpersonal sensitivity Influence strategies Persuasive ability
Self-management	Self-control Self-confidence Tenacity

Source: Carol Dubnicki, Hay Associates, 415-945-8220

For physicians to work in teams, they must appreciate:

- The activity as being essential to their success as leaders;
- The importance of each member's contribution;
- The need to establish boundaries of responsibility and accountability for the group and its members;
- The place and degree of flexibility necessary for teamwork; and
- The maximum contribution from each team member that they reap when coaching others.

Therefore, effective physician team leaders are most often process oriented, honest and trustworthy, good facilitators, flexible, hard working, courageous, innovative and humble. If they are to act on such attributes, physician leaders must make the following transitions:

- Soloist to orchestra conductor;
- Anecdote to fact;
- Controller to participant;
- Talker to listener;
- Teacher always to learner often;
- Decision maker to enabler; and
- Fear to trust.[25]

Create a Team Culture

The environment the team creates should motivate team members to excel and support their efforts to achieve their goals. The following six characteristics in the working environment stimulate team members to embrace:

1. Flexibility: Minimizing unnecessary procedures, policies and formalities and allowing freedom to expand on new ideas;
2. Responsibility: Permitting people in work units to do their jobs and take calculated risks;
3. Clear standards: Perceiving management to be committed to quality, setting challenging goals and encouraging people to improve their performance;
4. Rewards: Basing compensation on performance excellence—recognition and praise outweighing threats and cynicism;
5. Clarity: Ensuring open and clear communication about procedures, expectations and plans; and
6. Commitment: A feeling of pride in the work unit and the willingness to devote extra effort when necessary.[26]

Some useful insights to guide physician team play are observations that leaders:

1. Manage the dream: communicate the vision, recruit meticulously, reward, retrain, reorganize;
2. Embrace error: Failure is not the crime; low aim is;
3. Encourage reflective backtalk;
4. Encourage dissent;
5. Possess the Nobel factor: optimism, faith and hope;
6. Understand the Pygmalion effect in management: Subordinates, more often than not, appear to do what they believe they are expected to do;
7. See the long view;
8. Understand stakeholder symmetry: They must balance the competing claims of all the groups with a stake in the organization; and
9. Create strategic alliances and partnerships.[27]

Physicians are recapturing power lost during the past 20 years to health plans and hospital administration.[28] To continue this trend, however, physician leaders will need to master new competencies in building and leading teams. The new breed of physician leaders can not only be clinical team leaders, but role models for the next generation of practitioners and collaborators of those designing management teams in the health care organizations of the future.

A physician leader's work is rarely complete. The challenge of excellent performance is one of continuous process improvement. Continuously enhance competency at team leadership and gauge team effectiveness by encouraging group members to answer the following questions:

- Is the group growing?
- Are you experiencing personal and professional growth?
- Do you feel appreciated?
- Are you learning?
- Are you laughing?
- Are you saying "we" instead of "I" and "they?"
- Do you feel that if you drop the ball someone else will pick it up if he or she is able, without blaming? and
- Are leaders giving all the credit and taking all the blame?

In summary, team building is more art than science. That said, it remains an essential competency for physician leaders to master if they are to be effective.

◆ ◆ ◆

References

[1]Lyons, M.F., Ford, D. and Singer, G.R. *The Physician Executive*. September 1996.

[2]Farrell, J., and Robbins, M. "Leadership Competencies for Physicians." *Healthcare Forum Journal,* 39-42. July/August 1993.

[3]Khols et al. *Transformational Leadership*. Chicago: American Hospital Association, 274, 1995.

[4]Robert Siver, as reported in Khols et al. 103, 1995.

[5]Ibid., 120.

[6]Biskupiak, J.E., Chodoff, P. and Nash, D.B. in Todd and Nash, eds. *Disease Management*. American Publishing, 210.

[7]*"An Introduction to Systems Thinking."* Hanover, NH: High Performance Systems, 1-10, 1996.

[8]Ibid.

[9]Flanner, T.P., and Williams, J.B. "The Shape of Things to Come." *Healthcare Forum Journal*. September 1995.

[10]Thompson, C.J.C. and Zondlo, J.A. "Building a Case for Learning Teams." *Healthcare Forum Journal*. September 1995.

[11]Thompson, C.J.C., Ibid.

[12]Ibid.

[13]Young, R. and Eckman. "Patients, Physicians and Professional Knowledge: Implications for CQI." *CQI*, Hospital and Health Services Administration, 40. Spring 1995.

[14]Vavala. "Physician Executives: Managers First, Clinicians Second." *Physician Executive*, 31-35, Feb. 1994.

[15]Farrell, J.P. and Robbins, M.M. "Leadership Competencies for Physicians." *Healthcare Forum Journal*, 39-42, July/August 1993.

[16]Zahner, C.A. *The Physician Executive*, 10, September 1996.

[17]Hartfield, J.E., as reported by Baker, S.B., Sentara Health System and Eastern Virginia Medical School.

[18]Heifetz, R. *Leadership Without Easy Answers*. Harvard University Press. 1994.

[19]Berwick, D. as reported by Baker, S., Sentara Health System, in a 1995 talk.

[20]O'Connor, K.E. "The Best Leaders." *The Physician Executive*, 4, April 1997.

[21]Kholes, M.K., Baker, W.G., Jr. and Donaho, B.A. *Transformational Leadership*. American Hospital Association. 1995.

[22]Ibid., "The Best Leaders."

[23]Tagiuri, R. "Managing People." *Harvard Business Review*, 73:1, Jan/Feb 1995.

[24]Dubnicki, C. Hay Associates. 415-945-8820.

[25]Berwick, D., as reported by Baker, S., Sentara Health System, in a 1995 talk.

[26]Dubnicki, C., op. cit.

[27]Bennis, D. *An Invented Life: Reflections on Leadership and Change*. New York: Doubleday. 1990.

[28]Rice, J.A. "A New Era of Power." *Modern Physician*. May 1997.

ABOUT THE AUTHORS

Through The Governance Institute, Dr. Rice is working with physicians, leaders and boards throughout the country for leadership performance improvement. He remains active in international health policy reforms through Cambridge University in England and the World Bank. He previously served as a senior officer of one of the healthcare systems that founded Allina in Minnesota.

Medical Informatics—An Evolution for the Physician Leader

by Ed Lowenstein, MD

"Computers are on the move—from the back office to the front office to the physician's desktop, and finally to the exam room."

In this chapter the author explains what this "marketing speak" means and its significance for the practing physician.

◆ ◆ ◆

In the early days of office computing, the technology was limited in scope and served mainly billing functions (i.e., back office). As systems grew in functionality and prices moderated, computers migrated out to the front office to manage chores such as patient scheduling, patient reminders, etc. Over the past few years the movement has continued, with microcomputers appearing on physicians' desks. These personal computers (or Macintosh computers) bring clinical applications, access to expert systems (journals online, etc.) and other functions that allow physicians to improve the quality of medical practice.

Estimating the number of users who have migrated to this point would be difficult, but they are still among a small minority of practicing physicians. The next wave—computers in the exam room—is at the cutting edge. Because of issues of cost, technology (e.g., computer network development), user and patient acceptance and so forth, the migration process here has been exceptionally slow and may continue to be for the near term. Nonetheless, an evolutionary process is under way, and it will be increasingly important for physician leaders now and in the future to grasp the underlying concepts at work here. Their leadership will be crucial in guiding their organizations through the profound technological changes of the information age. This chapter will, hopefully, lend some understanding to this process.

Changing Paradigms

It might be instructive to begin with a discussion of the paradigmatic changes anticipated in the technological evolution we face. The "migration" of technology from back office to physician's desktop will be accompanied by equally significant changes in the ways we design and implement the information systems of the future. Consider the "then" vs. "now" paradigms in Figure 1 on page 312.

FIGURE 1: CHANGES IN PARADIGMS	
Current mode	**Future mode**
accounting system-based	workflow-based
based on fee-for-service reimbursement model	supportive of fee-for-service as well as prepaid, managed care models
limited in ability to interact with external entities	easily interactive with outside entities and platforms (e.g., Internet capable)
based on proprietary technologies	based on PC local area network, client/server and Windows platforms
purchased and used by billing and administrative staff	purchased by integrated delivery systems with physicians as key stakeholders
distributed by more than 1,500 currently small local and regional vendors	distributed by 30 large national vendors
IS expenditures <2 percent% of revenues	IS expenditures >3-4 percent of revenues
customers indifferent to technology	customers dependent on technology
physicians blind to technology	physicians lead technology implementation

These evolutionary changes will have profound effects on our organizations, and we, as physician leaders, must embrace and come to adopt a leadership role in them. To do this knowledgeably we should understand them better.

Beyond Billing

Accounting-based orientation's underlying premise is that the only legitimate use for automation is to allow the billing department to improve collection of billed charges. Although revenues are the lifeblood of the organization, this view is outdated and somewhat arrogant. Clearly, billing systems must improve and allow the flexibility needed as the mix of payers grows in number and complexity.

This, however, is only one of a vast number of issues that information systems (IS) must address in the coming years. The clinical information "spun off" as a byproduct of the billing process is wholly inadequate to meet the demands of the quality improvement initiatives. Therefore, IS companies whose software was written decades ago, when billing information drove the development process, must be viewed extremely critically by those empowered to evaluate and purchase systems for the next decade.

The movement from the traditional, fee-for-service billing mode to the prepaid one is profound. The motivation is no longer to maximize the billable procedures performed, but to manage successfully on a prepaid "budget" for all healthcare expenditures. This is an entirely different and much more complex undertaking. Physicians must be profiled and compared with recognized standards for utilization based on knowable aspects of the patient population (demographics, morbidity characteristics, etc.). Systems must have the capability of analyzing and prompting physicians "real time" as they work through the patient encounter. This requires a complete redesign of the data collection and management system.

"Client/server" is a term in serious need of explanation and understanding. Legacy systems built more than five to 10 years ago are considered "host-based." The computer software code for the particular application (billing, scheduling, patient index systems, etc.) as well as all of the data (the actual records of the patient encounters, demographics, etc.) live in one central place—on a large mainframe or "midframe" computer. This is connected to small "dumb" terminals dispersed throughout an organization.

In client/server architecture, the applications and the data are distributed between "servers" (somewhat larger and more powerful PCs) and "client" PCs. The distribution scheme is entirely flexible and designed according to the needs of a particular organization. If each facility needs to function independently, then all the functionality lives at that facility. Conversely, it is possible to have all the data and applications live on a large "central" server in one location, thereby simulating a host-based architecture. The basic premise of client/server computing is to present to the user any and all information he or she may need to carry out the specific task at hand—whether that user is a receptionist setting up a patient appointment, a physician fielding a follow-up call from a patient or an accounting department clerk talking to a patient about his or her bill. The physician in this case might need to refer to a radiologist's report and a lab test result and simultaneously check the patient's present medication list, making additions or alterations to it. In the "old world" of computing this would require access to possibly four discreet systems—a practice management system, a radiology system, a pharmacy system and a lab system. Furthermore, each system might require its own logon procedure and separate searches for a specific patient identity. The interfaces might be quite different, and the possibility that the physician will get all the relevant information from one user-friendly "desktop" is remote at best.

In traditional, host-based legacy systems, proprietary departmental solutions and core mainframe-based business systems quickly reached the limits of growth and accessibility. This challenge was historically addressed by simply adding another layer of host-centric computing—such as a clinical data repository or data warehouse—that attempted to extract information from a group of disparate proprietary systems and then made it accessible to users through a new "client/server" interface. This solution was prone to a number of problems including interface complexity among subsystems, scalability (it may work at low volumes and crash at larger ones) and contention between analytic users and transaction users (i.e., the people using the system with patients standing in front of them wait while the system addresses requests from back office staff doing studies on the same data). A system that prevents all of these potential problems is prohibitively expensive.

Because of cost issues, compromises are made. The approach to create a virtual "Fort Knox" of data is somewhat farfetched because the underlying database design won't support it. Meanwhile, there are many legacy system vendors with a lot at stake. The potential loss of marketshare among users with large IS budgets is staggering. Thus, attempts to remedy the situation are equally robust. Be careful to evaluate the actual functionality of all such integrated systems from vendors; they potentially may be selling "lipstick on a bulldog," which just won't work.

Client/server computing is the most effective vehicle for bringing all information to the physician's desktop in an integrated fashion, providing access from any workstation to any server containing relevant information without the user needing to know how it's done behind the screens. A modern, distributed approach tends to leave the data where it was collected and is likely to be used again while providing access to the data for all other authorized users.

This is essentially the same as architecture of the Internet. When you surf the Web, for example, you access a global search engine and follow pointers to the information you seek. In healthcare, the search engine becomes a global master patient index with structured links to various pieces of the patient's record stored in various systems throughout the enterprise. While there is certainly a place for the data warehouse, it is confined to its appropriate use as an analytic tool.

Systems Evolution

There have already been tangible advantages to client/server computing noted by users. Traditional systems require that system configuration be sized to accommodate expected growth at the outset. Thus, a large capital investment has to be made on day one for reserve processing power and capacity that may not be needed for years to come. Client/server systems allow incremental capital investment, with additional servers being added as system utilization increases. With the constantly improving price/performance curve of hardware there is a double benefit here—conservation of capital and improved purchasing power for later system expansion. Further, client/server computing brings with it a broad set of standards that not only makes inter-system operability easier but ultimately delivers lower cost solutions than proprietary systems. ODBC (open database connectivity) and relational databases set standards for accessing disparate information stores. TCP/IP (a data transmission protocol for use on the Internet and elsewhere) sets standards on how computers communicate with each other. Microsoft's Windows operating systems and Internet browsers set standards for how users interact with the system. These emerging standards then allow system designers to focus on the high-level system functions specific to healthcare, thereby reducing development costs ultimately passed on to users.

The easier communication among systems enabled by client/server technology allows system developers to deliver "closed loop" processing. For example, an electronic medical record system used by a physician can not only initiate and submit an order for a diagnostic test, but it can track the status of the test all the way to completion and publication of the result, and further, to notification of the patient.

Legacy systems typically were designed from the database outward. A systems analyst would work with an organization to define the appropriate data elements. Once known, the database was designed, and then user screens were then tacked up on top of the database. The design was a rather static one wherein subsequent changes in design, layout or base information meant an expensive overhaul of the system. Today's need for information moves much too fast for this old environment. For example, modern healthcare organizations are being asked to produce HEDIS quality data. (*For more information on HEDIS, see Dr. Tanio's chapter on page 223.*) To get these data from legacy systems will be a massive task, whereas modern relational systems will fare better in responding to this and other challenges. Today's client/server systems allow a design process that moves from the user inward toward the database and incorporates a perspective of the user's workflow into all aspects of the development process. There is an additional benefit in sharing a common infrastructure with the overall office automation and communications framework of the enterprise. The electronic medical record is delivered on the same workstations and with the same user interface features as the electronic mail, word processing and spreadsheet applications that the healthcare organization uses for its messaging and administration.

The Advantages and Challenges of Making the Transformation

To look at a real-world example of client/server architecture in action, consider the following information from a case study published by C.J. Singer and Associates, a Gartner Group company specializing in healthcare computing. The firm studied a 90-physician group in central Florida with a large prepaid population. The medical group transformed from essentially no system to an enterprise-wide practice management client/server system encompassing medical records functions, scheduling, billing, etc.

The business benefits are:

- Increased productivity
  Provider productivity increased by 5 percent, returning approximately $20,000 per provider annually to the bottom line.
  Medical record productivity also increased by 36 percent.

- Reduced resource consumption
  The number of FTE's required to support each clinical facility was reduced by 3 percent.
  Telecommunication costs were reduced by 51 percent owing to a decrease in the number of calls transferred between departments, reduced telephone activity in medical records (from 200 chart requests per day to 20), and centralized scheduling reducing telephone sets and supporting circuits by more than 70 percent.

- Improved financial performance
  Through tracking and closed loop checking, bad debt expense was reduced by 20 percent.

- Reduced malpractice exposure
  Automation of follow-up activities enabled a decrease in the number of failure to follow-up incidents, a key quality measure, by 70 percent. This allowed for a renegotiation of malpractice premium rates.

- Improved quality of care
  Chart availability increased by 18 percent and redundant lab testing was virtually eliminated.

- Increased patient and staff satisfaction
  Automated front desk enhanced patient flow; online documentation improved hand-offs between clinicians and staff; elimination of data reentry reduced patient wait times.
  90 percent of phone calls were returned in what members perceived to be a timely manner, and 72 percent of patients reported that exam room waits were "better than expected."

One might ask whether the investment in the kind of technology outlined here makes economic sense. That is, while we might all agree that this technology is desirable, is there a "return on investment" that makes practical sense and allows us to move along in our planning process?

A. D. Little is an accounting and consulting firm that looks at these issues. It was quoted in an April 1992 *Wall Street Journal* article, "Desktop Doctors" by Ron Winslow, and it estimated a $5 to $7 /patient visit savings from the automation of systems. For the organization analyzed above, based on 4 million visits between 1993 and 1998 at least $20 million might be saved. This translates to a return of investment of 300 percent over 5 years.

With the above background into modern computing design theory and practice, let us consider the potential impact on the futures of our organizations. The "factoids" in Figure 2 on page 317 provide some perspective. They are collected from a variety of current information technology journals.

FIGURE 2: FACTOIDS FOR MODERN COMPUTING

- Every physician visit creates 13 pieces of paper.
- Nurses spend 1/2 their time on paper, physicians spend 1/3.
- Paperwork consumes $10 per office visit.
- In the past decade purchase of patient care systems grew by 170 percent while purchase of accounting systems fell by 60 percent.
- Healthcare information companies will gross $13 billion this year.
- 86 percent of all healthcare organizations will implement an electronic record in next few years.
- 75 percent of group practices with more than 20 physicians will do the same.

What this suggests is that the day-to-day operations of healthcare organizations will undergo the technological transformations already seen in other service organizations. For example, can you imagine a large grocery store without scanning technology at the checkout stand? Can you imagine that inventory management might still be done by clerks who walk along store shelves counting the boxes of corn flakes left to sell?

While we have adopted modern technology in retailing situations, we are woefully behind in healthcare. There are a number of reasons for this. First, physicians determined the expenditures for new technologies, and they were more interested in using technology for direct patient care (diagnostic machines, etc.) than automating and improving the processes of care. This is no longer adequate to meet patients' and payers' demands. Secondly, there is a complexity to the delivery of healthcare not imagined in the world of business. Clerks, nurses, lab technicians and doctors are all managing the same patient in their own distinctive ways, yet the work of each must be transparent to the other, build on the other and not contradict the other. There must be specific rights that flow to each user (e.g., physicians may enter a diagnosis, clerks cannot). The tables that support the database must be infinitely flexible (e.g., years ago we did not track whether diabetics got their eyes checked; now this is mandatory). The flexibility to modify and add tables to the database structure is crucial. Software must be written to allow the user to perform basic table edits quickly and easily.

Perhaps the most profound difference between normal "commerce" and medical "commerce" is the issue of security and confidentiality. While it is desirable that the public not be aware of our individual food-purchasing habits, it is crucial that we keep our knowledge of our medical records absolutely secure. For example, it is now known that insurance companies have denied coverage to patients who are HIV positive and have obtained the information from the "data mining" of online information containing diagnosis and treatment histories. Banks have used information from medical databases to call loans due on mortgages for those patients with chronic diseases. News organizations are hungry for the kind of information contained within medical records to expose the weakness of a target politician or to simply satisfy the prurient interest of its readers. This appetite for information and its misuse will make the job of information security paramount. At the same time we could err by making the data "too secure." For example, it is in our best interest that data on our medical conditions be made available to an emergency room treating an acute situation. Lack of information here could be lethal.

Consider another technical issue for healthcare computing. There will be an increasing need to have elements other than pure data available in the online clinical record. There are graphics such as EKG strips and scanned elements, such as reports coming into the organization on paper from outside specialists. There are large data files such as digitized x-rays and CT and MRI scans. Additionally there are sounds (e.g. dictations, heart sounds, etc.). These files are extremely large and are referred to in technospeak as BLOBS (binary large objects). Because the telecommunications lines used to link us together are of limited bandwidth, there is a real danger of clogging the networks with the attendant loss of speed of data transmission. Think of it as a water pipe of limited capacity trying to carry a huge volume of water to many users at the same time. Delays are to be expected. The present cost of building larger "pipes" is still prohibitive for most organization budgets. The needs will drive improvements in technology, but the constraints are real and should not be minimized.

The Future

These peculiar issues in healthcare make the role of informatics unique and challenging for designers and physician purchasers alike. Thankfully, technology will provide answers that simplify our task. The Internet is an excellent example. Until this technology became prevalent, there was an almost insurmountable problem with disparate systems talking to each other. A host-based system couldn't easily download data to a PC environment for local PC users to analyze their own data. A UNIX-based hospital system couldn't communicate with an insurance company mainframe. The designers of the Internet perfected TCP/IP, a communications protocol that solved this "Tower of Babel" phenomenon. Currently we have PCs and mainframes passing data back and forth over the Internet, conducting commerce across secure links benefiting both ends of the transaction. This creates the vision of a virtual medical record that exists as a series of pointers into disparate systems but one that comes together in one common interface for the benefit of the user.

Imagine the patient in the emergency room. The physician calls his or her name up from a master patient index living in a database maintained in Washington, DC. He then requests lab data living on a mainframe laboratory information system in Philadelphia, and subscriber profile information living on a mainframe with the Blue Cross organization in Ohio. The physician sees one screen with all requested data organized for his immediate use and is indifferent to the links established in the background connecting the underlying systems. As he works with the patient, he "publishes" new data on the new clinical situation to this virtual record so that it will be available to the patient's primary physician next week at his appointment. To the patient, all the advantages of the interconnectivity accrue. The system would have "prompts" to remind each user that the patient is due for a specific procedure. This is done through "decision support" software that analyzes each patient and makes recommendations based on the patient's demographics and current disease states (e.g., it knows that a 40-year old woman needs to have a mammogram on file and that a 40-year old man with cancer needs to have a specific immunization done).

This futuristic view of healthcare informatics is not as fanciful as it might seem. The technology for everything stated above is currently in use to a limited degree in existing organizations. The problem is that there is currently no suprastructure of healthcare entities with the power and insight to organize the construction of an infrastructure needed to support such a vision. With multiple vendors there is still fierce competition and little cooperation necessary to produce the standards to build such a structure. Furthermore, there are still sufficient concerns about data protection to make many potential users sit back and wait for better answers to the security issues. Last but not least, is the issue of the initial expense required to build the telecommunications and workstation hardware and software to support such a system. With the cutbacks in reimbursement associated with managed care medicine, there is little discretionary income to apply to large scale informatics efforts. Increasing IS expenditures to 3 percent to 5 percent of revenue for most ambulatory healthcare systems would be prohibitive. There would have to be a general acceptance of the absolute need to invest in this new technology. Absent all users seeing this need in unison, there is fear that one organization might allocate inordinately more toward informatics than another. Without a commitment on behalf of all users, the dream of the virtual record cannot be realized. Perhaps the most important force to drive these initiatives will be that of the marketplace. That is, those organizations that show the patients and payers their commitment to informatics improvements will have access to managed care contracts while those that do not will lose this marketshare. It will be done in the name of improvement of the quality of care and should be easily explained to the various key stakeholders in the healthcare delivery process.

Only through the concerted efforts of physician leaders in healthcare organizations will there be the kind of effort necessary to produce this evolutionary change. It's necessary for us to be on the front line of these initiatives. Our organizations will depend on our judgment to deliver on the promises we make to our patients.

About the Author

Ed Lowenstein, MD, is president in CEO of the Orlando Health Care Group. Dr. Lowenstein is a member of the American College of Physician Executives, the Orange County Medical Society and the Florida Medical Association.

The Physician Leader's Role in Medical Technology Assessment

by Kathleen Ciccone

Technology in healthcare is exploding in both diversity and quality, and physician leaders have to help sort it all out. In this article, the author describes a seven-step model for medical technology assessment, focusing on the role played by the medical staff during the assessment process.

◆ ◆ ◆

Telemedicine technology is redefining the geographic boundaries around "access to care." Although primarily used to transmit findings from such things as radiological exams, it enables physicians in rural hospitals to collaborate with experts in almost any medical field by electronically linking them. This capacity is proving particularly valuable in caring for patients with acute exacerbation, such as psychiatric illness or in long-term treatment for conditions such as certain cancers. Installing the hardware for telemedicine technology can cost several hundreds of thousands of dollars per site, not to mention costs associated with its use and ongoing maintenance. Although this technology can revolutionize healthcare, the costs are significant for most hospitals. Potential use, market opportunities and implications of the technology should be carefully considered.

How will your medical facility decide whether to invest in telemedicine technology?

Innovations in minimally invasive surgical techniques, such as endoscopic and laser surgeries occur at a dizzying rate. The adoption of these procedures into daily practices is a seemingly overnight occurrence. New techniques for cardiac surgery, a $30 billion a year business, have the potential to transform traditional approaches to open heart surgery. Analogous to the rapid transformation of laparoscopic cholecystectomy from cutting edge to standard practice, post-access coronary artery bypass (PACAB) and minimally invasive direct coronary artery bypass (MIDCAB) have the potential to become standard fare over the course of the next few years.

These procedures greatly reduce patient discomfort, result in lengths of stay of three to five days as compared with the standard seven to 10 days and enable patients to recover in less than four weeks (standard recovery can last up to 12 weeks). However, new equipment costs, limited patient selection factors, physician and staff training needs and impact on existing techniques all need to be carefully considered by hospitals and their medical staffs. Should your medical facility be one of the early adopters of these new procedures? If the FDA approves the use of laser treatments or photodynamic therapy for bladder cancer, will your facility be in the vanguard of those using such techniques?

A recent article in *Crains New York* illustrated the competitive nature of hospital technology. Under a headline that sounded more like a child's taunt —"My Robot's Bigger, Faster and Better than Yours"—healthcare executives described the complex evaluations factoring into their decisions to acquire and convert human laboratory functions to a multimillion-dollar robotics system. According to the article, industry experts believe that because a robotics laboratory—which can run 24 hours a day—increases efficiencies, boosts capacity and reduces turnaround times, it can yield savings of millions of dollars per year. The laboratory information system also will assist physicians to identify the most appropriate follow-up laboratory tests for their patients and link with other computer systems across the healthcare system. Clearly, the system has far reaching implications. How do you decide who should be involved in the decisionmaking process?

FIGURE 1: TIPS FOR EVALUATING NEW MEDICAL TECHNOLOGY

- Consider the organization's mission and long-range goals.
- Set up a multidisciplinary assessment committee.
- Avoid personal or departmental bias.
- Consider updating existing technology.

Midazolam is a benzodiazapian class agent used in surgery Unlike diazepam, midazolam is water soluble so patients do not experience pain during injection. Furthermore, midazolam is more potent and shorter acting; patients recover from anesthesia more quickly and experience fewer problems with nausea and vomiting. The down side is expense. A pre-anesthetic patient dose of midazolam can cost as much as 13 times what diazepam does. Multiplied over the thousands of surgeries performed at your hospital each year, that cost could be significant. Similar questions arise about the cost and patient benefits associated with the use of midazolam and lorazapam for conscious sedation. What are the factors you should consider about the use of these drugs at your healthcare facility?

These scenarios illustrate the challenges posed by new medical technology. Advances in diagnostic and therapeutic technologies are being introduced at a dizzying rate. In many cases, the benefits are great, but so are the costs. Every facility cannot afford to have every new technology. Moreover, the comparative medical efficacy and cost effectiveness of competing technologies are often unclear when new drugs, procedures and equipment come on the market.

Hospitals, group practices, nursing homes and HMOs are increasingly looking to a formal process of technology assessment to help them make objective decisions in this area. As a physician leader, you may be asked to serve on a technology assessment team or supply clinical expertise as part of the assessment process. This article provides a brief overview of technology assessment. It describes one technology assessment model and delineates the specific questions that you as a physician leader may be called upon to answer. The model described here was developed and published by the Hospital Association of New York State (HANYS). For further information, readers may wish to consult *Medical Technology Assessment: A Model for Informed Decision Making.*

What is Technology Assessment?

Technology assessment is a process healthcare organizations follow to determine whether, when and how to acquire and adopt, update or maintain medical technology. In this context, medical technology refers to new clinical procedures, drugs, service delivery systems and equipment that affect the quality of patient care. The goal of technology assessment is to provide better quality patient care, not simply to acquire more equipment.

Figure 2: Cost Comparisons — Diazapam vs. Medazoliam

	Diazapam	Medazoliam
Per Unit Costs	$1.36	$18
Surgical Volume	3,000-4,000	3,000-4,000
Total Costs	$4,080-$5,440	$54,000-$72,000
Potential Annual Cost Implications	$49,920-$66,560	

What is the Technology Assessment Process?

Meaningful technology assessment is a multidisciplinary process that requires a careful, fact-based analysis of how new technology affects the quality of patient care, the practice of medicine and the internal operations of the organization. The organization needs to consider:

- How the new treatment or procedure meshes with long-range strategic objectives;
- Whether it fills a community need; and
- Whether adequate staffing and other operational recourses are in place to support the new technology.

The technology assessment model developed by HANYS is organized around seven components. (*See Figure 3 on page 324*).

1. A **medical assessment** determines whether the technology makes sense from a clinical and epidemiological perspective.
2. A **community assessment** examines external factors, such as community need and alternative providers, that may affect the success of a new acquisition.
3. A **facility assessment** determines space, staffing and training requirements, as well as other practical considerations involved in implementing a new technology.

4. **A vendor/equipment assessment** evaluates prospective suppliers and specific equipment or systems under consideration.
5. A **financial assessment** analyzes the costs, projected revenues and other financial aspects of the planned acquisition.
6. An **integration of assessments** helps leaders reach a final decision based on the recommendations from the previous assessments.
7. A **reassessment** periodically reevaluates the technologies acquired.

FIGURE 3: FLOW CHART OF THE MEDICAL TECHNOLOGY ASSESSMENT MODEL

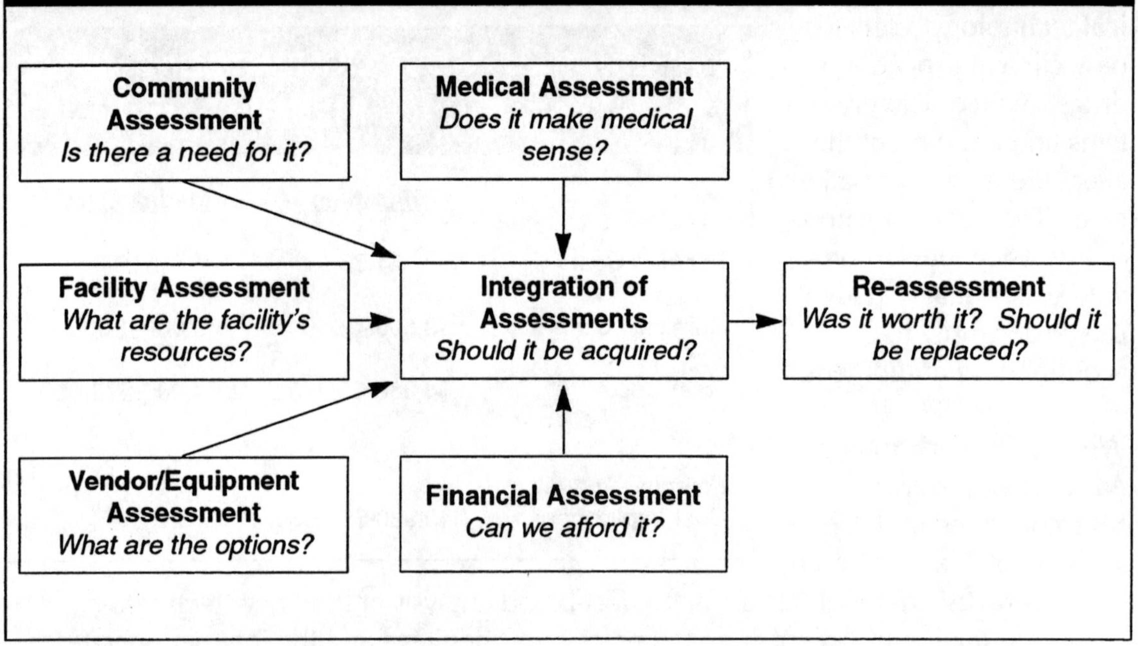

The Medical Assessment

Physicians often drive the technology acquisition process because they frequently are the first to learn of new medical advancements and are able to clearly see their potential benefits. Still, the interests of an individual physician or department must not be allowed to dominate the technology assessment process. The medical staff's role in the assessment process is to determine whether the new treatment or procedure makes sense from a clinical and epidemiological perspective, given community need and the organization's mission and goals. Others in the organization will develop cost projections, as well as data on staffing requirements and information concerning any special training needs.

The medical assessment phase for a new treatment or procedure usually begins with an in-depth review of the clinical literature. Hospitals with limited medical libraries can often access computer-based literature searches. Particularly valuable are studies comparing the new technology with alternative treatments or procedures. Following these initial reviews, physicians involved in the assessment process need to carefully consider the following six issues.

1. Are alternative approaches available? No, a healthcare organization needs every new technology. The ultimate goal is to improve patient care. Perhaps the organization would be best served by updating existing equipment rather than purchasing state-of-the-art equipment. Literature searches and discussions with knowledgeable medical staff members can provide these answers, as can discussions with peers using the technology at other organizations or involved in research on the subject.

2. Is the new technology efficacious? In evaluating a new treatment or procedure, it's important to determine how well it will perform under ideal conditions. Vendor reports and professional journals are good sources for this information. Healthcare providers should be suspicious, however, of vendor claims that are not substantiated in the clinical literature or by the experience of other, objective users.

3. Is the new technology effective? A key step in the medical assessment is determining whether the new technology improves the quality of patient care. How well does it perform under "real world" conditions? Are there data to demonstrate effectiveness? Is our organization likely to have similar results, given our patient mix, the qualifications of clinical staff and our organizational delivery system?

4. What are the potential risks? By their very nature, certain treatments and procedures carry great risks for patients and may result in adverse patient outcomes. Other new technologies may pose risks to staff. Physicians involved in the medical assessment must carefully estimate the degree of risk for patients and staff alike. It is also important that they differentiate between risks associated with varying skill levels of staff and those that can be attributed to system or organizational factors.

5. Is the technology accurate? Sensitivity—the degree to which a new diagnostic technology identifies all diseased cases—and specificity—the degree to which it does not identify healthy cases as being diseased—are important considerations when assessing new diagnostic advances. To what extent does the new technology reduce uncertainty as well as the need for additional testing? Reliability and the ability to perform consistently to specification are also important factors to consider.

6. Under what circumstances will the new technology be used? Few new technologies are equally useful in all clinical situations or in all operating environments. It is important that the organization clearly understand the capabilities and limitations of all new technology. Vendor performance claims should be discounted unless they are supported in the clinical literature or by other organizations using the equipment.

Reporting the Physicians' Findings

Usually, one or more physicians from the department that requested the new technology is called upon to conduct the medical assessment. However, if there are concerns that department or personal interests will bias the assessment, a physician(s)

Figure 4: Medical Assessment Form for a Medical Technology Acquisition Request

MEDICAL TECHNOLOGY ACQUISITION REQUEST
Medical Assessment Form

(Fill in all areas that apply and submit to Medical Technology Assessment Committee.)

This form aggregates clinical information about the technology.

Reference #______
Due ______ **date**
MTAC Receipt ______ **date**

Prepared by: ______ Department ______ Name/Title ______ Date

A. Overview

1. Describe the nature and scope of the technology (include uses and benefits). Continue on separate sheet if necessary.

2. What supporting equipment or additional resources will be required?

3. Qualitative assessment
NOTE: Attach documentation for all responses. Provide detailed supporting information.

Will this technology improve patient outcomes?	☐ Yes	☐ No	☐ Undetermined
Will it increase patient comfort?	☐ Yes	☐ No	☐ Undetermined
Will it enable practitioners to make more accurate or faster diagnoses?	☐ Yes	☐ No	☐ Undetermined
Will it positively affect patient or staff safety?	☐ Yes	☐ No	☐ Undetermined
Does this project meet a medical education need?	☐ Yes	☐ No	☐ Undetermined

4. For diagnostic technologies, what is its sensitivity and specificity?

5. What is the source of your information?

☐ literature (attach supporting documentation)
☐ peers (attach names and comments)
☐ vendors (attach documentation)
☐ other

6. What are the alternatives to this service, including technologies already available in the facility?

7. Describe why they were not selected. Describe benefits, hazards, and cost effectiveness.

Source: Hospital Association of New York State. Medical Technology Assessment: A Model for Informed Decision Making. *Rockville, MD: Bader & Associates, Inc., 1992.*

from another department or specialty may be asked to complete or assist in the assessment.

The findings and recommendations are then reported back to the individual or committee that has organization-wide responsibility for medical technology assessment, usually the medical technology assessment committee. The sample medical assessment report form that appears in Figure 4 on page 326 is a useful format to follow.

Other assessments. As part of *The Physician Leader's Guide*, this article focuses only on the medical assessment components. Readers interested in the community, vendor, financial or other assessment should consult the HANYS manual.

Your Role as a Leader

As a physician involved in technology assessment, you may be called to render opinions about technology you, a colleague, or a competitor will use. At the time you are asked for your assessment, information on clinical efficacy and cost effectiveness may be incomplete. Here is some advice to think about as you conduct your assessment.

- Recognize that the organization is depending on your clinical assessment.
- Recognize that the medical assessment is only part of the acquisition decision. The organization must also look at strategic, community, financial and other factors in reaching its decision.
- Make use of resources—such as literature searches performed by the organization's medical library—as part of your research. Talk to colleagues knowledgeable about the technology.
- Be as objective as you can. Don't just state a conclusion (e.g., acquire/don't acquire), but also explain why, in terms nonclinicians can understand. Remember, executives and trustees without clinical training often have the final decision about expensive new technology.
- Be candid about any conflicts you have, or whether you'll benefit from the technology being available or be adversely affected by it.

◆ ◆ ◆

References

Altman, L.K. "Cheapest Anti-Clot Drug Is Found To Be the Safest." New York Times, B9, March 4, 1991.

Lumsdon, K. "Beyond Tech Assessment: Balancing Needs, Strategy." *Hospitals*, 20-26, August 5, 1992.

AHCPR #97-R0068. *Medical Care*, 472-89, May 1997.

Hospital Association of New York State. *Medical Technology Assessment: A Model for Informed Decision Making.* Rockville, MD: Bader & Associates, Inc., 1992.

About the Author

Kathleen Ciccone is vice president of quality and research initiatives for the Healthcare Association of New York State.

Preparing the Medical Practice for the 21st Century

By Ralph O. Bischof, MD, MBA
A. Douglas Bender, PhD, and Robin L. Smith, MD

The American healthcare system has undergone an unprecedented change over the past two decades. The face of medical delivery is being reshaped by the growth of managed care, the formation of integrated delivery systems, an emphasis on primary care and outpatient medicine, greater emphasis on medical quality and the restructuring of the composition and size of the health care work force. Nowhere is the impact of all these changes more important than at the level of the physician-patient relationships and in the medical office.

In this chapter, we will address several issues that are basic to the effective management of a medical practice in the next century.

- *Recognizing the need for change;*
- *Providing effective leadership;*
- *Dealing with provider groups and coalitions;*
- *Incorporating a patient focus into the practice;*
- *Integrating effective care and changing roles for providers; and*
- *Organizing and positioning the practice to meet the challenge of providing quality care that is cost effective.*

◆ ◆ ◆

Before any process of change can begin, the need for change must be recognized. There is no doubt that some traditional types of practice will remain unchanged. For example, there probably will be a number of small practices that have developed niches in particular services or in a specific geographic area. They may maintain their competitive advantage without change. The vast majority of medical practices, however, will transform themselves in response to the environment or, preferably, at the initiation of the physician or physicians.

Physicians and their practices have a clear choice—to lead or to follow. But even after the need for change is recognized, old organizational structures, outmoded processes, policies and habits must be replaced by structures, processes and policies better suited to the demands of a new delivery system. For those practices willing to change, there will be a greater chance of success.

For the physician, the implications go beyond recognizing the need for change; it means a shift from the role of victim of change to the role of leader of change. Leadership for the changes that have already occurred has been provided by others who filled the void left by an absence of physicians. Leadership is needed in practices, in physicians organizations, in negotiating alliances and coalitions to provide care, in defining processes to deliver better care and in constructively dealing with the issues of rising healthcare costs.

New Forms of Organizing

With the uncertainties created by new forms of payment and the need for contract negotiation skills, physicians have created new types of physician organizations. At first, these organizations tried to balance the negotiating power of size with continued practice autonomy. This attempt resulted in such entities as independent practice associations (IPAs) and management service organizations (MSOs). These entities focused on very specific needs, such as negotiating with managed care organizations, billing mechanisms and other specific administrative services. The focus has been expanding and evolving. Today, the focus of physician organization is changing from loosely knit groups formed only for negotiating contracts to organizations that are taking the lead in terms of care management, integration and quality measures.

To buy or sell? During recent years, many hospitals and systems have been purchasing medical practices. One of the most significant decisions facing many practices is whether to sell the practice to a hospital, system or managed care organization. While the details of selling a practice are beyond the scope of this chapter, a couple of points need to be made.

First, there may be benefits to selling a practice. Doing so frees the physician from many of the practice's administrative hassles and sole financial responsibility for it. For many physicians, selling also spells decreased working hours. In fact, many hospitals and systems have watched productivity dip by 10 percent to 15 percent after the purchase of a practice. Another incentive to the physician selling a practice is that current prices for practices in some markets may be very attractive. In an effort to compete and survive, most hospitals and health systems have adopted a strategy of acquiring primary care practices. Further, physician practice management companies (PPMCs) have entered the market. These firms, usually backed by Wall Street money, purchase the assets of the practice and in exchange provide management services. The hope is that the PPMC will be able to produce enough efficiencies to pay its freight and pay dividends to its shareholders as well.

That discussion brings us to the downside of selling a practice. Foremost is the loss of control that usually accompanies such a transaction. But of course, loss of autonomy is not an issue confined only to the sale of a practice; many other transactions can require a doctor to surrender at least a portion of his or her autonomy. The pros and cons of selling a practice must be evaluated and weighed carefully.

Alliances. There are, of course, choices other than selling or doing nothing. The decision to align with other provider groups is based on the negotiating power of larger groups, cost reduction through consolidation or outsourcing of management services, the reduction in the many management tasks and responsibilities of physicians in smaller practices, and the perceived safety of being part of a group that strategically may be better to adjust to any future change. These benefits vary in value to each physician. As noted earlier, there are a variety of organization formats that range from full integration (pooling of equity) to loose alliances such as PHOs, IPAs and MSOs that preserve some physician practice autonomy. Each physician must make a choice; there is no magic formula. The choice may also vary with geographical location.

Any one of these physician organizations must make strategic sense. Groups formed in reaction to the current craze or change in market conditions run the risk of being obsolete when other conditions prevail. To survive change, an organization must be built on common values, focus on the patient, achieve efficiencies through integration, enhance quality and be based on a strategic plan to address changing market conditions.

Many hospitals and systems offer an MSO. MSOs can offer a wide range of services varying from simple assistance with billing to just short of purchasing of the practice and assuming all administrative functions. MSO services are often structured so that one can pick a la carte to suit the practice's needs. For hospitals or healthcare systems, this offers a way to align physicians who are currently not interested in selling their practice. It also offers a way for them to show how "closer" arrangements with the current hospital or system would be advantageous to the practice. For independent practice, it offers the opportunity to investigate the possibility of a closer alignment, in addition to providing valuable administrative and contracting services to the practice.

Focus on the Patient

The patient, as customer and as utilizer of services, has become a focal point for providers. In both roles, interest in patient satisfaction has increased. A high level of patient satisfaction may be a reflection of provider attitudes toward access, participative relationships with patients and patient education efforts. Having satisfied patients should lead to better patient outcomes and more appropriate utilization.

Although the word "customer" in medicine conjures up negative images, the concept of the customer can provide a focal point for improving both the quality and success of the medical practice. While patient satisfaction alone is not an adequate measure of medical quality, it does have a place in the assessment of quality. The key indicator of patient satisfaction is physician-patient communication. Communication will become an essential skill for physicians as they increasingly must compete for market share.

Patient satisfaction can reflect some very simple processes that are usually taken for granted. For instance, how many times must patients call before they get beyond a busy signal? How long does the phone ring before being answered? If you have an automatic system, are the prompts logical and easy to use? Once callers get through to a human being, are they put on hold? For how long? And the questions go on, including how long are waits for routine appointments, are weekend or evening appointments available and so forth. While there are many more urgent factors in delivering quality medical care from a doctor's standpoint, service issues can be equally important.

There are other ways of measuring the front line interaction between the patient and your practice. Walk up to the building on a pair of crutches. Is parking readily accessible? Is it easy to get into the office? Is the office comfortable? How long do patients wait? Many managed care organizations survey patients and ask questions such as these about waiting time, accessibility and hours of availability and the number of patients that change physicians and the reasons why. Many managed care organizations provide this type of feedback to physician practices. It can be very valuable information.

Staffing for Integration and Different Levels of Care

With pressure to reduce the cost of healthcare, while at the same time maintaining quality of care, different ways to provide and integrate care are being investigated. Thus, new roles have emerged. The nurse practitioner, the physician assistant, the hospital intensivist and the case manager are now important in the delivery of quality care.

The traditional solo practitioner often performed nearly all of the work in the practice on his or her own. This began to change as medical technology advanced and as insurance and paperwork became a major factor in healthcare. Receptionists, nurses, technicians, billers, office managers and other staff became commonplace. As in any other group undertaking, it is often advantageous to divide labor and responsibilities.

Nurse Practitioners

More recently, however, there has been the need or opportunity to add other types of providers and staff. Nurse practitioners and physician's assistants are one example. There is concern among some physicians that these types of providers will decrease the need for physicians. However, they can play a very valuable role in the office and can provide excellent care for the majority of medical conditions. They can help alleviate some of the burden of patient volume without adding on another "costly" physician. They can handle many routine aspects of medical practice, leaving more complicated medical issues for the physician's attention. Indeed, many practices have been using nurse practitioners and physicians assistants quite effectively for a number of years. It may be worthwhile to investigate this option with a colleague who is using these types of providers.

These practitioners can be useful in settings other than the outpatient setting. Tertiary care advance nurse practitioners function in the hospital setting. Many specialists have found nurse practitioners to be a valuable asset to the inpatient care team. The nurse practitioner in the hospital setting can be valuable in many ways, such as providing immediate access to care when the physician is unavailable, tied up in surgery, at a different facility, or in the outpatient office. They also can be very valuable in providing medical education to patients and facilitating discharge and home care, areas for which physicians often find they are short on time.

Hospital Intensivists

There has been considerable activity over the past several years in establishing the hospital intensivist. Just as the different medical specialties divide the labor of medical care and recognize the complexity of medicine, there is an important distinction between outpatient and inpatient care. A division of labor along the lines of inpatient/outpatient care also may be appropriate. A number of practices and hospitals are now using hospital intensivists exclusively for inpatient care. These hospital intensivists perform inpatient services only. This allows the physicians in the primary care practice to concentrate their efforts on the outpatient practice of medicine. In theory, the hospital intensivists are able to be more up-to-date on the technical and medical aspects of inpatient care. However, many primary care physicians are reluctant to give up inpatient care; it has traditionally been an integral part of most primary care practice. With pressures to see more patients and advances in technology, delineation of inpatient and outpatient responsibilities is becoming an important issue. For physicians in larger practices, it is relatively easy to add a hospital-based intensivist who assumes responsibility for all inpatient care for the group. Some practices rotate physicians monthly between all outpatient and all inpatient duties. Integrated delivery systems or other large organizations may offer this type of hospital-based intensivist to their primary care practices.

Case Managers

Coordination of outpatient and inpatient care and communication between hospital- and practice-based physicians are critical to the success of an integrated delivery system. They enhance the quality of care and decrease cost through increased efficiency in the delivery of care. Case managers can help to ensure that communication channels are open and effective. They track and monitor the work that is done, ensure that patient information and data are communicated to the appropriate provider and ensure that the transitions from outpatient to inpatient to outpatient are coordinated.

Other Staff

Other, more traditional types of division of labor in the office include the use of a nutritionist, a social worker and a nurse educator. These are not particularly new concepts, but have been economically more difficult for smaller groups to adopt. Practices in general are becoming larger, however, making it easier to justify these types of providers on an economic basis. Their use is also becoming more important in providing services that traditional medical practice has not adequately addressed in the outpatient setting. As outpatient medicine continues to receive increased attention in the new healthcare system, the role for these types of providers has become much more important.

Organizing and Positioning The Practice

To respond effectively to these many changes, physicians must create organizations that are able to meet the demands placed upon them. This means:

- Developing an organization that is flexible, works as a team and is focused on a clear mission;
- Creating processes that improve quality and efficiency. This includes improved patient management, billing and chart management processes;
- Implementing information systems that provide data to those who need it in a timely manner. Traditionally, information systems have been devoted to billing and financial management of the practice. Tomorrow these systems must be designed to help in the case management process, the monitoring of outcomes, and the analysis of costs; and
- Communicating the directions of the practice and information needed by employees and patients.

Organizing the Practice—Structure, Process and Policies

Despite all the changes that have occurred, few practices have designed the structure of their organization, their clinical and business processes, and written their policies and procedures in a way that fits these changes.

Structure

Physicians and their practices need to address the issue of organizational structure. Initially, physicians need to work as a team, to define their vision for the practice and, with the employees, create a mission statement that helps all in the practice to work toward a common goal and direction. Physicians who work on different agendas and have different ideas for the practice create problems for the organization that result in inefficiencies and frustration. Further, physicians must work more closely with their employees. Physicians who choose to disassociate themselves from the working of the practice limit opportunities to enhance quality, lower cost and improve the working relationships within the office.

Processes

In addition to structure, physicians and their staffs need to spend time on developing processes critical to the performance of the practice. Developing of these processes helps those in the practice to see their roles as team members and to understand the value of working together. Four processes are critical to the practice. They are:

- **Planning**—Setting the direction and goals for the practice and implementing change;
- **Patient Management**—Identifying all of the steps in the practice that impact the patient and how this process can be improved to enhance the quality of care and patient satisfaction;
- **Billing and Documentation**—Identifying the steps involved in billing and in documenting the medical record; and
- **Quality Improvement**—The process by which the practice focuses on improving the quality in all areas of office operations.

All of the processes are linked together. The goal is to provide better quality of care and lower costs.

There should also be a specific process for quality improvement. Quality improvement should be based not only on a one time improvement effort, but also on a continuous program of quality improvement, according to the principles of continuous quality improvement (CQI). While many would agree that quality of improvement is a very important element of a successful practice, many would often agree that is often difficult to devote enough time to this effort. Having clearly delineated quality improvement policies and procedures is one step in the right direction and sets the stage for future improvements and requirements.

Office Policies and Procedures

Policies and procedures can ensure quality and the proper function of a practice. While many offices have policies and procedures, they are often informal and unwritten. Assembling them in written form in an office policy and procedure manual allows staff members to be aware of what is expected of them. These policies and procedures can include almost any process that happens in the office, and may include staff and human resource related functions, hours of work, vacation and leave policies, etc. It is advantageous to have a vision and mission statement, which allows the staff to focus on the main purpose and goals of the practice. Policies and procedures can emphasize how patient inquiries are handled, standards for waiting times on the phone and in the office, handling of laboratory specimens, hours of operation, how many patients are booked per hour, handling of patient complaints, etc. Policies also can be useful in guiding patient expectations and in satisfying patients.

The Practice Newsletter

A practice newsletter can be a very valuable tool to communicate with patients. Newsletters can update patients on changes in staff, hours or other changes important to patients. They also offer a vehicle for disseminating information on specific diseases and preventive issues. A practice newsletter also can be an excellent vehicle for marketing to patients as well as referring physicians. It can be distributed as a way of advertising the practice. Such advertising and marketing will become very valuable as practices face increased competition and particularly for practices and physicians that want to establish a niche or remain independent.

There are many ways to produce a practice newsletter. Some businesses will produce and mail the entire newsletter with minimal involvement from the practice. A staff member could produce and mail the newsletter. Many software packages are available that produce an excellent newsletter. Other sources of information for newsletters can be public health announcements. From time to time, government agencies issue information to practitioners and the public that also can be incorporated into the practice newsletter. As practices negotiate with managed care organizations and other systems, special outreach services to patients, such as this type of a newsletter, can be very valuable. This type of outreach demonstrates commitment to quality and the patients in the practice.

The Role of Systems in the New Healthcare Order

Systems have become a key element in the evolution of healthcare. For many years, healthcare has been referred to as a "system." A system can be defined as a collection of related processes. Systems can be either well functioning or poorly functioning.

Healthcare has been more of the latter. While we often talk about the "healthcare system," the individual components of the system have traditionally not functioned in a coordinated fashion. The physician did his or her own thing. The specialist saw patients, but often did not communicate with other specialists or the primary care physician. Care of the patient in the hospital setting often took place in a vacuum and did not consider the context of the patient's healthcare in the outpatient setting. Each department within the hospital functioned relatively independently, often not communicating with other departments. Any alternative care received by patients was often ignored by traditional medical practice. The list goes on and on.

The new healthcare system recognizes that the components of the system need to function well and in concert with each other. There needs to be effective communication and coordination of care. The gatekeeper model is one expression of this. The gatekeeper is a primary care physician who functions as a facilitator and coordinator of care, negotiating the healthcare system on behalf of the patient. There are shortcomings in this model. There is no formal training for primary care physicians to learn how to be a gatekeeper. As a result, there is much variation in how well physicians function as a gatekeeper. The term gatekeeper itself has come to hold many negative connotations, such as limiting access to specialists. The term gatekeeper has fallen out of favor, but the need for this function remains.

Healthcare Delivery Systems

Systems are becoming more important in other aspects of healthcare. Networks of doctors, other providers and facilities are forming. Many hospitals have formed integrated delivery systems, which can coordinate and provide all of the care needed by patients. Managed care has also formed large networks that can provide all of the care for patients. And, indeed, there are many subsystems of providers and facilities within larger systems.

A key for success of the practice in the 21st century will be to define an effective role within the system. The practice also needs to consider its role in the larger healthcare system as a whole. What are the needs of the practice? What are the needs of the systems? What are the needs of the patient? How can the practice balance and satisfy all of these needs? The practice needs to consider these different needs in deciding where it fits into a system and how it will function effectively.

Communication in Systems

There are some practical things to consider for the medical practice in improving its function in the system. How good is the communication to other elements of the system? When patients are referred or referrals are received, is there prompt and appropriate communication through the provider being referred or for whom the referral is received? Is there appropriate communication between the outpatient practice and any hospitals to assure a smooth transition between the inpatient and outpatient settings? Are patients satisfied; have there been any surveys of patient satisfaction? How is the communication between the practice itself and the larger system that it belongs to? Questions such as these will go a long way in identifying how the practice become a better functioning and coordinated part of any system of which it is part.

Information Systems

With the exponential growth in information technology (IT), physicians have more opportunity than ever before to incorporate IT into their practice to gain efficiencies, reduce costs and be successful in an environment heavily weighted toward managed care. Because time constraints and expense physicians have been reluctant take advantage of IT. As physicians are increasingly becoming accountable for the care they deliver, collection of data will give physicians the opportunity to collect data and track care.

The majority of practice management systems (PMS) on the market today provide a wide range of administrative capabilities and services (practice finance and part of managed care). The wave of word processing and administrative efficiencies that can be gained through use of computer technology have been demonstrated and proven in industries throughout the world. True to form, the healthcare industry has finally been convinced that a capital investment to decrease paperwork and administrative overhead may be the wise business decision. Therefore, software companies have developed a number of administrative systems.

A few software companies have taken the initiative to develop state-of-the-art tools and mechanisms to collect and track clinical data, as well as facilitate communication among other healthcare service providers (pharmacy, laboratory, etc.). Other services have built in preventative health reminders and patient notification capabilities. In spite of its usefulness, only 7 percent of physicians report using technology to maintain clinical records. Today, most physicians still believe it to be easier and less cost prohibitive to write prescriptions and maintain paper charts since the cost of equipment outweighs the volume of currently documented benefits in patient care savings; however, this mentality is likely to rapidly change over the next five years.

◆ ◆ ◆

References

Bischof, R.O and Nash, D.B. "Managed Care: Past, Present and Future." *Medical Clinics of North America*, 80:225-244, 1996.

Brooks, R.J., Kahn, J.A. and Smith, R.L. "Practice Management, Health Maintenance and The Use of Computers in Today's Medical Office." *Medical Clinics of North America*, 80:279-297, 1996.

Carne, S.C. PAS/NPS: Forging Effective Partnerships in Managed Care Systems. *Physician Executive*, 21:23-27, 1995.

Edelson, J. T. "Physicians Use of Information Technology in Ambulatory Medicine: An Overview." *Journal of Ambulatory Care Management*, 9-17, July 1995.

Fabius, R. *A Physician Executive's Guide to Patient Management for the 90's and Beyond*. Tampa, FL: American College of Physician Executives, 1995.

About the Authors

Ralph O. Bischof, MD, MBA, is medical director with Prudential HealthCare in Cranbury, New Jersey. He is also a lecturer in Health Policy at the Widener University Graduate School of Business Administration in Chester, Pennsylvania. From 1995-1996, he was U.S. Quality Algorithms Managed Care Fellow at Jefferson Medical College. He is a member of the American College of Physician Executives.

A. Douglas Bender, PhD, is an associate professor of management at Widener University School of Business Administration, where he teaches courses in strategic management and managed care organizations. He is also president of Thayer Group Inc., a consulting firm that helps physicians and medical practices develop and implement strategies to meet the challenges of a changing health care system. Dr. Bender is a member of the editorial board of the Journal of Medical Practice Management.

Robin Smith, MD, is a Specialist Project Consultant to the Department of Health Policy and Clinical Outcomes at Thomas Jefferson Medical College. She is a Primary Care Attending at the Wilmington Veteran's Affairs Hospital in Delaware and an Associate Medical Director at Aetna-U.S. Healthcare.

Ten Ideas for Planning and Conducting Effective Meetings

by Barry S. Bader

Running effective meetings is essential for a good physician leader but, unfortunately, it is also easier said than done. In this article, the author presents 10 strategies that physician leaders can use to make medical staff department and committee meetings as productive and efficient as possible.

◆ ◆ ◆

Meetings are an inescapable fact of life for organizational leaders whether they are physicians, trustees, or executives. Comedian Jack Benny once said a committee is a group that keeps minutes and loses hours. Physician leaders typically deplore the length and number of meetings they're required to attend; at the same time, all of us are quick to complain if we're not informed or involved in key matters. Medical staff meetings deal with a wide range of important subjects, from new quality assurance rules to proposed new clinical services to medical education. The fact is, no matter how time consuming or tedious they may be, meetings are unquestionably necessary for communication, collaboration, education, and democratic decision making. The alternatives are an organization that stumbles from poor communication or autocratic leadership by a few.

The Leader's Role

Running meetings is a major responsibility for the chief of staff and the heads of clinical departments, sections and committees. Yet, as with other management skills, the art and science of running a good meeting are not taught in medical school or residency. Here are some ideas physician leaders can apply to make the meetings they chair more interesting and effective.

1. Take charge. Think of all the nonproductive meetings you've been to. What made them ineffective? Develop a list of "meeting killers," like starting late, wandering off the agenda (*or having no agenda!*), disruptive individuals, an outspoken minority that dominates a silent majority, meeting at inconvenient times and so forth. Then, as leader, plan and conduct meetings to prevent or control these negative factors. Take charge of the meetings for which you're responsible.

2. Be prepared to answer the question, "Why are we here, anyway?" Many medical staffs have too many committees, departments and subsections and, hence, too many meetings. As a leader, consider whether you're chairing an entity that really needs to exist. Does it perform a needed function? If so, does it need to meet as often as it does? Could its function be done more efficiently with fewer meetings or by another entity or the medical administrator? For instance, medical staffs have found that some peer review functions are better performed by designated reviewers than by entire committees. Similarly, combining small subsections into departments, merging committees doing related work and delegating parts of credentials investigations to a medical director can cut down on the number and length of meetings.

Taking this one step further, the medical staff structure isn't set in stone. It needs to be periodically reassessed and changed as appropriate. *(See IDEA 10, page 343.)* "Many committees have been appointed in one year and gone on working well into the next decade," wrote the late Lewis Thomas, MD, "with nothing much happening beyond ... extended, uninterruptible displays by each member of his special behavioral marks." Leaders should take the initiative to eliminate meetings and structures that serve no current purpose.

3. Write role statements and annual goals. To guide meetings and agendas, all departments and committees should have a written role description clearly setting out their purpose and accountability. This includes the medical executive committee (MEC), the senior medical staff policy-making body that makes recommendations to the board of trustees. Role statements clarify to everyone at the table just why they're there and what they are expected to do.

In addition, leaders need "job descriptions." CEOs and vice presidents have them, and because physician leadership is an administrative function, job descriptions are helpful here, too. The chief of staff and the chairs of clinical departments, sections and committees should have a statement of their roles and responsibilities. *(Sample position descriptions appear in Conflict and Cooperation: The Medical Director and the Chief of Staff As a Team, by Kenneth C. Cummings, MD.)*

Annual goals. While role statements are useful, they are by nature broad and do not reflect specific priorities needing attention over time. Chairs can supplement the department or committee's role statement by annually developing a limited number of goals, based on input from members and subject to their review and approval.

Written annual goals have several components, including a clear objective, an assignment of responsibility, and a target completion date. Figure 1 shows sample goals for a surgery department.

By pursuing a number of desired goals, a committee or department is likely to find its meetings become more purposeful and interesting. Some goals will be generated from within a department or committee; others will come as part of a broader medical staff effort. The medical executive committee might devote one meeting a year to discussing achievement of last year's goals and delegating new goals to various departments and committees. For instance, the MEC might ask:

- The credentials committee to review the process for considering privilege requests for new clinical procedures;

Figure 1: Sample Annual Goals— Department of Surgery

1. Review the departmental on-call policy and recommend changes, if needed. *Assigned to:* Ad hoc on-call policy committee. *Date due:* Draft recommendations by ________(date)

2. Review outcomes for laparoscopic surgical procedures, disseminate the data for educational purposes, and recommend revised privileging criteria, if necessary. *Assigned to:* Surgical QA Subcommittee. *Date due:* Draft report and recommendations by ________(date)

3. Develop ideas for new surgical suites, as part of the hospital's strategic planning process, and make recommendations. *Assigned to:* Ad hoc committee. *Date due:* Draft report and recommendations by ________(date)

- All departments to develop quality improvement plans, in cooperation with the medical director and QI department; or

- The library committee to assess whether sufficient access is available to medical databases.

Writing roles and goals may sound bureaucratic, but a little thoughtful planning and communication once a year can facilitate meetings *for the next 11 months*. Try it, and see if the time isn't worth the effort.

4. Develop and follow an agenda. Routine business and major goals should be reflected in written agendas and developed in advance, usually by the physician chair and an assigned staff person. Meeting agendas should be circulated to members ahead of time, along with background information on topics to be discussed. While there may be limits on sharing confidential peer review information in advance, many other reports can be circulated ahead of time and then discussed at the meeting on a more informed basis.

5. Promote communication, trust and respect. Controversy and diversity of views can be productive, but they can also get out of hand and hinder group dynamics. Set a positive, democratic tone for meetings. Establish a climate in which all views are encouraged and respected. Personal attacks should be prohibited by the chair and not tolerated if they occur. Communication flourishes only in a climate of trust and respect.

When it comes to dealing with peers who are disruptive at meetings, be firm. Some physicians mistakenly attempt *laissez faire* chairmanship. They are reluctant to exert control over their colleagues. In fact, physicians' time is valuable, and meeting participants will respect tactful but strong leaders. As George David Kieffer writes in *The Strategy of Meetings*, "Control is not a dirty word."

6. Do your homework and expect members to do theirs. If difficult or controversial proposals are expected to be discussed, talk to key members in advance. Prepare them; solicit their views and ideas on how to handle the topic. Similarly, if management is making a report or proposal likely to stir controversy, alert the executives in advance so they can be prepared. There should be no surprises. Good preparation leads to productive meetings. Similarly, insist that members do their homework, reading minutes and other reports sent out in advance.

7. Balance participation and closure. As chair, encourage discussion. Seek out views on important matters, especially from quieter members; their ideas could be the best. At the same time, do not tolerate those who monopolize discussions or go off on tangents unrelated to the agenda or the matter at hand. Start meetings on time and stick to the agenda. If the meeting is dwelling excessively on a minor point, assert leadership and recommend the meeting move on. Schedule the most important issues early on the agenda, to allow flexibility for longer discussion and debate if necessary.

As chair, you are always looking to balance participation with meeting efficiency. Unlike the parameters in medical science, there's no meeting science to say when discussion has been sufficient and it's time to vote or move on, but be aware when the discussion grows repetitious. As chair, move the group to closure on important issues.

8. Make use of administrative staff. Physician leaders should rely on staff who have the appropriate training—such as a medical administrator, medical staff services personnel and quality assurance staff—to draft agendas, assemble data, draft minutes, prepare reports and disseminate materials for review. As a general rule, physicians should review and approve minutes drafted by staff, not write the minutes themselves. Today, medical directors, QI staff and medical staff services personnel have been trained in proper documentation techniques to meet legal and accreditation requirements. Make use of their skills.

To be effective, administrative staff need to attend the meetings they support and become a partner with the leader in meeting preparation and follow-up. Sometimes. you'll hear physicians say, "We don't want administrative staff there. These are *our* meetings." Such statements usually indicate a lack of trust between the medical staff and the organization. They also suggest a lack of understanding of the medical staff's role in the organization. These issues need to be worked out; they are a foundation for building an effective organization of physician leaders. Barring administrative staff at the door solves nothing and perpetuates a lack of communication and trust.

9. Depart from the ordinary on occasion. Enliven meetings by inviting guest speakers who might educate the group on innovations, hot topics, or educational issues. Schedule round table discussions on topics of interest, so members can share their views. Once a year, ask for input and consensus on the annual goals. Consider opportunities to invite other disciplines, hospital management and even hospital trustees in order to build communication and stimulate thinking. Dare to be different!

10. Evaluate and improve. Informally, ask members after a meeting how it went and what ideas they have for improvement. Consider formal evaluation as well. Occasionally or regularly, distribute a brief evaluation form for members to complete after the meeting. (At the end of medical staff committee meetings at George Washington University Hospital, each member rates the meeting, an evaluation technique familiar to QI team members.)

In addition, medical staff organizations should periodically make a thorough self-assessment of their entire structure, communications mechanisms, selection procedures and so forth. This process may lead to bylaws changes, streamlining of committees and other improvements that will lay the foundation for more effective meetings.

"Time is money," said Ben Franklin, and that is never more true than when physicians leave their patients and practices to attend medical staff meetings. Consequently, physician leaders need to make every effort to make meetings as productive, efficient and interesting as possible.

About the Author

Barry S. Bader is a governance consultant and speaker based in Potomac, Md. He has advised many hospitals, health systems and physician groups on improving board performance.

Yesterday, Today, and Tomorrow: Personal Development for Physicians in Changing Times

by Alfredo Czerwinski, MD, and Joan Lawson, CMSC

Yesterday, the physician needed to be concerned only with clinical development and expertise. The medical, economic and moral issues of patient care were relatively simple and straightforward: The patient would seek help for a particular health problem, and the physician would give the patient the best hands-on care he or she had been trained to provide. In return, the physician would be paid a fee for that service.

Today, clinical changes, economic changes, regulatory changes and advances in technology require the physician to develop new thinking and behaviors. Healthcare is shifting from episodic individual treatments to long-term population care. Increasingly, the doctor is responsible for a much larger collection of patients, healthy as well as sick, whose care is contracted to the healthcare "provider," often for a preset fee. Patient care decisions have become more complex as a result of the need to control costs and keep pace with new technologies. The physician must give more careful consideration to whether a specialist should be consulted, whether generic drugs can be substituted and whether the patient should be cared for in the hospital.

Tomorrow will bring more dramatic changes. Every physician will need to be concerned with personal development and continued learning because future success will demand skills in a number of different arenas beyond basic clinical competencies. Whether the goal is to better manage a clinical practice, to become a leader among peers, to become a physician executive, to evaluate managed care contracts and analyze buyout offers, or to invest in healthcare ventures, physicians who want to be successful will have to pay explicit attention to personal progress.

A personal development plan will be an important tool for adapting to change and ultimately thriving in a variable environment.

◆ ◆ ◆

The sweeping changes taking place in healthcare are particularly difficult for physicians to weather because their training was designed for a simpler time. For example, most physicians were schooled in the value of autonomy rather than teamwork. They were trained to be analytical rather than intuitive, to do as opposed to delegate, and to be healers, not helpers.

Reaction to change can best be explained in stages, similar to those Dr. Elizabeth Kübler-Ross described for death and dying:

Anger: The first stage often takes the form of anger. To illustrate, many physicians express outrage about the changes in healthcare delivery and payment introduced by managed care plans.

Denial: Most physicians proceed to the denial stage as they choose to believe that managed care will not visit—or at least will not further penetrate—their local market area. Many, however, have witnessed new economic arrangements become a driving force in the profession. When denial eventually becomes impractical, the bargaining stage is triggered.

Bargaining: In the bargaining stage, the physician attempts to hold on to old ideas and often becomes stuck. Symptoms of being stuck are blaming and complaining about change. They waste valuable time in this stage because, while physicians are stuck, others, such as regulators, health plans and competitors, are shaping their future.

Depression: Despair sets in as the physician hears that healthcare needs to be "fixed", because he or she did not consider it "broken" in the first place.

Acceptance: Success in a tumultuous environment can be achieved only in the acceptance stage. Acceptance shifts the focus and helps the physician become a *change agent*. As change agents, we target the possible rather than stonewalling and railing against what we believe should not be done.

Personal development is critical because change can be controlled and modified. Physicians add tremendous value when they participate in both clinical and non-clinical healthcare decisions. But to be effective change agents, physicians must acquire new knowledge, and develop new skills and attitudes.

New Knowledge

Yesterday, physicians viewed most management techniques as contradicting their individualized patient care skills. Practice development and office management were not taught; they were skills to be learned later. As a result, physicians understandably resisted learning most management practices, and those who did seek to attain management skills were derided by their colleagues as "turncoats.

Today, many physicians lack general business and management knowledge, a deficiency that is swiftly becoming a handicap for most physicians striving for success in what has become the healthcare "industry." Physicians find themselves increasingly uncomfortable when confronted with difficult business decisions that will significantly alter patterns of healthcare delivery. Similarly, they struggle through negotiations involving their livelihood because they are at a serious disadvantage.

Basic management studies in cost accounting, data collection and analysis, human resources development and contracting are necessary for a better understanding of the new challenges in healthcare. Business knowledge can help in anticipating the future and identifying leverage points during negotiations. In essence, the physician must learn to think with the shrewdness of an accountant, delegate with the efficiency of an administrator and protect patients' interests with the zeal of an attorney.

Tomorrow, computers will cut through the redundancy and inefficiency of paper systems. Information technology will provide a method for tracking costs and measuring treatment effectiveness and outcomes across the continuum of care. Medicine will become a more data-driven process, wherein accurate profiles of the patient population will influence many treatment decisions. In an era of information overload, the physician will have to discriminate which information to retain and how to readily retrieve it. The ability to sort and analyze patient care data will be essential in creating and optimizing tomorrow's continuum of care.

Honing Skills

Gaining knowledge is considered a concrete process because it can be accomplished through reading and attending seminars and measured through testing. By contrast, the acquisition of new skills is a softer process. Because they are hardly concrete, skills are less readily learned and measured.

Yesterday, physicians were allowed to be eccentric, often arrogant, and self-involved, perhaps even unreasonably discourteous. Of course, not all physicians behaved in that manner, but there was certainly tremendous leniency when it came to the limits of acceptable physician behavior. The family doctor was chosen based on location or a recommendation from a friend, not from a list provided by a third-party payer. Patients were expected to sit in the waiting room for an unpredictable and probably unreasonable period of time, after going through an equivalent experience on the telephone to arrange the appointment. There were no patient satisfaction surveys to record patient displeasure, and so their umbrage went unrecorded.

In addition, management by objective, conflict resolution and education about group dynamics were absent from standard medical school curricula. These so called "people" skills are abstract, and so learning them involves an unfocused process, which presents a challenge for physicians trained as *clinical scientists—not social scientists*.

Today, competition and the demand for comprehensive healthcare are forcing physicians and other healthcare providers to re-engineer their capacity to care for the patient population. Coordination among all parts of the delivery system is essential. Success, translated, is delivering the best healthcare to the most people at the lowest price. This new paradigm demands not only clinical expertise but also managerial and human resource skills. Physicians are being called upon to influence colleagues, facilitate system thinking, build consensus and align incentives. The key to these and the skill from which all other interpersonal skills are derived is communication.

Good communication involves the ability to deliver a clear, meaningful message. It requires maintaining perspective, setting priorities and staying flexible. Such communication includes listening and the capacity to understand what others are saying. Attentive listening can turn a defensive reaction or premature judgment into a learning adventure; it can lead to new ideas, the realization of mutual values or goals, and compromise in an otherwise adverse situation.

Tomorrow, skillful communication will be indispensable because it is the best way to influence the behavior of others. It is essential for building teams, supervising allied health personnel, negotiating with third-party payers, and developing a productive workforce to address patient needs.

Changed Attitudes

Yesterday, most physicians were upbeat about their professional future. Graduation from medical school practically ensured financial success and above-average social status. Hospitals were more like hotel accommodations for patients than working partners in the continuum of care. Nurses stood when a physician walked into the room, and patients looked to the physician for every medical need. Cost containment was not an issue, and physicians felt in control of their destiny.

Today, managed care and other cost-control programs are significantly changing the roles and responsibilities of the physician, the nurse and the hospital. The new economics of healthcare dictates how patient care will be delivered and how fees will be set. New allied health professions have evolved, blurring the definition of healthcare "provider." What was once called "alternative medicine" has won a certain respectability. Many physicians feel disempowered, with the resulting attitudes of pessimism, confusion and frustration. Herein lies yet another reason that a personal development plan is important for success.

Tomorrow's physician must behave like a leader, modeling optimism, commitment and responsibility. The physician who is acting as a change agent takes responsibility for the results produced. He or she becomes an advocate, problem-solver and opinion leader, as opposed to a disenfranchised bystander. The transition is difficult to make. Successful attitudes in tomorrow's healthcare environment will include being positive about change, taking pride in being an expert, respecting others as colleagues and team members, striving to be patient during the course of change and being humble enough to learn from colleagues, support staff and patients. Hand in hand with these attitudes goes humor: Humor releases stress, brings perspective to challenging situations and is usually quite contagious.

Healthcare in the 21st Century

Change is a process, not an occurrence. It is a deviation from the norm that can result in unpredictability and turbulence. Transformation can threaten current goals, values and belief systems, but it is among the greatest sources of creativity. Change emerges from an existing problem (the need to reduce healthcare spending), passes through a transitional phase (managed healthcare), and culminates in a new state (high-tech, population-based healthcare).

Physicians in the 21st century are experts who know how to manage business and delegate authority. They are business people as well as clinicians. They continue to work on pathways to standardize important tasks in disease management. They delegate authority to the most appropriate patient care resource. They watch the bottom line and realize that expensive care is not necessarily quality care. They have found that together they have superior strength because they are able to combine their knowledge and experience to deliver a high performance approach to medicine.

Getting from Here to There: Your Personal Development Plan
New roles offer physicians opportunities to make a positive impact on healthcare delivery, quality and outcomes across the continuum. To ensure success in those roles, physicians need a plan for personal development, which will function as a road map to keep them moving in the appropriate direction. The following is an outline provided to help physicians plot their course.

DETERMINE THE ROLE(S) TO WHICH YOU ASPIRE:

Take time to consider the areas in which you are expert as well as what you would like to be doing five years from now. Balance the years left in your medical career with the approximate amount of time required to learn a new role or roles. Strategically target one or more roles.

- ❑ clinician
- ❑ teacher
- ❑ researcher
- ❑ group practice manager
- ❑ medical staff leader
- ❑ executive
- ❑ board member
- ❑ politician
- ❑ investor
- ❑ newscaster
- ❑ other ______________________________

IDENTIFY SPECIFIC AREAS FOR DEVELOPMENT:

You may want to perform your own 360-degree evaluation to accurately determine those areas in need of development. Accomplish this type of evaluation by asking two to four coworkers and two to four friends (e.g., supervisors, professional partners, subordinates, colleagues, a spouse or significant other) for a candid appraisal of your abilities in each area. Make note of areas that need work.

Knowledge:

- ❑ clinical medicine
- ❑ medical economics
- ❑ cost accounting
- ❑ strategic planning
- ❑ database management
- ❑ data analysis
- ❑ contract negotiations
- ❑ risk allocation
- ❑ risk management
- ❑ human resources
- ❑ other ______________________________

Skills:

- ❑ oral communication
- ❑ written communication
- ❑ listening
- ❑ leadership
- ❑ conflict resolution
- ❑ management by objective
- ❑ consensus building
- ❑ group dynamics
- ❑ team building
- ❑ other ______________________________

Attitude:

- ❑ positive thinking
- ❑ commitment
- ❑ responsibility
- ❑ pride
- ❑ respect
- ❑ humility
- ❑ patience
- ❑ humor
- ❑ other ______________________________

REVIEW YOUR PERSONAL RESOURCE ALLOCATION:

Only a limited number of waking hours can be expended on personal development. It is important to STOP and evaluate the effectiveness of each current activity with regard to your personal development. Use a time management approach to attain your targeted goal(s).

- Keep things in perspective and strive for overall balance in your life. List the personal, professional, institutional and community needs that are most important to you.

Professional	**Institutional**	**Community**
____________	____________	____________
____________	____________	____________
____________	____________	____________

- Take inventory. List your current assignments, meetings and commitments.

____________ ________________________

____________ ________________________

____________ ________________________

- Become strategic about your career and the assignments you take. List those items that offer no reward and stop doing them.

____________ ____________ ____________

____________ ____________ ____________

- Determine the best use of your time. Target areas where you can develop methods that help people help themselves.

____________ ____________ ____________

____________ ____________ ____________

DESIGN YOUR PERSONAL DEVELOPMENT PLAN:

Keep in mind that you must be an active participant in the learning process. Learning is not automatic, and it is best accomplished by using many different approaches simultaneously:

Target Area	**Learning Approach(s)**
Medical Economics (for example)	❑ formal education programs ❑ seminars ❑ books and articles ❑ self-study ❑ mentors ❑ role models ❑ networks ❑ coaches ❑ other_______________
Strategic Planning (for example)	❑ formal education programs ❑ seminars ❑ books and articles ❑ self-study ❑ mentors ❑ role models ❑ networks ❑ coaches ❑ other_______________

SHARE YOUR PLAN:

Sharing ensures commitment.

- Communicate your goals and the details of your plan to your most respected colleagues or business associates, close friends and family members. By sharing your plan, you create a support system of coaches and cheerleaders. This will better ensure your commitment, and you will find it more enjoyable to stick to the plan.

PRACTICE AND PROMOTE:

At this stage of personal development, you are becoming a change agent. Exercise your new skills. Practice and gain confidence. Be patient with those who may not be accustomed to your new role and accomplished skills. Do not be afraid to inform those around you that you are taking an active role in managing change by changing your own behavior.

- Put new knowledge into practice by speaking up at meetings or giving presentations.
- Initiate new work processes that are efficient and facilitate your goals, incorporating your new skills in delegation.
- Promote yourself. If you don't believe in yourself, no one else will.
- Use influence to guide others by getting involved in collaborative activities.
- Foster a network of change agents. Form a group of like-minded colleagues and meet regularly.

EVALUATE YOUR PROGRESS:

You have determined your goal(s), designed your plan and have taken necessary actions. From time to time, you should explicitly review the effectiveness of your personal development plan. Ask the following questions on a learning basis. Occasionally, it may be beneficial to perform another 360-degree evaluation. Weaknesses should be targeted for further development.

- ❑ What steps have you taken?
- ❑ What has not worked?
- ❑ Is the over-all plan working?
- ❑ How can it be improved?
- ❑ Has anyone noticed or commented upon your new knowledge and skills?
- ❑ Have you connected with other change agents?
- ❑ What steps have you taken outside your comfort zone?

Change is an ongoing process. Be willing to be coached, go outside your comfort zone and be flexible. Keep in mind that knowledge combined with coordinated efforts will result in manageable chaos, and you will be on the road to success—today and tomorrow.

ABOUT THE AUTHOR

Alfredo Czerwinski, MD and Joan Lawson, CMSC are principals with Lawson & Associates, a consulting organization of experienced healthcare executives and physician leaders based in California. Lawson & Associates was established in response to the demand for effective management solutions by healthcare organizations in transition, which include physician development programs at the individual as well as the organizational level.

The Role of Physician Leaders in Strategic Planning

By Richard K. Keck, Jr., M.H.A.
and Lisa M. Corrente, R.N., M.B.A.

While the healthcare industry is undergoing dramatic restructuring, change in how healthcare organizations develop strategy is moving at a much slower pace. A critical success factor for organizations in the future will be their ability to involve physicians in strategic planning at a level that is still, for many, inconceivable. While the strategic planning processes do not need to be changed (i.e., assessment, vision, strategy formulation, implementation planning and evaluation), participation in the process must undergo a dramatic shift. At a minimum, three fundamental principles must be followed. These principles involve a joint commitment on the part of both physicians and healthcare executives to basically change how they "behave." (See Figure 1 below.)

FIGURE 1: FUNDAMENTAL PRINCIPLES FOR INVOLVING PHYSICIANS IN STRATEGIC PLANNING

- Strategic and Economic Partners
- Committed to "behaving" differently
- Empowered to develop and execute solutions

This article examines what it means for healthcare executives and physician leaders to follow these fundamental principles. Strategic planning is no longer an inside-out, self-absorbed process whereby health systems obtain physician input by including a few of them on the strategic planning committee. Strategic planning is a joint effort that aligns physicians and healthcare organizations to develop and execute strategies that enhance healthcare in the community and ultimately the market position of the providers.

◆ ◆ ◆

In the past, physicians who participated in a strategic planning process were really planning for the health system's business, not their business. True, certain groups of physicians did benefit by investment in various equipment and programmatic initiatives. But the strategic and economic interests of physicians and the local health system were not aligned. Today, hospitals and physicians are in the same business—managing covered lives.

As demonstrated in Figure 2, "Building an Integrated Delivery System," health system and physician strategic and economic interests are becoming aligned to effectively manage care. Patient care is a continuum rather than artificial groupings of services and locations (e.g., inpatient care, outpatient care, physician services, etc.). Competition is for a share of the premium dollar and covered lives, rather than market share of inpatient admissions and office visits. Providers (health systems and physicians) must work together to successfully compete for a share of this business.

FIGURE 2: BUILDING AN INTEGRATED DELIVERY SYSTEM

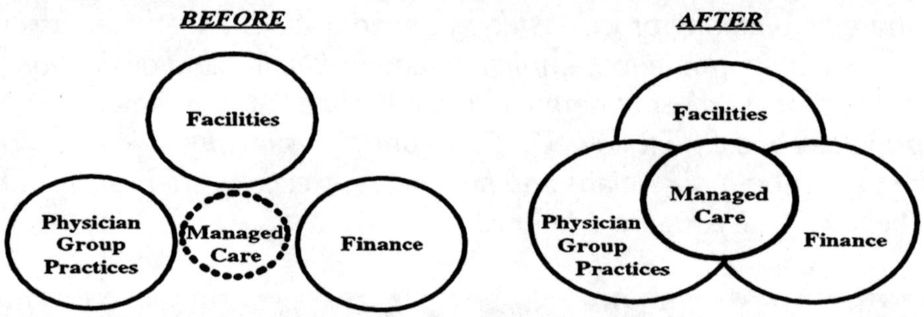

Before		After
Physician as Customer	⇨	Physician as Partner
Hospital or Hospital System	⇨	Healthcare Network
Clinical Services	⇨	Care Continuums
Market Share of Admissions	⇨	Financial Risk for Covered Lives
Single Site Service Line Management	⇨	Multi-Site Service Line Management
Core Facility Cost/Quality Performance	⇨	Regional Network Cost/Quality Performance
Horizontal Integration	⇨	Vertical Integration
Associated Management/Governance	⇨	Integrated Management/Governance
Joint Ventured Assets	⇨	Pooled Assets
Manage Care Delivery	⇨	Manage Financial Risk and Care Delivery

The transformation in the way physicians practice medicine is influencing physician involvement in strategy development. Hospitals and health systems can no longer assume physicians will participate in strategy development with their local healthcare system. Today, it is likely that some physicians may not be able to participate in a health system's strategic planning process. Physician practice management companies, multi-specialty group practices, managed care companies, publicly traded hospital chains and even pharmaceutical companies are all vying to be physicians' strategic partners. These organizations are now the most significant competitors to hospitals in many markets. A large multispecialty group may admit patients to the local hospital, but if it is owned by a physician practice management company, the hospital or health system must evaluate whether it wants people who are essentially their competitors at the table when business strategy is developed.

In traditional strategic planning, hospitals and health systems worked on a noneconomic basis with all members of the medical staff. Business relationships with the medical staff were on a temporary/contractual basis. The new paradigm dictates that hospitals and health systems work on a selective basis with some members of the medical staff. The new model also says hospitals and health systems will develop permanent economic partnerships with select members of the medical staff. This will require new types of physician and healthcare leaders.

Physicians and Healthcare Executives Must Commit to "Behaving" Differently.
If healthcare organizations hope to successfully embrace the new world order, they must introduce a new brand of leadership at every level of the organization. Physicians and healthcare executives entrusted to carve out the strategic direction for an organization, must put aside outmoded ways of interacting and transform into true leaders. Physicians can no longer come to the table complaining about past grievances; they must leave baggage behind. Likewise, healthcare executives can no longer plan in a vacuum, without involving physicians as participating partners in the process. What is the essence of transformational leadership? Scott A. Mason, D.P.A. and Edward J. Schumacher, Ph.D., writing in *The Medical Leadership Forum* (Summer 1994), identified several key *attributes* of noted transformational leaders:

- **Revolutionary.** Transformational leaders are willing to completely "dismantle" management processes and structures and undergo a "total demolition" of previous management styles and approaches, according to quality guru W. Edwards Deming.
- **Courageous**. In serious pain and dissatisfied with past performance, transformational leaders muster the courage to change, observes Deming. These leaders willingly "break out of line," even to the point of being exiled or abandoned by their peers and colleagues.
- **Aggressive.** Not content to develop short-term treatments for symptoms, transformational leaders work diligently to overcome the root causes of problems and craft long-term solutions.
- **Creative and Collaborative**. Transformational leaders reach beyond traditional boundaries and old-fashioned techniques of management control and direction. Instead, they work collaboratively with others to achieve ever increasing levels of performance.
- **Visionary.** Above all, transformational leaders anticipate, invite, embrace and champion change. "Innovative accomplishments stretch beyond the established definition of a 'job' to bring new learning or capacity to the organization," writes Harvard business school Professor Rosabeth Moss Kanter in *The Change Masters*. "They invite change, a disruption of existing activities, a redirection of organization energies that may result in new strategies, products, market opportunities, work methods, technical processes, or structures," she says. In short, by extending their vision to others, transformational leaders will bring about fundamental cultural, behavioral and organizational changes.

Most physicians have built their success on independent, entrepreneurial actions and are now asked to work interdependently within integrated delivery systems.

Embracing transformational leadership is not easy. It requires embracing fundamental concepts that run counter to the education, culture and attitudes of most physicians. Writing in *The Healthcare Forum Journal* (March/April 1993), James P. Farrell and Morley M. Robbins suggest six key "change agent" attributes that apply to physicians in particular:

- **Group Leadership**. No longer "lone wolves" roaming the clinical "frontier," physician leaders must move from independence to interdependence and from a narcissistic focus on personal income gain to a group-oriented or partner-oriented distribution of both risk and income. To do so will demand that physician leaders develop the savvy to launch, coordinate and facilitate groups and task forces, and work cooperatively with other groups, agencies and organizations. Right or wrong, only physicians can deliver this unique brand of leadership to physicians. Non-physicians, in contrast, have limited credibility to deliver this type of leadership.

- **Direct Persuasion**. Physician leaders must utilize every available logical and ethical argument to motivate other physicians to accept dominant paradigm shifts. The sooner physicians are able to dismiss fee-for-service medicine as a moral issue, the sooner honest discussions about risk-sharing and capitated arrangements will come about. Physician leaders must help their colleagues understand the deep need for change in such areas as shared and capitated risk, quality management, economic credentialing, peer accountability and continuous quality improvement.

- **Organizational awareness.** Already skilled at navigating rough clinical waters, true physician leaders have enough perspective to grasp an organization's priorities and points of view. In communicating with physician colleagues, they can advocate for a balance between physician, organization and community interests. However, many physicians—especially busy primary care physicians—complain about the sacrifice of time and income involved in participating in decision-making activities. While physicians might complain less if organizations were to give meetings a sharper focus and waste less time in seemingly endless conversation, their grievance still has merit. Physicians are justifiably concerned with loss of time and income. As a result, some organizations have begun to pay physicians per-meeting fees or some other type of compensation in exchange for their involvement in decision-making.

- **Initiative**. Blessed with a knowledge of medicine and the respect of their medical colleagues, physician leaders can forge strategic partnerships by demonstrating their willingness to assume financial risk, through either contracting and employment, or the sale of practice assets. Without such risk-taking, it is doubtful that physicians and hospitals will get close enough to establish the trust needed for shared risk arrangements.

- **Relationship Building**. Just as physicians can initiate ventures, they can also sustain relationships with community groups, insurers, employers, physicians and other healthcare organizations. However, doing so will demand that they blend their hands-on clinical expertise with the mission and values of a regional healthcare network.

- **Planning and Organization**. Physician leaders must participate fully in the development of comprehensive strategic plans designed to catapult a healthcare organization into a regional integrated delivery system.

Scott A. Mason and Edward J. Schumacher (*The Medical Leadership Forum*) wrote that each of these "change attributes" calls for physician leaders to assume new roles, competencies, and behaviors. But none is more important than the role of a strategic business partner. This role calls for full integration of clinical, managerial, governance and strategic expertise. Each area of expertise is described below:

- **Clinical.** Instead of serving as patient advocates, physicians must be willing to assume roles as care managers. All too often, the patient advocate role implies that the system is out to harm patients and that physicians must protect patients from the system. While physicians must sometimes act in the protector role, physicians functioning as care managers have a different point of view. They acknowledge the system's shortcomings, but embrace their power to actively manage healthcare through care mapping and clinical protocols. Further, they recognize the truth of the axiom: "Good quality costs less, not more."

- **Managerial**. Unfortunately, many physicians still view management not as a valued skill but as an attribute most people are born with, not unlike the ability to breathe. How else could one explain the disarray or unmanagement state that characterizes many physicians' offices? Stories abound of physicians who routinely force patients to wait hours for an appointment, allow significant receivables to lapse and permit dysfunctional employees to operate the practice. Since most physicians view management as "overhead," only the most progressive physicians understand how and why good management improves quality, patient and employee satisfaction and access to enrollees. As a result, physicians often have little regard for anyone with the title of manager. And when they do hire managers, they often hold them back from doing their jobs. Still, these troubling realities may change with the coming explosion of physician managers.

- **Governance**. Successful physician board members possess several traits. They tend to focus not on their own interests or those of their peers, but on the best interest of the community or on good patient care. While they claim no special status as patient advocates, they recognize that everyone is an advocate for good patient care. They not only concentrate on patient care issues, but also appreciate their obligation to learn more about the overall system. In doing so, they participate fully in the policy making process—not as a physician member of the medical staff, but as a board member who is also a physician.

- **Strategy.** Stories detailing the absence of business savvy among physicians are as frightening as they are numerous. The dearth of business skill is a function of an antimanagement mindset and the complete absence of business training in medical schools and other college programs. Is it any wonder that the relatively limited number of entrepreneurial physicians acquire tremendous followings? They know how the entire system works and how to exploit it to their advantage. Still, learning how to make money in a small segment of healthcare, such as regional reference labs, doesn't always translate into grasping the "ins and outs" of the total system. Moreover, because physicians view hospitals as bureaucratic, inefficient and slow to respond, they view them not as partners but as roadblocks or competitors.

The continuing challenge for healthcare leaders is to put together an interdependent team that can effectively develop and execute a vision for the organization. As more and more executives and physicians embrace these behavioral changes, it will become easier for executives and physicians to work together to the ultimate benefit of the communities they serve. But what are the key steps to empowering physicians to develop and implement solutions?

Involving Physician Leaders in Today's Strategic Planning

Participation in today's strategic planning should involve physician leaders with a strategic and economic interest in the outcome, rather than only a member of the medical staff in good standing. This is not to say that hospitals and health systems should not seek to involve and understand the perspective of the broadest possible number of physicians. With today's computer and communication technology, receiving effective input from a large number of physicians can be relatively easily accomplished. But final selection of physician participation must be influenced by those that are willing to understand the complexities of the organization and, more importantly, share in the risk associated with the selection and execution of strategies.

FIGURE 3: TRADITIONAL BARRIERS TO STRATEGIC PLANNING

- Mistrust
- Failed Past Ventures
- Perception that Hospitals have Difficulty Making Timely Decisions
- Traditional Physician/Hospital Differences
- Difficulty some Hospitals have in Sharing Power with Physicians

As hospital and health systems seek meaningful involvement and physician commitment in strategic planning, they must recognize and overcome some traditional barriers. These include:

- **Mistrust.** Physician/hospital relations have been filled with real and perceived mistrust over the years. In this era of heightened tensions and real competitive threats, mistrust by both parties is one of the major hurdles to overcome. In fact, the key to successful physician relationships is developing trust. Taking that leap of faith, when all the research is completed and the strategy is formulated, and moving on to a relationship of mutual trust and understanding is most important in successful strategic planning.

- **Failed past ventures**. In many markets, there is a venture that, for whatever reason, was not successful in the eyes of one or both parties. The ventures range from medical office buildings to PHOs, MSOs and other types of joint ventures where dollars may have been put at risk and lost. Many times these ventures are five or 10 years old. But they come to the forefront as the hospitals and physicians enter into new discussions about creative strategies to align their economic incentives. One of the biggest issues is leaving old baggage behind.

- **Perception that hospitals have difficulty making timely decisions**. Many physicians believe that hospitals and healthcare executives have a difficult time making prompt, effective business decisions. Many times, past performance by hospitals has tended to support that understanding. The challenge is to demonstrate to physicians that even though there may be a history to the contrary, the hospital or health system is prepared to make efficient strategic decisions in a competitive market.

- **Traditional physician/hospital differences**. In the current healthcare system, the strategic and economic incentives of physicians and hospitals are not aligned. This has led to many of the traditional differences we see today. Physicians work in a low margin, high volume business. Great attention is paid to overhead and productivity. Physicians have limited access to capital and are essentially running small businesses. Hospitals are low volume, high margin businesses with huge cash flows and, in many cases, have substantial financial resources. Hospitals are supported by a complex, confusing and often inefficient decision-making system. Joining two fundamentally different businesses with different cultures, operating parameters and case reimbursement systems is always a challenge.

- **Difficulty some hospitals have sharing power with physicians**. Many markets have a history of joint ventures with physicians where the hospital always insisted on a majority control and/or ownership. To be successful, physicians and health systems must develop true business partnerships between equals. In many markets, hospitals and hospital management continue to believe that the hospital needs to control its physicians either through governance, capital or reserve powers. Physicians are looking for true partnerships with their strategic and provider partners.

Remember that despite your best efforts, this baggage is likely to remain for some time. Notwithstanding this, health systems still need to involve physicians in strategic planning.

In addition to physician leadership, a successful strategic plan requires creative strategies and precise execution. These two factors should guide the method by which health systems gain physician involvement in strategic planning.

Remembering that the purpose of strategic planning is to accomplish something, health systems must think about execution as well as strategy development. In other words, how are we going to get this done? *(See Figure 4 below.)*

FIGURE 4: INVOLVING PHYSICIANS IN TODAY'S STRATEGIC PLANING

- 50/50 representation
- Select physicians based on criteria
- Involve as many physicians as possible
- Include opponents and detractors
- Involve those who "think outside the box"
- Choose those who can impact execution
- Develop organization structure that facilitates physician involvement
- Delegate responsibility and authority

- **Create a focused strategic planning committee with 50/50 representation.** The planning committee, which will ultimately recommend strategies to the board, should be composed of at least 50 percent physicians, and the other 50 percent composed of hospital executive management and lay board members.

- **Select physicians based on key criteria.** Physicians should be selected based on three major criteria. These include:

  - ✓ Their strategic and economic commitment to the hospital or health system. Do they have a relationship with the health system beyond membership on the medical staff?
  - ✓ Their willingness to assume responsibility and authority for executing portions of the strategic plan. Are they willing and able to undertake the hard work of leading implementation efforts?
  - ✓ Their potential to significantly influence the strategic plan or its implementation. These may be elder statesmen or women, key admitters or informal leaders whose stature can influence board members and other physicians. Local circumstances will ultimately dictate the exact number and composition required for effective strategic planning.

- **Involve as many physicians as possible.** The more physicians who are involved increases the odds that there is a shared vision for the future of the organization and that there is meaningful commitment in executing that vision. Take advantage of computer and communication technology. Utilizing today's communication technology makes this task much easier. Physician involvement can take many forms, including:

- ✓ Interviews
- ✓ Medical advisory group
- ✓ Membership on task forces or work groups
- ✓ Opportunities for presentations to the planning committee
- ✓ Questionnaires/surveys
- ✓ Ad hoc meetings or presentations to small groups of physicians
- ✓ Clear and effective communication channels back to physicians on the medical staff and to other physicians in the community
- ✓ Responding to concept papers

- **Always include opponents and detractors.** Sometimes the messenger, or the messenger's delivery, drowns the content. Listen to your opponents. That ensures that you have listened to all sides of the debate of the issue and that they are on record as having been included in the process.

- **Look for individuals who think outside the box.** Breakthroughs in strategic planning come from creating new industries or new visions rather than incremental market share increases in the traditional businesses. Be sure to include the "contrarian" and the "iconoclast" in the strategic planning process.

- **Include physicians with the ability to have an impact on execution**. Ensure that opinion leaders and those with economic or political clout are an integral part of the process. Key physicians are those who can affect the outcome and execution of the strategic plan. In each market, this is a different set of physicians. Most health systems can readily identify who "needs to be included." Make sure this happens. It is better to begin working with them up-front rather than during execution of the plan.

- **Institute an organization structure that will facilitate execution of the strategic plan.** In most hospitals and health systems, the only formal organization for physicians is the antiquated medical staff structure. Some hospitals and health systems have developed physician organizations or physician councils led by a physician executive who is a senior member of the health system management staff. Members of a physician council are most often representatives of groups of physicians who have made a strategic and economic commitment to the organization, including selling all or part of the practice, entering into a economic joint venture with the system or making a long-term contractual commitment. Those with the most economic and strategic commitment to the health system will have greatest motivation to help execute the strategic plan.

- **Delegate responsibility and authority**. Hand over real responsibility and authority to individual physicians and physician groups for executing key portions of the strategic plan. This requires that physicians are provided with the power, financial and other resources, tools and recognition to accomplish a given goal or strategy.

References:

Mason, Scott A. and Edward J. Schumacher , "Physicians as Change Leaders: Challenges, Barriers, and Strategies," *The Medical Leadership Forum*, pp. 13-14, Summer 1994.

Farrell, James P. and Morley M. Robbins, "Leadership Competencies for Physicians," *Healthcare Forum Journal*, pp. 39-42, July/August 1993.

About the Authors

Mr. Keck is a principal with NHA and Practice Leader for Physician Partnering Strategies. He has multi-faceted experience in healthcare consulting and executive management. In his almost 20-year career, he has held senior positions with two international consulting and healthcare management firms, one of the leading integrated healthcare systems and a nationally recognized academic medical center. Mr. Keck is a frequent speaker on a variety of healthcare issues, and is on the faculty of State University and a guest lecturer for the Wharton Business School. He holds a master's degree in hospital and health care management from George Washington University.

Ms. Corrente is a senior consultant with NHA. She has more than 15 years of clinical and management consulting experience in the healthcare industry. Ms. Corrente is a diplomat of the American College of Healthcare Executives and a member of the American Association of Healthcare Consultants and the Medical Group Management Association. She graduated with honors from Pennsylvania State University and received an M.B.A. from the College of William and Mary.

Appendix A
Glossary

Glossary of TQM, CQI and Managed Care Terms

Accountability: To take responsibility or be answerable for an action.

Allowable costs: Charges for services rendered or supplies furnished by a health provider that qualify as covered expenses.

Analysis of variance: A statistical method for analyzing data from experiments in which the total variation of the data set is divided into components according to specific sources of variation.

Analytic approach: Use of the scientific method; in total quality management, it is used to determine the basic causes of unsatisfactory outcomes of a process and seek permanent improvements to that process.

Ancillary charge: The fee associated with additional service performed before and/or secondary to a significant procedure, such as lab work, x-rays and anesthesia; or a charge in addition to the copayment that the member is required to pay to a participating pharmacy for a prescription which, through the request of the member or participating presciber, has been dispensed in nonconformance with the plan's maximum allowable cost list.

Bar chart: A graphic display using bars to show the rankings (y-axis) of each element being measured (x-axis); often used to illustrate measures of time, magnitude, increases, or declines.

Benchmarking: The process by which an organization continuously compares and measures its specific operations, processes, or products against those of an organization that is "best in class" for that element in order to obtain the knowledge necessary to improve its own performance.

Bounds: Numerical limits that define what is considered acceptable variation from expected values; established by those who compile reports on outcome data.

Brainstorming: A technique of generating as many ideas on a specific problem as quickly as possible early in the problem-solving process by having each member of a quality improvement team or group write down all their ideas at once. Criticism of an idea is prohibited during the initial discussion, after which all ideas are worked through.

Capitation: In the strictest sense, a stipulated dollar amount established to cover the cost of healthcare services delivered for a person. The term usually refers to a negotiated per capita rate to be paid periodically, usually monthly, to a healthcare provider.

The provider is responsible for delivering or arranging for the delivery of all health services required by the covered person under the condition of the provider contract. *Base capitation* is the stipulated dollar amount to cover the cost of care less mental health/substance abuse services, pharmacy and administrative charges.

Cause-and-effect diagram: A detailed depiction of the relationship between some outcome, or *effect*, and all the possible contributors to or *causes* of that effect. Also known as a **fishbone diagram** because the major effect is listed on the right side of the diagram as the "head" of the fish, and the major causes and related subcauses are listed on the left side as the connected "bones" of the fish. Also called an **Ishikawa diagram** after its Japanese inventor.

Closed access: A type of health plan in which covered persons are required to select a primary care physician from the plan's participating providers. The patient is required to see the selected primary care physician for care and referrals to other healthcare providers within the plan. Typically found in a staff-, group-, or network-model HMO. Also called *closed panel* or *gatekeeper* model.

Common causes: Sources of variation that are built into the structure of, or otherwise always present in, a process procedure. Usually, these sources of variation can be corrected only by changes to the process itself (see also **special causes**).

Community rating: A method of determining a premium structure that is not influenced by the expected level of benefit utilization by specific groups, but by expected utilization by the population as a whole. An *adjusted community rating,* on the other hand, is a community rating that is influenced by group-specific demographics.

Comparative process analysis: An examination among two or more organizations of the similarities and differences in the way each performs a process or procedure—for example, the process for a coronary artery bypass graft—in an attempt to identify superior practices.

Continuous quality improvement (CQI): The use of incremental and breakthrough quality management techniques to constantly improve processes, products, or services provided to internal and external customers and thus achieve higher levels of customer satisfaction.

Control chart: A **run chart** that illustrates the measure of a process over time with *upper control limits* and/or *lower control limits* calculated by plugging averages from sample runs of the process into a specific formula. The averages from sample runs and the upper and lower controls are drawn as lines on the chart; if any of the average points fall outside the control limits, the process is said to be **out of control**.

Copayment: A cost-sharing arrangement in which a plan member pays a specified charge for a specified service, such as $10 for an office visit. The member is usually responsible for payment at the time the care is rendered. Typical copayments are fixed or variable flat amounts for physician office visits, prescriptions, or hospital services. Some copayments are also called *coinsurance,* but coinsurance is more accurately defined as a specific percentage of the charges for services.

Cost of poor quality: The four categories of costs associated with providing products or services of poor quality: *internal failure costs* (those from defects found before the product or services reaches the customer); *external costs* (those from defects found after the product reaches the customer); *appraisal costs* (those incurred to inspect or otherwise determine the conformance to quality requirements); and *prevention costs* (those incurred to keep failure and appraisal costs to a minimum.

Cost sharing: A general set of financing arrangements via deductibles, copays and/or coinsurance in which a person covered by the health plan must pay some of the costs to receive care.

Critical path (also called clinical path, care path): Clinical protocols that describe the "best" or ideal management of a specific disease or procedure. They are designed to reduce undesirable variation in the treatment of individual patients.

Critical processes: Those processes within an organization that are determined to be crucial to the final output and/or meeting customer needs.

Cross functional: A term used to describe **process or improvement teams** that are organized along system or process lines, rather than **departmental** lines. Such groups include members from various disciplines involved in the process being studied.

Customer: Anyone who benefits from or is otherwise affected by the processes, products, or services provided by an organization or a portion of that organization.

Customer satisfaction, delight: The former describes the result of meeting customer requirements of a product or service; the latter describes the result of exceeding customer requirements or expectations with an unexpected benefit.

Customer-supplier partnership: A collaboration between a buyer and a supplier that results in lower costs and improved products for the buyer and assured customers for the supplier. The buyer agrees to establish a long-term contract and use fewer suppliers; in return, the supplier implements quality improvement/assurance initiatives to provide goods of a consistently higher quality and also contributes to the design of better products and processes.

Departmental: A term often used to refer to process improvement teams that are staffed according to profession or organizational section, rather than along **cross-functional** or multidisciplinary lines.

Deployment: Generally, the term refers to the act of positioning strategically; in TQM, it refers to the process of operationalizing the commitment to TQM throughout the organization.

Diagnostic and remedial journey: The clinical language version of the **plan-do-check-act-model** for making process improvements. Borrowing from the works of J.M. Juran, the model has two parts: *diagnostic journey*: 1. Examine the process; 2. Diagnose it. *Remedial journey:* 1. Write a prescription for what needs to be done; 2. Determine a prognosis for the expected outcome; 3. Treat the process; 4. Monitor the results.

Distribution: The population or sample from which observations are drawn, categorized into cells and forming identifiable patterns. In a *bell-shaped curve,* which indicates normal distribution, the greatest number of observations fall in the center (which may also represent the average), with fewer and fewer observations falling evenly on either side of the average.

Drug formulary: A listing of prescription medications which are approved for use and/or coverage by the plan and which will be dispensed through participating pharmacies to a covered person. The list is subject to periodic review and modification by the health plan.

Empowerment: A concept in which employees are given authority commensurate with their job responsibilities and, further, in which they accept responsibility for their actions. Empowerment enables employees to improve their work processes, drive out fear (one of Deming's **fourteen points**), and build employee **ownership.**

Encounter: Face-to-face meetings between a covered person and a healthcare provider where services are provided or rendered. The number of encounters per member per year is calculated as the total number of encounters per year/total number of members per year.

Enrollment: The total number of covered persons in a health plan. The term also refers to the process by which a health plan signs up groups and individuals for membership, or the number of enrollees who sign up in any one group.

Exclusive provider organization (EPO): A term derived from the phrase **preferred provider organization (PPO).** In contrast to a PPO, an EPO provides coverage only for contracted providers; hence, the term "exclusive." Technically, many HMOs can also be described as EPOs.

Experience rating: The process of setting rates based partially or wholly on evaluating the previous claims experience and then projecting required revenues for a future policy year for a specific group or pool of groups.

External customer: In contrast to **internal customers**, external customers are those traditionally identified as customers because they consume the outputs of the organization intended for outside consumption. In healthcare organization, patients are primary external customers.

Fee maximum: The maximum amount a participating provider may be paid for a specific healthcare service provided to plan members under a specific contract. A comprehensive listing of fee maximums used to reimburse a physician and/or other provider on a fee-for-service basis is called a *fee schedule.*

Fishbone diagram: See **cause-and-effect.**

Flow chart: A diagrammatic representation of a process that shows every step in the process and how the steps relate to each other. The development of such a chart can aid process improvement teams in reconciling different views of the process so that they agree on what problems or variations exist.

Force-field-analysis: A diagram of the relationship between the forces in a given situation that are driving change of that situation and those that are impeding change. Such an analysis can clarify all the facets of a desired change and encourage a consensus about the relative priority of factors on each side.

Fourteen points: Fourteen guidelines for management and the continuous improvement of quality formulated by W. Edwards Deming, one of the founders of the total quality management philosophy. The points are:

1. Create and distribute to all employees a statement of the aims and purposes of the company or organization. Management must demonstrate constantly its commitment to this statement;
2. Learn the new philosophy, top management and everybody;
3. Understand the purpose of inspection—for improvement of processes and reduction of cost;
4. End the practice of awarding business on the basis of price tag alone;
5. Improve constantly and forever the system of production and services;
6. Institute training;
7. Teach and institute leadership;
8. Drive out fear. Create trust. Create a climate for innovation;
9. Optimize the efforts of the teams, groups and staff areas toward the aims and purposes of the company;
10. Eliminate exhortations for the workforce;
11. a. Eliminate MBO (management by objective). Instead, learn the capabilities of processes and how to improve them;
12. Remove barriers that rob people of pride in workmanship;
13. Encourage education and self-improvement for everyone;
14. Take action to accomplish the transformation.

Gatekeeper model: A situation in which a primary care physician, the "gatekeeper," serves as the patient's initial contact for medical care and referrals. Also called *closed panel* (see also **closed access**).

Group-model HMO: A healthcare model involving contracts with physicians organized as a partnership, professional corporation, or other association. The health plan compensates the medical group for contracted services at a negotiated rate, and that group is responsible for compensating its physicians and contracting with hospitals for the care of their patients.

Histogram: A type of bar graph that displays the frequency distribution of a characteristic or occurrence, or how frequently each observed value occurs. The histogram reveals the amount of variation that any process contains; a bell curve pattern in the graph indicates normal variation in a process that is in control; a pattern that is "skewed" to one end of the graph or the other indicates unexpected problems or inefficiencies in the process.

Hospital affiliation: A contractual agreement between a health plan and one or more hospitals whereby the hospital provides the inpatient benefits offered by the health plan.

Hoshin planning: A strategic planning process developed in Japan in which an organization develops up to four **vision statements** for the next five years that then serve as the basis for the development of the company goals and daily work plans.

In-control process: A process that, over time, consistently operates within a certain range of variation attributable to **common cause** variables/events. A process in control may not necessarily meet quality standards; it simply does not exhibit variations outside the set limits that are due to **special** (unusual) **causes** (see **control chart, out-of-control process**).

Indicator: A characteristic of a process that serves as a measure of the quality of that process. Also called a "performance measure."

Individual practice association (IPA) model HMO: A healthcare model in which the HMO contracts with an individual practice association to provide healthcare services, and in turn, contracts with physicians who continue their existing individual or group practices. The IPA may compensate the physicians on a per capita, fee schedule, or fee-for-service basis.

Internal customer: A member of an organization's staff who is the consumer of products or recipient of services produced by another department or organization. For example, in healthcare, a physician is often considered an internal customer of a hospital's services; similarly, the billing department may be an internal customer of the admissions department, from which it receives documentation.

Ishikawa diagram: See **cause-and-effect diagram.**

Kaizen: A Japanese term for gradual, unending improvement; *i.e.*, whether the improvement by doing little things better and setting and achieving increasingly higher standards.

Maintainability: In continuous quality improvement, a characteristic of a process improvement; *i.e.*, whether the improvement in performance resulting from change in the process can be maintained over time.

Malcolm Baldridge National Quality Award: A national award to recognize manufacturing firms, service firms and small businesses that "excel in quality achievement and quality management." Established in 1987 and named for a late U.S. Secretary of commerce, the award was is based on an examination of seven categories of organizational characteristics and operations.

Managed healthcare plan: One or more products that integrate financing and management with delivery of healthcare services to an enrolled population; employ or contract with an organized provider network that delivers services and that (as a network or individual provider) either shares financial risk or has some incentive to deliver cost-effective services; and use an information system capable of monitoring and evaluating patterns of members' use of medical services and the cost of those services.

Mean, Median, Mode: The *mean* is the average of a set of values; the *median* is the middle value in the distribution of the values above and below which there are an equal number of values; the *mode* is the most frequently occurring value.

Mission: For an organization, the stated purpose or reason for operation.

Monitoring and Evaluation (M&E): The Joint Commission for the Accreditation of Healthcare Organizations' (JCAHO) 10-step process to assess and improve the quality of healthcare services on a continuing basis.

Multivariate control chart: A control chart for evaluating the stability of a process in terms of the levels of two or more variables or characteristics.

Network model HMO: A healthcare model in which the HMO contracts with more than one physician group and may contract with single- and multi-specialty groups. The physician works out of his/her own office. The physician may share in utilization savings but does not necessarily provide care exclusively for HMO members.

Nominal group technique: A problem-solving method used when team members have different opinions and goals. Participants offer alternative solutions to a problem in writing, and these are read, recorded and discussed only to clarify them; then the team votes on each to rank order the solutions.

Norm: A statistically validated standard of performance.

Open access: A term describing a members' ability to self-refer for specialty care. Open access arrangements allow a member to see a participating provider without a referral from another doctor. Typically found in an IPA HMO. Also called *open panel*.

Organizational culture: The overall pattern of operation and behavior within an organization that develops from the goals and values, business environment, rituals, formal and informal leaders, and modes of communication within the organization.

Outcome indicator: Precise measurements that verify that an outcome has or has not occurred (for instance, in healthcare, a specific health status of an individual); *clinical outcome indicators* are used to measure the quality of medical care.

Outlier: An entity having a rate of outcome occurrence that is much better or worse than the norm, usually ± two standard deviations.

Out-of-control process: A process that, over time, frequently operates outside the limits of variation (control limits) attributable to "common cause" variables/events (**see control chart, in-control process**).

Ownership: In quality improvement, an individual who is involved or who participates in the services or production process, e.g., physician, manager, employee, or board member; the individual who understands the process and who is accountable for it—the "process owner."

P value: A statistically calculated expression of the probability, or certainty, that an observed effect or value exceeds a magnitude that could be explained by chance fluctuations alone. Low P values are said to be an indication of the *statistical significance* of the result or effect.

Pareto chart: A special form of bar chart in which elements are arranged in descending order of significance. Useful to display relative frequency of elements or of problems in order to determine which is most important or which to solve first.

Pareto principle: The concept, named after 19th-century economist Vilfredo Pareto, that most effects result from relatively few causes; that is, that 20 percent of the causes create 80 percent of the problems.

Participating provider: A provider who has contracted with the health plan to provide medical services to covered persons. The provider may be a hospital, pharmacy, other facility, or physician who has contractually accepted the terms and conditions set forth by the health plan. A *non-participating provider* (non-par) is a provider that has not contracted with the carrier or health plan to be a participating provider of healthcare.

Performance measures: Precise measures of key characteristics of a process that determine its quality.

Plan-Do-Check-Act (Shewhart or Deming) Cycle: A four-step process for continuous quality improvement developed by statistical quality control pioneer Walter Shewhart and introduced to the Japanese by TQM pioneer W. Edwards Deming.

Point-of-service plan: A type of health plan allowing the covered person to choose to receive a service from a participating or non-participating provider, with different benefit levels associated with the use of participating providers. Point-of-service can be provided in several ways: An HMO may allow members to obtain limited services from non-participating providers; it may provide non-participating benefits through a supplemental major medical policy; a preferred provider organization may be used to provide both participating and non-participating levels of coverage and access; or various combinations of the above may be used.

Preferred provider organization (PPO): A program in which contracts are established with providers of medical care. Providers under such contracts are referred to as "preferred providers." Usually, the benefit contract provides significantly better benefits (fewer copayments) for services received from preferred providers, thus encouraging members to use these providers. Members are generally allowed benefits for non-participating providers' services, usually on an indemnity basis with significant copayments. A PPO arrangement can be insured or self-funded. Providers may be, but are not necessarily, paid on a discounted fee-for-service basis.

Primary care network: A group of primary care physicians who have joined together to share the risk of providing care to their patients who are members of a given health plan.

Process: The combination of people, raw materials, machines and equipment, and methods that makes up a sequence of tasks that produces a product or service.

Process capability: The inherent, measured ability of process to yield a consistent product or exhibit some other characteristic. Once the statistically determined pattern or distribution of the capability is calculated, it is compared to specification limits to determine if the process can consistently deliver a product within those limits.

Process improvement (PI) team: A group of employees who are all involved with the same process, established to make improvements to that process through the use of continuous quality improvement methods.

Quality: The degree to which a product or service conforms to accepted standards and/or to the requirements of internal and external customers.

Quality function deployment (QFD): A method of quality planning in which a matrix is used to organize the needs of internal and external customers and translate them into technical requirements for each stage of a production or service process.

Quality trilogy: A term coined by quality expert J.M. Juran to describe the three interrelated stages of managing for quality: *planning,* or developing processes that will yield the products and services required to meet customer needs; *quality control,* or consistently satisfying product and process goals through such activities as product inspection; and *quality improvement,* or the achievement of higher levels of performance through the application of statistical analysis and process improvement techniques.

Random sampling: A common technique for developing a sample for testing in which all the units in the population have an equal chance of being selected for the sample.

Random variation: Differences or deviations cause solely by chance and not attributable to specific factors.

Range: A simple measure of the degree of variability in values in a data set, determined by subtracting the smallest value from the largest.

Referral provider: A provider (usually a specialty physician or other health entity) that renders a service to a patient who has been sent to him/her by a participating provider in the health plan.

Reliability: The probability of a product performing its intended function or a service operating as intended under stated conditions for a specified period of time.

Retrospective review: A method of determining medical necessity and/or appropriate billing practice for services that have already been rendered.

Risk analysis: The process of evaluating the expected medical care costs for a prospective group and determining what product, benefit level and price to offer to best meet the needs of the group and the carrier.

Run chart: The simplest form of graph, used to display data collected on one measure over a specified period of time. Run charts can help identify meaningful trends or deviations from the average.

Scatter diagram: A type of diagram used to examine whether there is a relationship or correlation between two variables. The "cause" variable is usually displayed on the horizontal axis, and the "effect" variable on the vertical axis. The values from the sample are plotted as points on the diagram; the resulting pattern indicates (but does not prove) the nature of the correlation or lack thereof.

Seven tools of quality: Statistical analysis tools that help organizations assess and improve their processes. The tools are the cause-and-effect (or fishbone) diagram, check sheet, control chart, flow chart, histogram, Pareto chart and scatter diagram.

Severity: The seriousness or degree of illness; when assessing the quality of clinical care, comparative data on adverse events should be adjusted for the relative severity of illness in the sample.

Special cause: A cause of variation in a process that arises from a special, unpredictable set of circumstances and is not an inherent part of the process; a special cause is not likely to recur regularly. For example, if it took 1 patient in 100 two hours longer than an average to go through the admissions process because the patient could not speak English, that constitutes a special cause variation.

Staff-model HMO: This healthcare model employs physicians to provide healthcare to its members. All premiums and other revenues accrue to the HMO, which compensates physicians by salary and incentive programs.

Standard deviation: A measure of the degree of variability of values in a data set.

Statistical significance: See **P value**.

Storyboards: First developed by Japanese companies involved in continuous quality improvement, these are typically poster displays that summarize a quality improvement process in a standardized format, usually with graphics and brief captions.

System: In the quality improvement process, this term refers to a group of related processes—for example, the system comprised of the admissions, transfer and discharge processes.

Total quality management (TQM): A management system for continually improving quality and satisfying customers that is directed from the top levels of the organization and involves all its members in the improvement of processes, products and services by focusing on systemic problems, not the performance of individual employees. The term was initially coined by the U.S. Naval Air Systems Command in 1985 to describe its Japanese-style management approach.

Trends: Patterns of continual rise or fall of a series of data points, such as are found in a **run chart** or **control chart**. Such patterns merit attention when they exceed a statistically based, predetermined number of data points.

Values: In an organizational context, the beliefs and philosophy that form the basis for the organization's operation and provide guidelines for employees' daily behavior.

Variation: A difference or deviation in the actual performance of a process or product from the expected or standard performance. Variations require further analysis to determine the cause—either a **special cause** or a **common cause.**

Vision: An organization's statement of its goals for the future, described in measurable terms, that clarifies the direction for everyone in the organization.

Work redesign: Comprehensive changes to a work operation or system—such as the simplification of tasks; changes in staffing, materials, and systems; and changes in physical layout—to improve efficiency and quality. For example, some hospitals have performed work redesign to create "patient-focused care units."

World-class quality: A term used to indicate the "best of the best;" often used in the **benchmarking** process to refer to a product, process, or system with superior performance.

Zero defects: A term for a defect-free product; also a performance standard developed by Philip B. Crosby to promote improved quality in all areas of production or other processes, rather than a "close enough" attitude.